Performing the Great Peace

Performing the Great Peace

POLITICAL SPACE AND
OPEN SECRETS
IN TOKUGAWA JAPAN

LUKE S. ROBERTS

UNIVERSITY OF HAWAI'I PRESS
HONOLULU

© 2012 UNIVERSITY OF HAWAI'I PRESS
All rights reserved
Paperback edition 2015

Printed in the United States of America

20 19 18 17 16 15   6 5 4 3 2 1

Library of Congress Cataloging-in-Publication Data
Roberts, Luke Shepherd.
Performing the great peace : political space and
open secrets in Tokugawa Japan / Luke S. Roberts.
p. cm.
Includes bibliographical references and index.
ISBN 978-0-8248-3513-2 (hardcover : alk. paper)
1. Japan—Politics and government—1600–1868.
2. Japan—History—Tokugawa period, 1600–1868.
3. Political culture—Japan—History. I. Title.
DS871.R64 2012
952'.025—dc23
2011040192

ISBN 978-0-8248-5301-3 (pbk.)

Designed by Julie Matsuo-Chun
Printed by Sheridan Books, Inc.

FOR YACHIYO

Contents

Map of domains, daimyo clans (italicized), and cities of Japan
discussed in the text. *Produced by Andrew Roberts*

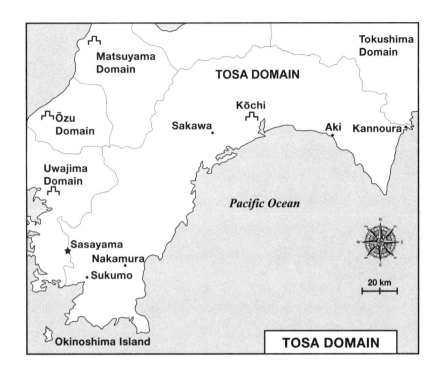

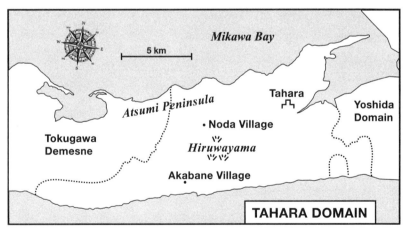

Maps of Tosa domain and Tahara domain.
Produced by Andrew Roberts

Acknowledgments

This book began as an attempt to resolve some problems posed by my first book. Three scholars provided me with key departure points: While I was doing an article on the abolition of Tosa domain at the time of the Meiji Restoration, Professor Mitani Hiroshi provided a thoughtful critique and advice concerning differences between the Tokugawa period and the Meiji period. Professor Watanabe Hiroshi's research on Tokugawa governmental ideology then supplied fundamental inspiration and my start at a methodological approach to historical terminology. Professor Ronald Toby's critique of my use of the notion of "country" to mean "daimyo domain" in my first book forced me to rethink the relationship between governmental space and language use. Additionally, along the way of my investigations, I also found particularly helpful inspirations in the research of Ōhira Yuichi on law, Peter Nosco, Alan Grapard, and Haga Shōji on religion, Takagi Shōsaku and Kasaya Kazuhiko on warrior society, and Philip Brown and Herman Ooms on political culture, all of whom I would like to mention here with particular thanks. This is just the tip of the iceberg of my intellectual debt, and I acknowledge many other scholars' valuable research in the footnotes.

I have taken many years to research and write this book, and I have incurred a tremendous debt of gratitude to many people and institutions. The following institutions contributed crucial financial and other support: The Japan Foundation provided me with a Faculty Research Fellowship in 1994–1995, thanks to which I began research on this and another project. During that year the Faculty of Economics at Doshisha University supplied me with all of the benefits of visiting scholar status. The American Philosophical Society gave me a Sabbatical Leave Fellowship in 2004–2005 for a year of further research and writing. The National Museum of History and Ethnography in Sakura, Japan, provided a summer fellowship in 2008 at its institution, during which time I made my final key research advances. The UCSB Division of Humanities and Fine Arts and the UCSB Academic Senate offered important support at various times during this project. The staff of Kōchi University, Kōchi Prefecture Library, Kōchi City Library, and the Yamauchi Shrine Treasury and Archives all gave me the finest assistance possible whenever I showed up. The secretarial staff at the Tahara Municipal Museum were most helpful when I visited.

Thanks to the following people for assistance and advice at various stages: Dani Botsman and Tsukada Takashi in Osaka, Kurushima Hiroshi and Hoya Tōru in Tokyo, and Ōhira Yuichi and Fujita Teiichirō in Kyoto. My friends and teachers in Kōchi—Akizawa Shigeru, Ogi Shin'ichirō, Takahashi Shirō, Uchikawa Kiyosuke, Yorimitsu Kanji, and Moriguchi Kōji (a dear friend who passed away while I was working on this project)—all helped me immensely with their learning, kindness, and generosity. Thinking on them and my other friends in Kōchi reminds me daily why I love Tosa so much. James Baxter, James Brooks, Suzy Cincone, Joshua Fogel, Helen Hardacre, Tsuyoshi Hasegawa, David Howell, Kate Nakai, Constantine Vaporis, and Anne Walthall all provided assistance and comments concerning drafts of various chapters. My mother, Betty Roberts, and my sister Peggy Roberts greatly improved the readability of this book by providing careful editing of the near-completed manuscript. My brother Andrew Roberts created maps and figures for the book. Thanks also to Patricia Crosby and the staff of the University of Hawai'i Press, as well as copy editor Rosemary Wetherold, for their kind assistance and support and for improving the manuscript in its final stages. What mistakes remain are purely my own responsibility.

Thanks to Yachiyo for helping me in life throughout, and to our children, May and Ken, who give me much pride and happiness.

Names, Dates, and Units Used in the Text

Names are written in the Japanese fashion, with family names first and personal names second. Following conventions of Japanese history writing, when one name is used, it is usually the personal name rather than the family name, so the daimyo Yamauchi Tadayoshi is referred to as Tadayoshi rather than Yamauchi. I refer to a daimyo household as a clan or house, and to the territory they ruled as a domain or realm. When I put a "the" in front of the family name, for example "the Yamauchi," I am referring to the clan. The Yamauchi clan is also known as the Yamanouchi clan in modern times. I use the former reading because it is the way that the Yamauchi call themselves and was the common and official usage in the Tokugawa period. The Yamanouchi reading originated in modern Tokyo. Note that modern libraries and bibliographies romanize both ways but tend toward the Tokyo reading.

All translations in the text are my own from the cited sources unless otherwise noted.

The early modern Japanese used a different calendar from the modern one. Each year included twelve months of thirty days, and sometimes an inserted intercalary month as well, to make up for slippage in the lunar and solar cycles. An intercalary seventh month, for example, followed the normal seventh month. Each month of the early modern year usually began about one month later than the corresponding month of the modern Western calendar. For example, the second day of the twelfth month of the fifth year of Meiji was the same day as December 31, 1872. The next day, January 1, 1873, the Japanese began using the modern Western calendar.

Years were counted by a succession of eras. The eras were decided, not according to reigns, but by astrological considerations and might change mid-year. The shortest era in the early modern period lasted only one year, and the longest lasted twenty years. I have given the Japanese days and months and the most approximate Western calendrical year in the following manner: I write the fourteenth day of the fifth month of the first year of the Tenmei era as 1781/5/14.

I have used the Edo-period gold currency unit *ryō*, which equaled 4 *bun*. I have used in the text the following early modern units of measurement. Their approximate Western equivalents are as follows:

silver weight: 1 *kan* = 1,000 *monme* = 3.75 kilograms = 8.25 pounds
rice volume: 1 *koku* = 180 liters = 5.1 bushels

One *koku* was considered to be the volume of rice that one adult male would eat in a year. Although prices fluctuated, one *ryō* of gold could buy roughly one *koku* of rice throughout most of the Edo period.

Introduction

I found information on the following incident of the Tokugawa period (1600–1868) in the castle diary of Tahara domain, which was ruled by daimyo lords of the Miyake clan: In the autumn of 1792, the Grand Inspector of the Tokugawa government entered the Edo residence of the childless daimyo Miyake Yasukuni on a mission to certify that although Yasukuni was ill, he was of sound mind when he personally chose whom he would adopt to assume his position and inherit the domain. The Grand Inspector brought government physicians to evaluate the state of Yasukuni's health and mental fitness. A roomful of domain doctors and Miyake clan relatives waited to witness the adoption ceremony, when the bedridden Yasukuni would imprint his personal seal on a document naming his choice of heir. The law stated that if a bedridden daimyo did not personally choose his adopted heir while in the presence of the Grand Inspector, then the Tokugawa government would terminate the lineage and confiscate the daimyo's domain. For the Miyake who ruled the small domain of Tahara in Mikawa province, this misfortune could cause hundreds of retainers and their families to become homeless and masterless. Merchants in the domain might go bankrupt if the daimyo's loans went unpaid, and villagers would wonder if their advance payments of taxes would be honored by whomever the Tokugawa overlord chose to install as successor. The certification staked the interests of the clan and the domain against the authority of the Tokugawa government, whose chief legal official presided over the tense ceremony to make sure that everyone present respected Tokugawa law. On this particular occasion the ceremony went smoothly, younger brother Miyake Yasutomo was certified as heir, and the Grand Inspector notified the Senior Councillors of the Tokugawa government. The Miyake clan in Edo let out a collective sigh of relief. The clan was safe: Yasutomo would be named the next daimyo when Yasukuni died. Miyake clan officials sent a letter by express post to chief officials of Tahara domain with the happy news. The same letter also reported the sad news that immediately following the ceremony lord Yasukuni's illness had taken a sudden turn for the worse and, despite the best efforts of the doctors at hand, he had died that very night, surrounded by relatives who were, as the letter noted, "speechless with grief." However, the next paragraph of the same letter stated that Yasukuni had *not* died that night following the ceremony; that—as all samurai in Tahara had been told many weeks earlier—he had actually died fifty-five days earlier. When I first read the castle diary and the letter recorded within, this incident and the letter itself that blithely reported in two paragraphs two conflicting versions of the lord's death puzzled me greatly.[1]

After much research, I discovered that, thanks to the performance of the Tokugawa inheritance ceremony, the discrepancies in Miyake Yasukuni's two dates of death did not matter. Nor did it matter that the Grand Inspector and government doctors knew of the earlier death and that their superiors most likely were also well aware of the situation. Ever after, all participants in the ceremony would say that they had performed it in full compliance with the law. Furthermore, all available Tokugawa sources on this event reveal nothing happening out of order with the death and the adoption and the requirements of law. Nor do they record that Yasutomo was not actually Yasukuni's younger brother, that he was not the age he purported to be, or that, eventually, he too officially "died" long after he died. We can learn these facts only from Miyake clan documents that were intended to be read only by clan insiders.

The official records produced by the Tokugawa government are "wrong" on most of the facts of Miyake Yasutomo's adoption, as indeed I have found they are inaccurate about a large proportion of daimyo deaths, adoptions, and identities. Not only were inheritances regularly carried out in ways not according to the law, but a surprisingly large number of daimyo appearing in Tokugawa records were actually a succession of two individuals who were fit into one official identity. On such matters Tokugawa sources, such as the official history, the *Tokugawa jikki,* and the lineages of its retainers, such as the *Kansei chōshū shokafu,* are useless for modern historians. They are records that present ceremonial and seemly "facts" as if they were reality.[2] Yet just as a daimyo could be both dead and alive at the same time, the Tokugawa sources are both useless and useful. If we put the right questions to the documents, they instruct us in the political culture of the day.

When I first read the Miyake clan diaries, I thought that the above adoption ceremony was a strange waste of time and money. The Miyake were not concealing the premature death in earnest, so why so much pretending when just about everyone involved was in the know? Daimyo adoption and inheritance were governmental processes, not a theatrical play. Yet, as I grappled with this and similar problems, I came to learn the functional meanings of such ceremonies and that, in fact, the "play" was the thing of government. The ability to command *performance* of duty—in the thespian sense when actual performance of duty might be lacking—was a crucial tool of Tokugawa power that effectively worked toward preserving the peace in the realm. Real political struggle between parties occurred in the connections between *performance* and performance.

Such *performance* of obedience helped make the Tokugawa regime one of the most stable governments of the early modern world. For more than two centuries rebellions against Tokugawa authority were almost unknown. Praise for this peace was plentiful in the day, encapsulated in the epithet "the Tokugawa Great Peace" (*Tokugawa taihei*) or simply "the Great Peace" (*taihei*). This expression reflected thanks for freedom from the incessant warfare that had afflicted the preceding era of Warring States (1467–1590), a time when the archipelago was divided up among many competing warlord states and samurai houses that had powerful traditions of independence and violent ambition.[3] The late sixteenth-century conquests of the succession of three unifiers, Oda Nobunaga, Toyotomi Hideyoshi, and Tokugawa Ieyasu, eventually restored central authority, and the Tokugawa government of the early to mid-seventeenth century gave the new order a long-lasting political stability. This new era has two common names, which I use synonymously in this book. It is known as the Tokugawa period, when named after the clan of the overlords, and also as the Edo period, when named for the capital city of the Tokugawa government, a city today known as Tokyo.

Institutional historians have provided us with a clear outline of the Edo-period government: Tokugawa Ieyasu and his allied daimyo warlords defeated his enemies at the Battle of Sekigahara in 1600. He immediately punished the enemy daimyo by confiscating their domains completely or in part and rewarded himself and his allies with these spoils, making them all lords of larger realms. In 1603 he received the title of *seiitaishōgun* (chief of all samurai generals, hereafter called shogun) from the emperor who resided in Kyoto and was the nominal ruler of Japan, albeit a ruler with hardly any worldly power. The Tokugawa shoguns ruled from the city of Edo in a highly bureaucratic feudal government known to us as the shogunate or the *bakufu*. A shogun ruled his own massive domain within Japan and also was lord over the hundreds of daimyo who ruled the remaining four-fifths of the islands. Underneath this Tokugawa hegemony, the daimyo ruled their own separate domains with a degree of independence but were subordinate to the broad framework of shogunal directives, the supreme law of the land.

The society was organized into hereditary status groups. At the top were the titular emperor and his aristocratic court, who lived under samurai control in Kyoto. They possessed almost no temporal power themselves but were respected for being descended from people who had actually ruled Japan several hundred years earlier. The Tokugawa and the daimyo were hereditary samurai who jealously held the real governing power over Japan, while regarding the emperor and aristocrats as their status superiors and seemingly delighting in being allowed to participate in aspects of Kyoto court protocol and culture. The Tokugawa had thousands of high-ranking samurai retainers called bannermen, many of whom served as prestigious government officials in the shogunate alongside some daimyo who were also chosen to serve in shogunate offices. Beneath the bannermen were samurai called housemen, who served as guards, scribes, and the like for the Tokugawa government. Daimyo likewise had their own ranks of samurai retainers who served their own houses and domain governments as officials and guards. The collective role of the samurai class was to govern and defend Japan. Beneath the samurai were the demilitarized commoner classes of villagers and townspeople who farmed, manufactured, and engaged in commerce and services and entertainment as ways of living, all subject to the injustices of samurai "justice" that defended the regime.

The first fifty years of the regime saw much change and innovation, but all major government institutions had been put in place by the middle of the seventeenth century. A succession of fifteen Tokugawa shoguns reigned over a stable regime for centuries. Daimyo governed their domains over a similar stretch of generations as long as they escaped punishment from the shogun, something that became rarer as the era deepened. Commercial growth created financial and morale problems for the samurai and encouraged both social disorder and a vibrant culture among the commoners, but the regime itself lasted unchanged in its basic outlines until its downfall during the Meiji Restoration of 1868. If political and institutional change is the mark of vibrancy, then the regime itself seems to have begun two centuries of stagnation and long, slow decline in the 1660s.

Although the institutional structures of the political order have been well studied by historians, there remains much room for research on the cultural logic by which the regime operated. This book looks at seeming contradictions in political events and analyzes them by comparing Tokugawa-produced documents with various daimyo-produced documents so as to explore the assumptions meaningful to the participants and thereby approach an understanding of the cultural logic of their politics. In the process I particularly focus on exploring what has often been described as the tension between the centralized and decentralized nature—sometimes called the centralized feudalism—of the Tokugawa order that was expressed in the division of authority between the Tokugawa shogun and the daimyo. An examination and an analysis of both the autonomy of daimyo and their subservience to the Tokugawa government takes a central place in this book.

I have discovered that there are two difficult elements to describing my findings, for which I need beg the reader's patience and indulgence: One is that a study of culture must rely heavily upon the language and terms of the Tokugawa period and their contextual nuances. So there is a plethora of Japanese terms. Where I think appropriate, I use translations, but because translations often carry their own inappropriate cargo of meaning, I occasionally remind the reader of the original terms and their contexts of usage. There are a few words so important to the analysis that I must use them in their original more often than not, because no translation can express more than a small aspect of the word's meaning. The second narrational difficulty arises from the fact that people of the Tokugawa period held very different notions of the spaces of politics than modern people do. This is so difficult that people living in the modern national world almost *need* to forget this and reinscribe the Tokugawa order into nationally framed forms of political space so as to describe that order in simple terms. Because the concept of "space" is crucial to understanding Tokugawa political culture, I must use it in ways that may be unfamiliar to the reader, and I set out its parameters below.

The politics of Tokugawa feudal space

Alternate definitions of political space are key to understanding how the roles of inferiors in this hierarchy could simultaneously express both "autonomy" and "complete subservience." Autonomy was described in the Tokugawa era largely in terms of space, and the language of active politics was largely composed of spatial metaphors. The Tokugawa government delegated ruling authority over realms and houses to warlords, thereby forming a governmental organization that thinkers of the day termed *hōken:* a polity of delegated and "sealed-off spaces" of governance. Subsequent scholars have translated this term as "feudal," and I follow their lead.[4] The "sealed-off spaces" permitted interiors and exteriors to be incongruent, in such a way that a daimyo could be both dead and alive at the same time, as long as the conditions were divided by the political spacing of "inside the clan" and "outside the clan." Manipulation of space allowed many such contradictions. For example, a daimyo retainer might regard his lord's realm as a "country" (*kuni*) on the same day as he regarded the Japan into which it was integrated as a "country" as well. Such situations seem paradoxical when we try to understand them with the terms of modern national discourse, but they were part of functioning politics of the Tokugawa world.

The contradictions did not interfere with the Tokugawa government's key goal of maintaining peace and hierarchal stability. The government strictly enforced numerous rituals of submission by the responsible leaders of feudal spaces in order to contain potential disorder in the smallest spaces of authority possible and encourage stable self-management of the many lesser polities that Tokugawa rule contained. This policy of containment began by delegating strong ruling authority to daimyo lords over their realms and houses in order to limit samurai and commoner disorder. However, the ambitions of these same lords, their kin, and samurai in general and the power that they might derive from their local territories posed a potential threat to Tokugawa hegemony. The regime developed various institutions to restrain the ambitions of powerful samurai: a hostage order, the alternate attendance system, periodic inspections of domainal management, control of courtly ranks and office, control of marriage and inheritance, supreme judicial authority vested in an overarching high court, and many other things that indirectly exerted authority over all of the Japan of the day. These institutional controls that enforced the subservience of daimyo and other powerful political players have been well and ably explored by scholars of the past century, but I argue that because the logic by which these institutions operated has been understudied, their political functioning and the nature of the documents produced by this system have been significantly misunderstood.[5]

This book is concerned with how politics operated within these institutions of control according to indigenous understandings of political behavior. How did the politically active players of Tokugawa Japan imagine, describe, and perform their governments? Throughout this book, I use some common terms of the day that have hitherto been largely ignored by historians in Japan and in the West: *omote, uchi,* and *naishō. Omote* generally means "surface" or "interface" and refers in Tokugawa politics to the location of ritualized relations between an inferior and a superior where the inferior party should act out subservience to the superior's will. *Uchi,* its opposite, means "inside," and its political usage refers to the acknowledged space of authority held by the inferior party in a hierarchic relationship of power. The character for *uchi* is read as *nai* in compound words, and the space of authority held by its leaders was often called *naibun*, meaning "one's portion of competence." *Uchi* frequently carries the nuance of informality and is part of the most useful word for analyzing the negotiations and agreements of Tokugawa politics: *naishō*, which means "inside agreement" and refers to the arrangements that could not be allowed to appear in *omote* situations. Behavior in *omote* situations and behavior in *uchi* spaces often contradicted each other. A lord might profess total compliance with an order from the Tokugawa government and yet ignore it back in his realm. This fact alone might be interpreted as mere disobedience or corruption or as weakness of the central regime—interpretations that have been common in historical writing—but for two things: first, there was usually a mutually arranged management of this "disobedience," and second, the difference was not merely about submission to power but also about the various situational discourses of lived reality.

Omote and *uchi* involved both behavior and management of personal, social and political space; they referred to situations and sometimes physical locations such as domains and houses. One crucial aspect of Tokugawa politics was keeping *uchi* activity and *omote* activity separated. When this was achieved, then enacting subservience in *omote* did not mean full-time submission; it was the reassuring *performance* of signs that one accepted the hierarchy and general order of the higher authority. *Omote* was the ritual framework that statically bound disparate *naibun* compartments of authority together. The informal *naishō* agreements that were made concerning what could and could not be actually tolerated were what dynamically bound the realms of *omote* and *uchi* together in living political action. The boundary between acceptable and intolerable deviation was subtle and sometimes shifting, and the stuff of politics was discovering just where this boundary lay for whom and at what moment. The cautious political players relied upon investigating and following the precedents of earlier *naishō* agreements among communities of daimyo or within their own pasts, and the ambitious worked to set new standards for acceptable deviation.[6] Because inferior parties felt the need to record precedents of informal arrangements, relevant documents of this hidden side of politics are plentiful. Conversely, the formal records kept by politically superior parties can be misleading because they primarily record *omote* activity.

This state of affairs can be disconcerting for modern historians who tend to look for politics of open contestation. Rarely would someone in the Tokugawa period object to or attempt to change an *omote* rule of behavior, because to do so would damage one's case. A person who disrupted an *omote* situation would most likely be seen, at best, as lacking knowledge and decorum and, at worst, as a criminal challenging or sullying the legitimacy of the overlord. *Omote* was a homonym for "face" and "honor," and indeed it is evident from the documents that the meanings of ritual interaction, face, and honor intertwined within samurai culture in ways that linked personal identity and political behavior. The performance of respect was so crucial to the order that a lord would much more likely be punished for the status affront of wearing a bit of tiger pelt into Edo castle than for breaking Tokugawa laws back in his domain. The key demands of the Tokugawa were for everyone to hold up a front of compliance and respect and to see that disorder did not erupt into the outside of their realms and households. Politics usually took the shape of asserting compliance with Tokugawa demands in formal *omote* situations, while at the same time informally negotiating actual needs.

Deviance in *omote* could be a form of political behavior, but it was disruptive, uncivil politics and always called for punishment. Such deviance was most often used strategically by people poorly placed in the hierarchies of power, typically commoners engaging in public disorder as a tactic to cause their superiors to "lose face." Illegal petitioning, protests, and riots could be effective tools in collective bargaining because they exposed a ruler's inability to maintain the peace.[7] Such disruption often achieved demands, but always at a heavy cost. The rituals of resolution of such conflicts involved punishing some representative of the inferior party for the crime of insubordination so that reinstatement of the hierarchy could be affirmed. Leaders of protests therefore expected to receive punishment and had to be willing to sacrifice themselves for the collective good.[8] This book primarily explores daimyo and samurai politics but also delves into some cases of commoner protest where the politics of *omote* and *uchi* operated.

National space and its narratives

The problem of nationalism is a muse to many modern historians from Renan to Hobsbawm, Anderson, and Duara and many others to whom I am indebted.[9] The present-day profession of history is the type of history that has its origins in the nineteenth century and continues to take shape within the era of nationalism. It is worth reflecting on national presumptions about space and how they affect our narration of history. Nationalizing the past essentially involves a process of translating the past into terms and relationships easily understood within an accepted frame of reference that is some nation. Nations need storied pasts, and historians create these. They write pasts of "our nation" for members of the same country, pasts of foreign nations to help them understand international relations historically, pasts of international order and disorder, and pasts that press local regions to be safely contained within national history. Stories, categories, and ways of thinking from prenational pasts that are not easily translated into this framework tend to be devalued, overlooked, and erased. This nationalizing influence is certainly not monolithic—there are many exceptions—but it is dominant and powerful enough to deserve serious reflection on how its perspective affects the analysis and interpretation of pre-modern history.

My intent in this book is to bring a dialogic method to narrating the prenational past. I think of my research as a conversation with the people of the past, through which I desire both to understand them in my terms and also to learn about my present from their terms. Like most contemporary historians, I do not think that one can just recount the "bare facts" of the past; rather, I think historical narration inevitably transforms the past into present concerns. I understand positivism to be an attempt to master and dominate past histories with present knowledge, and relativism to be an attempt to frame historical knowledge so that narrative power goes both ways. Using this notion of dialogue, I have asked the people of the Tokugawa era to contribute to my self-understanding on the following issue: What is the nature of my nationalism, and how does my nationalism affect the way that I interpret and narrate the past in general and specifically the past of the Tokugawa period? This question has framed the narration of the whole book.

The nation of Japan today seems so relentless in its assertion of "Japaneseness" that it seems somewhat absurd for historians to say that there were numerous "countries" within the archipelago as recently as the Tokugawa period. Modern Japan has no easy way of incorporating smaller countries within, because the modern nationhood of Japan is unitary, and Japan is emphatically a nation that contains regions. Discursively, Japan possesses a national past and present, and its regions possess regional pasts and presents. The power of the present national discourse makes it difficult for modern historians to perceive and comprehend, let alone question, the extent of the difference between the political spatial consciousness of the prenational Tokugawa order and that of national modernity.

To explore this issue, I use "nation" and "national" in this book to identify Japan from the Meiji period on, and other nation-states such as began to appear in the Americas and Europe from the end of the eighteenth century. Certainly, protonational elements were present in prenational countries, but the fuller complex of elements formed around, and promoted by, a nation-state did not yet exist. Many individual elements, later transformed and woven into Japanese nationalism, certainly originated in the Tokugawa period and earlier, including some ideas that had been scaled to fit the conceptual space of "Japan" and some to fit the space of "domains" and "houses" as well. For example, as Mary Elizabeth Berry has observed, the "imagined communities" of Japanese print culture certainly emerged in the Tokugawa period.[10] Political and religious traditions of an imperially centered country of Japan have deep lineages explored by many scholars, and as this book argues, certain practices later appropriated by the Japanese state's official religion of Shinto originally developed in daimyo-ruled domainal countries of the Tokugawa period. As my earlier book on domainal political economy, *Mercantilism in a Japanese Domain,* argues, some daimyo domains developed mercantilist forms of political economic nationalism, which were later appropriated into the service of modern Japanese nationalism.[11] However, the existence of these elements, which can be described historically as protonational, made neither "Japan" nor any domain a "nation" in the understanding of this book. Under the feudal politics of the Tokugawa period they were variously and situationally referred to as "all under heaven" realms, military states, daimyo realms, countries, kingdoms, dukedoms, houses, domains, fiefs, and private property. One purpose of this book is to discern the logic that underlay this variety of terms so as to better understand the politics of the era.

The influence of nationalism on the narration of even recent premodern pasts is evident in the language scholars used to describe the Tokugawa world. This is true in both Japanese and English historiography, for David Lowenthal's dictum that "the past is a foreign country" to modern people certainly applies to the Japan before Meiji.[12] Modern Japanese-language descriptions of the Tokugawa era involve an implicit consensus to translate basic terminology of government to fit the national space. Modern Japanese use of such terms as *han* to mean daimyo domain, *bakufu* for the Tokugawa government, *shōgun* for that government's ruler, *tenryō* for that government's demesne, and *tennō* for the emperor obscures the fact that they either were not commonly used in the Edo period or were then used in very different ways and contexts than in the present. Many of these staple terms of Japanese historiography are even much used in English-language writings, ironically imparting a sense of historical authenticity and accuracy and, more to the point, effectively inscribing an overriding sense of Japanese space to that past.[13] The victors of the Meiji Restoration who destroyed the Tokugawa government chose these terms to narrate Tokugawa history, and they have reigned over modern historical consciousness ever since.[14]

One may ask why this choice of different terms to describe the history of the Tokugawa era is significant, thus leading to the question of what were the original terms anyway and where and how can we find them? First, one must note that because Tokugawa-era discursive political space was different from a present-day national sense of such space, and because, in general, words take on meaning within an unspoken frame of reference, it is impossible to give a one-to-one translation between modern terms and Tokugawa-period terms. The modern reader's assumed frame for these political terms is the nation of Japan, but the Tokugawa-era frames of reference were divided among feudal spaces, and political terms were deployed according to the location of the speaker and the listener within that feudal hierarchy. For example, neither the modern term *han* for domains nor the term *bakufu* for the Tokugawa government was commonly used in the Tokugawa period. *Han* is an amalgamation of many premodern terms with distinct meanings: territory (*ryō*), territorial portion (*ryōbun*), personal territory (*shiryō*), country (*kuni*), government (*kōgi*), state (*kokka*), daimyo house (*ie*), and others (see Table 1). Each word was used in certain contexts, some divided by *omote* and *uchi* considerations. The common Tokugawa-period term for *bakufu* was *kōgi* (government). Because *kōgi* was sometimes used to mean daimyo government in domain internal discourse, use of the term can be confusing in a national framework. *Bakufu*

Table 1. Modern terms and Edo-period governmental terms

ENGLISH TERMS	MODERN JAPANESE TERMS	EDO-PERIOD TERMS
lord, daimyo	*daimyō*	daimyō, kō, uesama, tono, shujō
domain, realm	*han*	ryō, ie, kokka, kachū, ryōbun, ryōgoku, kuni, shiryō, zaisho, fu, seifu, kōgi
shogun	*shōgun*	kubō, shōgun, kō, uesama, taikun, shujō, tenkasama
shogunate	*bakufu*	kōgi, kōhen, kokka, chōtei
emperor	*tennō*	tenshi, mikado, shujō, tōgin
court	*chōtei*	kinri, chōtei

and *han* (or the English "shogunate" and "domain") give the concepts immediate, clear distinction within modern Japanese space.

Other differences between modernity and premodernity are also at work in the word choices. The modern historical terms unify the distinct Edo-period concepts of "territorial government" and "household government" by subsuming the "houses" (*ie*) within the daimyo territorial state and its bureaucracy. Houses, families, and households are "private" matters under the state and its bureaucracy in national modernity around the world and in Japan. But in the Edo period all samurai houses were themselves feudal governmental institutions that possessed legal and administrative authority. A daimyo house would survive intact a transfer to a new territory, where it would build a new territorial state. Some daimyo even held no territorial realm at all but ruled houses, merely receiving stipends from the Tokugawa, such as the early Tayasu Tokugawa house, or from a "parent" daimyo such as the Satake Iki no kami branch daimyo lineage of the Satake clan, who ruled Akita domain.[15] Most daimyo ruled both house and realm. House law (*kahō*) existed alongside domainal realm law (*kokuhō* or *ryōchū hatto*) in the language used under daimyo authority. The former was the law concerning retainers of the lord's household, a privileged group within any domain, while the latter was the law applying to the territory and all of the people of the domain. As with domainal territories, houses also possessed a *naibun* inside portion of competence. For example, members of a daimyo's house were subject to his house punishment even if they committed crimes while in Tokugawa territory. The authority of daimyo superseded that of the Tokugawa in these cases, such that Tokugawa officials could not enter the official residences of daimyo in the capital city of Edo with impunity. In the terminology of this book, samurai houses generally constituted a feudal "political space," an authority that ran by rules potentially contradicting the higher *omote* rules.

Although they coexisted as polities in the Tokugawa period, "governmental houses" had a much longer lineage among samurai than did "territorial states" historically, going back to the Kamakura era (1183–1333). Territorial states were forms of rule forged during the Warring States period and continued in modified form into the Tokugawa period. The status system of the Tokugawa period was based on houses and helped continue samurai dominance over other status groups even as the relative importance of territorial state rule expanded.[16] We can see in the multiple and changing meanings of the term *kokka* (made from two characters meaning "country" and "house") over history a long, evolving shift in balance from house governments to state governments. Originally *kokka* commonly referred to the house that ruled a region. Beginning in the Warring States era it also gained the meaning of the territorial state. The *kokka* of a domain could variously mean the daimyo house, its house government, and its territorial state government, meanings that continued throughout the Tokugawa period. In modern Japan, however, *kokka* means solely nation-state, and houses are subsumed within, existing as private entities.[17]

Because the term *han* used today subsumes and obscures this pair of house and state government types that were active in the Tokugawa era, it makes certain historical tensions less visible. This is problematic because these tensions gave shape to endemic political struggles important to the people of that era. My first book about the emergence of mercantilist thought (*kokueki*) in domains explored the struggle between the sometimes differing interests of the samurai household government and the territorial state in fiscal and economic policy. In order to do that analysis, I had to reject use of the historiographical term *han* and rely upon the indigenous house/state distinction to understand the dynamic of class interests at stake in the emergence of the *kokueki* ideology. The economic interests of the samurai-focused house and those of an increasingly commercialized domain filled with mercantile commoners were often at odds, and their interaction created and shaped *kokueki* thought. Following the conceptual work of Fujita Teiichirō, I described domains as existing as countries within an international trading order that was Japan. And following the analysis of Miyamoto Mataji, I relied on the indigenous terms of the day to describe domainal autonomy and to argue that while the domain of Tosa was a *kuni* (a country), the space of Japan was by contrast solely a *tenka,* a term that literally means "all under heaven" and is translatable as "empire."[18] I argued that this polity ruled by the Tokugawa was not a state but a space imagined as a universal realm, an international order of domainal countries subjected to the overarching authority of the Tokugawa hegemon.

Some historians have criticized this view, most clearly Ronald Toby, who pointed out the many Tokugawa-period examples of calling Japan a *kuni* and a *kokka* in a political sense.[19] Although I had described Japan as a cultural, linguistic, and religious country, I had come to rely too singularly on the domainal perspective with regard to political economy and thereby did not recognize or value evidence that the Tokugawa government was also described as a political *kokka* at times in the terminology of the day and therefore that Japan was rhetorically politicized as a territorial country in addition to being politicized as a *tenka.* My assumption was that if domains were politicized countries, then Japan had to be something different, because there could not be something so conceptually strange as hundreds of domainal political countries within what was also a Tokugawa political country. So with much evidence of the use of *tenka* at hand I decided that the latter must be something akin to an empire. My first book was focused on economic policy, and to me the "real" countries in that sphere of activity were domains and not the Tokugawa *tenka*. Although I had been concerned to identify and use indigenous terms in my analysis, when contradictions arose in terminology identifying which was the country or not, I felt compelled to resolve it in one direction. Likewise, critics of the description of Japan as an international order have said that Japan is the "real" country while domains were at best quasi states. Toby, for instance, writes, "Japan, I shall argue was 'the Nation' and the *bakufu* 'the State' in early modern Japan, while domains were neither 'states' (except in the sense that Texas and Massachusetts are 'states') nor 'nations,' but local or regional units within the political and discursive bounds of 'Japan.'"[20] This too was attempting to re- solve the multiple discourses existing in the sum of surviving evidence, but in the other direction, so as to rhetorically unify Japan as a "nation."

Resolving the multivocality in the evidence so as to frame interpretation to fit the modern nation-state of Japan is common in modern historiography. As an example, historian Mizumoto Kunihiko begins his book on the Tokuga- wa period with the vigorous assertion, "At the beginning of the seventeenth century a nation-state [*kokka*] was born. Begun by Oda Nobunaga, Toyotomi Hideyoshi, and Tokugawa Ieyasu, the creation of a unitary state was com- pleted in the era of Tokugawa Iemitsu. . . . The countrymen of the Tokugawa nation-state called themselves 'Japanese,' and they thought of their state and society as 'Japan.'"[21] Most of Mizumoto's statements are well evidenced, but his evidence is selective and ignores the vast amount of counterevidence in Edo-period documents that does not fit his scheme. As is demonstrated in this book, many "countrymen" (*kokumin*) also thought of their state and so- ciety as the domain in which they lived or as the ruling house or daimyo state (*kokka*) they served. Selectivity is part of historical interpretation, and Mizu- moto's particular interpretive bias comes from living within the conditions of worldwide nationalism and its associated forms of imperialism. This unitary imagination leads modern people to insistently pose the question, "Which is the authentic nation and which is not, and how can we know by locating origins?" This question shapes the power struggles of modernity in our world and reinscribes a national identity onto the past, but what interesting pasts are obscured by nationally narrating the history of prenational times?

In summary, this book attempts to work through the geography of politics in the Tokugawa period by understanding how its political and social spaces were imagined and understood by the people of the day in all its diversity.

Omote and *uchi* and related terms are keys that unlock many significant—and sometimes, to modern eyes, curious—aspects of the Tokugawa past. Political behavior that may appear on the surface to be banal, powerless, desperate, or just plain silly begins to look meaningful, powerful, and serious when understood in terms of the concepts of *omote* and *uchi* as they operated in the Tokugawa period. These words are left to us as flotsam from a sinking world, and they have since been largely overlooked in historiography. However, the reasons why they have not appeared valuable to understanding politics of the Tokugawa era are due not to their lack of explanatory power but to the preoccupations of modernity and the historiographical traditions that national modernity engenders. Thus, not only does exploring the use of these terms in the Tokugawa period allow us to more directly access the thought of the people of the time, but, furthermore, the process of narrating this past to people in the twenty-first century uncovers our own nationalistic preoccupations and makes the past a mirror reflecting our modern condition.

Organization of this book

The current book analyzes in each chapter various power arrangements and struggles of the Tokugawa period in terms of the politics of *omote* and *uchi*.[22] It does so to explore how the Tokugawa order politically worked and held together, but primarily from the perspective of large and small daimyo domains rather than the perspective of the Tokugawa clan, commoners, or the imperial house. Chapter 1, "The Geography of Politics," describes the institutions of the feudal government, with a focus on the politics of spatial containment of conflict. It shows that the identity and subjectivity of actors changed radically, depending upon whether they were operating in an *omote* space or an *uchi* space, and reveals that the character of political units themselves were likewise expressed differently according to *omote* and *uchi*. Chapter 2, "Performing the Tokugawa Right to Know," explores the information regime of the Tokugawa government. This highly bureaucratic system collected and managed vast amounts of data from all of the parts of Japan under Tokugawa direct and indirect rule. The chapter evaluates the nature of this information collection in terms of accuracy and its role in guaranteeing submissiveness of daimyo and maintenance of the peace. The daimyo often supplied inaccurate information with the full complicity of Tokugawa officials, and this was done from very early on in the period. The disjuncture between the local truth and the submitted information, clearly evident in the more fully surviving documents of the latter half of the Tokugawa period, has been interpreted by most historians as a sign of systemic decline and the waning power of Tokugawa authority. Yet I argue, through analysis of seventeenth-century examples of information collection, that the disjuncture was an important part of the desired order from the beginning and that the main purpose of touring inspections by Tokugawa officials and other data collection was the performance of rituals of subservience and obedience, and the creation of arrangements for service rather than the quality of the information itself, suggesting that the data this regime produced need to be understood by historians in terms of *omote* and *uchi* interactions. The next chapter, "Politics of the Living Dead," explores the politics of *omote* and *uchi* on occasions of daimyo inheritance by adoption, a problem at the highest levels of interaction between daimyo and the Tokugawa government. It shows how the formal system of inheritance set up by the Tokugawa government was truly dysfunctional and thus would have doomed all daimyo houses to extinction and would likely have led to an early revolution against the Tokugawa. Nevertheless, this *omote* dysfunction was deliberate, reducing violent conflict among samurai within domains through requiring their thespian performance of subservience to seemingly impossible *omote* demands. As a result of this order, the lineages of daimyo and bannermen submitted to the Tokugawa are by necessity images of *omote* "performance" and not of actual reality. This example of disjuncture between inside realities and external performance also has broad implications for the reading of Tokugawa-era documents.

Chapter 4, "Territorial Border Disputes," explores the operation of the Tokugawa legal system in the resolution of territorial disputes between villages and between daimyo. One focus is on how consolidation of domainal territorial membership in the seventeenth century was fostered by the requirements of secrecy during the management of these trials. Another is on how, on the one hand, the system repeatedly discouraged litigation and encouraged resolution at the lowest possible level through the deployment of various *omote* rules to suppress disorder in the hierarchy, yet, on the other hand, the system customarily permitted informal ways around the rules so as to let troublesome cases come to adjudication and be resolved. Participants performed acceptance of the sometimes impossible formal rules and thereby were disciplined in their behavior even as they engaged in rule-breaking conflict. The importance of preserving the formal peace was a sword that could cut up and down the hierarchy of power. It mostly worked to suppress dissent by inferiors in the political hierarchy but also gave particular force to social disturbance created by inferiors such as villagers, because their superiors were held responsible for maintaining the appearance of peace and harmony. This chapter explores a dispute between villagers and their daimyo that the villagers managed to bring to the Tokugawa court against all *omote* rules. Inferiors who were willing to submit to a final punishment for offending the hierarchy could frequently win their demands by causing their immediate superior to lose face for failing to manage the problem internally.

To say that the politics of *omote* and *uchi* were normative is not to say that the institutions of the Tokugawa period were static. Chapter 5, "Daimyo Gods," is framed around an argument of significant changes occurring in the Tokugawa era. It engages the transformation of daimyo lords into deities (*kami*), an illegal act according to Tokugawa *omote* rules but one that occurred in many domains nevertheless. Unlike earlier chapters that focus on seventeenth-century evidence and attempt to convey a sense of a functional system rather than an evolution, this chapter looks at the evolution of deifications over the whole Tokugawa period in order to reveal the creative and adaptive potential of this political order. It was an order that allowed innovation to happen in *uchi* spaces even while appearing hidebound in *omote* interaction. The evolving relationship between religious understandings of power and the political order played a significant role in the development of domain rule in the latter half of the Tokugawa period. Changing notions of Shinto religiosity due to the spread of print culture and other factors intersected with and contributed to the creation of an emperor-centered Japan in popular consciousness that figured importantly in the Meiji Restoration, and their manifestation in domain state politics subsequently influenced religious policy of the new Japanese state.

The final chapter, "Histories," shifts gears to reflect on the relationship between historical narration and political order. It first analyzes a number of histories created in the Tokugawa period and relates their narration to the politics of *omote* and *uchi*. It shows that the accuracy of information in most of the Tokugawa histories is the accuracy of recording various *omote* truths rather than the truth as we moderns would regard it. There is much overlap with modern truth, but certain types of facts are likely to be what we today would call fiction. This was due not to a lack of skill of the historians of those days but rather to their different goals in writing history. The chapter also studies the rapid changes made in historical narration in Japan during the Meiji Restoration and reveals how some aspects of the language of modern history writing were adapted from imperial *omote* history of premodern times. The book's conclusion looks at the process of destruction of the feudal order itself and offers some thoughts on what happened to *omote* and *uchi* within Japanese culture in the transition to modernity. The political underpinnings of the culture of *omote* and *uchi* were mostly destroyed, but these concepts and associated modes of behavior continue to operate with less intensity.

This book is not exactly a "regional" history, but it is part of a comparatively recent wave of regional histories by Western scholars on Tokugawa-era Japan that began with Philip Brown's 1993 book, *Central Authority and Local Autonomy in the Formation of Early Modern Japan,* and continued by Kären Wigen, David Howell, Edward Pratt, Mark Ravina, and others whose works are among the inspirations for this book.[23] In one important aspect this book is a continuation of Brown's original project to use a noncentral perspective in order to understand the broader political order. He noted in his book the difficulty that historians have in addressing what seemed a key contradiction between the extensive claims of the overlords and the actual weakness in enforcement of a large degree of those claims. Brown described the Toyotomi and the Tokugawa regimes as "flamboyant" governments because they claimed to be able to do much more than they could. Brown wrote, "Even unchallenged proclamations do not imply an effective implementation of policy. . . . The potential for a positive evaluation of such [nominally strong but actually weak] states is substantial and should be taken seriously."[24] One of the purposes of this book is to further Brown's argument by analyzing the logic of that flamboyance so as to understand that it was not merely bluster and vanity but functioned as *omote* ritual control to ensure the stability of the regime.

Local or "regionally" produced documents and narratives of the Edo period were essential evidence for this book about the culture of Tokugawa politics. In the methodology of this book, local history is not merely a "case study," nor is it simply a history of a smaller "piece" of Japan that provides local color and gives the national story more nuance. I argue that because of the way that *omote* and *naishō* influenced politics, respecting the local and the hierarchically inferior perspective is essential to understanding the politics of the "center." One simply cannot know how the "center" functioned using only the sources that it produced.

1

The Geography of Politics

The Japanese have a word for all of the things carried out in
secrecy—that is, as insider secrets. They call it *naibun*, which is
translated into the Dutch as *binnenkant* (inside). This is because
the laws are so severe that they cannot be applied to the letter,
as actually carrying out the law would cause things to become
great incidents. The word that means the opposite of *naibun*,
inside, is *omotemuki*, which means outside. When an incident is
made public and treated as *omotemuki*, then the legal case must
be treated according to the public rules and then it becomes
impossible to lessen punishments.

—J. F. VAN OVERMEER FISSCHER (1833), clerk in the Dutch Factory on
Deshima[1]

The above quotation comes from a book written by the Dutchman J. F. van
Overmeer Fisscher in 1833, a clerk who had lived in Nagasaki for about nine
years in the 1820s. Here he describes the operation of the legal system of the
Tokugawa period and reveals that the rulers themselves considered their laws
too severe to regularly implement, but rather than changing the laws, they instead manipulated the metaphors of "inside" and "outside" in a way to keep the
peace and prevent incidents in the realm. Secrecy and knowledge were formal
in character and were tied to an anxious management of political, geographical, and social space. If things were mishandled and appeared in *omotemuki*,
then everyone was bound to follow *omote* formal prescriptions, and this might
be disastrous for all concerned.

This pattern was indeed basic to the operation of not merely law but also of politics and identity in the Tokugawa period. The containment of disorder and "incidents" was managed through a political system that delegated generally heritable authority over people and/or territory to powerful individuals in return for their service. The entrusted "inside" spaces existed in such institutional forms as domains, houses, occupational organizations, and villages, and the heads who ruled or represented them were such people as daimyo, samurai, village headmen, outcaste group leaders, and monopoly merchants. The leaders of such units were preoccupied with benefiting from their own position; performing duty, which meant funneling wealth up to their superior; and ensuring that they prevented disorder from breaking out of their spaces of authority and becoming, as Fisscher notes, *omotemuki*, outside knowledge. Such disorder brought higher authority inside and negated internal authority. This pattern was repeated down a branching hierarchy of leaders and institutions, creating spaces within spaces within spaces, such that some historians have described the political order as a "compound state."[2] Although at its governmental heights this order was primarily a set of what we think of as feudal relations between samurai, it existed in varied similar manifestations extending throughout society, interrelated with a social culture invested in inside/outside dichotomies of behavior.[3] The goal of the political order was not centralized direct control, and so the Tokugawa government in charge would, for example, assist daimyo in the containment or suppression of disorder if possible, but it would also hold daimyo responsible for any egregious breaches in their authority. Those lower down in the hierarchies were treated similarly by their lords. All leaders were beneficiaries of, and hostages to, the Great Peace. This tension gave a character to the politics and disorder of the period.

The politics happening in the Tokugawa period are easy to overlook because, in general, duties to superiors were clearly spelled out and rights of inferiors were at best revocable privileges or appeals to precedent. It is possible with a modern sensibility to mistake the authoritarian despotism of the Tokugawa as leaving an inferior little legitimate recourse for resistance against a higher authority. Certainly the *omote* claims of superiors seem limitless, and it is possible to consider the regime to be markedly centralized and absolutist if judged on those formal claims. But asserting "rights" was not the common mode of resistance. Inferiors regularly resisted higher *omote* claims without denying their validity, and furthermore resisted unwanted burdens and control sometimes with the full complicity of their superiors, in a pattern of behavior that held not only in the years of supposed decline but also in the mid-seventeenth century when the Tokugawa regime was in its moment of power most ripe. This chapter introduces the discursive structure of a complex network of political spaces integrated into the Tokugawa government.

Our explanation of Tokugawa-era political space should begin by teasing out the various parts of government in terms of their *omote* demands on inferiors and the spheres of authority and competence that inferiors held. The imperial *omote* based in Kyoto was the highest, having a recorded tradition of supremacy that went back a millennium, but it held very little actual power. The Tokugawa clan was formally beneath the emperor but held such vast authority that Westerners who visited Japan, such as William Adams in the early 1600s and Commodore Matthew Perry in the 1850s, reasonably called the Tokugawa ruler the "emperor" of Japan and relegated the figure in Kyoto to the role of spiritual leader. All daimyo were subject to the Tokugawa government and its *omote* demands, and they ruled their realms and houses as their *naibun* units of competence. Beneath the daimyo were other samurai who ruled their own houses as *naibun* units, but most of them had lost territorial control. Under the *omote* management of the Tokugawa and daimyo (and a small number of enfeoffed religious institutions and retainers) were commoners who were subject to three simultaneous and overlapping modes of organization: geography, house, and occupational status. Through geography, commoners were organized by membership into villages and towns represented by headmen. Through houses, they were represented by (usually male) family heads and organized according to gender and personal relation to the head. Commerce and other occupations were likewise organized through delegation of internal management to leaders in return for service to whoever authorized them. Although each of these institutions of management had different historical origins and at times even represented mutually incongruous ideologies of authority, they were integrated into the politics of the Tokugawa world. Sometimes people would play the various ideological discourses against each other for political ends, but mostly they coexisted and their incongruities were partitioned through manipulations of metaphorical space.

Imperial authority and its space

Imperial authority and traditions provided the most encompassing framework of Tokugawa rule, even as it subordinated the Tokugawa. The imperial court was the highest *omote* interface demanding ritual obedience in the Tokugawa period, even though the emperor and the aristocracy were, in terms of power, clearly subordinated to the Tokugawa government. Imperial tradition was mostly based on institutions that had flourished from the seventh to the twelfth centuries. These included various ministries of central government in Kyoto and a system of aristocratic governors dispatched to administer the more than sixty provinces (*kuni*) into which the emperor had divided Japan. The actual political power of the imperial and aristocratic order began a period of accelerating decline in the twelfth century with the appearance of limited warrior government based in the city of Kamakura. By the fifteenth century the emperor and the aristocracy held almost no governing power outside the city of Kyoto, as the islands fractured into chronic civil war and daimyo warlords developed their own regional authority.

Yet even in these times warlords used imperial traditions and garnered proclamations of ranks and duties when it suited their needs, and the imperial aristocracy remained a continuing source of legitimacy.[4] The exigencies of war and local politics required Warring States daimyo to be practical, inventive, and local. Effectively independent of each other and of any actual imperial control, they nevertheless lived and fought together in a general environment imbued with the memory of the formerly functioning Japanese imperial system and the continued presence of the greatly diminished authority of its descendants. Lords continued to jockey to receive court rank from the impoverished Kyoto court, and countless more people just assumed and asserted possession of imperial court ranks and titles because it was a widely understood language of prestige and authority. The overall disorder was evident in that such titles as Governor of Awa Province, Master of the Emperor's Tax Offices, Master of the Emperor's Warehouses, and the like were claimed by local warriors throughout Japan, and even the basest male villager was likely to have a name deriving from lower titles identifying him as a guard of a gate, such as Jinzaemon, or a soldier of the imperial army, such as Kichibei. As the early unifiers conquered Japan in the latter half of the sixteenth century, they rebuilt the forms of imperial authority and put them under their control.[5]

Toyotomi Hideyoshi refurbished the imperial government in Kyoto so as to situate himself as an aristocrat and Imperial Regent and thereby exercise control over the symbolic language of authority.[6] Hideyoshi ruled samurai and civilians as Regent and thereby ideologically unified the civilian and military aspects of rule under a single title. However, he did not revive the actual governing machinery of the imperial government. For example, an aristocratic Minister of the Right dealt only with imperial household matters, and the empty title "Provincial Governor" conferred no actual authority over a province. Daimyo ruled only domains, which they received in fief directly from Hideyoshi. When Tokugawa Ieyasu grabbed the realm away from Hideyoshi's child heir in 1600, he also made use of the imperial court's authority, but in a slightly different way that more clearly separated military and civilian discourses of rule. As military ruler he used the imperial appointment and rank of shogun, and as civilian ruler he used the high civil office of minister of the emperor's government.[7] Each of his heirs in the dynasty began his inheritance with the rank of Minister of the Interior and moved up through Minister of the Right, Minister of the Left, and ultimately (although for many posthumously) Grand Minister of State and a status rank, Senior First Rank, equal to the emperor himself. The general appellation that derived from directly representing the emperor was *kubō*. The Tokugawa primarily used this moniker to identify their role as rulers, but this has been obscured by modern historical practice, which relies solely on the term "shogun." The Tokugawa monopolized the term *kubō* in their day so that it effectively meant themselves as "ruler of Japan." The Tokugawa *kubō* and his government used the discourses of imperial civil rule in a broad spectrum of their governance of Japan. Most of its information collection was carried out according to the imperial government framework. Maps and cadastral registers were compiled along the lines of imperial provinces and counties. Plaintiffs who appeared in Tokugawa courts identified their addresses using this geographical indexing rather than the domainal fief system. For all their actual power, successive generations of Tokugawa *kubō* regularly performed *omote* rituals expressing their subservience to their lord (*shujō*) the emperor.[8]

The Tokugawa restricted the possibility of alliances forming between daimyo and aristocrats by prohibiting or mediating all formal contacts between them. The Tokugawa also controlled the disbursement of imperial court ranks to the daimyo and other leading samurai. They segregated the system of imperial court ranks for samurai lords from the equivalent imperial court ranks disbursed within the aristocracy. These samurai appointments were prestige ranks that influenced seating precedence when they sat down together, but they conferred no actual government authority.[9] For example, the daimyo Miyake Yasukazu held Junior Fifth court rank and passed through appointment as Governor of Bitchū Province (Bitchū no kami) to Governor of Tsushima Province (Tsushima no kami) in his "imperial" government career, but this conferred no actual relation to those provinces and were merely statements of status. His actual realm was a fief on the Atsumi Peninsula granted him by the Tokugawa and was a small portion of Mikawa province, and his real duties were serving the Tokugawa.

Tokugawa and daimyo authority emerging from
warrior territorial state traditions

The Tokugawa utilized their formalized subservience to imperial authority, but they also had forms of authority that originated in warrior government of the Warring States period. These forms structured the bulk of Tokugawa *omote* authority vis-à-vis the samurai and commoners under their control. Their government had a dual structure that included both a house government to rule warriors and a warrior state government to rule and tax the people of its own demesne. The "two governments" of the Tokugawa were deeply intertwined with each other and with the imperial order as well, but they nevertheless maintained separate discursive and administrative elements that have significant implications for understanding how the government functioned. The warrior house government naturally emerged out of military organization honed in the Warring States era and had become with the advent of the Great Peace a collection of all military houses arranged in hierarchies of obedience and servitude that led to the Tokugawa shogun at the top. The civil government was fashioned out of Warring States traditions of territorial state rule mixed with the preexisting discourses of ancient imperial authority and the continental Chinese discourses of government to which Japanese imperial rule itself historically had been deeply indebted.

Daimyo of the Warring States era developed traditions of territorial rule over their domains. At lower levels of regional power samurai asserted rights of taxation and juridical authority over the residents of territories, and more powerful warriors guaranteed such rights as fiefs (*chigyō*) to their samurai retainers. Fief villagers provided the samurai with agricultural land taxes, labor duties, and other incidental taxes. The samurai managed his fief as his territory and was to use this income to serve his lord. At higher levels of authority many daimyo lords asserted their position as the *kōgi*, the government, and the *kokka*, the ruling house of their domainal state. This ideology made use of the political language of the original Chinese Warring States era of the fifth through third centuries BCE. They called their realms *ryō, kuni*, and *ryōgoku*, countries of a premodern fashion, and issued laws to the residents. They waged war and conducted relations with other lords of Japan and, when they could, with non-Japanese powers and authorities from outside the islands.[10]

Some of these traditions ended in the Tokugawa period. For example, by submitting to the Tokugawa, the daimyo lost their rights to wage war and carry out independent foreign relations. In general, the usage of the pair of words *ōyake* (read as *kō* in compound words and meaning government or ruler) and *watakushi* (read as *shi* in compound words and meaning personal or selfish) directly speaks to the nature of Tokugawa public authority at its own *omote,* where the governmental *kō* always referred to the Tokugawa, and the personal *shi* always to the daimyo. The Tokugawa asserted that it was the only government (*kōgi*) and that it provided its daimyo with the only source of authority over their fiefs. A daimyo had to "personally" manage his territory within the confines of Tokugawa law. The 1643 version of the Laws for the Military Houses, which the Tokugawa issued to daimyo, makes this clear, using the word *watakushi* as the pronoun for daimyo. This usage appears in its various prohibitions against "personally" deciding marriage and inheritance, "personally" waging suits against others, and "personally" creating toll stations and trade embargoes, ending with the order "Everything shall be carried out in all locations of every province with complete respect and accordance with the laws issued from Edo."[11] So although daimyo territorial control remained the norm through infeudation, daimyo discourses of being ruling houses of "domainal states" were not recognized in formal relations with the Tokugawa, who instead generally described a daimyo's authority as "personal management" (*jibun shioki*) of "personal territory" (*shiryō*). This authority of "personal management" given to daimyo was no small thing. It allowed almost complete rights of ownership of the domain and its people. Daimyo were permitted to enact death penalties on their people without bothering to query the Tokugawa government, for example. However, this was not the full extent of daimyo territorial authority. Warring States era discourses of ruling domainal countries continued to survive within some domain boundaries as "inside knowledge." These internal discourses were not merely vestigial identities but contributed, as we shall see, to new developments on the islands in the eighteenth and nineteenth centuries.

In contrast to this Tokugawa rhetoric to which they submitted, daimyo were frequently spoken of as *ōyake* or in other terms expressing a public governmental identity within the space of their own realm and household. One might interpret this solely as identifying them as governmental representatives of Tokugawa law and authority, but for the fact that their authority was mostly spoken of in Tokugawa *omote* as personal and for the fact that these daimyo governments issued and enforced many laws that directly contravened Tokugawa law. Subsequent chapters of this book describe many instances of breaking the above 1643 law code, such as the frequent "personally decided" inheritances and the waging of legal suits against other daimyo. In an earlier book I explored the "illegal" setting up of toll stations and trade embargoes that were key to controlling the commercial economy and were activities that show a relationship between the inside terminology and the actual functioning of daimyo governments independently of the legal system of the Tokugawa government.[12] As we shall see, the very same daimyo who served as key officials in the Tokugawa government simultaneously participated in all of these types of behavior in their own realms and houses, clearly indicating that this dichotomy was not adversarial in an anti-Tokugawa way but was part of normal politics.

The inside/outside distinctions and incongruities that retainers learned were not simply samurai expressing allegiances to different lords. Instead they organized varying political subjectivities for different situations. A samurai of the Yamauchi clan of Tosa domain frequently meant the Yamauchi lord when he said ōyake and Yamauchi rule when he said kōgi, expressing the lord's authority to rule house and realm, but if he were an official of his lord engaged in interactions with outsiders, he would apply those terms only to the authority of the Tokugawa overlord. All daimyo with realms large and small took as a matter of course—and with the tacit encouragement and participation of the daimyo in charge of Tokugawa government—that the character of their inner authority and their external subservience would be different. An example from Tosa domain in 1787 illustrates this logic, as well as the manipulation needed to attain political goals. That year the lord of Tosa, Yamauchi Toyochika, began a reform program designed to improve the troubled government of his domain. Not only was the government deeply in debt and on the verge of default to its creditors, but widespread rioting and protest in Tosa had revealed the declining legitimacy of rule. The lord was supposed to depart for his alternate attendance duty to the Tokugawa, but he wished to remain in Tosa an extra three months to ensure that the reform began solidly and also to save his government money by shortening his stay away in Edo. The delay meant that he would not fully carry out duties to the shogun, so Toyochika's Edo ambassador sent queries to the Elders of the Tokugawa house. They told him that Toyochika must make his request for a delay in terms of his having an illness requiring recuperation at a spa in his realm. The lord writes about creating this spurious reason for delay in his diary in the following way:

Of course, [our needs] were spoken of off the record [*nainai*] to the government authorities in order to gain the proper information. They replied that if such needs were heard to be spoken freely, it would be difficult to grant the request, [and] that I should instead send a formal request saying, "Although my illness has largely improved, I remain somewhat in pain and the long journey to Edo

26

would be difficult. I am being treated by my doctor, taking medicines and bathing in the waters of a hot spring in my home province. If I get the least bit better, I will quickly set my palanquin to the journey."

The domain lord's request to shore up his local rule was regarded by the chief Tokugawa officials as "too selfish a circumstance" (*tsugō jiyū*) to authorize a delay in departure. However, these officials were mostly daimyo themselves and certainly understood his needs. Therefore they instructed him that in the formal request he had to say he was sick and needed to remain in his domain a while to recuperate, promising, however, that the moment he recovered his health, he would return to duty.[13] Clearly, in the Tokugawa government his public duty was alternate attendance, and issues of managing his own domain were personal and "selfish" matters. Strangely enough, the only way he could carry out effective local government was to plead illness, a legitimate personal reason that was acceptable in the *omote* rules that defined him as a personal servant of the Tokugawa. The actual political negotiation happened informally and was unmentionable in all *omote* records. As it eventuated, Toyochika remained in the domain, working hard to repair local government; after five extra months in the realm he sent a message to the Tokugawa Elders announcing his recovery, and he departed to Edo. Tokugawa officials were fully aware of the inside story through informal negotiation, but they required that in *omote* documents and interaction everyone had to perform the ideal relationships of Tokugawa authority. "Personal management" of one's territory could not take precedence over the duty to serve the Tokugawa, because putting domains first might lead to centrifugal tendencies and ultimately to disorder in the Tokugawa state.

While the legitimacy of the territorial government of daimyo was thus circumscribed as private management in formal Tokugawa discourse, the territorial rule of lesser samurai went through even more change during the late sixteenth-century era of transition to the Tokugawa period. As daimyo strengthened their own domainal states, they gradually worked to decrease the fief rule of their retainers.[14] They limited the juridical authority of fief holders and restricted their freedom to decide types of taxes and the tax rates themselves. Daimyo increasingly required fief holders to live away from their fiefs and within the towns around the daimyo's castle, and it became normal in many domains for daimyo to appoint intendants to manage whole districts of fiefs on behalf of retainers. The retainers themselves were reduced to collecting payments of their taxes from the daimyo warehouses.[15] By the early Tokugawa period the disbursement of fiefs to samurai became very limited in scope. Generally only daimyo themselves, who received their domains in fief from the Tokugawa, a few thousand senior Tokugawa bannermen retainers, and a few handfuls of senior daimyo retainers had significant authority over fiefs.[16] In the large domain of Tosa, for example, by the year 1700 only three retainers, who held realms the size of those held by small daimyo and bannermen, had strong fief rule. The remaining 300 enfeoffed samurai held almost no ruling authority.[17] Many samurai of large peripheral domains such as Tosa held similar attenuated fief rights. However, the majority of daimyo, such as the Miyake of Tahara domain, disbursed stipends to all of their retainers and ran their realms as a single judicial and administrative entity. They gave honorary "fief-holding" status to their samurai houses, but in reality developed bureaucracies to manage their whole realm and disbursed pay to those samurai a few times a year.[18] Throughout Japan, retainers who held lesser status than samurai—such as musketeers and foot soldiers, a class who made up 90 percent of the retainers in any daimyo house—were almost all stipendiaries and, together with the samurai, came to govern commoners only when they served as members of the administrative machinery of their lord's domain. Curiously, even though daimyo authority had become "private" in Tokugawa *omote* discourse, it was becoming locally more centralized and powerful.

Thus in the Tokugawa *omote* the keys of territorial government in this period existed in the hands of the head of the Tokugawa clan, and his house was administratively and ideologically expressed in the following three ways: as the highest minister administering Japan on behalf of the emperor; as a warrior government *kōgi* who disbursed, in personal fief, domains to the daimyo and smaller fiefs to some temples and shrines and to some aristocrats and bannermen; and finally as a kind of daimyo manager of his own demesne. The fiefs were "private" and operated with a recognition of *naibun* competence, so that the boundaries of the fiefs were situationally opaque, so to speak, to the Tokugawa eye.

Tokugawa and daimyo authority emerging from warrior house traditions

These various ideologies of territorial and civil government coexisted with ideologies of house government. Samurai houses also organized the military, the economy, and politics, and generally their affective power over members mobilized personal identity and honor more strongly than the imperial and samurai territorial traditions of civil rule. There was a branching hierarchy of houses in servitude beneath the shogun that was built on the idea of having each samurai individually serve his own immediate lord. The fief rights and the rights of disbursed income held by daimyo and samurai were revocable, but they were generally inherited over generations of a house lineage. The master of the house disbursed his income among members of the household and also governed the people of the house. Those members might also be heads of their own houses and disburse income to members of their households whom they also governed. This meant that all samurai were simultaneously rulers and caretakers of inferiors while existing as mere servants of and dependents of their superiors.

In the eyes of the Tokugawa government a daimyo's territorial rule was private "personal territory" and personal management, but his house rule was somewhat more public in character, which is to say it was expressible in Tokugawa *omote* discourse. Headship of a house conferred the right to rule its members but also the duty to contain disorder and keep the peace. A daimyo was far more likely to be punished for mismanagement of the house than for mismanagement of his realm.[19] As head of his house the daimyo was the master, lawgiver, and chief judge of all of its members, but he had to manage this house so that it caused no problems to his superior. He might be held responsible for the crimes of people of his house, for instance. "Failure to manage the house" was a frequently cited crime leading to the punishment or even attainder of daimyo and other samurai who had unruly retainers in their households. Naitō Nobuhiro was disenfeoffed in 1650 when it was discovered he had hired a Christian samurai into his household without a proper background check, and numerous daimyo such as Date Munekatsu of Ichinoseki domain in 1661 and Matsudaira Chikayoshi in 1682 were disenfeoffed because retainers in the house could not stop fighting among each other for power.[20] When a lord was punished, all members of his household suffered. Retainers would lose honor if their daimyo was reprimanded, and they would lose home and income if he was disenfeoffed. Average samurai had similar responsibilities to control their own house members. The Tosa samurai Nakajima Jingoemon had his 300-*koku* fief confiscated and found himself banished from his lord's realm in 1693 because, in the words of the court judgment, one of his servants "broke domain law to such a degree that [Jingoemon] should be punished with death, but will be shown lenience." Another Tosa samurai, Miyakawa Kojūrō, was punished in similar fashion in 1706 when his daughter and a male household servant ran away from the castle town to a village in order to live together secretly. When this was discovered, Kojūrō was banished from the realm for the crime of "letting his house law degenerate and losing his will."[21] The widespread nature of such incidents indicates that, unlike fief rights, which attenuated or disappeared in Tokugawa Japan, the system of authority of common samurai over their own households continued to be supported by daimyo.

Although the lord might be subject to punishment for either his own misdeeds or those of members of his household, his recognized sphere of "inside competence" buffered the immediate application of Tokugawa authority. More often than not the Tokugawa government worked extensively, sometimes for years, to help repair a disturbance within a daimyo's house before resorting to actual punishment.[22] The Tokugawa government also never officially permitted a retainer to accuse his own lord of a crime. The system provided no normal path of moving up in the world by harming one's lord. Because retainers would lose their positions if a household head became attaindered for his personal faults, they became invested in controlling their lord's behavior even while serving him. These conditions necessarily fostered a strong sense of group membership framed as duty to the personal head of the house but in reality geared more to maintaining the institution of the house itself. Occasions of retainers keeping their wayward lords under arrest in order to protect the house were not unknown. This was all managed internally and informally so as not to affront the *omote* order that guaranteed a retainer would be completely subservient to his lord.[23]

Because average samurai were to manage themselves and their houses with proper regard to their formal duties and appearances, the importance of maintaining distinctions between *omote* behavior and behavior in informal/inside (*uchi*) situations was made manifest to samurai in their daily life, a way of educating and disciplining them into an awareness of the culturally deep and resonant distinctions of a social outside and a social inside. In domain public life the governments regularly identified situations as *omote* formal or *uchi* informal and enforced an accompanying code of behavior. For example, Yoshida domain in Mikawa province noted the following in one of its codes issued to its samurai in 1769: "When you are not on *omote* business and serving informally, then you do not need to wear your formal jacket [*haori*] but may dress as you please." Okayama domain instructed its samurai to use high-quality paper in documents addressed to outsiders and medium- to low-quality paper in documents for use inside the domain.[24] Every samurai home was built with an *omote* set of front rooms for formal interactions with outsiders, and the remainder of the house (*oku*) was reserved for use by family and servants and informal interaction with close friends. Rules of behavior differed for each space and issues of access had serious legal ramifications. If outsiders were allowed access to the inner parts of the house and some incident occurred, the granting of that access in itself could invite punishment of the homeowner. The Tosa samurai wife Fukuoka Shō discovered this when she killed a man of lesser status in the back of her home in 1824. She claimed he had been insolent to her and, as she was a samurai and he of lesser status, that she had the right to slay him for rudeness. The domain acknowledged this right, yet the government punished her for the crime of allowing this outsider into the back of the house in the first place. Furthermore, all of the menservants of the house were punished for this reason as well, because they should not have permitted an outsider to enter the back of the house. Her husband was away in Edo at the time, but the domain deemed him responsible for failure to manage his household. He was relieved of office, reduced in fief, and sent back home to Kōchi to live in house confinement.[25] This extreme incident reveals that a commonly held set of assumptions about proper formal and informal behavior and location was worked into the tenor of daily life. As these examples show, the distinctions of behavior and situation were deeply embedded in samurai daily life and sustained informed participation in the associated forms of samurai politics.

The metaphorical insides and outsides of houses were tightly bound to a sense of personal honor and dignity. There is even a consonance between the term for formal ritual interface, *omote,* and the term for personal "face" and "honor," read as *omote* but written with a different ideograph. A personal *omote* was a social interface that represented one's competence and authority and therefore needed to be carefully protected. It was part of a widespread pattern of respect for the autonomy of samurai that was tied to their notions of honor.[26] The following anecdote related by the daimyo Matsura Seizan in his miscellany *Kasshi yawa* illustrates how autonomy and honor were tied to the preservation of the distinction between inside knowledge and outside knowledge. When Tokugawa Tsunayoshi became *kubō,* he forced the chief adviser to the previous *kubō,* Sakai Tadakiyo, into retirement. Before long it was reported that Tadakiyo had died of illness, but there was also gossip that he had committed ritual disembowelment (*seppuku*). Tsunayoshi was angry to hear this, because *seppuku* was legally to be done only at the command of one's lord, so he ordered his Grand Inspectors to the Sakai residence to check the body in order to make sure that Tadakiyo had not killed himself. Tadakiyo's nephew, the daimyo Tōdō Takahisa, was at the front of the house at the time and asked the Inspectors why they had come. They told him, and he would have none of it. Takahisa told them to go back to Tsunayoshi and tell him that Takahisa said it was illness. "This is the word of a samurai, so there is no reason to believe anything different. Even if you saw the body, it would be none other than he died of illness!" The browbeaten Grand Inspectors returned promptly to Tsu-nayoshi, who sent them right back to inspect the body. By this time Takahisa had seen to it that the body had already been taken to the temple and cremat-ed.[27] Tsunayoshi was more autocratic and much less respectful of the politics of *omote* and *naishō* than other *kubō,* frequently surprising people by his judg-ments, and such character is evident in this story.[28] Of more general impor-tance is that during this negotiation the Grand Inspectors' initial response was to respect a samurai's portion of competence, here clearly tied to the notion of samurai honor. Takahisa asserted that Tadakiyo died of illness, not because an inspection of the body would prove so, but rather because a samurai's word was at stake. That word was true not because it reflected reality but because to doubt that "truth" was to offend the honor and autonomy of the samurai. This truth was also tied to proper governmental *omote* relations.

The Grand Inspectors' respect was also for the spatial autonomy of the daimyo's property, in this case one of his Edo residences. Even though they were representatives of the *kubō* who had granted that residence to Sakai, they could not barge in with impunity—they could have done so only as an action of last resort involving the severe punishment of the lord. A lord's residence was part of his area of competence and as such had a high degree of inviola-bility. This is made evident in Kasaya Kazuhiko's research on the customary practice of samurai outlaws gaining protection by running into domain resi-dences in Edo. If the head of a house refused entry or denied the presence of an outlaw, then Tokugawa authorities could not force entry into the residence and were constrained to take the samurai at his word.[29]

This independence was true whether the lords were hereditary servant (*fudai*) daimyo or outer (*tozama*) daimyo. One aspect of samurai house or-ganization was the arrangement of vassals into longtime lineages and recent lineages, and this functioned in the organization of daimyo as vassals of the Tokugawa. *Fudai* were daimyo who had descended from hereditary vassals of the Tokugawa and could serve as officials in the Tokugawa government. They were more fully incorporated into the Tokugawa household but nevertheless retained degrees of independence as rulers of their own domains and houses. *Tozama* were daimyo descended from people who had either sided against Tokugawa Ieyasu at the Battle of Sekigahara in 1600 or chosen to ally them-selves with Ieyasu not long before the battle. They could not serve in Edo gov-ernment, and their history of "recent" submission to the Tokugawa made them popularly regarded as less trustworthy supporters of the Tokugawa cause. The difference was formalized but in reality was not necessarily a sign of degree of either independence or trustworthiness.[30]

Village space

The majority of the population in villages in the Tokugawa period also lived in a world distinguished by inside/outside dichotomies that shaped their political behavior. Villages in most regions of Japan during this time were largely self-administered. The village headman served as the community's interface with higher authorities, and he was personally answerable for maintaining public order in the village. The payment of taxes to the overlords was a corporate rather than individual responsibility, so what one villager could not do, the rest in the village had to make up in ways managed by the headman.[31] Likewise, most villages held a degree of judicial and penal authority. Minor legal infractions that could be addressed with fines or banishment were all handled within villages, while only major crimes were supposed to be dealt with by higher samurai authorities. In reality many major crimes were often dealt with "unofficially" within villages as well. Such village self-administration had its origins in the Warring States period and was indeed the foundation of the early modern political order.

The long era of civil war before the Tokugawa period had done much to strengthen patterns of local community solidarity, especially regarding local administration and relations with outside authorities in villages across much of Japan.[32] Villages and towns developed into self-administering corporate entities, and samurai dominance was achieved in part thanks to a degree of acquiescence to the communal solidarity of various commoner groups. Elizabeth Berry has appropriately called this the "culture of civil war" in her exploration of urban Kyoto.[33] In the system of subcontracting local management (*mura-uke sei*), villages promised an agreed-upon amount of taxes to be paid via the village headman to the samurai rulers in return for autonomy in internal affairs. The term *mae* (front; respectable identity) can be found in many village documents and has overlapping meanings with *omote*; it identifies an interactive identity that protects a space of acknowledged respect and competence for villagers, as in the term *hyakushōmae* (one's identity as a tax-paying farmer). This arrangement of a certain local autonomy went hand in hand with the urbanization of samurai, their separation from fief control, and a division of commoner and samurai into more clearly separate economic and cultural spheres. Village and town local autonomy somewhat paralleled the legal autonomies possessed by samurai over their realms in that, ideally, internal matters were not to erupt into the formal *omote* space of their daimyo or Tokugawa seigneurs. Villages had local law codes and local means of punishment for internal crimes.[34]

Just as the law of daimyo for their houses and realms did, village codes had to profess to be in accordance with the law of the Tokugawa or their daimyo. They actually were so, more or less, but they contained substantial degrees of autonomy and differentiation that could exist as long as they did not trouble *omote* relations. Herman Ooms describes this aspect of village politics in *Tokugawa Village Practice,* in which he writes about the "intravillage/extravillage dichotomy":

> Villages had two sets of regulations, laws with an extramural origin and internal codes. With regard to village justice, penal practices in principle existed by sufferance from the overlords and often functioned in "illegal" ways. Certain informal practices suggest that the overlords silently acknowledged some of these irregularities. Probably more often than not, village authorities were in mutual agreement about administrative matters, whether openly or silently.[35]

Ooms' emphasis on "practices," taking inspiration from the theories of Pierre Bourdieu, brings to the fore this inside/outside dichotomy. A focus on formal structure is less likely to reveal this dichotomy, because it tends to neatly organize arrangements, making contradictions, when they appear, seem corrupt or exceptional. Ooms put "illegal" in quotation marks because although *omote* rules declared them illegal, such contradictions were a basic, essential part of the compartmented political order, and they would have been illegal in the modern national context into which we translate the past.

The basic dichotomy of "formal interface" and "inside competence" in politics was accepted practice in villages and operated in ways analogous to daimyo territorial and house rule. Samurai rulers remained in control of villages via the village leaders and at times when intravillage conflict caused the headman to lose face, which is to say that when the village could no longer operate according to *omote* rules, rulers often held the headman personally accountable for disturbances that burst beyond the village boundary, in much the same way that the Tokugawa held daimyo accountable for their household and territorial "mismanagement."

Samurai normally controlled just the formal exterior of a village, and this meant they had broad latitude to intervene in village external relations and in the behavior of villagers outside of their villages. As an example, in one situation described in Ooms' book certain powerful members of the village of Hozu in Kameyama domain were legally regarded as samurai in the village codes, but this held true only within the confines of the village that they controlled, where they wore swords and leather sandals. Facing outward toward the lord of the domain, they were merely commoner peasants and had to behave appropriately toward his officials. When they visited the castle town, they had to dress as commoners and show proper respect to the samurai they encountered. The domain had laws prohibiting people whom it did not regard as samurai from displaying the symbolic accouterments of status such as wearing two swords, but the domain officials had little interest in peering into and controlling such behavior within the village. Only when internal village struggles between these "samurai" and the other villagers repeatedly showed up on the domain government's doorstep was the ritual interface broken and the domain officials most reluctantly became involved in the issue of status distinctions within the village.[36]

Occupational status and space

The status system was another key form of authority that integrated Tokugawa Japan, and has been a major topic of historical research in recent decades. As can be seen from the above example of people who were samurai within Hozu village but commoners without, the status system intersected with and was influenced by the inside and outside of spaces of authority. Various special occupational status groups as well, such as outcastes and mendicant entertainers, were integrated into the larger political order through a system whereby occupational status leaders administered their own members and served as the "face" of the status group to higher samurai authorities. Many of these groups geographically transected the authority spheres of numerous daimyo, villages, and towns but retained varying degrees of judicial and punitive autonomy over their members independent of the local administrations within which they operated. This was similar to the way that daimyo held "house authority" over their retainers even in nondomain territory. In this way we can see that the various "insides" and "outsides" of authority groups were not neatly packed inside one another like Russian dolls but rather had a complex, overlapping character more like a Venn diagram.

Occupational group status is somewhat different from the four statuses of samurai, peasant, craftsman, and merchant cherished in Japanese-style neo-Confucian thought. Neo-Confucian thought had some relevance to people's ideas about society, but recent historiography has emphasized that the actually functioning system of status in the Tokugawa order was rather different.[37] The legal and political system was organized around the broad status groups of aristocrats, clerics and mendicants, warriors, townspeople, villagers, and outcastes, as well as a multitude of status groups based on categories of oc-cupation or duty. Some of these status groups were organized into hierarchic legal groups with symbolic heads: the aristocrats headed by the emperor, the clerics by the leaders of their various temple sects and shrines, the warriors by the Tokugawa shogun, and the outcastes by Danzaemon.[38] The overlapping character added complexity to the play of authority. Buddhist monks in any daimyo realm, for example, were somewhat subject to their head temple in Kyoto and somewhat subject to their local samurai authority. Members of out-caste groups had similarly complex spheres of authority. The exact degrees of jurisdiction were often the object of negotiation and contestation. These sta-tus groups each created a feudal "space" whereby members were subjected to the direct legal authority of their heads, who were in turn answerable to their superior. Of course the vast majority of people held status as townspeople and villagers, but these statuses did not function as corporate status groups in the same way: Atomized onto separate villages and wards, locally they were di-rectly administered by their respective headmen, but as commoners they had no encompassing head of their own status. At any rate, the patterns of delega-tion of authority stretched across the islands in an intricate web of powers, and all groups answered directly or indirectly to the authority structure centered on the Tokugawa and were required to support their Great Peace.

Gender and space

Gender authority was like status in that the patriarchal household system systematically operated throughout the space under Tokugawa authority. In general, because the ideal was that a man represented a house, women were formally regarded as "inside" and had *omote* roles only rarely. When they did have recognized *omote* authority, it usually emerged because of a temporary lack of men in the household. The most common such moment was for wid-ows with no sons. This tendency held most strongly in samurai households and to a lesser degree in households of other status groups.[39] Two of the com-mon words for samurai "wife," *oku-sama* and *naishō-sama,* indicate the "inside" nature of womanhood in the spatially organized political system: the former is a metonymic way of respectfully naming people of power by the residence that they control, in this case the non-*omote* portion of the house, and *naishō* identifies the internal competence that she might hold in the household. Even when a woman actually held significant power within a house, her ability to be a public face of the house was highly circumscribed and unlikely to appear in formal records.[40] This is one reason why official *omote* documents produced by women are extremely uncommon. Not only were such documents uncommonly produced, but the memory of the moments of public roles for women tended to be erased over time.

Ikeda Mitsumasa of Okayama domain gendered the inside and outside of houses when he called high-ranking samurai to the castle so that he could encourage frugality in their lives. His rhetoric is a good example reflecting how political struggle was carried out in terms of the proper balance of inside authority and outside duty, and furthermore in a way that linked these identities to notions of gender. He noted that samurai were living frugally in *omote* interaction as he had requested, but remained extravagant with regard to "internal" expenses of their own households. He encouraged further frugality by threatening their masculinity. Although the notion of "inside" was not always feminized, his message of the need for frugality inside samurai houses was made in a way that reduced the legitimacy of the inside concerns by feminizing it and by relating it to a common rhetoric in samurai society that women were extravagant. Mitsumasa situated his critique in a "natural" gendered order, writing,

> The energy of Heaven and Earth is lively in spring and summer and withdrawn in fall and winter. Likewise, with birds the males are brilliant and the females are without decoration. I hear that these days in our country the *omote* is frugal but the *naishō* is rich. Some people seem to think that their fiefs are income designated to pay for their wives' adornment. This news portends the collapse of the country. I order you all to sign oaths regarding this point.[41]

As shall be seen below, the naming of women also was regulated according to inside and outside dichotomies.

Inside and *omote* naming and identities

Another way to approach the importance of *omote* and internal discourses of political space is through analyzing naming practices of individuals and their titles in the Tokugawa period. In modern Japan the governor of Okayama prefecture is called governor (*chiji*) by anyone. An employee of the local history museum and the prime minister of Japan address him with the same title and call him by the same family name. The character, duties, and accouterments of his office are publicly describable by anyone in a way that makes the governor fit seamlessly into the space of Japan. Naming during the Tokugawa period was different. A daimyo's subjects would commonly call him one thing, and the Tokugawa overlord and people of other domains would call him something quite different. His duties and office might also be described quite differently by people inside and outside of his sphere of authority. This was in part a product of the status system, because certain forms of address were for inferiors to use. However, the feudal politics of space were also decisive. An Edo city commoner would call the daimyo by a rank and style assigned by the Tokugawa in a way that implicitly expressed that the commoner belonged to the Tokugawa order rather than the daimyo's order. Even the daimyo's family name might be different inside and out. For example, the daimyo of Okayama domain were called by the family name "Matsudaira" out in the Tokugawa realm by commoners and samurai alike but were called by the hereditary family name "Ikeda" within their household and realm. "Matsudaira" was Tokugawa Ieyasu's original family name that he bestowed upon the Ikeda as a way of incorporating them into the Tokugawa household. A similar difference occurred at the imperial *omote*. When facing the imperial aristocracy, the Ikeda formally used the lineage name "Minamoto," which situated the Ikeda clan as of a famous warrior lineage of imperial family origin and allowed the Ikeda to formally interact with the aristocracy. Therefore historians seeking to understand for which *omote* a document was produced can look at family name usage and thereby infer the nature of the information within the document.

Inside and *omote* naming had further dimensions beyond family name usage that paralleled the usage of political terminology for daimyo authority. The basic structure can be represented by a schematic image showing the terms that operated inside a daimyo's space and linking them with the terms that operated at the Tokugawa *omote*. Figure 1 shows some of these *uchi/omote* distinctions with regard to the daimyo realm of Tosa and the Yamauchi clan. As the upper right portion of the diagram indicates, some Tokugawa *omote* terms for "lord" were *daimyō, shin* (retainer), and *ryōshu* (territorial master). These terms situated the lord as a feudal retainer of the Tokugawa. Two other terms, *kokushu* (provincial master) and the quasi-imperial court rank Tosa no kami (Protector of Tosa), identify the Yamauchi as a servant of the imperial court mediated by the Tokugawa overlords in their status as government ministers. All of these terms might be used within the Yamauchi house and domain inner discourse, but insiders more commonly employed words identifying their servitude to the Yamauchi rulers such as *kami-sama* and *tono-sama,* meaning "my lord," and terms identifying his place as head of government such as *kōgi-sama.* In inner discourse, people influenced by the continental classics occasionally used terms such as prince (*kimi*), divine prince (*seikun*), and even great general

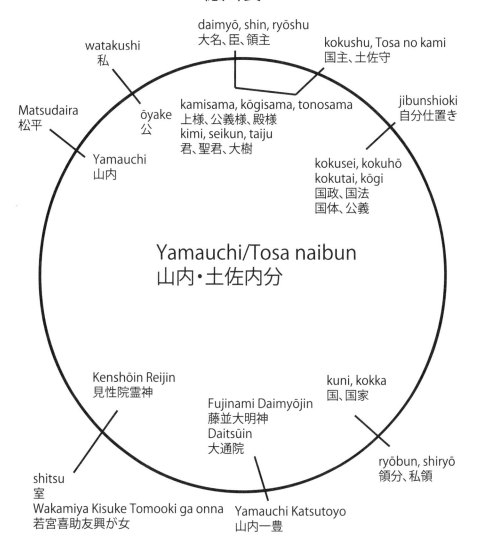

FIGURE 1. The Tokugawa omote and naibun of Tosa domain.

(*taiju*), a term often used to refer to the Tokugawa shogun that derived from the name of a famous general of the latter Han dynasty. For example, Tosa retainer Hirabayashi Chōshin praised his lord's choice to create a petition box in 1759 by writing, "It is truly a sign of the safety of our state that you, divine prince, have now asked to hear the opinions of those beneath you!"[42] Such words could be used only for the Tokugawa shogun in *omote* space because they expressed a role of leadership, and daimyo subjectivity in *omote* space was a private identity expressing faithful servitude to the Tokugawa.

Because of the hierarchal arrangement of spaces of authority, the use of such internal words as "divine prince" did not preclude identification with outside *omote* realities for any member of the Yamauchi clan or any subject of Tosa domain. A scholar of Tosa might identify with a notion of Japan as an imperial country and simultaneously identify Tosa as a domainal country ruled by a lord possessing divine authority. For example, the scholar Nakayama Sazō wrote the following to his lord in 1759:

> It has been acknowledged from ages past that the princes dispatched
> to all of the provinces of the divine country rule their states with
> virtue and benevolence as the parents of their people and by foster-
> ing the land and sea. . . . Indeed my prince, by the virtuous influence
> of your great benevolence and humanity, the deities of heaven and
> earth have responded in sympathy and made your state safe. As
> we can see, the five food grains are flourishing and we are deeply
> grateful.[43]

Because the layering of space was hierarchal, Nakayama could use the language of higher imperial authority within the lesser space of his daimyo's authority, but the opposite could not be true. In a formal letter addressed to the Tokugawa, the words "prince" and *kokka* could not be used to identify the lord of Tosa because they would be an affront to Tokugawa authority.

The use of family names among the Yamauchi house paralleled that of the Ikeda daimyo mentioned above. The Tokugawa granted the second lord, Yamauchi Tadayoshi, and his descendants the family name "Matsudaira" in 1610. It was simultaneously an honor and an erasure of Yamauchi identity. Thereafter Tadayoshi and his heirs were required to use the Matsudaira name in correspondence with the Tokugawa and other daimyo, but in inner discourse people continued to use "Yamauchi," as a sign of the hereditary authority of the Yamauchi house itself. Not shown in the diagram, which represents only the Tokugawa *omote*, is that in correspondence with the Kyoto court the

Yamauchi had to use the Fujiwara lineage name of their putative aristocratic ancestry, giving them the right to directly contact the court; both "Matsudaira" and "Yamauchi" were too base for this purpose. This imperial *omote* of naming represented the highest *omote* in the hierarchy, one to which even the Tokugawa were subject. At lower levels in the hierarchy, different *omote* had associated naming practices as well. For example, the Yamauchi constructed their own *omote* vis-à-vis retainers and subjects, and this also affected name usage. Many chief samurai retainers of the Yamauchi house had been granted the Yamauchi name, which they were required to use in formal contact with the Yamauchi, but within their own houses they used the original family names of, say, "Hayashi," "Inui," and "Sakai." Similarly, commoners who might use family names in correspondence with each other were mostly not able to use those names at the Yamauchi *omote*.[44] Modern historians tend to use the "inside" names for all of these people in part because doing so reflects modern values about houses and makes it easier to distinguish them from each other in an undistinguished national space of narration appropriate to modernity. Indeed all of these houses rejected their various granted names and reverted to their original names following the Meiji Restoration.

A similar regard for distinctions of Tokugawa *omote* and daimyo *uchi* was also preserved when naming deceased daimyo. The founding daimyo of Tosa under the Tokugawa, Yamauchi Katsutoyo, was known historically to outsiders and at the Tokugawa *omote* by his unadorned name, but to insiders he was known by various terms of numinous identity. His posthumous name early on was the Buddhist "Daitsūin," and he was also called the Founder (*ganso*). His descendants likewise were referred to by Buddhist posthumous names. This distinction had a direct correlation to their worldly power. The power of the Yamauchi filled Tosa but did not extend into the rest of the islands. The higher, invasive power of the Tokugawa was evident in that deceased Tokugawa rulers were also locally numinous. Ieyasu was the combinatory Buddhist/Shinto deity Tōshō Daigongen, with a shrine to him set up in Tosa, and later generations were known by their Buddhist posthumous names. Up to this point the distinction of spatial usage of naming might be seen as simply one expressing respect of the status hierarchy. It was, after all, perfectly legal and consistent with *omote* demands for lords to have such Buddhist posthumous names, and they were required by the Tokugawa to have Buddhist rites when they died. However, as we shall see in Chapter 5, it gradually became common in many domains to refer to founding daimyo by deity names following Shinto deifications that were explicitly prohibited by the Tokugawa government. In Tosa a triad of founding figures—Katsutoyo, his spouse, and his son—were deified in 1807, and locally Katsutoyo came to be called the deity Fujinami Myojin and, from 1836, Fujinami Daimyōjin. This directly contravened Tokugawa law but was tacitly permitted as long as the naming did not exceed the space of Yamauchi authority. Furthermore the divine nature of the Yamauchi rulers to insiders was not merely a development of the late Tokugawa period. Even before the deification, samurai of Tosa in the eighteenth century, as noted earlier, variously described their lord as deriving authority from the deities of heaven and earth (*jingi*) or from the Confucian heaven itself (*ten*), and as a man who brought fecundity to the land and sea through his virtue.[45] Such language could not have been used at the Tokugawa *omote* and clearly reflects not merely the status hierarchy but also the *hōken* feudal nature of daimyo rule.

Ways of naming individuals also illustrate the intersection of gender and these compartments of authority. In general it was extremely rare for a woman's independent identity to be expressed in higher *omote* situations. Rather, women tended to be named in terms of a generic association with a particular man regardless of the status of her house. When Tosa domain Elders were required to submit familial hostages to Edo in 1647, the domain submitted a report of this to the Tokugawa Elders. The descending order of the ability to appear as oneself in the *omote* shows that designated heirs were listed with surname and common-use name, noninheriting brothers were listed as "brother" with common-use name but no surname, and daughters were designated simply as "true daughter" with no name at all.[46] Even with regard to a woman as well connected outside as Katsutoyo's wife, this rule held true. She was known posthumously as Kenshōin (and from 1807 as the deity Kenshōin Reijin) within Tosa but was known in the Tokugawa *omote* either as "wife of Katsutoyo" or, in answer to the question "Who was his wife?" as "daughter of Wakamiya Tomooki." However powerful Kenshōin was due to her status within the realm and the household, her *omote* identity was limited to being an extension of an associated male.[47] This held true for all daughters and wives of daimyo; they remain nameless in lineages submitted to the Tokugawa *omote*.[48] Even within the domain a woman of status might frequently be identified by a term of association with a male power because of the strongly patriarchal order, but it was still possible for her individual name to be used in various situations. This gendered pattern of naming functioned at many levels of *omote*, where, for example, retainer women and villager women were primarily known to the daimyo *omote* by similar patterns of nameless masculine association. In their daily life they were identified by a mixture of such associational names with personal names, and in internal-use lineages of the family women might be identified by personal name.[49]

Kuni as a province and as a daimyo country

Awareness of the politics of exterior and interior identities can be applied to resolve recent historiographical debate concerning the meaning of the word *kuni* (read as *koku* when used in compound words) in relation to daimyo realms. Some historians consider all early modern uses of *kuni* with regard to domains as deriving from its meaning as province. Yamamoto Hirofumi writes, "In early modern terminological usage, when a domain is called a *kuni*, it is simply a reference to the [imperial] province and county system. Is not the fact that *han* are without exception referred to as 'houses' evidence indicating that Japan was the state made out of a grouping of houses?"[50] As noted in the introduction, Ronald Toby has made a similar assertion concerning the meaning of domainal *kuni*.[51] Other scholars such as Mark Ravina and myself have made claims for one meaning of *kuni* as domainal country being separate from its meaning as province. The disagreements emerge from the nature of the sources that the scholars gave priority to and used, depending on whether their perspective was Tokugawa-centered or daimyo-centered. What is argued here is that Yamamoto and Toby correctly identify Tokugawa *omote* usage and that Ravina and myself correctly identify various forms of internal usage.[52] In the actual Edo period both discourses existed. Exploring how they were deployed helps us better understand the contemporary political culture.

It is clear from language use in Edo-period documents that domains held varying degrees of an inside nature as *kuni*, used to mean a domainal form of country, that could not be expressed in the Tokugawa *omote*. Clarifying this particular meaning is made a bit difficult because *kuni* had many other common meanings as well. *Kuni* referred to the Japan reigned over by the emperor, as well as to the various lands ruled by foreigners, and these uses have been translated into English as "country." *Kuni* also referred to the districts of administration created by the imperial government in the seventh century, and this has normally been translated as "province." When *kuni* appeared in documents referring to a daimyo's territory, it was translated either into English as "domain" or into Japanese as *han* and was used that way in English historiography. That some daimyo were formally known as "province-holding" (*kuni-mochi*) makes it even more difficult to tease out the difference between *kuni*'s meaning as province and its meaning as a daimyo domainal country.

Imperial provincial administrations were defunct, but the provinces remained as spatial constructs regularly referred to in literature by people of all classes in Japan in ways that linked the present historically to local and imperial pasts. As noted above, the Tokugawa also put provincial boundaries to administrative use when it gathered information on population, village distribution and size, and produced maps organized along the boundaries of imperial provinces and counties. Because actual daimyo realms rarely matched provincial boundaries, daimyo had to cooperate with other daimyo and Tokugawa intendants in the province to organize their information before submitting a finished map or set of data to the Tokugawa government. Daimyo and bannermen were issued documents of enfeoffment that identified the provinces and counties within which their territories lay. Such examples reveal the continuing importance of the imperial division of geography in the Tokugawa order and support claims that the Edo-period usage of *kuni* essentially meant province.

However, domainal *kuni* identity also derived from Warring States daimyo discourses of rule and from continental traditions of political thought, but these identities were not formally expressible in the Tokugawa order and continued only in domain internal discourse. The independence of this discourse from "province" may best be illustrated with an example of such a *kuni* in a samurai government with no direct tie to the Tokugawa *omote* at all. Iwakuni was the 30,000-*koku* realm belonging to the Kikkawa clan, who served within the large Mōri clan of Hagi domain. It was a realm created purely by "private" subinfeudation and was not even recognized as a branch domain by the Tokugawa, yet the retainers of this realm sometimes referred to it as a *kuni* in conscious alignment with discourses from ancient China. When the lord Kikkawa Tsunenaga asked a retainer to discourse on public morality, the retainer wrote, "The way we have come to our territory is similar to the infeudations of the Shang dynasty. Especially because we are a *kuni* made by infeudation of territory from our parent *kuni* [of Hagi domain], it seems obvious that primarily we should base things on the Shang-era infeudation system." He thereafter referred to the Iwakuni territory in his missive as a *kuni* while discussing various points of governing the *kuni* as learned from continental political philosophy. This was all done in a context recognizing Iwakuni domain's situation within and dependence on the parent domain of Hagi, and Iwakuni's indirect relation to the Tokugawa and the imperial *shinkoku* (country of the gods) of Japan, but it has nothing to do with provinces, nor with being an emissary of the Tokugawa government.[53] The author's acceptance of the three higher layers of *omote* discourses vis-à-vis Hagi domain, the Tokugawa, and imperial Japan did not erase the *uchi* discourses that he and other retainers utilized to preserve degrees of real political autonomy from the parent domain. This relative independence was such that at the Battle of Sekigahara in 1600 the lord of Iwakuni secretly sided with Ieyasu against the interests of the parent domain, and the same domain also operated somewhat independently of the parent domain during the final years of the Tokugawa in the 1860s, in the end serving as a mediator between the Tokugawa and Mōri clans during the war between the two.[54] As the quotation above indicates, this was authorized by appeal to traditions of feudal *kuni* in ancient continental history that were a continuing source of inspiration for use within domains in Tokugawa Japan.

Similar examples exist for daimyo retainers of the Tokugawa who were not of "province-holding" status. Kyōgoku Takaakira was lord of the relatively small 50,000-*koku* Marugame domain, situated in Sanuki province on Shikoku. He was not a province-holding daimyo, but in 1825 he issued an official declaration of domain reform in which he referred to the *kokusei* (government of the country) and described his role as "the model for the samurai and commoners of this one *kuni*." Without doubt, Takaakira was referring to his realm and not the province that it was situated within, which contained the domain of another daimyo of much greater public stature. In his missive he quoted passages from the ancient classics of continental learning as models of good government that guided his policies.[55]

The use of domainal *kuni* for internal discourse was merely an option, and not all lords of small domains used *kuni* as a term defining their realm. This was true for the diminutive 12,000-*koku* domain of Tahara, ruled by the Miyake clan, that figures prominently in this book. A survey of a nearly unbroken two-hundred-year run of domain diaries reveals consistent usage of *ryō* and *ryōbun* as terms identifying the realm in internal legal discourse and no self-referential use of the term *kuni* in official proclamations. Each domain had its own internal configurations and development, and it is likely that the daimyo of many small domains chose not to make official use of domainal *kuni* discourse. Yet such was always an available resource readily understood by any daimyo. Even in Tahara the domain Elder Watanabe Kazan admonished his lord with the need to care for his *kuni* if he wished to be picked to serve in Tokugawa government office, writing, "The pride of the *bōfū* plant is that it continues to sprout new leaves to the very end of its life. The logic of a samurai serving his *kuni* and that of a lord serving the [Tokugawa] *tenka* is basically like this. But if there are no roots, then there is no way to keep the plant alive, and samurai serving their *kuni*, and lords serving the *tenka*, cannot maintain even themselves without roots. . . . For samurai to take care of their houses and lords to take care of their *kuni* is maintaining the roots, and thus you must put your heart into caring for your state [*kokka*], and this will work far better toward having you chosen for a [Tokugawa] government post than paying bribes to the powers that be."[56] Here Watanabe was positing his domainal country as a site of resistance to aspects of Tokugawa politics, namely the prevalence of bribery in daimyo acquisition of posts and rank, a circumstance he did not like. The translation of this kind of domainal *kuni* as "country" expresses the agency implicit in the term, as well as the ruling authority of a daimyo over his territory that developed separately from house rule and separately from the provincial *kuni* of imperial rule, even as the lord was a servant of the larger Tokugawa order.

Domainal *kuni* discourse was also derivative of provincial *kuni* discourse. Of the roughly 250 daimyo of Japan, 15 to 22 lords (depending on the era) held status as a province-holding (*kunimochi*) daimyo. The territories of many of these daimyo roughly equaled or neared the area of a province or two, but some held less than half of a province. Province-holding status came with many ritual marks of prestige. For example, such daimyo could use in official correspondence with the Tokugawa the phrase "return to the province" (*kuni ni kaeru*) rather than the more common "return to the residence" (*zaisho ni kaeru*), which lesser daimyo were required to employ. They were allowed to attain the court rank of Junior Fourth and sit in a higher-status waiting room in Edo castle. They also frequently used the word *kuni* when referring to their domain in local laws, whereas it is very uncommon to find self-referential use of *kuni* in legal proclamations from daimyo governments that had no province-holding status in the Tokugawa order. Such domains consistently issued "house laws," or their territorial laws referred to the domain as *ryō, ryōbun,* and like terms that were also expressible within the Tokugawa *omote*.[57] The legal discourse within domains thus suggests that the connection of *kuni* to province-holding rank—if not actual possession of a province itself—was important to the language of local daimyo law. Whether to translate this law as "provincial law" or "domainal law" or "law of the domainal country" is complicated by a number of factors. Only "province holders" often called the laws they issued *kokuhō,* which would suggest that "provincial law" would be the best translation. However, the *kokuhō* that they issued applied only to their domain territory and not to the province, which would suggest that "domainal law" would be more appropriate. On the other hand, calling it "domainal law" would not distinguish between the *kokuhō* laws of these daimyo and the house laws and territorial laws of daimyo who did not extensively use *kuni* discourse internally. Nor would it be able to suggest the resonance of this legal order with the many other *kuni*-related terms utilized by daimyo with large holdings, terms that could be used only in their internal discourse and not vis-à-vis the Tokugawa.

It is clear that province-holding daimyo were able to use the term *kuni* more freely than other daimyo, and close attention to usage is required to fig-ure out the term's meanings as a domainal identity or as a provincial identity. For example, province-holding status did not mean that daimyo could refer to their governments as *kokusei* facing the Tokugawa, yet they regularly did so locally to express a type of inside autonomy. The content of the laws and proclamations of province holders clearly shows that they were not merely "provincial" extensions of Tokugawa law. Despite *omote* orders and promises that the content of local law would be in accord with Tokugawa law, the inside truth was often different. The difference was not a formalized distinction of authorities whose details were contestable in courts, such as exists in mod-ern nations—for example, in the relations between the state of Massachusetts and the U.S. government. When there was conflict between the authority of Tokugawa law and that of daimyo law, the struggle was not carried out in terms of daimyo rights of government, for their authority could always be viewed by the Tokugawa government as merely "private." As we shall see in subsequent chapters, the actual content of local government was subject to negotiation according to the rules of *omote* and *naishō* interaction.

One key method of ascertaining autonomous domainal discourses of *kuni* is to learn which words were usable in formal documents vis-à-vis the Tokuga-wa and which were not. The Yamauchi daimyo were province holders in both name and reality. The boundaries of their domain and Tosa province were identical, so the "domainal country" nature of much "inside" use of *kuni* can be even more difficult to separate than for other province-holding daimyo. For example, in Tosa an eighteenth-century document refers to Kōchi as *kokufu* (*kuni* administrative office) and as *kunimiyako* (capital of the *kuni*) and the ruling house as *kokka,* but whether the *kuni* in these words means the prov-ince or the domainal country might not be immediately apparent to a modern reader. However, none of these words could be used in Tokugawa *omote,* and they were often used locally in association with proposals and laws that would themselves have been illegal in *omote* discourse.[58] Saga domain covered a large territory ruled by the province-holding Nabeshima clan. It was within Hizen province but not contiguous with it. Yet members of the domain frequently called it a *kuni* and used the term in various ways indicating a degree of gov-ernmental autonomy not expressible in the Tokugawa *omote.* The eighteenth-century author of *Hagakure,* a collection of the sayings of the domain samurai Yamamoto Tsunetomo, used *kokka* to mean the domain or the lord's family, *kokugaku* to mean study of the domain, *kokushu* to identify the lord of the domain, and *kokusei* to mean domain government. Yamamoto was clearly identifying his domain in this usage and was not referring to other parts of

Hizen province. Furthermore, none of these words could have been used with the Tokugawa government.[59] The Ikeda of Tottori domain ruled a realm that spanned the two provinces of Hōki and Inaba. Sometimes in their proclamations they used the word *ryōgoku,* or "two provinces," to identify their realm, but at other times they used the expression *kuni* for their realm, reflecting a consciousness of the domain itself as a single *kuni* conceptually different from a province.[60] Uwajima domain was merely a single southern county of Iyo province, a province of fourteen counties, but the Date rulers, who held honorary province-holding status, regularly used *kuni* and *kokka* to identify the realm and its government, and they reminded their people of their "debt to their *kuni,*" by which they meant their domain. In one document they ordered performers of their own *kuni* not to perform in Ōzu, another domain within the same province, thereby highlighting that the association with domainal *kuni* could take priority over its meaning as provincial *kuni.*[61]

The example of Morioka domain of the Nanbu clan is particularly instructive because various documents produced by the domain express a keen awareness that the relevant terms were different for inside use and outside use, and because of the nineteenth-century rise in status of the Nanbu clan to province-holding. Morioka domain was within Mutsu province, which the Nanbu shared with the province-holding Date clan of Sendai domain and about ten other domains as well. The Nanbu clan did not have province-holding status throughout most of the Tokugawa period. But in 1808 they learned that, thanks to their recent efforts in the defense of the Ezo region against Russian incursions, the formally accepted productive value of their realm (*omotedaka*) would thenceforth double to 200,000 *koku.* This was done without granting one iota of land to the Nanbu clan and was purely a statement of increased status. The status gains were actually a mixed blessing because changing the productive value in the *omote* meant increased amounts of duty formally demanded by the Tokugawa. However, the benefits it brought related to other forms of ranking as well, including that the Nanbu clan would thenceforth have honorary status as a province holder. Not long after this the lord of the domain ordered his retainers to stop using the term *zaisho* (residence) and begin employing *kuni* in correspondence with the Tokugawa government, "so that we may be in accord with our peers."[62] This indicates a direct link between province-holding status and the ability to use the term *kuni* as self-description vis-à-vis the Tokugawa government. Yet, long before the rise in status, the lord's ancestors were referring to the realm as *kuni* and reminding its people of the generations of debt that they owed their *kuni* (*sūdai no okokuon*) for its management of their welfare.[63] Their awareness that such language was not appropriate for use with the Tokugawa can be seen in the proclamation of 1806 made only months before the elevation to province-holding status:

> With regard to our territory, traditionally we called it *kuni,* but in re-cent years it has become more common to call it only *zaisho.* At Edo *omote* when in relations with other samurai houses it is common for people to call their territories *zaisho,* and—because this is easy for both sides—naturally people have come to use *zaisho.* However, we think that it is rather a good thing to call our realm *kuni* and not lose the old ways. Of course, when facing the [Tokugawa] government we must not use this indiscriminately and should continue in all ways as before, but other than this, certainly within our *kuni* and also in relations with other samurai houses, henceforth we should follow the old ways and call our realm *kuni.*[64]

This *kuni* of internal discourse was unrelated to province-holding status and to actual provincial boundaries, but it was a term used politically to mobilize people in the service of domainal culture, economy, and politics. This exhor-tation reveals that the lord was quite aware of the impropriety of using such language toward the Edo government. He was also aware that *omote* ways were potentially corrosive of a domain *uchi* identity and urged his subjects to strive to maintain a distinct local identity through the assertion of "inside" linguistic practices. The separation between inside and outside the domain was neither isolation nor total resistance but rather was mobilized to mediate outside in-fluence in ways that the domain leaders saw as advantageous when it suited them.

The former usage of *kuni* in internal discourse, as noted in the lord's state-ment, is evidenced in domain documents. A survey of proclamations from be-fore 1808 illustrates common use of such Tokugawa-approved terms as *zaisho* and *ryōbun,* yet there are also numerous instances of the use of *kuni* to refer to the realm.[65] An example from 1741 shows a preoccupation with preserving language and customs of the domain in terms of a *kuni* consciousness. The lord admonished his retainers that they were "losing the language of the *kuni*" because people laughed at their dialect in Edo. He then advised, "Edo is under the authority of the shogun, and therefore act accordingly there, but when in the *kuni* you should keep to the ways of the *kuni,* and do not lose them!"[66] This concern for preserving domainal culture is repeated in later proclamations and reflects a common concern among various domains with managing the beneficial and corrosive influences of the effects of the alternate attendance system that tied together Edo and domains in many ways.[67] The differential use of inside/*omote* language was not limited to the term *kuni* of course but was part of a broader pattern of ritual subservience. Morioka domain internally used the term *rōjū* for members of the governing council of domain Elders between 1753 and 1797. This term was identical to that used for the Tokugawa Elders, and perhaps the initial choice to use the term rather than the more common *karō* (house Elder) was to lend them prestige locally. Yet *rōjū* was only for internal use, and vis-à-vis the Tokugawa and other domains Nanbu officials were instructed to use the less problematic term *toshiyori* (Elder). This proved cumbersome, and the domain later reverted to using *karō*, a term acceptable inside and out, but the attempt to use *rōjū* was symptomatic of the feudal political culture.[68]

The notion of domainal *kuni* was often politicized in border control and immigration issues. When the Morioka domain economy deteriorated in the mid-eighteenth century, the government issued a 1742 prohibition against the immigration of people of other *kuni* into the domain, to prevent them from competing for insufficient local resources. Local resources were so scarce that Morioka domain had the opposite problem of its people fleeing to other domains. Neighboring Sendai domain, which was in the same province, complained about the influx of Morioka people into "this *kuni*" of Sendai. Shamed by this admonition, some Morioka people criticized their government for its poor rule, arguing that "we need government that will make people of other *kuni* come here, not one that makes the people flee our *kuni*."[69] We can see from these documents that a domainal country consciousness expressed in the term *kuni* included the notion of domainal subjects as members and of nondomain subjects as foreigners who might not be admitted, and that in this ideology of the domainal *kuni* the ruler had responsibility to ensure the welfare of his subjects.[70]

The term *kuni* was also used to politicize new forms of government intervention in the economy in ways that had nothing to do with "province" and everything to do with the political economy of the domain. This is evident in its use in the terms *kokusan* (products of the country) and *kokueki* (prosperity of the country), which merchants used to influence their domain governments and which those governments used to influence the people they ruled concerning management of the commercial economy of the domain. These terms were used in Morioka domain from before the Nanbu clan's rise to province-holding status. Furthermore, even after the clan's acquisition of province-holding status, the usage of *kokueki* had nothing to do with the *omote* demands of either the Tokugawa or the province of Mutsu. The borders of *kokueki* were domainal, and as the domain's economic policies often functioned directly against the interests of the Tokugawa government, they can hardly be said to be the work of daimyo engaging in government as provincial emissaries of Tokugawa authority. Similar policies were common in many domains. Such intervention in the economy justified by *kokueki* ideology often was extensive enough that it threatened to cause serious political problems for the domain, as occurred with eighteenth-century Tokushima's management of its indigo industry.[71] In many realms *kokueki* was an ideology of resistance to the Tokugawa-designed economy, which was organized around the service of daimyo to their overlord. The increasing use of *kokueki* ideology was part of a local movement to alter the goals of daimyo government so that they emphasized taking greater responsibility for care of the local economy regardless of the *omote* duty owed to the Tokugawa.[72] This rhetoric can be found in small domains as well, although certainly less frequently. The 30,000-*koku* Ichinoseki domain, a branch realm of the large Sendai domain, made use of *kokueki* mercantilist thought and policy and had subjects who called their daimyo realm "my *kuni*" in their economic struggles.[73]

It should thus be clear that there were many overlapping meanings of *kuni* and that one of the meanings was a politicized domainal *kuni* that existed separately from either actual provinces or the ritual province-holding status. This meaning derived from Warring States traditions of daimyo and from ancient Chinese literature describing kingly autonomy before its imperial era. For some large domains *kuni* also derived from province-holding status, but domain internal usage of the derived term did not mean that in associated policies the daimyo was therefore necessarily ruling the domain as an emissary of Tokugawa government. Because people of the Edo period accepted and utilized the variety of meanings of *kuni* for various political ends, the modern nationalist desire to find out which is the "real" *kuni* is misguided if our aim is to understand the politics of the Edo period. Stakeholders in this regime such as daimyo were required to perform full "private" subservience to Tokugawa government desire in *omote* situations but were informally permitted to deploy various independent identities such as that of the domainal *kuni*.

The independence of daimyo and the degree of difference between inside and outside were influenced by the lord's place in the Tokugawa hierarchy. Politics involve power, and the more powerful the lord, the greater the habitual degree of independence in discursive practice, policy, and action. The Yamauchi of Tosa were relatively high-ranking daimyo who ruled a geographically large, contiguous realm and who likewise had a high degree of distinction between inside and outside discourses. The Miyake lords of the small domain of Tahara in Mikawa province ruled in ways more closely in line with the *omote* political discourse of samurai house servitude, but there are many examples of their participating in the politics of *omote* and *naishō*. For example, like the Yamauchi, the Miyake too formally pleaded personal illness at appropriate times in order to manage domain and family politics. Yet the arrangements of power are sometimes difficult to discern. With regard to inheritance politics, the Miyake actually operated far more at variance with Tokugawa *omote* rules than the Yamauchi did. These two contrasting domains are touchpoints throughout this book, marking degrees of subservience and autonomy that were expressible in this system.

It is quite possible to continue to do institutional history of "Tokugawa Japan" without reference to the spatial consciousness of the Edo period. One could narrate the same order by taking the perspective of either the Tokugawa gaze or the retrospective gaze of imperial Meiji Japan, the latter having indeed been the dominant mode of historiography since the late nineteenth century. Many excellent histories have been and will continue to be written from those perspectives. However, one aspect of the Tokugawa form of politics that no historian can afford to ignore is its influence on the record keeping of the day and on the documents we use to understand the Tokugawa past. The Tokugawa era produced voluminous documentation and data. An extensive regime of information collection was one of the hallmarks of the Tokugawa government and one of the expressions of its authority and power. The next chapter explores the effects of the Tokugawa mode of politics on its enormous data collection systems and shows that the records must be understood in their *uchi* and *omote* contexts of meaning and production.

2

Performing the Tokugawa Right to Know

"Itemized list of possible reports of the income from our two
provinces"
Item. 296,374.2030 koku assessed agricultural base
     The tax income from this at 50% would be 148,187.1015 *koku.*
     One report you can submit based on this calculation attached.
Item. Increase the above assessed agricultural base by 40% and we
have a domain amount of 423,391.7182 *koku.*
     The tax income from this at 35% would be 148,187.1015 *koku.*
     One report you can submit based on this calculation attached.
Item. . . . [four more calculations]

From 1605 Hagi domain memorandum to domain ambassador on what he
might submit to the Tokugawa government's request for domain tax data[1]

The Tokugawa government collected much information about the conditions
and management of daimyo domains. It used such data in the formation of
government policy, as the basis of extraction of services and resources from
daimyo, and, on occasion, to intervene in the daimyos' control of their domains. For their part, daimyo likewise collected much information from villages and towns of their own domains. This regime of information collection
was more thorough in its pretensions than anything in Japan up to that time,
and it bequeathed numerous documents that allow modern historians opportunities for statistical and analytical study. This information had a degree of
accuracy that was admirable and useful, but the accuracy was also systematically affected by the processes of the politics of *omote* and *uchi.*

One example familiar to any student of the era is the domain's official assessment of agricultural production (*omotedaka*). This assessment of a daimyo realm's productivity was the basis for calculating many Tokugawa exactions from daimyo, and it also strongly influenced a daimyo's status among his peers. Historians contrast this with the internal productivity assessments (*uchidaka*) made by daimyo, which were often higher than *omotedaka.* One common explanation for the difference is that as land development increased yields, the internal assessments rose while the official assessment remained the same. Many historians have also pointed out that the original *omotedaka* (established by the Tokugawa for many domains in the first decades of the seventeenth century) for some domains were only loosely based on the late sixteenth-century land surveys, which themselves were of dubious quality.[2] The document quoted in the epigraph of this chapter was produced by the Mōri clan of Hagi domain at the beginning of the Tokugawa period. Clan officials sent it to the domain ambassador in Edo, who was going to make an official report to the Tokugawa of domain tax income and the agricultural base of the domain. The numbers were calculated down to the fourth decimal and purport to present domain tax income and agricultural production, but they present two options that differ by more than 120,000 *koku* in the amount of agricultural land. Both numbers were politically produced themselves, and the clan's ultimate *omotedaka*—a product of informal negotiations—ended up being different from either.[3] The seeming precision of these numbers is beguiling, and it is tempting to use them as if they are direct products of the land surveys of that era, but this would be problematic. In truth, some daimyo *omotedaka* seem to be near the amounts of the actual surveys of their land, and others were obviously highly manipulated.

The example of *omotedaka* suggests that the *omote* pretensions of the Tokugawa government obscure how a daimyo's "inside" authority kept much information hidden from official notice. Lords had to declare that they would offer up all sorts of information upon request, but then strove to gain their desires through *naishō* informal negotiations rather than by challenging *omote* rituals. The Tokugawa government ran smoothly by forcing subordinate parties to play their parts in the rituals of order and submission and simultaneously diverting its eyes from full apprehension of the inner realities of *uchi* spaces. True deceit also existed in government relations, but many of the discrepancies in documents were simply the result of negotiated fictions.

This chapter first looks in detail at the Touring Inspectors of the Tokugawa government, whose job was to gather a great variety of information about domains in Japan. It then discusses daimyo inspections of the villages of their own domains and, finally, briefly surveys various other forms of information collection such as demands for reports of agricultural productivity, tax income, and territorial maps. Most of the information comes from relations between the Yamauchi government of powerful Tosa domain, the Miyake government of tiny Tahara domain, and the Tokugawa government, but information from other realms is also included where appropriate. These events span the two and a half centuries of the Edo period so as to show a basic continuity in the use of *omote* and *uchi* politics and to explore its various dimensions. There was a decline in the degree of accuracy of some key economic information over time, which can be related to the fiscal pressures on daimyo caused by economic change, but most of the information comes from the middle of the seventeenth century, and some—such as the document quoted in the epigraph of this chapter—from the very start of the Tokugawa regime, to clarify the argument that the incorrectness of the information was not in itself a sign of the decline of Tokugawa authority. The Touring Inspectors have had a visible place in many historians' arguments of Tokugawa decline, and all historians have regarded the inspection system as having degenerated into a mere formal show by the nineteenth century, but this chapter reveals that the itinerant inspections were consistently not about the "inspection" but about putting on the right "show."

Another aspect of this political culture was how it functioned in the formation of group identity. The constant management of two sets of information, *omote* and *naibun,* made special the feeling of membership in the community. In this sense the politics of *omote* and *uchi* are a perfect example of an indigenously articulated, self-conscious system of boundary maintenance and identity creation that illustrates Fredrik Barth's theories of how boundaries maintain group identity by controlling and shaping interactions with the outside.[4] The political culture of information management fostered a group identity not merely at daimyo domains but at many levels of the hierarchy in ways that served the interests of its various stakeholders. The relationship between villages and daimyo governments, though dealt with only occasionally in this chapter, is done so in order to suggest that this mode of politics was endemic to the whole political system. Key work on that front has already been done. With regard to the accuracy of economic information submitted by villages to daimyo, Thomas Smith's seminal article on the land tax in the Tokugawa period described broad areas of tacitly accepted dissimulation whereby villages protected their interests.[5] Smith saw in this relationship a record of decline, which was only somewhat true. Philip Brown has shown in his work on cadastral registers and the management of village commons that there was a large degree of mutually accepted inaccuracy in the reports from the very beginning of the Tokugawa regime.[6] The relative village autonomy of the contract local management system (*mura-uke*) had a different shape from that of the relative daimyo autonomy of the feudal house system, but this chapter explores some daimyo-sponsored tours of their own realms to illustrate some of the similarities and how the politics of *omote* and *uchi* worked at the domain/village level of interaction as well.

Tokugawa touring inspections

In 1667 the Tokugawa ruler sent Touring Inspectors across Japan to survey conditions of rule in all provinces of Japan. These grand feudal processions advertised the *kubō's* interest in implementing good government and were a statement of Tokugawa sovereignty over its demesne and the territories of all daimyo. In preparation for the 1667 tour, the Tokugawa presented each daimyo a document with an extensive list of items that would be inspected: the quality of their domain management; enforcement of anti-Christianity policies; whether high prices and commercial taxation were causing hardship; whether anything subverted the intent of Tokugawa laws; whether speculation and commercial hoarding of goods were happening; the price of precious metals; whether placards proclaiming the fundamental Tokugawa laws were displayed in sufficient numbers in the domain; and whether the writing on the placards was not faded with age.[7] The picture that emerges, based on this *omote* document, is of a very intrusive Tokugawa government that ruled a unitary state with little space for independence in the lordly management of realms.

The first such tour happened in 1633 under Tokugawa Iemitsu, and the tour of 1667 was under his son Ietsuna. Thereafter the Tokugawa authorized a tour of inspection at nearly every change of ruler in the Tokugawa dynasty until the final tour in 1838.[8] Most scholars of these touring inspections see a history of declining effectiveness and would say that in the seventeenth century the tour was a rigorous and severe inspection but gradually in the eighteenth century it became a "formalized and ritualized" parade with little real observation carried out at all.[9] Within this body of literature some scholars see this change as a symptom of decline in Tokugawa authority and some see in the highly ritualized tours statements of continuing Tokugawa suzerainty over the daimyo that confirmed order and stability at each change in Tokugawa overlord.[10] Yet there is evidence that the tours were always highly formalized and ritualized, that scrutiny was not high on the list of Tokugawa objectives, and that from the very beginning the most significant feature of the tours was that they were a drama of submission by daimyo to Tokugawa ruling authority.

Touring inspections in a large *tozama* domain

When the Tokugawa Elders announced the 1667 tour, they informed the Edo ambassador of the *tozama* (outer daimyo) Yamauchi lord of Tosa that the inspection was going to be more thorough than the previous tour of 1633 and that the dissimulations of that time would not be tolerated on this occasion. The lord conveyed this warning to the senior administrators in Tosa, who replied to his assistant with a letter expressing their intent to comply and to permit no attempts at fabrication:

> At the time of the previous inspection it reached the ears of the Tokugawa Elders that domainal management was poor, and our country hid its defects by having samurai dress up as villagers. The lord has heard that the Inspectors have been told to keep this in mind and investigate things carefully, and they are determined to ask many questions of farmers in each of the places they visit, and if they cannot get clear answers there, they have been ordered to query the rural magistrates and intendants. We have been told not to alter anything in the slightest and let all be just as it is. We are respectful of the lord's concern and promise that here we shall answer questions just as if we were wild monkeys without the slightest dissimulation and will state things about our country just as they truly are. So please convey to the lord that he can put his heart at rest on this matter.[11]

Based on this document alone, it seems that Tosa domain would not repeat the obfuscations of 1633 and this time would comply with full transparency.

Tosa officials were aware that the 1633 tour had indeed involved a large amount of charade. On that occasion the Tokugawa *kubō* gave a direct order to the Inspectors not to accept any food or special care from domain officials. The Inspectors were supposed to purchase their own food and provisions locally and find their own lodging. The Tosa lord Tadayoshi was in Edo and sent a letter home noting these commands, but in the same letter he ordered his chief officials to learn from neighboring domains what food and special care they would provide and then to be sure to do them one better. He had heard that this was not going to be an inspection to unsettle things in the domains, and he wrote that the main thing was to entertain the Inspectors: "I hear that this investigation of the domains is not something to worry about. Just know that they will ask about the general outlines of things in the domains and they are not going to be ordering any changes. Put all of your energy into treating them well, and as I have said before, check out what the neighboring domains are doing!"[12] Tadayoshi met informally with various representatives of these Inspectors as soon as he could. With a suggestion that expresses the delicate balance of interests, one of the Inspectors told him that when Tosa fixed up or made new lodgings and repaired roads and bridges, they should do so with a particular nuance: —"Make it look as if you are ordering these repairs and other things secretly."[13] The Inspectors informally signaled that they wished to have a good time and that the domain could protect its interests and gain a good report by satisfying this desire, as long as it was done with enough seemly obedience to *omote* strictures. Thus, despite many formal orders not to be excessive in fixing things up, numerous items of furniture and food were bought in the Kyoto-Osaka area to furnish the rooms along the tour. The Inspectors had been ordered neither to visit the castle town nor to socialize with local samurai, so that they could be impartial, but the chief retainers of the domain had some informal negotiations with the Inspectors, who ended up staying in the city for two nights and visiting with most of the domain Elders. Tadayoshi himself was in Edo but secretly exchanged letters with the Inspectors not only afterward but even during the tour itself.[14] Following the event, the domain records concerning the Inspectors (including one daimyo, two bannermen, and their combined 346-person retinue) noted that, "We put great care into fixing the roads and bridges, and the food and other care was not negligible. The three Inspectors left letters to lord Tadayoshi thanking him." These were the same Inspectors who had received regulations issued directly from the *kubō* stating, "You will not indulge yourselves on this journey!" and "In every domain and location wherever you go you will not accept any entertainment or food."[15] Subsequently, Tadayoshi wrote a number of letters praising the domain administrators because he heard from the Inspectors and their relatives about how well everything went with the preparations, and he gleefully noted gossip that the food and preparations were found wanting in a number of other domains in Shikoku. "I am very satisfied!" he wrote.[16] As far as Tadayoshi was concerned, and he seems to have been well informed, the success of the tour was judged on the merits of the preparations for receiving the Inspectors rather than on governance of the domain and household.

Tosa domain did not want scrutiny of its rule, and it had reason to worry. It was still suffering the aftereffects of a crippling debt load to lenders in Kyoto and Osaka that peaked at more than six years' annual regular income of the domain in 1620. The domain raised numerous taxes and corvée duties and created new taxes to increase income. It extricated itself from debt by the end of the decade but maintained the higher level of taxation, which created many tensions within the domain.[17] The domain official in charge of resurveying agricultural land met so much resistance from samurai and villagers that he fled the domain in fear. The villagers themselves were fleeing Tosa in such large numbers that Tosa negotiated extradition treaties with its neighbors in the 1630s in an attempt to bring them back.[18] Scrutiny would have uncovered numerous shortcomings in domain rule, so Tadayoshi told the domain officials to secretly decide what sort of answers to use for the Inspectors' anticipated questions.[19] He was worried about villagers and not only told the domain officials to make sure that the farmers looked no worse than those in neighboring domains but also repeatedly told his officials to make sure that all the villagers and townspeople answered satisfactorily.[20] Surviving documents of the 1630s reveal no orders that samurai be dressed up like villagers, but the Yamauchi were suspicious of what untutored and uncontrolled villagers might say. Two years earlier a senior statesman of the domain, Fukao Izumi, wrote in a letter of advice to the lord regarding various Tokugawa officials who were coming to the domain, "They have been informally ordered to stop and ask many questions of the villagers along the roadside. Villagers are stupid complainers, and I am very worried what they might say."[21] Anxiety over commoner complaints led Tadayoshi to order that some steep crop taxes be lowered in advance of the tour and that samurai be given a one year reprieve of their labor tax, but he added that these measures should all be spaced out and done informally and secretly.[22] There was also worry over expressions of disorder among the samurai. After two Tosa samurai had a swordfight over a personal grudge not long before the Inspectors arrived, Tadayoshi ordered the victor to kill himself. In authorizing this judgment, he wrote, "For those two to engage in a fight near the domain border, and just before the Inspectors arrived, means that there is no other way of dealing with this."[23] The Tosa retainers worked very hard to make sure that their stories to the Inspectors matched. On one occasion during the tour they presented some written information on how many samurai were in the Yamauchi household. The Inspectors refused to believe it, thinking the numbers improbably large, so in addition to attempting persuasion on the spot, the Tosa officials sent copies of the stated numbers to other Tosa retainers and even to the lord in Edo so that everyone's responses to later queries would match and there would be no loss of face.[24] The inspection of 1633 was thus a ritual, but it was nevertheless a spur to create better government: bridges were built, roads were repaired, tax relief was granted, and disorder was controlled and suppressed.

Tokugawa Iemitsu himself likely understood that this would be the actual character of the tour. It is curious, for example, that in his original order to the

Touring Inspectors he included one important article of explicit limitation to investigation. The Inspectors were not to entertain petitions or suits from any party. This certainly saved the Tokugawa courts much time, but by allowing no formal petitions and only on-the-spot conversation, it also was a way to prevent communication between local people and the Inspectors that had any guarantee of safety for the speaker afterward. For along the whole trip the Yamauchi made sure that many of their own people accompanied the Inspectors as guides, doctors, and carpenters to keep an eye on things. In addition, the Inspectors themselves were chosen from among daimyo and bannermen whose own realms were simultaneously in the process of being inspected by others.[25] This suggests that Iemitsu was perhaps not deeply interested in getting to the bottom of things in the lands of his retainers, but rather that the main interest of this very first Japan-wide inspection was to parade his authority into daimyo territories. He certainly had daimyo worried, made them spend much money and energy devoted to satisfying his representatives, and made them enact numerous rituals of submission to his authority. Despite its purported function, the 1633 tour eventuated in no punishments of any daimyo in Japan, even though rule was clearly poor in a number of domains. Not long after, in 1637, the impoverished people of Shimabara and Amakusa domains went into open war against their excessively harsh rulers in what became known as the Shimabara rebellion, but the Inspectors of that region were not reprimanded for making a poor investigation.[26]

However, the Tokugawa Elders' warning to the Yamauchi government in 1667 seems to have put it on notice that this second occasion of inspection would be thorough. This was arguably the decade when Tokugawa authority was at its height. The residual disorder of the unification era was gone with the last open rebellions of lordless samurai in the 1650s, and institutions such as the religious inquisition and the outlawing of fealty suicides were being introduced over all the realm of Japan. The threats against samurai dominance that emerged from commercialization and the cultural ramifications of peace and stability were not to enter loudly into public discourse for a few more decades. What kind of inspection represents this time when Tokugawa rule was unquestioned?

On the same day that the Inspectors were appointed to their various circuits, the Yamauchi lord in Edo sent a letter by express post to senior Tosa officials telling them to make preparations.[27] They contacted neighboring domains and the head of the domain mission in Osaka to collect information on the preparations of other daimyo. The earliest reports suggested that the main focus of this tour would be Tosa's ports rather than inland towns and villages, so the Tosa officials immediately began arranging boats for all contingencies, even though as yet they did not know when the tour would come or even whether it would arrive in Tosa from Osaka, from Tokushima domain to the northeast, or from Wakayama domain across the bay. Within two weeks domain officials had assigned over eighty samurai to tasks such as making sure that lodgings, rest houses, transport, and supplies would be appropriate at all possible stops and preparing documents detailing the answers one should give to Inspectors' queries. A number of retainers were in charge of making sure that utensils for the tea ceremony—the main form of refined entertainment on the road—were prepared, and one was given the tasks of reviewing the documents of the previous tour and being in charge of gifts.[28] A number of these items were expressly forbidden by the Tokugawa orders concerning the tour, just as they had been in 1633, but Tosa officials still prepared.

Meanwhile the daimyo in Edo, Yamauchi Tadatoyo, employed family and friends with connections to learn what the likely eventualities would be. The Tokugawa prohibited direct contact with the Inspectors beforehand, so Tadatoyo was delighted to learn that a friend, the Tokugawa bannerman Kuwayama Sadayori, had offered to assist in any way he could. Sadayori wrote that one of the Inspectors was his son-in-law, another his neighbor, and the third a close friend. "So if you have any business, I'll let them know the details."[29] Sadayori was friendly with the Yamauchi because, through a quirk of fate, his older brother, Kuwayama Sadakatsu, had become a retainer of the Yamauchi clan back in 1650. Ultimately, this same brother went to the domain border to greet the three Inspectors on their arrival, one of whom was his nephew by marriage. He was assigned to ask informally about their wishes, his case perhaps best exemplifying the many connections of family, neighbors, and friends that could enter into managing informal negotiations.[30]

Tadatoyo had sent warnings home about what was to be officially prohibited: no complementary food or entertainment, no tea utensils, no house Elders going to the domain border to greet the Inspectors, and no planning of the Inspectors' route for them. They should be given maps so that they might inquire with the owners of lodgings. He repeatedly noted that especially housing, food, and entertainment should be handled in accord with Tokugawa orders. This was useful information, but the officials back in Tosa tried to break these limitations when they could. They prepared some food and entertainment, but during the actual tour the Inspectors refused almost all of this and were very careful to pay for firewood and other supplies. They also prepared facilities along the route. Where new rest houses needed to be built for the convenience of the Inspectors, Tadatoyo had ordered that "old wood should be used so that they look like they have been there a long time."[31] Tosa officials planned the route—ultimately the same as in 1633 but with no nights in the castle town—and found lodgings for the Inspectors. Their list reveals that many of the houses where the Inspectors were to stay were not commoner residences, as Tokugawa orders required, but were the more commodious official travel residences of the daimyo or the homes of samurai or tax officials. For example, in Aki port the Inspector Kawaguchi Genbei stayed at the lord's own travel residence. Written in small characters beside the description of the lodging are the words, "Say this is the village headman's house." Tōdō Shōhei stayed at the house of a rural samurai and beside the notation of this are the words, "Say this is the house of a village Elder." All other stops on the itinerary were of a piece. One sees beside the descriptions of each of the night's residences on the list such marginal notes as "Say this is a merchant's house" or "Say this is a village headman's house."[32] As the architecture of these buildings would have been unmistakably "samurai" in ways regulated by custom and law, it is inconceivable that even the densest of Inspectors would not have recognized the fiction. During the tour, not everything went smoothly. The domain had planned to have the Inspectors stay at the port of Akaoka, but the Inspectors wanted to take a tour the next day of Tosa's finest temple, Gyūkōji, with a scenic view across the bay likened to that of the famous Mount Wutai of China. From there, they pressed on to the nearby village of Noichi, where two homes of rural samurai and one of a wealthy merchant were quickly prepared and used as lodging. The Inspectors then looked at their maps and attempted to choose the next lodging, at the village of Asakura on the other side of Kōchi, but the Tosa samurai noted that this would upset the prepared route all the way to the west end of the domain, whereupon the Inspectors concurred and followed the prepared route for the remainder of their Tosa tour.

When the Inspectors had first arrived in Kannoura port at Tosa's eastern border, the most powerful man in the domain, house Elder Haramiishi Mondo, currently in charge of domain government, "just happened" to be there inspecting roads and bridges. This fortunate coincidence was presented to the Inspectors "off the record" by Kuwayama Sadakatsu, who was uncle to the Inspector Hori Hachirōemon, and the Inspectors congenially agreed to have an audience. After his audience, Mondo tagged along "in the status of secret visitor" over the complete route of the tour through Tosa. The Inspectors knew "off the record" that he was present, but they could not formally acknowledge it because it was prohibited. That "secret" did not mean that Mondo had to slink around alleys and enter by back doors, however: indeed he was accompanied by a retinue appropriate to his status. The Inspectors invited him for another audience as they departed at the west end of the domain, but he refused, not wanting to display the many samurai of his own train near the border of the neighboring Uwajima realm, relations with which were strained due to recent border disputes in that region (explored in Chapter 4).[33] Because of his status as "secret visitor," Mondo and his retinue would not have appeared in any Inspector's report to the Tokugawa.

In the domain records there is no hint of any questioning taking place. When these records note observations made by the Inspectors, they are comments such as at Gyūkōji, "The Inspectors said the temple was beautiful and were impressed with the view," and in another location, "They saw the lord's palace in Urado and were impressed." In Nakamura, which had suffered a devastating flood the previous autumn, the records note, "They saw the marks of how high the water had risen and were very impressed."[34] The final comment as they left for the next domain of Uwajima was "Because the whole realm looks assiduously governed, there are no problems and we are happy with the tour."[35] Doubtless the Inspectors carried out their role of asking questions and receiving answers from the Tosa samurai, perhaps not knowing that these samurai had been ordered to memorize ten prepared texts of answers.[36] They certainly would have failed in their role if they did not query the commoners, but the effect of having Haramiishi Mondo looking on in his status of "secret visitor" must have dampened any desire for complaint. It is likely that in general the answers given were honest when inoffensive and prettied up when the reality was inappropriate.

Taken as a whole, the tour of 1667 was similar in character to the tour of 1633. With one night's exception they had traveled along the route chosen by the domain and had stayed at prepared housing and lunched at prepared rest houses, some new but made to look suitably old—a politically savvy *sabi* (weathered) aesthetic. It should not surprise us that this was a route along which homes had been ordered repaired and damaged fields restored, in the interest of reflecting Tosa's good government. In the end the Inspectors were satisfied that government was good, and they did not even accept presents from the Yamauchi, at least not until a few years later when each were sent five bolts of figured satin and their retainers, gifts of silver.[37]

The domain did not challenge the right of the *kubō* to demand full honesty and accountability, and it is clear that the inspection was an intimidating event to be met with an extraordinary mobilization of resources and care, yet Tosa officials continued to arrange "off the record" with the Inspectors themselves many aspects of the journey that did not meet Tosa interests. To call these arrangements the production of "lies" does not convey their integrating nature.

The "deceptions" were open secrets negotiated informally according to mutually acceptable practice in ways that separated the expectations of *omote* relations from those of *naishō* relations. Tosa officials promised full submission to the will of the *kubō* at the formal boundary of relations with the Tokugawa but then proceeded to negotiate off the record with the Tokugawa officials for exactly what they needed—in this case, respect for their control and little scrutiny of internal affairs. We can understand the political content of the interaction more clearly by observing the manipulation of the *naishō* relations and the formal *omote* relations, rather than through a search for overt contestation and resistance. To see the difference between *omote* promises and *naishō* arrangements as a sign of decline in Tokugawa authority or as an erosion of the social order, as many scholars of the much better recorded eighteenth-century tours of inspection have done, is to miss how political players of the day viewed and understood their own politics. To most of them the open secrets and negotiations were not a symptom of decline but rather an example of the proper harmonious functioning of government.

Touring inspections in a large *ichimon* domain

Some might think that the deceptions occurred during the tours because the Yamauchi were *tozama* daimyo less invested in the success of the Tokugawa regime and were more independent, with more to hide, than hereditary vassal *fudai* lords. The significance of the distinction can be addressed directly through an examination of the 1667 tour through Aizu, the domain of *ichimon* daimyo Hoshina Masayuki, who was a half brother to Tokugawa Iemitsu and, at the time of the tour, one of the most powerful figures within the Tokugawa government itself. *Ichimon* were regarded as having descended from Tokugawa Ieyasu and might be considered the most loyal of all daimyo, even more than *fudai*. Yet the inspections reveal patterns of behavior similar to those in Tosa. That Hoshina Masayuki was the guardian of his nephew the young *kubō* Tokugawa Ietsuna suggests that the "deceptions" had nothing to do with distance from the aims of the government that created the tour.

When the Hoshina clan officials in Aizu were informed of the upcoming tour, they immediately began repairing roads and bridges and sprucing up buildings along the likely route. They appointed the domain retainer Niwa Kan'emon, who by marriage was a relative of one of the Touring Inspectors, to informally arrange preparations and decisions in order to circumvent the *omote* directives concerning the tour. He began this assignment before the tour by negotiating the route the Inspectors would take, and he also accompanied them within the domain. As the day of the Inspectors' arrival neared, retainers dressed up as merchants and entered a neighboring domain to view the tour and report back, and the domain secretly prepared guides for the Inspectors and rewarded them with money afterward. The Inspectors refused a number of offers of food from the domain, but Aizu officials managed to have anyone selling food and goods to the Inspectors do so at a 30 percent discount, which the lord refunded at a later date. In the end, this is how domain officials summed up the tour: "At each location there was nothing of note in their questions: only about the tax rate, the number of houses, and occasionally the number of people. No villagers offered up any kind of petition, and there were no complaints about the guides. All in all, there was not the slightest problem, and it seems as if the inspection ended very well."[38] A similar experience to the tour of Tosa domain, the inspection displayed that no one would contest the Inspectors' right to investigate, while the Inspectors congenially showed little interest in knowing what was going on behind the performance. It was an inspection of sorts, but perhaps best understood as an inspection of how well the domain could manage the facade it wished to present—a key indicator of the political health of the household. Domains that could carry this off effectively were considered to be well managed.

Touring inspections in a small *fudai* domain

The "deceptions," or open secrets, practiced between the Tokugawa Inspectors and Tosa domain or Aizu domain were not a reflection of the power of their daimyo. Although they differed in being *tozama* and *ichimon,* the Yamauchi and the Hoshina were both among the top twenty most powerful daimyo in the Tokugawa order. But a very similar pattern of relations between Inspectors and daimyo can be seen in even such a minor *fudai* daimyo house as the Miyake of Tahara domain, which was composed of a mere twenty-four villages and the castle town of Tahara. In a pattern common to many *fudai* daimyo in the seventeenth century, the Tokugawa had moved the Miyake daimyo from realm to realm three times that century by the time they were enfeoffed with Tahara in 1664. The castle diaries for the inspection tour of 1667 do not survive, but the tour of 1681 is well recorded.

These diaries from Tahara domain are by their nature generally less revealing of negotiations with the Inspectors, but they nevertheless record local activity that displays a similar pattern of attention to pleasing the Inspectors, improving the appearance of local conditions without making it seem so, and attempting to instruct people of the realm into habits of secrecy and prepared answers. As soon as the Miyake learned of the impending tour of 1681, they issued orders to the chief domain officer: "Bridges, roads, etc. should be repaired, but make sure that they do not look like recent repairs. . . . Furthermore, the world these days is unsettled, so be sure to put especial interest in the villages."[39] Domain officials planned out the Inspectors' route through their territory, double-checked the list of items available for sale along the route, and provided tastier foods than what were available locally. They lent rice to poor villages to be sure they could feed the Inspectors. They checked the lodging houses in the realm to decide on necessary repairs. This included making the baths and toilets much finer than specified in the orders, but they also decided not to install new tatami matting in most places because they feared it would be a sign that their efforts were excessive. For the same reason they had the roads swept but made sure that the broom marks were erased. To ensure that the Inspectors' needs were satisfied, domain officials sent to each lodging site inkstones, paper, tobacco articles, and enough dishes to serve a hundred people of the expected retinue. They also sent screen paintings from the castle to the inns where the Inspectors themselves would stay. When unofficial reports arrived that some villagers were likely to present a suit to the Touring Inspectors, the domain Elders sent a message that they would entertain this suit, which they had earlier refused to hear. They also placed guards around the inns where the Inspectors would stay, and sent a domain Elder to meet the Inspectors at the border. As we saw in the case with Tosa domain, these Elders had the status of "secret accompaniment" (*shinobi*), but this level of "secrecy" still allowed them to stay in the same lodgings as the Inspectors. They kept their eyes out for suspicious characters such as a kimono merchant who wandered nearby the lodgings an unseemly number of times.[40] The Miyake in Edo learned that secret investigators (*kakushi metsuke*) would be inspecting separately from the formal tour. They immediately sent a secret message to the domain officials telling them to instruct all inns and villagers not to provide lodging to any unknown person, and they had the rural intendants of the domain quietly call village headmen one by one to their office so that they might inform them of the secret investigators and to warn them, "Be sure not to discuss the merits and demerits of the realm with the members of the retinue of the Touring Inspectors, and furthermore not with any people from outside the realm or even among yourselves in the villages."[41] When domain officials told villagers to beware of the secret inspectors, they revealed their assumption that as a matter of course the villagers should not complain to the Touring Inspectors. Thus we see that even for a small daimyo house recently moved into a new domain its pattern of

interaction with the Inspectors and its expectations of the people of the domain were not that different from those of a large domain. This suggests that
the pattern of activity was wholly acceptable to the Tokugawa rulers even
for minor daimyo and reflected a desirable generalized pattern of behavior.
Because correspondence does not survive, we do not have direct evidence
that these preparations were made according to informal prearrangements
with the Inspectors. However, the domain diary does contain repeated communications with neighboring daimyo concerning preparations and a desire
to be in accord with common practice.

Touring inspections and daimyo punishments

In support of the above interpretation of how the tours of inspection operated, it is worth noting that they resulted in very few punishments. One
scholar has observed that there were four attainders of daimyo ostensibly
occasioned by the inspections.[42] Each of these occurred in the seventeenth
century, and considering that there were 119 daimyo attainders during the
reigns of Iemitsu, Ietsuna, and Tsunayoshi—the *kubō* of the first three inspection tours—the role of inspection tours seems small.[43] Yet, upon investigation, the attribution of the four attainders to information uncovered by the
tours of inspection is problematic. The attainder of lord Matsudaira Mitsunaga of Takada domain in 1681 following the tour of inspection was caused
by a house disturbance (*iesōdō*) among the samurai disputing who should
be designated the daimyo's heir. In 1679 this had nearly erupted into a civil
war when more than four hundred samurai of one faction put on armor and
marched with weapons to the house of the leader of the opposing side. The
conflict ended without battle, but by then the Tokugawa government well
knew about the issue. For years the chief Tokugawa Elder Sakai Tadakiyo had
informally been using various daimyo in an attempt to solve the problem.
Tokugawa Tsunayoshi became *kubō* in 1680 and used this incident to force
Tadakiyo out of office in 1681, assert his own control of the government, and
pursue his overall penchant for dealing with daimyo *uchi* matters publicly.[44]
The Inspectors certainly noticed mismanagement of the household, but this
was hardly news to anyone, and the attainder itself was brought about because
Tsunayoshi declared himself willing to hear the suit presented by one of the
factions, thereby causing the conflict to be judged by *omote* standards. Fed
up with the interminable conflict, he ordered the leaders of both factions to
commit seppuku and confiscated the lord's domain. He also punished a number of government officials who had unsuccessfully tried for years to resolve

the disturbance informally, a convenient way to dispose of members of Sakai Tadakiyo's faction in Tokugawa politics.[45] The attainder was certainly due to misgovernment of the samurai household, but the tour of inspection was only incidentally involved.

The attainder of the daimyo Kōriki Sakondayū in 1668 seems the best case for arguing that information discovered on the tour was the cause. The Kōriki clan had been newly enfeoffed with the castle of Shimabara in 1638. The Touring Inspectors of 1668 found the populace unhappy with Kōriki's harsh government. This had been the site of the Shimabara rebellion less than thirty years before, a rebellion so strong that the armies of the *kubō* failed to subdue it for months and succeeded only after enlisting the aid of the Dutch to provide naval bombardment of the rebel stronghold. The Tokugawa were understandably particularly anxious about maintaining good government in the region. Yet even in this example, what decided the case was not villager complaint and visible hardship but complaints of misrule lodged by numerous Kōriki samurai retainers themselves to the Inspectors. The moral of these two stories is that a daimyo who could not keep even his own household in enough order to present a seemly *omote* interaction with the Inspectors was not worth retaining.

This leaves the two related punishments of Honda Masatoshi and Honda Toshinaga by Tsunayoshi in 1682. They were accused of excessively harsh rule, but like Kōriki's case, theirs depended on accusations from their own retainers. There was also a complicated backstory to Masatoshi's case, in which he had depended on the support of Sakai Tadakiyo to resolve an inheritance dispute. The resolution had been engineered in a way to upset many parties, and with the fall of Sakai and the rise of Tsunayoshi the stage was set for his attainder and that of his cousin and ally Toshinaga.[46] Investigation of the inside stories shows that all four of the attainders ostensibly resulting from tours of inspection required an extraordinary lack of order among the lord's own retainers and usually additional special circumstances as well.

Daimyo touring inspections of villages

Additional evidence that this pattern of political culture had deep roots is that a similar relationship existed between domain lords and the people of their own realms when it came to touring inspections. Most lords either took tours of their domains soon after accession to office or sent retainers in their stead as traveling inspectors. This was a formal display of interest in the management of the realm and a ritual that enacted local acceptance of the daimyo's authority. Villages competed to be pleasing and negotiated with the inspectors or the lord's retinue off the record so as to provide services and pleasures that were officially forbidden. For example, in 1816 when Miyake Yasukazu toured his domain in Tahara, his chief retainers issued to all members of the retinue a strict prohibition against receiving any sake from villagers. This was to prevent a sense of bribery and the possibility of drunken incidents, but it was, after all, a prohibition of one of the most common forms of sociability. The people of Akabane village did more than repair bridges and rest houses and prepare food. As the headman noted, "As for sake, Higashi village had informally served some, so we prepared it as well, but because it is severely prohibited, although we informally served it to some of the lord's representatives, we did not drink together."[47] Here we see that one village was checking with its neighbor to see what the actual *naishō* limits were with regard to making gifts of sake. It seems that they learned it would be safe to offer sake but not to join in the drinking, because the conviviality might give the appearance of collusion.

The key to success in all of these interactions during the tours was the ability to carry out an effective *performance* of peace, submission, and duty rather than the quality of a noninteractive domain or village "reality" that might be got at through investigation. The demand for *performance* is evident in a humorous story about one daimyo-sponsored inspection of his own territory. Lord Yamauchi Toyochika of Tosa commissioned two trusted retainers to travel around the domain as inspectors in 1788, one to the east and one, Mori Yoshiki, to the west. Among Yoshiki's duties were to issue documents of praise and to disburse rewards to villagers who were nominated by their headmen as being particularly laudable. When Yoshiki arrived in the village of Nishi Yoshihara, the headman Sanzō said, "Ever since it was reported to villages that you would be touring as the lord's representative and asking about filial people, one local man began pretending filial behavior. After investigating this thoroughly, I therefore decided that I have no one to report today." Yoshiki asked, "What was he pretending?" Sanzō responded, "Recently the lord has been giving money and rice to filial people in villages, and this man was jealous and plotted to get some for himself. I was going to report this insolence at a later date." Yoshiki then scolded Sanzō in a great voice, "You have got it all wrong! When people start pretending to be unfilial or pretending to raise a rebellion, then you should report it immediately, but the lord's intent is to have everyone pretend to be filial. That is why he rewards them. Your job is to arrange things so that people pretend to be filial! You have been completely wrong!"[48]

Other data sent to the Tokugawa

It is worth briefly considering further how domainal interests were protected by the information that they prepared for response to the Touring Inspectors. One of the pieces of information regularly told to Inspectors from Edo was the assessment of domain agricultural productivity. In the case of Tosa, the figure was consistent with written productivity reports sent to the Edo authorities in other situations, making a seemly truth, but it bore little resemblance to what the domain officials knew. This chapter began with a discussion of the *omotedaka* formal production records, but the Tokugawa government also occasionally requested information on internal records of production, three times in the form of cadastral books and accompanying maps. The final time Tosa domain submitted to the Tokugawa actual known production amounts was in 1644, when the village productivity cadastres (*gōchō*) of the Shōhō era recorded 259,180 *koku*. This was at a time when the daimyo Tadayoshi still had hopes that the Tosa *omotedaka* and consequently his status could be increased. At the next Genroku-era survey of 1701, Tosa reported only 268,486 *koku* out of a known 368,261 *koku,* and for the Tenpō-era survey of 1835 it reported 330,026 *koku* out of a known 473,952 *koku*. The reported amounts had financial significance on the occasions when the Tokugawa government demanded province-wide payments (*kokuyaku* or *kuniyaku*) based on these amounts, so underreporting effectively reduced the burden. For example, in 1808 when Edo demanded *kokuyaku* payments for the coming arrival of an embassy from Korea, the domain declared its production to be exactly 330,026.52 *koku,* of which 28,497.22 *koku* was presented as exempt from the tax duty due to field damage in excess of 20 percent in certain villages, leaving 301,529.30 as the basis for calculating Tosa's tax payment. The elegant calculations belie the fact that the numbers bore no relation to what the domain knew to be taxable realm production—a figure somewhat nearer 434,000 *koku*.[49] The 330,026.52 *koku* figure had not changed an iota since a report given to the Tokugawa in 1720 when one of its Inspectors visited.[50] Even in 1720 it was a significant understatement, but subsequently it was used as the basis whenever Tosa reported to the Tokugawa the amounts of crops and fields lost due to storm and drought.[51]

Tokugawa orders declare an interest in accuracy. The Tenpō-era order first issued in 1831 clearly demanded a full update on changes in productivity, "leaving nothing out."[52] All landowners enfeoffed by the Tokugawa and Tokugawa demesne intendants (*daikan*) had to submit updated agricultural production amounts village by village. These figures were then totaled and organized by county and province by a particular daimyo or intendant who had been assigned to organize the data into bound provincial registers, which he submitted to the Finance Office of the Tokugawa government. In sum they became a statement of the agricultural productivity of Japan. Based on Tokugawa *omote* assertions, scholars are tempted to use these figures at face value. A major encyclopedia of Japanese history describes the registers as follows: "These were the basic land production documents of government finances and presented the agricultural income of all the country in a clear and easily accessible manner. They were compiled on three separate occasions, revealing the increase in productivity, and are highly regarded for their documentary value."[53] Methodologically speaking, though, their documentary value can be grasped only through comparison with daimyo "inside" documents.

The 1830s case was, Japan-wide, the least accurate of all the submissions, and the bold evasiveness of the daimyo suggests serious problems in the Tokugawa government at the time. Without a doubt, the Tokugawa government inspired less fear in the 1830s than it did in the seventeenth century, and this allowed for more brazen resistance. However, not a single daimyo broke the rituals of submissiveness in *omote* exchanges nor asserted any claim to having a right not to report increased agricultural production. This was the first time in a century that a new survey had been ordered. The financially strapped Tokugawa government was clearly looking for new sources of funds and was hoping to increase the *kokuyaku* assessments. Few domains would desire to truly comply, but it was impossible and unproductive to openly refuse. The daimyo first checked with each other via their Edo ambassadors, and it seems they collectively chose to stall. Two years after the initial order, the Tokugawa Finance Magistrate again sent out the order putting down a deadline: the tenth month of 1833. All he received were more evasive answers. The Satake clan replied that their domain in Akita was too far away and too snowy to get the information on time. The Tokugawa then asked when it would be possible, and the Satake replied that fifty days would be needed. Time passed, and the Finance Magistrate called the Satake ambassador to court. "When we queried you last, you said it would take fifty days to finish, but sixty days have already passed. What an extraordinary amount of time you take!"[54] They again asked the Satake how long it would take, to which the Satake replied that they could not be sure. The Finance Magistrate then declared the end of the second month to be the new deadline, and immediately the Satake requested an extension to the end of the third month, to which the Magistrate acquiesced. At this point, instead of working to prepare the registers, the domain officials started negotiating off the record with two Tokugawa Senior Councillors and two Finance Magistrates to see if they could just submit a register identical to the first one they had submitted when they received the realm in 1602—that is to say, with no production reassessments at all. They justified this by appealing that all domain officials were busy dealing with famine in their realm and did not have time to carry out new surveys. They received a terse refusal in which the Finance Magistrate argued that the domain had to know recent annual productivity of each village as part of its internal management and tax collection. It is clear that the Satake did not want to let the Tokugawa in on Satake understandings of the productivity of their own realm.

It is also clear that most other domains were acting likewise, knowing that there was safety in numbers. In 1834 the Finance Magistrate called all domain representatives to his office to speak about the as yet unsubmitted maps and cadastral registers. "This should not have involved any special difficulties," he told them, "but it has now been four years since we issued the order. . . . You should certainly submit these very quickly."[55] The Mōri of Hagi domain (with an *omotedaka* of 369,000 *koku*) immediately sent a letter to officials back home, instructing them to do everything possible to delay things but at the same time noting the predicament of the Tokugawa government. It had on numerous occasions formally asked for registers with assessments of "real production" and there was no way to rescind the decree without harming the "august authority" of the Tokugawa. They therefore decided to begin an appearance of cooperation. Six months later the Mōri submitted registers that showed the highest production increases of any of the provinces in Japan. Why would a powerful *tozama* domain with no sense of debt to the Tokugawa reveal so much on this occasion? It turns out the Mōri were bound by a formal statement as well. Back in 1792 the Hagi officials had submitted to a Tokugawa Inspector a document stating that local production was 894,000 *koku*. In 1834 they knew a local production of 971,000 *koku* but decided that they would announce that there had been no production increases at all since 1792. The circumstances under which they had made the 1792 report are unclear but it was a formal "reality" that had to be lived up to.[56]

Many other domains were able to make far more modest declarations of growth, but it is certain that most declarations did not reflect knowledge internal to the domain, such as can be seen with Tosa, which submitted a number more than 20 percent less than what it actually knew. The powerful Shimazu daimyo of Kagoshima domain were the most protective of their actual autonomy while formally acquiescing and submitting reports. Internal documents demonstrate that Satsuma domain had knowledge of production rising by more than 130,000 *koku* between the early seventeenth century and

1722, and yet none of this increase is reflected in its reports to the Tokugawa.[57] The Shimazu flatly declared no change in the amount of production of their realm across the years 1645, 1697, and 1834.[58] If the difference between production recorded in the 1834 register and productivity declared to the Meiji government in 1873 is any indication, then the greatest underreporting existed most strongly in southwest Japan and somewhat strongly in northeast Japan, and more centrally, underreporting was in the provinces dominated by the powerful Matsue, Tottori, Owari, and Kaga domains.[59] The small domain of Tahara in central Japan seems to have honestly and promptly reported its known internal totals to the Tokugawa even at the 1834 submission.[60] There was probably somewhat of an inverse relationship between an honest report and the general prestige of the daimyo household. In sum, the reported numbers and their changes were due as much to political relations as to changing agricultural production, and this is the basic character of the Tokugawa data regime. The falsity in reported production was probably not of great importance to the Edo authorities because, with the exception of *kokuyaku* province assessments, almost all relations with lords were based upon the *omotedaka*.

The information regime of the Tokugawa government extended throughout the archipelago, but it extended feudally. There were often significant discrepancies between internal information of domains and the information they submitted to Tokugawa representatives. This tendency was strong from the very first century of the Tokugawa period and thus was not in itself a symptom of the decline of Tokugawa authority. Viewed through the lens of the politics of *omote* and *naishō,* the information collection can be understood as a performance of total submission to higher authority, and the objective quality of the data was a product of informal negotiation. The next chapter explores the politics of inheritance as another example of the nature of information formally used by the Tokugawa, and also investigates how these somewhat strange politics functioned to prevent conflict and maintain the peace.

3

Politics of the Living Dead

I was adopted by the Katsu family when I was seven years old.
My age was officially given as seventeen, and the hair at the
front of my head was accordingly cut off. As part of the adoption
procedure, Ishikawa Ukon-no-shōgen, the commissioner of my
unit in the construction reserve corps, and his assistant, Obi
Daishichirō, came to the house.
"How old are you and what is your name?" Ishikawa asked.
"My name is Kokichi and I am seventeen."
Ishikawa pretended to be taken aback. "Well—for seventeen you
certainly look old!" He burst out laughing.

—KATSU KOKICHI, *Musui's Story: The Autobiography of a Tokugawa Samurai*[1]

On the eleventh day of the third month of 1823 the daimyo Miyake Yasukazu of Tahara domain donated some gold to the memorial services of his great-great-great-grandfather.[2] Taking care of memorial services for ancestors was a routine responsibility of a daimyo. The only oddity about the event was that Yasukazu himself had died more than a month earlier. His death had been kept from *omote* formal notice, and in the eyes of the Tokugawa government Yasukazu died on the sixteenth day of the fifth month, nearly a hundred days after his actual death. The reason for this long delay was that he had no heir at the time of his actual death, and according to Tokugawa law a daimyo must have an heir approved while still alive or else the household and realm were forfeit.[3]

Indeed, in the first half of the seventeenth century the Tokugawa confiscated the domains of many daimyo for lack of having prearranged a suitable heir *before* falling mortally ill. The Tokugawa Elders changed this law in 1651, permitting deathbed adoptions and subsequently fewer and fewer daimyo were attaindered for this reason. Yet even the new inheritance law included many seemingly impossible obstacles to the long-term preservation of daimyo households. Indeed the obstacles made it likely that not a single daimyo clan in all Japan would have survived up to the Meiji Restoration. Nevertheless, most houses did survive. How this was achieved is the subject of this chapter, which explores the laws and phenomena of "deathbed adoptions" as a way of elucidating how the politics of *omote* and *naishō* worked to maintain daimyo feudal autonomy and the Tokugawa Great Peace.

Inheritance was an act of central importance to feudal politics. Factional politics often coalesced around the selection of an heir, and politically ambitious samurai strove to be well situated in a pyramid of human connections having the incoming lord at its apex. It was one of the few issues during the Tokugawa period around which strategic violence and occasional large-scale organized disorder erupted among samurai. "House disturbances" over inheritance held such a fascination among commoners and samurai that the real events quickly became transformed by authors and playwrights into lurid and embellished tales and theater.[4] Sex and personal ambition took the forefront in these versions, but the real mundane consequences for commoners and samurai alike were severe and of great importance. Homelessness and bankruptcy were the lot of many in the house and realm when an inheritance went awry. How this cauldron of ambition and turmoil came to be largely tamed in the seventeenth century in a way to best preserve in stable association the diverse interests of people who were dependent on daimyo households is the story of the first half of this chapter. The second half of the chapter examines well-recorded cases of deathbed adoption from the latter half of the Tokugawa period so as to elucidate the process in terms of the politics of *omote* and *naishō*.

Attainders for lack of heir, 1600–1650

In 1602 Tokugawa Ieyasu attaindered the large realm of *tozama* daimyo Kobayakawa Hideaki for lack of an heir when he died at age twenty-one.[5] By the 1615 destruction of the Toyotomi clan the Tokugawa had fully solidified their authority to approve the choice of an heir for every single daimyo, without which the daimyo's domain would be confiscated and his lineage terminated. Approval was guided by the following ideals and conditions: If the lord had his own sons, then the heir should normally be the eldest. Sons of concubines ranked after those of the wife. If no sons were present, then the heir could be adopted but should be a blood relative such as a nephew, a younger brother, or, in lieu of their availability, an uncle. Less ideal was an unrelated son who married the actual daughter of a daimyo, and the least preferred was a wholly unrelated man. An actual son might be permitted to inherit even without prearrangement, but an adopted heir had to be chosen by the daimyo and approved by the shogun while the daimyo was still healthy and active. Furthermore a daimyo had to have achieved an audience with the shogun before the daimyo had the right even to present an heir for approval. This audience normally could not happen before age seventeen, and if a lord died younger, then the lineage was ended.

Another stipulation of the first half century of Tokugawa rule was that a lord did not have the right to ask for an adoption while on his deathbed. This law was inherited from the Ashikaga government and had existed since at least the fourteenth century. The reasoning behind this draconian rule was to prevent factional disputes arising from meddling relatives who might take advantage of the weak state of a sick man to get him to choose an heir for their benefit. Furthermore, a last-minute adoption could also bring disorder into a house because the instant heir's own retainer band would not be organized and ready to take charge of house and domain.[6] This law remained in effect until 1651. However, another kind of disorder could be caused by this policy as well. People in this period frequently died young and suddenly, perhaps newly wed and expecting an heir to be born. Such people might not have arranged for an adopted heir because disinheritance was legally difficult and also because a named adopted heir could become a focal point for factional politics. Changes of plans commonly inspired violence. The potential for disorder from such a situation existed in even the highest houses, as evidenced in Hideyoshi's murder of his adopted heir, Hidetsugu, and all his concubines following the birth of Hideyoshi's own son, Hideyori.[7]

Subsequent to the dispositions of losers in the aftermath of the Battle of Sekigahara, lack of a recognized heir was the most common reason for the many daimyo attainders up to 1651. Sixty-one daimyo lords were thus attaindered between 1600 and 1650, representing 5,179,000 *koku* of domain *omotedaka,* or roughly about a fifth of the assessed production of Japan. About 150,000 samurai, one-fifth of all in Japan, lost house and home by these events, and large numbers of them traveled to Edo, hunting for new employment at the residences of successful lords. Many of these lordless samurai (*rōnin*) did not find new positions, and they were indigent, culturally violent men who were skilled in the use of weapons. They committed crimes in the cities and elsewhere, and in 1614–1615 and 1637–1638 many joined the anti-Tokugawa forces at the battles of Osaka and Shimabara.[8]

General dissatisfaction with the management of government was rising in the second quarter of the seventeenth century, especially concerning the treatment of daimyo, bannermen, and lesser retainers. The third *kubō,* Tokugawa Iemitsu, died in the fourth month of 1651, leaving behind a ten-year-old son, Ietsuna, to nominally take the reins. Iemitsu's half brother, Hoshina Masayuki, lord of Aizu domain, and three key Elders were named in Iemitsu's will as overseers of government during Ietsuna's minority. Although it was ethically very difficult for people of the day to criticize a *kubō,* the presence of a ruling council immediately allowed people to voice criticisms in terms of abuse of authority. Two events quickly followed in 1651 that had a great influence on the policy change concerning last-minute adoptions. The most unexpected event centered on Tokugawa Ieyasu's nephew Matsudaira Sadamasa, lord of Kariya domain. Early in the seventh month he submitted a protest document declaring that although he desired to serve Ietsuna, "I cannot agree with the way the Elders are governing these days."[9] He offered to return his domain to the government, asking that it use its wealth to succor poor bannermen retainers. The Elders instead declared him insane and entrusted him to his uncle, the lord of Matsuyama castle, where he lived in genteel retirement until his death in 1662.

Quick on the heels of this incident was the discovery of a plot for rebellion being planned by the military arts teacher Yui Shōsetsu and many other lordless samurai. Taking advantage of the minority of Ietsuna, they planned to set the city on fire and overthrow the Tokugawa in the confusion. The plot was uncovered by an informant, and the government immediately rounded up numerous alleged participants. For a while the plot took on unsettling dimensions, because not only *rōnin* but even retainers of various daimyo were students of Yui's school.[10] Vigorous investigations followed. No daimyo ended up being punished, but the events had raised awareness of the "*rōnin* problem" created by too many daimyo attainders. The Elders held a meeting near the end of the year, which Sakai Tadakiyo opened by saying that all *rōnin* should be chased out of Edo. Everyone present initially agreed, but Abe Tadaaki pointed out some of the problems: Edo was the only place for *rōnin* to search for work, and if they were all sent out into the countryside, they would be forced by poverty to become criminals and thereby lessen the august authority of the *kubō.* Furthermore, banishing *rōnin* would shame the government by making it look as if the government was afraid of a bunch of lordless samurai. The best thing was to leave things be. All consented, and the record of the day's conversation ends.[11]

More must have gone on in the meeting than recorded, however, because the very next day the Elders called all of the daimyo and captains of the bannermen to Edo castle for an announcement. They proclaimed that henceforth all direct retainers younger than age fifty would be permitted in certain circumstances to adopt an heir even while on their deathbed. On that very same day, they approved an unprecedented eighty-five retainer inheritances, half of which were for adopted heirs. Although the proportion of deathbed adoptions is unknown, it certainly set the tone of willingness to let samurai houses continue over generations.[12] These were all bannermen and housemen. The first daimyo to be allowed a deathbed adoption was that of the Sōma clan of Nakamura domain during the second month of 1652. The adoption had been pending approval, but there were complications (discussed below). Hozumi Nobushige and subsequent scholars have interpreted these events as evidence that the government had decided to reduce daimyo and bannermen attainders so as to lessen the *rōnin* problem.[13] The result was clearly a rapid decline in attainders. However, a difficulty remains with this interpretation of the law: the rules for deathbed adoptions remained far too strict to avoid the failure of daimyo houses.

Although not fully spelled out in the 1651 proclamation, from early on there were three key limitations to the deathbed adoption process. The one mentioned in the proclamation was the easiest to fulfill. It required a daimyo to choose an adopted heir before he reached fifty years of age. It was regarded as a sign of carelessness for one so old and without a natural son not to choose an heir, and the law being known, any daimyo reaching his forty-ninth year could effectively respond by naming an heir. This stipulation therefore provided no naturally insurmountable obstacle to succession. However, not mentioned that day, because it was already required, was that a daimyo must have had an audience with the *kubō* in order to be able to name an heir, and in order to have the audience, the daimyo needed to be at least seventeen years of age himself. This stipulation was made explicit in 1683, but it was applied as early as 1655 when Katagiri Jōsaku died at age fifteen and his line was terminated.[14] Ōmori Eiko's research has shown that attainders and the lesser penalty of fief reductions of daimyo houses for not satisfying this requirement happened with decreasing frequency after 1651, totaling eleven attainders and eleven reductions over the remainder of the Edo period. Only one instance occurred after 1730.[15] Considering that ten daimyo under the age of seventeen had been attaindered for want of an heir before 1651, this is a strange fact. Did daimyo gradually cease to die before this significant age seventeen? This is a problem to which we shall return.

The third condition was also unstated early on but became part of the system at least by 1683. It posed difficulties as problematic to daimyo as the age-seventeen rule. This was the requirement that the Tokugawa Grand In-spector (*ōmetsuke*) personally visit the daimyo at his deathbed, confirm that he was still alive, and also confirm the daimyo's personal wish by watching the ill man affix his seal on a document naming who should be the adopted heir. Once the Grand Inspector certified these facts, then the family could send the request to the Tokugawa Elders, and the lord himself could safely die. This event was called *hanmoto mitodoke,* which means "certification of impressing the seal," and it remained the official formula down to the end of the Edo pe-riod. The only formal exception to this rule was made for daimyo who might die on the road or while back in their domains. Before leaving Edo, a daimyo had to leave a sealed document with a Tokugawa Elder within which was a statement of who should become heir if he died. The contents were generally kept secret, and the statement was effective only if the lord died.[16] Although the deathbed certification system was a relaxation of the pre-1651 policy of total prohibition of deathbed adoptions, it still left much to be desired as a practical solution to daimyo attainders in the case of sudden death. Heart at-tacks, strokes, and many other fatal ailments could happen without warning. Falling off a horse or being struck by a bolt of lightning was not needed to destroy house continuity. Tokugawa *omote* records such as the compiled lin-eages of daimyo and bannermen, the *Kansei chōshū shokafu,* and the official Tokugawa history, the *Tokugawa jikki,* make it appear as if the law was applied according to formula, yet following 1651 a sum total of three daimyo within the age limits of seventeen and fifty were attaindered for lack of an heir.[17] The answer to this curiosity and the problem of deaths before seventeen is to be found in the politics of *omote* and *naishō.*

The *hanmoto mitodoke* deathbed adoption ceremony

A Meiji-era interview of a former Tokugawa Grand Inspector, Yamaguchi Na-oki, is instructive of how the certification was actually carried out. Yamaguchi first described how the law required that he make sure the lord was alive while making his request for adoption, but then the Inspector recounted how such events transpired in latter days: "Usually they were all dead and cold, but the family would lay him out on a futon behind a folding screen just as if he were alive. I act as if he is alive. . . . Some relative from behind the screen presses the lord's seal to a document as if he did it himself. That is your *hanmoto mitodoke.* . . . There are a lot of people who die without children. It can't be helped."[18] This interview confirms that the certification of the seal was a ritualized act in which all present played along in the fiction that the lord was still alive, even though the explicit (and seemingly only) duty of the Grand Inspector was to make sure that the lord was not dead. This curious performance of the way that things should be—even when they were not—engaged in by members on both sides of the hierarchy is the politics of *omote* and *naishō* in action.

The nature of *omote* and *naishō* politics made it unlikely that a Grand Inspector ever returned to a Tokugawa Elder and said something like, "The lord was really all dead and cold, but I pretended he was not." One interesting account by the daimyo Matsura Seizan indicates how this might have been received:

> When Matsudaira Sadanobu was in office, the Lord of Tsuchiura, lord Tsuchiya the Chamberlain, died, and there was widespread gossip that it was not a death from illness. Sadanobu ordered the Grand Inspector Ōya Tōtomi no Kami to carry out the *hanmoto mitodoke* at the time of request of an heir. This Ōya had formerly been an Elder in the Tayasu house and had been quite close to Sadanobu, so on this occasion he said privately to Sadanobu, "They say Tsuchiya died an unnatural death. If that is true, how should I handle this?" Sadanobu's face colored, and he said, "Here your Office is Grand Inspector and you say such sudden and unadorned words! You must go and certify the truth!" Ōya greatly regretted his misspoken words and later returned to say that there was nothing untoward at the *hanmoto mitodoke*.[19]

Sadanobu did not want to hear anything improper, even from a friend, while he was serving as Tokugawa Elder and that friend was functioning in his post as Grand Inspector. Performing these duties with decorum was crucial.[20] A similar incident, with a less happy ending, occurred in Tosa domain, where its own samurai were subject to the *hanmoto mitodoke* stipulation to receive inheritance. One of the domain Junior Elders, Andō Saori, had died of smallpox and had no son, and his relatives arranged an adoptable heir for the certification ceremony. The Captain of the Junior Elders, Teramura Kurōdayū, was responsible for verification, and he certified the request without incident. However, three weeks later at a party he became drunk and confided to the domain Elder, Gotō Geki, that Andō had been dead at the time. Geki's face colored, and he stood up and said, "You are my son-in-law, so you and I are like father and child, but that is a private relation. Insofar as I have been appointed domain Elder, I cannot irresponsibly act as if I had not heard that!" He then reported Kurōdayū's words to the other Elders and the lord. In the end Kurōdayū was relieved of office, and Andō's line was ended.[21] Given this desire to have officials perform, in the thespian sense, their office vis-à-vis their superiors, an understanding of the value of reticence and reserve was key to the successful operation of this kind of politics, lest it degenerate into open cynicism. It also meant that documents held in the collections of superiors rarely recorded the inside truths of those below them.

Another late Edo-era example sheds more light on the certification ceremony itself. A diagram in the archives of the Yamauchi daimyo of Tosa domain illustrates the spatial arrangements of the moment of the pressing of the seal.[22] It comes from the year 1848, most likely drawn for the occasion of the death of the thirteenth lord, Yamauchi Toyoteru, in the middle of that year but possibly drawn for the death of his heir, Toyoatsu, shortly after arriving in Edo that same year to become the fourteenth lord of the domain. Both deaths required a rush adoption, and numerous records survive recording activities that will allow us to explore in detail the operative politics.

Figure 2 is based on the diagram and shows the rooms in the Yamauchi Edo residence where the ceremony took place. The participants are indicated and positioned in ways reminiscent of Tokugawa-era diagrams of forces on the battlefield. The Yamauchi clearly have the upper hand in this peaceful contest. The lord's futon is laid out toward the back of his room. Screens wrap around three and a half sides, revealing to the front of the room only the area of the lower half of the lord's body. Before the futon lies the document naming his choice of heir, and behind the screen in front of the pillow is the lord's personal seal. His Chamberlain sits near the foot of the futon, and one of the domain Elders also sits in the room near the entrance. Other screens and domain samurai are positioned strategically in the hallway and rooms so that the Grand Inspector sees as little as possible of the inside of the residence—a kind of protection of the "inner space" that the Tokugawa representative should not violate. The Grand Inspector himself is seated in the next room about four yards away from the mattress. He would have entered from the hallway in the upper right of Figure 2, where one of his servants remains holding his swords. Also in this room are three bannermen to the Inspector's right who serve as representatives of the Yamauchi. Two are "messenger bannermen" (*sakite hatamoto*) whose general duty is to serve as messengers and mediators between the Tokugawa Elders and the daimyo. Each daimyo had a particular set of such messengers who served as go-betweens on almost all issues of negotiation.[23] The center *hatamoto* is Yamauchi Toyokata, of a collateral house descended from Tadayoshi, the second daimyo of Tosa. Following the ceremony, these three would convey the certified document to the residence of the Tokugawa Elder on duty. Other Yamauchi relatives sit to the left and rear of the Grand Inspector witnessing the event. Lined up against the back wall are five Tokugawa doctors, and closer to the lord's room, within the screen, sit two of the daimyo's own doctors. The Tokugawa doctors are there to certify the nature of the lord's illness and that he is alive. They are presumably backups for the judgment of the Grand Inspector and checks on possible subterfuge by daimyo doctors. They will even jointly sign detailed statements of medical evaluation. On the day of Toyoatsu's ceremony, we learn from the certified statement that his arms and legs hurt and that he is using various medicines to improve his condition. Nevertheless, they note, he suffers from coldness and has trouble eating. There is some black humor in the last observation, in which unintentionally the truth of Toyoatsu's mortal situation is expressed.[24]

That such doctors were expected to stand by their evaluation even under pressure is evident from the story that Matsura Seizan tells about the Tokugawa doctor Ōyagi Den'an. Den'an wrote the diagnosis of a daimyo's illness that accompanied the daimyo's request for an inheritance approval. Later, gossip circulated that led the Elders to ask him if anything was actually different from what he wrote. He then turned red with indignation and said, "I who have long served as doctor of the inner quarters have never said anything different! What is truly strange is that you should be asking!"[25] This was enough to quiet those who certainly had guilty consciences themselves, but it reveals that excessive gossip could create waves, and therefore seemliness was enforced strictly.

In the document upon which Figure 2 is based there is no lord, only the futon from which we can infer his presence. This may be a diagrammatic convention of the times to show respect to his person, but it inadvertently depicts a fact: The lord was almost certainly not there, even as a corpse. Toyoteru's ceremony was performed in midsummer twenty-four days after his death. Toyoatsu's ceremony happened in winter, but a full ninety-six days after his own sudden demise. It is unlikely that a body could or would be kept so long, but no surviving records indicate how the Tosa lords' bodies were treated in the interim between actual death and *omote* death.[26] Perhaps there was a retainer playing the part of the enervated lord who would then reach out his hand to grab the seal and press it to the document, or perhaps there was (as noted in Yamaguchi's interview) a relative hiding behind the screen whose hand would come out with the seal. The ceremony ostensibly was to find out if the lord was really alive, yet everyone, even the doctors, cooperated in performing the missing lord's living presence.

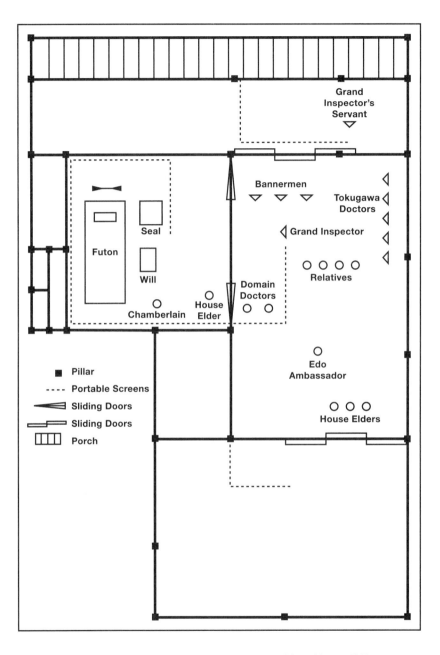

Grand
Inspector's
Servant

Bannermen

Tokugawa
Doctors

Seal

Grand Inspector

Futon

Will

Relatives

Domain
Doctors

Chamberlain

House
Elder

Edo
Ambassador

■ Pillar
- - - Portable Screens
Sliding Doors
Sliding Doors
Porch

House Elders

FIGURE 2. Hanmoto mitodoke ceremony—Tosa's Edo residence, 1848.
Produced by Andrew Roberts

Maintaining order by performing order

Was the acting at the ceremony merely, as suggested in Grand Inspector Yamaguchi's interview, a sign of late Tokugawa decline, where the system was falling apart and people no longer feared the Tokugawa? Much as with the touring inspections, many historians have written that the deathbed adoption ceremony originally functioned as intended but later became lax. Yet there is not much evidence for this. More convincing is that, as noted above, after 1651 only three daimyo houses were extinguished for want of an heir when the dying man was between seventeen and fifty. Furthermore, even the very first "deathbed adoption" under the new system involved hiding the lord's death until his request had been safely delivered to the Elders. This was the succession following the death of Sōma Yoshitane of Nakamura domain. Yoshitane died without a natural heir in early 1651 while in Edo following a ten-day illness. The law prohibiting deathbed adoptions was still in effect at that time, but hoping for an especially benevolent treatment, Yoshitane had time to write a will expressing his desire to adopt an unspecified heir and listing the names of more than a dozen relatives from collateral houses. The surviving relatives and chief retainers chose Tsuchiya Naokata, the second son of a maternal relative, saying—perhaps truthfully—that this was Yoshitane's orally given choice.[27] They intended to have Naokata wed Yoshitane's daughter Okame. Yoshitane died on the third day of the third month, but his retainers delayed his official death by two days so that when they delivered his request to the Tokugawa Elders on the fifth, he would still be officially alive. Government decision was put on hold because Tokugawa Iemitsu died at this time, but thanks to many familial connections with highly placed people in the Tokugawa government and to the new policy begun at the end of 1651, the succession was finally approved in the second month of 1652, following nearly a year-long wait. Exploration of the process in this example suggests that more important to the Tokugawa than the lord's own expressed will was maintenance of peace within his household. This goal could be achieved more effectively by having the people who held large stakes in the succession agree to perform "the lord's will" than by having his actual will itself.

It was difficult to prevent disorder in the Sōma house while awaiting Tokugawa judgment. The chief domain Elders maintained the appearance of being in agreement, but lower in the hierarchy many other retainers and people of the domain were upset with the choice of heir, Tsuchiya Naokata, because he had no blood from the male Sōma line. If instead Sōma Kumanosuke, the grandchild of one of Yoshitane's uncles, were adopted, then the Sōma male bloodline, understood at that time to have lasted more than twenty generations, would continue. To keep protest under control, the domain Elders had all retainers sign an oath swearing not to speak their opinions on these matters to anyone else as long as the inheritance remained unapproved, and not to "form bands and plan unrighteous activities toward the government."[28] "Unrighteous activities" certainly referred to protest over the choice of an heir and especially to taking that protest to the Tokugawa Elders. Months later the domain Elders threatened people of the domain with death or jail if they became unruly while the fate of the house was in question—certainly a sign of brewing trouble. The conflicting ambitions of outside relatives added further divisive complications to the inheritance. In the year of his death Yoshitane had refused a request by his brother-in-law Kamio Motokatsu to adopt Motokatsu's grandson. It was also known that Yoshitane suddenly fell ill immediately after he went to a dinner at Motokatsu's residence, and gossip went that perhaps he was poisoned. Motokatsu had later threatened the house with extinction if his grandson were not chosen as heir. The Sōma clan was potentially divided into three camps: one for Tsuchiya Naokata, one for Sōma Kumanosuke, and one for Kamio Motokatsu's grandson. Motokatsu's sister was Yoshitane's widow and a power in the household. He had hoped for her assistance, but she fended off his demands by saying that Yoshitane's verbal will was for Tsuchiya Naokata to inherit.[29]

The end-of-year declaration in 1651 by the Tokugawa Elders that deathbed adoptions would be approved in certain cases must have given confidence to all in the Sōma clan and brought the conflict out in the open. In the first month of 1652 two different groups of people from the domain presented direct appeals to key Tokugawa officials in Edo, one a collection of over forty temple priests and mountain ascetics and the other a group of over eighty rural samurai and villagers, both asking for the inheritance to go to Sōma Kumanosuke. They presented evidence that when Yoshitane was residing in the domain the previous year, he had told numerous relatives that he intended to adopt Kumanosuke as his heir. They also noted that Yoshitane had already promised to marry his daughter Okame to Satake Yoshitaka's son, who would become lord of Akita domain. Tokugawa Elder Sakai Tadakatsu responded that Kumanosuke's grandfather had displeased shogun Tokugawa Hidetada so much while serving him that he had been spared self-immolation only by going into retirement in a village, and therefore he had no heirs in the eyes of the government. Another Tokugawa Elder, Matsudaira Nobutsuna, told them to be happy because Yoshitane's daughter would wed Naokata and therefore the bloodline would not end. Closing off with a statement that everyone should just be thankful that the house was not attaindered, they pushed through the inheritance of Naokata, who then became the next daimyo and changed his name to Sōma Tadatane. It is quite clear from the events that neither the lord's being alive nor his will was crucial to the permission.[30] The key requirement seems to have been a performance of agreement among senior retainers and key relatives that it was the lord's last wish. In this case, only their word held that Yoshitane's last wish was for Naokata, despite much evidence to the contrary. This requirement of unity among the chief survivors is also evident in another case in 1677, when the daimyo Doi Toshinao of Ōwa domain named his nephew as heir in a deathbed adoption. Despite his having actually fulfilled the legal requirements, the government attaindered his domain simply because "he did this without consulting relatives and they were not in agreement."[31]

Conflict over the choice of heir often resulted in violent house disturbances in the early seventeenth century, and this led to the government's preoccupation with managing a formal consensus. The famous Mogami house disturbance that began in 1617 ultimately ended with the attainder of the domain in 1622 by Tokugawa Hidetada despite his own efforts to defuse the conflict. Hidetada had ordered the Mogami numerous times to restore harmony to a house divided over the choice of the next heir. Many retainers directly refused Hidetada's order, and thus the domain was confiscated. The scholar Fukuda Chizuru sums up the significance of this event: "The real reason for the attainder was the response of the retainers to Hidetada's first judgment. It was that they had directly refused the directive of their superior. They did not need to be told this, but for retainers to explicitly go against his judgment meant a complete loss of face for the shogun."[32] The appearance of harmony showed respect for the overlord's judgment, and visible disharmony could be a defacement of Tokugawa authority itself. The inheritance reform of 1651 in effect required key members of the household to create a decorum of agreement with the lord's wish and to keep their conflicts behind the scenes.

The few subsequent failures of inheritance due to lack of an heir were mostly the result of an inability to keep up appearances. The case of the attainder of the Mori clan of Tsuyama domain is instructive. In 1696 the lord of one of the Mori branch domains died. The succession would have gone well, but his adopted heir refused to proceed to Edo to attend his father's funeral. To have picked such an heir was a sign of incompetence. The Tokugawa declared this son to be insane, and they ended his line and associated branch domain, but the fief amount itself was returned to the main domain of Tsuyama in a gesture of generosity. Shortly on the heels of this incident, the daimyo of the main domain, Mori Naganari, fell ill in early 1697, childless at age twenty-seven. A deathbed adoption was arranged so that one of his great-uncles, Mori Atsutoshi (who was nevertheless two years younger than Naganari), would be heir, and this was approved by the Tokugawa. The heir remained in Tsuyama for a while, because Naganari seemed to be recovering following the deathbed ceremony. However, Naganari died midyear after his condition worsened suddenly, and Atsutoshi was ordered to depart for Edo. Halfway on the journey at Nao village in Ise province, he refused to go further. Yet again the Mori clan had chosen an heir badly. Domain officials sent letters to Edo saying that he had contracted a fever and was resting, but Tokugawa Elders had heard through other routes that he had gone insane. After two weeks Mori Nagatsugu, the eighty-eight-year-old retired former lord of Tsuyama domain who was living in Edo, asked the Elders to change the inheritance to someone else, but the game was up. The daimyo Naganari had been allowed to formally die, and his arranged choice would not proceed to Edo to accept inheritance. The Mori clan found no way to pretend around the matter, and the shogun confiscated the domain.[33] Bad luck also intervened to doom the Mizunoya clan in 1693. The daimyo Mizunoya Katsuyoshi had died, but relatives successfully carried out a deathbed adoption of a branch family's son, Katsuharu, and then allowed Katsuyoshi to formally die. Just days later, however, Katsuharu contracted smallpox and died before holding an audience with the *kubō*. Because he had therefore not yet become a retainer, it was difficult to find a proper way to deal with the problem, and the clan was attaindered.[34]

Other households became more inventive in such difficult situations. Ōmori Eiko's research on inheritance problems in daimyo houses where the daimyo was less than seventeen years of age reveals the many extraordinary ways that appearances could be kept up.[35] One common method, as exemplified in the epigraph of this chapter from the autobiography of Tokugawa retainer Katsu Kokichi, was to lie about the age of the new adopted heir. Age seventeen was the safest age to announce, as was used for the seven-year-old Kokichi. The government allowed bannermen and lesser retainers to delay reporting births of children until they were as much as age eighteen or nineteen, a policy these retainers found very convenient.[36] Generally, daimyo had to notify the Tokugawa Grand Inspector when a child was born, but this act would naturally fix the child's age and was undesirable in light of the age-seventeen rule for permitting adoption. The loophole was a custom called *jōbutodoke*, where a notification was sent to the Grand Inspector that a child had been born earlier but had been so sickly that they had not thought it worth notifying the Tokugawa while they waited to see if the child would live. This document would say the child had become healthy and the daimyo now informed the Tokugawa of the birth. At this moment, many daimyo would inflate the ages of those children. Most daimyo were more circumspect than Kokichi's parents and added on only a few years. For example, the Tosa Yamauchi clan reported Toyotsune's age as four years older than he was, which saved the domain difficulties when Toyotsune died at an official age of nineteen in 1725.[37] His contemporary, Ikeda Tsunamasa, lord of Okayama, was two years younger than officially reported, but lived much longer.[38] A later Tosa lord, Yamauchi Toyooki, also was officially reported to be three years older than he really was. He had reached an actual age seventeen when he died in 1809, but the Tokugawa regarded him as twenty.[39] The advantages of being older were such that many daimyo regularly waited a few years to report a birth and then added on a few years for insurance.

More daring were unreported inheritances. These sometimes occurred when a daimyo died before reaching an officially reported age seventeen and therefore was ineligible to choose an heir. To solve this dilemma, domain officials would slip a new person into the dead daimyo's clothes, so to speak, and in the Tokugawa *omote* world this meant that two individuals would share a biography as a single person. Ikeda Masafusa was the three-year-old lord of Ikusaka domain, a branch domain of Okayama, when he died in 1777. The main family then decided they could spare a six-year-old son, Tetsujirō, who had not yet been reported as born. They sent him from Okayama to the Edo residence with a retainer in the guise of that retainer's son. Shinmeiin, the mother of the deceased lord Masafusa, then paid a visit to Okayama domain's Edo residence, and when she returned in her covered palanquin to the Ikusaka residence, Tetsujirō was secretly inside with her. She thereafter treated him as her son. Tetsujirō took on Masafusa's identity, and there was no need to negotiate with the Tokugawa. In later years he changed his name to Masayuki, but as changing names was common practice among daimyo, this would not have caused any notice. The Tokugawa record of daimyo lineages, the *Kansei chōshū shokafu*, has these two people existing as one individual. Lineages made for circulation only within the Ikeda clan relate the truth but point out that the inheritance was kept from the Tokugawa (*kōhen naibun sōzoku*). No records indicate negotiation with Tokugawa parties regarding this inheritance. Perhaps it was truly a secret to outsiders, but it could have been engineered only within the framework and possibilities of *omote* and *uchi* politics.[40]

A yet more surprising inheritance was accomplished in the Sagara clan of Hitoyoshi domain. The daimyo Sagara Mitsunaga was officially eleven years old (actually eight) when he was adopted into the Sagara clan from the Akizuki clan in 1759. The Sagara had no appropriate heirs within the clan and chose Mitsunaga through a maternal connection. Mitsunaga had been ill for a while, however, and he had become blind in one eye and nearly blind in the other. Domain officials prepared for the worst, which was wise, because in 1761 he died at an official age of thirteen. They checked with the Akizuki clan again but found they had no more sons to spare. Lineage remained important, so they then thought to check with the aristocratic Washinoo house in Kyoto. The Washinoo were, like the Sagara, a branch of the Fujiwara lineage and more than a century earlier had sent daughters to wed into the Sagara house. Hitoyoshi domain's Osaka Ambassador garnered the help of a local merchant and a Kyoto doctor to ask if a son might be available. Washinoo Takahiro indeed had a second son, Isomaru, who had just secretly returned from an unsuccessful placement within an Osaka temple. This made him somewhat invisible in the public realm. He was the right age, twelve years old, and healthy, and he had, as the merchant noted, "a strikingly beautiful face." Normally the Washinoo house would be required to send a large sum of money along with the son (the going rate to have someone adopted into a daimyo house was at least 3,000 *ryō*), but the Sagara were quick to say that they needed no money. What they did require was that the whole deal be kept secret. Isomaru was to assume the identity of the dead Mitsunaga. The parties reached agreement, and Isomaru traveled to Edo as the son of a domain retainer. Not long after, domain records report that Mitsunaga "had been suffering from eye disease up to 1761 . . . but in 1762 he completely recovered." Coincidentally, Mitsunaga's miraculous recovery had also resulted in his becoming more handsome. He later changed his name to Yorisada, and he lived long enough to officially reach age seventeen and receive an audience with the *kubō* Ieharu, thus formally assuring the continuity of the Sagara house. Only two years later, though, he died without a natural heir and needed a rush adoption ceremony to secure one, but this proceeded with much less difficulty than his own chance transformation into a daimyo. The *omote* and *uchi* of the daimyo Sagara Mitsunaga thus encompassed three birthdays, three death dates, and two human bodies, an existence that makes sense in the spatial management of politics of the era. Such private inheritances were not all that uncommon. Ōmori provides numerous other examples of daimyo—such as in the Sō clan of Tsushima, the Inaba of Usuki, the Nanbu of Morioka, and the Mori of Akō domain—who in the Tokugawa *omote* records were one daimyo but in reality were a succession of two individuals.[41] This practice also was likely given tacit acceptance by the government. Tokugawa Yoshimune was once told secretly by the Elders that the daimyo Honda Tadamura had died of smallpox before reaching age seventeen. To which Yoshimune twice said, "The faces of many people are changed by smallpox," and had this message sent to the Honda house Elders. Honda's retainers did not understand the hint, however, and formally reported that their lord had died. Yoshimune was left with little choice but to reduce the daimyo's fief by half, but his cryptic response suggests that filling the clothes of deceased daimyo was not so uncommon in his day.[42]

Maintaining *omote* within the domain and its relation to status

Deathbed adoptions for a daimyo who had reached his majority were simpler, but they still required substantial manipulation of facts and performance. The extensive collection of office diaries of the Miyake clan provide a close view of how such inheritances were handled in Tahara domain. When the twenty-six-year-old lord Miyake Yasukazu, mentioned at the beginning of this chapter, died in Edo in 1823, he had no son. Yasukazu had two younger brothers who were back in Tahara, but the brothers were there without official permission, which was in itself a crime because officially they were hostages in Edo. The necessity of getting one of them secretly back to Edo so he could be chosen as heir further contributed to the delay in the formal announcement of Yasu-kazu's death.[43] The domain diaries surrounding these events are fascinating because they illustrate the complexity of the local management of the facts of his death. They present a local "*omote* truth" as could be formally known by the low-status sub-samurai secretaries who recorded them. This local *omote* at first seems to coincide with the *omote* truth that the Tokugawa received, but has an important twist in the end that suggests how the status system was integrated into this form of politics.

The subtle beginning of the incident in the domain diary is hardly notice-able. The diary records that two letters sent by domain officials from Edo on the eighth (the day the lord died) and ninth days of the second month in quick succession reported "nothing special."[44] A full month later, a letter arrived with first intimations of something wrong, saying, "The lord has not been feeling well, and from early last month his condition has become slightly unfortunate. Of course, it is not anything special. The doctor Nakagawa Jōshun and his son are providing medicines, and Sugimoto Chūon is also doctoring the lord." All domain samurai were called to Tahara castle on that day "to inquire after the lord's health." The next day, a retainer was ordered to Osaka "on the lord's busi-ness," probably to drum up money for the expenses of burial and inheritance. A flurry of letters between Tahara and Edo followed, those from the domain officially conveying the retainers' wishes for the lord's full recovery, and those from Edo occasionally mentioning the efforts of his doctors. Suddenly domain officials in Edo decided that "there were not enough retainers in Edo" and requested additional staff. Two new pages were assigned to the lord but were instructed to practice by serving the lord's younger brother Hachizō in Tahara. Then they decided that Hachizō should depart to Edo to inquire after the lord's health, which he did on the first day of the fifth month. Soon after his arrival there, a letter sent home noted that the lord's condition had worsened, and he was preparing to adopt Hachizō (who would become the daimyo Yasuaki). A letter sent on the seventeenth noted that on the previous day the Tokugawa Grand Inspector had arrived at the Edo residence, where the lord took Buddhist vows surrounded by numerous relatives and two "messenger bannermen" as witnesses. The Inspector certified the document declaring that Yasukazu was alive and had declared his desire for Hachizō to inherit, which the two bannermen immediately took over to the house of the Tokugawa Elder on duty, where the request was accepted. The letter continues: "That very night, the lord's condition took a turn for the worse, all efforts at care failed, and he passed away at the hour of the boar. Everyone was speechless with grief." Up to this point, with the exception of Hachizō's secret journey, the story presented in the domain diary was in accordance with official Tokugawa knowledge, but what follows reveals the local management of information.

The diary next records the subsequent lines from the letter:

Of course, as retainers above the rank of *monogashira* have earlier been informed, the inner truth [*naijitsu*] is that the lord died at the middle of the hour of the bird on the eighth day of the second month. We should have told everyone immediately, but discussions by letter over succession and financial matters took much time and only now are we making this known. Even though there was this delay, all is now safely processed, and everyone should be at peace and without worry.

Retainers above *monogashira* rank in the Miyake clan were all the retainers who received fiefs rather than stipends, about the top twenty samurai houses of the domain. Beneath them were about seventy-five houses of samurai who received stipends, including the secretaries who kept the domain diaries.[45] We can discern three circles of "insideness" to which the truth formally emanated in succession in the Miyake house. The first circle was likely only the most senior retainers and interested relatives who were in the know at the time when letters declaring "nothing special" were arriving, the period in which they were deciding who would be the heir. Other retainers might have noticed something strange in the rapid succession of letters from Edo and may have wondered what secrets were enclosed in sealed letters to more highly placed people in the domain. The second circle was the enfeoffed retainers, who most likely formally learned the truth when they were called to the castle "to inquire after the lord's health." These retainers were privileged by status with greater access to the "inner truth" of things, and many of them were assigned to various tasks from that time forward. Certainly the parents of the youths told to "practice" being pages, for example, were discreetly pleased at the prospect of their children becoming close attendants to the next daimyo. However, the secretaries who recorded events in the domain diaries did not report the real news from that moment, because their rank as stipendiaries meant they were part of the "third circle" of retainers who could not formally know the inner truth until the announcement of the completion of the rush adoption ceremony. We see here how the performance of *omote* and *uchi* functioned not merely to mediate relations with the Tokugawa but also to reinforce the many hierarchies that structured relations within the domain.

One reason for the local reticence during the process is that the domain should not appear to make light of Tokugawa law. This fear of showing disrespect to higher authority is one element that makes the politics of feudal compartmentalization so nuanced and complex. Laws might be broken, but decorum must be maintained. As we saw in the examples above concerning higher officials' management of gossip, it could be dangerous to misunderstand the necessary degree of decorum. It should by now be obvious that the Tokugawa Grand Inspector, his doctors, and the Tokugawa Elders generally knew the real fact of death but played their roles, officially noticing nothing out of order. They could lose face if news of the lord's early death were bandied about too freely or expressed so boldly in Miyake house ritual that other daimyo houses and people in neighboring domains would know about it. To make local knowledge too public and official would express disrespect of the Tokugawa order itself, rather than expressing a desire to work within the order through informal compromise. This is likely why all lesser Miyake house retainers were officially informed of the actual death date only after the succession problem was resolved.

The local maintenance of *omote* appearances in ritual even continued for a while afterward. Needless to say, the burial ceremonies for Yasukazu's ashes could take place only after his official death. Likewise, the stipulated period of mourning began from the *omote* death date. Retainers were told to shave their pates and refrain from parties, construction, and various other activities for periods ranging from twenty-seven to thirty-five days out of respect for their deceased lord. Officials sent an announcement to all villages, telling them that the lord had died on the Tokugawa *omote* date and that they should engage in appropriate mourning activities. Commoners of the domain thus constituted a fourth circle of insideness created by status considerations. The boundary against commoners' official knowledge may not have been erased for a full year, when at the first anniversary of the lord's death on 1823/2/8 everyone in the domain was brought into the cycle of official memorial observance of the real death date.[46] This process of revelation in stages indicates how status and political space intersected at the *omote/uchi* boundary to maintain a proper face toward the Tokugawa and simultaneously reinforce the local status hierarchy, while fostering layers of a local inside identity that ultimately included all subjects of the daimyo. Concerning knowledge of the lord's death, local status differences were gradually diffused over the year, but vis-à-vis the Tokugawa, the official reported death date continued to hold validity until the end of the Tokugawa regime.

The marking of status differences through the stepped expansion of circles of local *omote* knowledge of the lord's actual death date is an important phenomenon, but this *omote* was not equivalent to informal local knowledge of the facts. It is likely that real knowledge was wide ranging and quickly acquired, easily inferred from the suddenly rapid pace of exchanges of letters between Edo and Tahara, the rush of promotions and appointments among retainers, and the frequent prayers at temples and shrines throughout the domain for the lord's recovery. Even the least well-connected of village officials likely learned of the death, at the latest, more than a month before the rush adoption ceremony, when they were called to have their villages make special donations of money to the Miyake.[47] The scribes of the domain diaries could have inferred the death from precedents recorded in their own books. Yasukazu himself became daimyo when his actual father Yasutomo died 1809/3/20, but only after more than a month of delay that is shrouded in mystery because all of the relevant diaries are missing. Yet the scribes knew that Yasutomo's *omote* death was 1809/5/6, the day after the request to have Yasukazu recognized by the Tokugawa. A step back in time, and Yasutomo became daimyo when his brother Yasukuni died without an heir on 1792/2/29 and officially died on 1792/3/23.

The scribes would have seen that the pattern of events and messages following Yasukuni's death was so similar as to be a template for Yasukazu's. Like Yasukazu, Yasukuni also took care of ancestors' memorial rites before his own official death.[48] Four days after Yasukuni's death in Edo a special delivery messenger arrived in Tahara. The scribe wrote in the domain office diary that the letter said that the lord's condition had worsened and that all enfeoffed retainers should immediately show up at the castle to inquire after the lord's health. Domain officials in Edo and Tahara rapidly exchanged letters over the next month and a half. Many of those from Edo contained detailed descriptions of the lord's obstinate illness and the valiant efforts of doctors to aid the lord in his recovery. Letters from Tahara described the frequent religious services offered for the recovery of the lord. In the meantime it was decided that there were not enough retainers living in the Edo mansion, and a few senior retainers in Tahara were ordered to go there as fast as they could make it, but the domain doctor, who earlier had been ordered to travel to Edo, was told that his services were no longer needed. Fifty-six days after Yasukuni's death a letter arrived in Tahara saying that the lord's condition seemed not to be improving and that, after consultation with relatives, it was decided to name his younger brother as his heir, with a formal request to be made soon. Two days later a letter arrived saying that the lord had died. It noted that on the twenty-third of the third month (there had been an intervening intercalary second month, so this was nearly two months after the actual death) at the hour of the snake, with four relatives and four bannermen present as official witnesses, the lord took Buddhist vows and shaved his head, with the Grand Inspector present to confirm authenticity. The letter continued: "On that very day there was a change in the lord's condition, which worsened severely, and the lord died at three in the afternoon, despite all efforts at care. Everyone was speechless with grief." The diary next records a message that everyone should prepare for the burial following the arrival of the lord's ashes, and adds, "Of course, as all *monogashira* had been informally told earlier, the lord actually died on the twenty-ninth of the second month. We should have made this known immediately, but there were negotiations concerning the inheritance and finances, . . . so we are making this known now, and everyone should be comforted."[49] The extraordinary similarity of the unfolding of events reveals that the inheritance process and its associated local reportage were strongly guided by precedent, observation of which helped minimize the danger of indiscretions that could invite misfortune.

Tahara domain had more than a century of experience managing the difference between Tokugawa *omote* memory and domainal memory (Table 2). Of all the domain lords to die in the Edo period, only the first died on his official day of death. The rest—even in cases of direct descent—had different actual and *omote* death dates. Tahara was small and famously poor, and perhaps even in the best of circumstances the domain needed days to prepare funds while the lord was still "alive."

Table 2. Recorded deaths of Miyake-clan daimyo of Tahara domain

GENERATION	NAME	ACTUAL DEATH DATE*	HEIR	OFFICIAL DEATH DATE (DIFFERENCE)
4	Yasukatsu	1687/8/9	Son	Same
5	Yasuo	1726/10/4	Son	1726/10/6 (2 days)
6	Yasutoku	1753/12/1	Son	1753/12/3 (2 days)
7	Yasutaka	1791/3/14 (ret.)	Adopted	1791/3/21 (7 days)
8	Yasusuke	1803/8/9 (ret.)	Son	1803/8/16 (7 days)
9	Yasutake	1785/9/12	Rush adopted	1785/9/21 (9 days)
10	Yasukuni	1792/2/29	Rush adopted	1792/3/23 (55 days)
11	Yasutomo	1809/3/20	Son	1809/5/6 (46 days)
12	Yasukazu	1823/2/8	Rush adopted	1823/5/16 (98 days)
13	Yasuaki	1827/7/10	Rush adopted	1827/10/23 (104 days)

THE FOLLOWING DIED AFTER THE MEIJI RESTORATION

14	Yasunao	1893/8/9 (ret.)	Adopted	Same
15	Yasuyoshi	1895/1/23	—	Same

Source: Compiled from clan lineage in Tahara-chō Bunkazai Chōsakai, *Tahara-chō shi, chūkan* (Aichi Pref., Tahara-chō, 1987), pp. 1189–1205.

*"(Ret.)" means the lord was living in retirement when he died, and his inheritance was already processed.

The final rush adoption that occurred when Yasuaki died in 1827 involved a passionate struggle for control of the Miyake house. Yasuaki had a younger brother, Kōzō, who was healthy, educated, and next in line to inherit. Many members of the domain, including the domain Elder Watanabe Kazan, wanted Kōzō to be chosen as heir. Up to this time adoptions had been kept within the clan, and this faction considered keeping the Miyake bloodline intact a duty to the Miyake ancestors. Nevertheless, because the Miyake were extremely poor, another group of retainers wanted to adopt a wealthy outsider who would bring with him a large adoption gift. Sakai Tadamitsu, lord of Himeji domain, was wealthy and well connected. He had numerous children, and he wished to have his sixth son, Sakai Inawaka, adopted into the Miyake house. After much negotiation in the domain the faction supporting Inawaka won the argument.

Because Kōzō's existence was formally known to the Tokugawa, domain officials declared him to be physically unfit to inherit so that they could request an
adoption from outside the clan. Kōzō was not happy and returned to Tahara
along with Kazan and another chief retainer, before their presence at the *hanmoto mitodoke* certification might be required. The ceremony in Edo succeeded, and Inawaka became Miyake Yasunao, fourteenth daimyo of the Miyake
clan. However, Kōzō's early return to Tahara meant that the new lord needed
to make extra effort to restore harmony within the domain. Yasunao immediately distributed gifts of money to all members of the household: enfeoffed
retainers each received more than two *ryō* in gold, and even lowly musketeers
received half a *ryō*. Yasunao then invited Kōzō back to Edo and provided him
with the status and perquisites of retired lord and the new name "Tomonobu."
These gestures failed to quell dissent, and finally Yasunao had to promise in
1832 to marry his daughter to Tomonobu's son, Shintarō, and adopt him as
heir to ensure the continuance of the Miyake bloodline. These compromises
likely prevented a serious house disturbance from erupting into Tokugawa
omote space.

The fragile nature of this containment of disorder is made clear by an
incident that happened in 1844. In 1840 Yasunao proposed to change his
choice of heir to one of his own biological sons. Retainers were forced to
choose between duty to the current lord and duty to the ancestral Miyake
house. Some allied with Yasunao, but other retainers resented his attempt to
break the agreement of 1832. Maki Sadachika, a friend and ally of Watanabe
Kazan (who was by this time dead), vowed never to return to Tahara, but
he was ordered to accompany his lord Yasunao on a journey from Edo to
the domain in 1844. On the road at the inn in Kanaya station, just before
reaching the home country, Sadachika threw a party for his retainers and
sent them to bed. He then wrote a document of appeal to Yasunao in which
he begged him to reconsider, placed it on the floor, and disemboweled himself before it. The blood-spattered document was delivered to the lord. This
act was tantamount to breaking the *omote* that existed between retainer and
daimyo and was likely to inspire disorder within the Miyake household. Yasunao was so moved and likely frightened by the protest that he reverted
to his original agreement and in 1850 retired in his adopted son's favor. He
had a memorial stone erected within the Miyake clan graveyard that read
in Yasunao's own script, "The Grave of Loyal Retainer Maki Sadachika," in
order to express his remorse publicly within the domain and restore a sense
of decorum.[50]

Informal negotiations with the Tokugawa

The surviving records for the Miyake clan reveal the activities and the process of revelation of various rush adoptions back in the domain, but they do not disclose much about the negotiations with Tokugawa officials. Documents for the Yamauchi clan of Tosa can help us better understand this aspect of the politics. The clan was afflicted with a succession of two daimyo deaths in 1848. The death of the thirteenth lord of Tosa, Toyoteru, followed the standard pattern for last-minute adoptions, but the sudden death of his successor, Yamauchi Toyoatsu, required particularly delicate negotiations. Yamauchi Toyoteru died at age thirty-four on 1848/6/16, and his only son was a two-year-old yet unregistered with the Tokugawa and living in Kōchi. Toyoteru's younger brother Toyoatsu was named as heir at the *hanmoto mitodoke* ceremony, but with the promise that he later adopt Toyoteru's infant son, whose existence had just been made known to the Tokugawa by *jōbutodoke*. The Tosa officials in Edo probably made this arrangement as a precaution to avoid the possibility of an infant heir dying before age seventeen, a worry that turned out to be sadly prescient. The infant son died the day after news of his father's death reached Kōchi. A messenger from the domain raced to Edo to convey the news but arrived after the deathbed adoption ceremony was complete. If they had picked the son as heir in the request, it would have been a very difficult situation for Tosa.[51]

On Toyoteru's death, domain officials sent a formal letter to Tosa saying that the lord was ill and that people should offer prayers for his recovery. A secret letter to the assistant of the retired daimyo, Toyosuke, who was living in Kōchi, said, "The lord's illness gradually worsened, and finally in the middle of last night he stopped breathing. It is unspeakably awful. Knowing this, please learn informally [the retired daimyo Toyosuke's] thoughts on the matter." They also noted that they were already going to proceed with the adoption of Toyoatsu. To make sure that there would be cooperation on the day of the deathbed adoption ceremony, domain officials in Edo began informal communications early in the seventh month. On the fifth day, they invited over to dinner at the Tosa compound the Tokugawa doctors and the messenger bannermen who would serve as contacts with the Tokugawa Elders, certainly to make informal arrangements. Over the next two days, they informally contacted the Tokugawa Grand Inspector and sent a message to the Tokugawa Elders saying that the lord was very ill and informally showed them the adoption request to see if all was in order. Only after making these quiet prearrangements did they formally request the Grand Inspector to come to a deathbed adoption ceremony on the ninth. Toyoteru then formally died on the following day so that mourning rituals could begin.[52] However, a problem then arose.

Toward the end of the month, the heir, Toyoatsu, departed Kōchi together with a younger brother, Toyokane, who was to be adopted into the branch daimyo house of Yamauchi Toyokata. They arrived in Edo over a month later, much delayed by rain and flooding. Toyoatsu had fallen ill on the road and had to send his daimyo cousin Toyokata to Edo castle in his place to accept notification of Toyoatsu's inheritance and the bestowal of the Matsudaira name from the Tokugawa. Only twelve days later Toyoatsu lay dead without even having had audience with the *kubō*. The Tosa officials in Edo were put in the curious position of having to formally order people in Kōchi to get on with construction, firing guns, and partying with songs and entertainers in celebration of the inheritance and the end of mourning for Toyoteru, while secretly sending news of the new daimyo's death to the retired daimyo, Toyosuke, to ask him what to do. News of Toyoatsu's death leaked quickly around Kōchi, and many were too nervous to party and expressed fear that the domain might be attaindered.[53] It is difficult to evaluate exactly what they thought the true dangers were. No major daimyo had actually been attaindered for this reason in well over a century.[54] Perhaps the politics of *omote* and *naishō* made people afraid because they knew propriety demanded that they should express fear or because something might, after all, actually go so wrong as to end up in attainder. Human foibles could cause an heir to be unable to perform. Toyosuke himself had been rush adopted in 1809 when he was sixteen and his elder brother, Toyooki, had died childless. His first response was to be so terrified that he refused to rise from bed for three days, but he finally steeled himself to duty and became a capable lord who even after retirement remained a major player in domain politics.[55]

The crucial problem was that the new daimyo, Toyoatsu, had not had the ceremony of audience. This omission meant that he had not yet fully become a retainer of the Tokugawa and was not qualified to choose an heir. Tosa's Edo Ambassadors informally queried other daimyo houses for precedents. The lord of Satsuma was a relative by marriage, and on hearing the news he suggested that they have the accompanying younger brother Toyokane secretly become Toyoatsu and then have Toyokane officially die.[56] For whatever reason, the Yamauchi rejected this suggestion and began investigating past inheritances of daimyo who had not achieved an audience. They discovered the request made by Tsuchiya Hironao, the lord of Tsuchiura domain, who died at age sixteen in 1810 but had been kept officially alive for a year until 1811. His rush adoption letter started by noting that he had requested an audience with the shogun but then discovered that he was too ill to actually carry it out. Despite the assistance of many doctors there was no hope of recovery, and he therefore asked to return his fief—to be attaindered in effect—but he and all of his house would be grateful if the shogun would show mercy and permit a rush adoption. This format was followed to the letter by Abe Masanori of Oshi domain, who died (officially at least) at age eighteen in 1823 without having had audience. The third example was the request of Date Chikamune, who had died at age fourteen in 1809 but was officially kept alive until 1812—and active enough in the interim that he became engaged to a daughter of the *kubō* Tokugawa Ienari! This letter was slightly different, with its writer, the supposed Chikamume, noting, "I am now seventeen, but it is difficult for me to request an audience.... There is no precedent for this request, and I am fearful and embarrassed, but it has been a very long illness with no change foreseeable in the future." The letter concluded by saying that he and all members of his household begged for merciful approval to adopt his younger brother. The response was that the request would be approved, but that they must follow precedent by sending a companion letter saying that the lord wished to return his fief. Tosa's Edo Ambassadors noted that this last example could not be directly acquired from the Date, who were secretive about the event, but that they managed to negotiate a copy from the hands of an outsider, presumably one of the Tokugawa Elders who received it.[57] The examples made clear to Tosa officials that one had to formally acknowledge the irregularity of the situation by offering to return the domain.

The retired daimyo Toyosuke played a key role from his residence in Kōchi. He arranged for a nephew, Yamauchi Toyoshige, to become the adopted heir and immediately sent him to Edo "to inquire after Toyoatsu's health," but he would not allow the phrase "I ask to give up my fief" to be put in the inheritance request. This had no clear precedent, although the Date clan example was close, insofar as it was on a separate document sent later. On the occasion of Toyoatsu's death Toyosuke's demand that there be no mention of returning the domain became the key issue in the negotiations that followed. To this end the Yamauchi first approached two powerful daimyo who were relatives: Kuroda Narihiro, lord of Fukuoka, and Shimazu Nariakira, designated heir to Kagoshima domain. Kuroda Narihiro was originally born to Shimazu Shigehide, daimyo of Kagoshima, but was adopted into the Kuroda clan. He was an uncle and a good friend to the similarly aged Shimazu Nariakira. Shimazu Nariakira's sister Kōhime had married Yamauchi Toyoteru and was thereby Toyoatsu's adoptive mother and an active and powerful presence in Tosa domain politics. One more daimyo who became involved was Kuroda

Nagamoto, lord of Akizuki domain, which was a branch domain of Fukuoka. Nagamoto was originally Toyosuke's younger brother but had been adopted into the Kuroda house. The Yamauchi, Shimazu, and Kuroda clans were all thus closely bound by marriage and adoption ties, and the Yamauchi hoped to depend on these relatives for political pull with Abe Masahiro, who had recently gained position as the most powerful Elder in the Tokugawa government. The relatives told the Yamauchi that their hands were tied because they were each already in the midst of delicate *naishō* negotiations of their own and could not stretch their political capital.[58]

Instead Narihiro and Nariakira called Date Munenari, lord of Uwajima domain, to a secret meeting in one of the waiting rooms of Edo castle. Munenari had no particular kinship relation with the Yamauchi clan, but they chose him because he was friends with Abe Masahiro. Uwajima domain bordered Tosa, but as we will see in Chapter 4, this circumstance could as easily provoke tension as friendship. Munenari only reluctantly took on the task and wrote a detailed memorandum of the first meeting and subsequent events concerning the adoption negotiations. Narihiro and Nariakira started the meeting by saying to Munenari that, "as you already know," Toyoatsu had died. That they expected him to know this secret, even though he had no ties to the Yamauchi clan, suggests how open the "secret," unspeakable in *omote* situations, had become two and a half months after the death. They explained to him that the Yamauchi wished to submit a request for adoption that had no mention of the desire to return the domain. Abe had already told them that the Tosa domain Elders should come to him to negotiate, but Narihiro and Nariakira did not wish to proceed in this way, because they were worried that domain samurai "were ignorant about all the ways [of negotiation] and would explain everything with all of the details," noting that "Tokugawa government officials do not like to go into negotiations with all of the details laid bare."[59] The Tosa Edo Ambassador had already somewhat botched things by formally (*omotedatte*) rather than secretly asking the Kuroda to intercede on their behalf, when the Kuroda were already in the midst of their own secret negotiations with Abe. Other Yamauchi relatives, such as Yonezawa lord Uesugi Narinori and Okayama lord Ikeda Yoshimasa, were not to be trusted with this problem, Narihiro and Nariakira said, so they begged Munenari to help them. After checking with his relatives in the domain and also with the Sendai Date house, which was the main branch of the clan, Munenari was given the green light to go ahead and help the process.

Narihiro and Nariakira wished him to show Abe a draft of request documents and get his informal approval. Some miscommunications ensued.

Munenari tried to meet Abe but was told that Abe was busy. Then, surprisingly, Kuroda Nagamoto told him that the Tosa Elders wished to informally submit the documents to Abe now. Munenari urged them not to and enlisted Narihiro to back him up, but they did so anyway. The next day, Munenari was able to meet Abe and asked if he had seen the documents. Munenari then told him that, "as you already know," the "inside story" was that Toyoatsu had died without having had an audience and that the people of the domain were worried that this might be the end. Even if the Yamauchi house were restored by an act of benevolence of the shogun, as sometimes happened in this kind of situation, this would mean that the heir would become the first generation of a restored house rather than fifteenth generation of a house that went back to the days of Sekigahara, and he argued that the Tosa people had too much pride to accept that diminution in prestige. Munenari pressed the point by saying that he knew from living in a domain next to Tosa that the people were old-fashioned and might cause disturbances if they had to request a return of the domain as part of the formalities. Abe relented but said that he would have to convince the other Tokugawa Elders. Therefore the Tosa domain Elders needed to come as quickly as possible and make a show of informally asking his thoughts on the issue, and he would discuss matters with them. Munenari thanked Abe and immediately informed all parties, and the Tosa Elders went the next day to Abe for discussions.

A week later, prearrangements had proceeded well enough that the branch domain relative Yamauchi Toyokata could formally present the request for adoption to the Elders at Edo castle, who approved it after a couple of days. Despite some apparent friction between the Tosa retainers in Edo and the various involved daimyo, the request concerning wording was approved successfully. This was an incremental change in *omote* rules, now a precedent for other houses in similar situations to use. One curious aspect of these negotiations was that all of the negotiators were *tozama* (outside daimyo). Normally some *fudai* lords and messenger bannermen would have been marshaled to assist in such negotiations, but Abe Masahiro was an unorthodox Tokugawa Elder who tried to build his power base with the support of outside lords.[60]

Enough tension remained that the rush adoption ceremony itself became unorthodox. The Grand Inspector, two messenger bannermen, Tosa house relatives and domain Elders, and even the missing Toyoatsu were present as was traditional, but many daimyo also were there and this was uncommon. Shimazu Nariakira, Tōdō Takayuki of Ise Tsu domain, Kuroda Narihiro, and Kuroda Nagamoto were present. The two daimyo Uesugi Narinori and Ikeda Yoshimasa, mentioned above as not being reliable for negotiations, were listed as promising to attend but not actually showing up. In addition to the five Tokugawa doctors and two Yamauchi doctors, there were four additional doctors—two from Kuroda Nagamoto; one from Shimazu Nariakira's father, Narioki; and one from Sengoku Hisatoshi of Tajima Izushi domain. Their presence was so atypical that the news made it all the way to a village headman in western Tosa, who wrote, "Lords from many houses came into the small residence, and it made quite a commotion."[61] These extra presences were certainly a show of support for a delicate, precedent-setting event. It was a precarious moment, but anyone who might wish to raise a stink about this change by "uncovering" the death of Toyoatsu would have to go against the word of numerous powerful people of the realm who were sitting in on the ceremony. Perhaps because of the importance of the event and its exacting and subtle nature, Toyoatsu remained publicly alive as retired daimyo well into the next year, busy sending gifts, emissaries, and financial support to family events and Tokugawa rituals. He was allowed to go to his final rest late in the second month. For his own part, the new daimyo, Toyoshige, made visits to his adoptive father, inquiring after his health down to the end, the moment when people could mourn and formally be speechless with grief.

One other result of this event was bringing Date Munenari into close political contact and action with Nariakira, Narihiro, and Toyoshige, and all of them into close working relations with Abe Masahiro. A number of years later they acted in concert to have Hitotsubashi Yoshinaga appointed heir to the *kubō* Tokugawa Iesada, so as to have a leader capable of dealing with the threat of the Western powers that had arrived with Commodore Perry in 1853. Their efforts ended in failure, and many were punished for their temerity, but one can see how the politics of *omote* and *naishō* helped foster such groups bound by mutual obligations and privacies.[62]

Remembering *naishō* and *omote* events

The above examples of rush inheritances have provided us views of events in the domain and the political negotiation in Edo. One final subject to address is the issue of memory, and this can begin with gravestones. The Miyake clan graves in Tahara are all inscribed with the actual death dates of their lords.[63] This is in line with the anniversary memorial rites for the lords being carried out in accordance with the actual death dates. Another daimyo house, the Honda of the 15,000-*koku* Ise Kanbe domain, had death dates inscribed on the stones of two of its lords that differ from the *omote* lineage records. These two were the only lords of that lineage that required rush adoptions, and it is likely that the stones reflect the actual death dates.[64] These examples suggest that there was a desire for memorial rites in accordance with actual rather than *omote* death dates even if the original burials had to, by political necessity, be carried out according to *omote* rules. Yet not all domains felt free to memorialize actual death dates, and it is clear that complicated memories were produced by these politics. The Yamauchi grave markers and memorial biographical steles in Kōchi generally display *omote* dates. Toyoteru and Toyoatsu's steles present *omote* histories, but Toyotsune's gives his actual birth date rather than his *omote* one.[65] However, Toyoatsu's first-year memorial service was held in the domain on 6/15 of the next year, his actual death date.[66] A selection of late Tokugawa and early Meiji histories of Tosa reveals a complex mix of reality and *omote* records, with some histories using one or the other, some noting both in asides, and some seeming to egregiously use an indiscriminate mix of both.[67] Other domains seem to have observed the *omote* death date as the actual one, even in local records. Many domain lineage records contain some suspicious facts. The number of daimyo who die within a few days of having a rush approval of an heir can be regarded as either impressive or disconcerting. The Hachisuka clan of Tokushima domain had a "secret history" completed in 1845, which nevertheless has suspicious dates. For instance, lord Munekazu died at age twenty in 1735, just three days after requesting approval of a rush adoption, and lord Yoshihiro died at age nineteen in 1754, two days after requesting a rush adoption. Both had been unable to appear at court for some time beforehand.[68] There is a similar pattern in the lineages of the Matsudaira clan of Matsuyama domain. Lord Sadataka died in 1763 on the same day he adopted an heir. That heir also died in 1763, one day after an emergency adoption. His heir died in 1779, two days after an emergency adoption. Then Lord Sadanori died in 1809 at age seventeen, just a day after achieving an emergency adoption.[69] The compiler of the lineage created in 1844 wrote in his preface, "I have largely relied on the lineage composed in the Bunka era [for facts up to that time]. However, because that lineage was submitted to the Tokugawa government, there are not a few things that were written with reserve. I have written the truth for some of these."[70] Nevertheless, the death dates he presents are in agreement with the Tokugawa *omote* record. If the lords actually died earlier than reported, then this suggests that the actual death dates remained an unpresentable secret even within the domain, a pattern quite different from that of Tahara domain. The complexity evidenced in these examples suggests that only further research can help us determine the considerations that went into creating and preserving memories.

It is certainly important for historians to be aware of the complex politics of *omote* and *naishō*, if only because these politics influenced the documentary record in ways that cannot be ignored. I have saved this discussion of the relationship between history writing of the Edo period and the politics of *omote* and *naishō* for the final chapter of this book, but I will summarize here some problems of information regarding daimyo lineages and personal histories in Tokugawa records. The formal fiction surrounding the deaths and inheritances of daimyo is the basis of Tokugawa compiled histories. All birth dates and death dates in the *Kansei chōshū shokafu* reflect the Tokugawa *omote* story. Its "truths" are the product of negotiations between daimyo and bannermen vassals on the one hand and the Tokugawa government on the other. The entry for Miyake Yasutomo, the adopted son of Miyake Yasukuni, is instructive. Beside Yasutomo's name is a parenthetical note that states "Really Yasuyuki's sixth son," that "really" refers to what the Miyake told the Tokugawa. In their own records he was "really" Yasuyuki's brother but had been adopted by Yasuyuki without *omote* notification and then adopted again by Yasukuni, as reported to the Tokugawa.[71] The facts in the official history of the Tokugawa clan and government, the *Tokugawa jikki,* are also *omote* facts. Like the lineages, it is a very careful history compiled by many of the best historians of the day. It does no disparagement to their skills to say that they recorded only *omote* facts— they knew very well what they were doing—but for modern historians to use this information as facts in the modern sense, as if the Tokugawa had worked according to the logic of a modern nation, is not being sensitive to how deeply history writing itself is bound by historical context. To read these documents correctly, it becomes essential to recognize *omote* facts for what they are, ritual statements of subordination to and general agreement with the order of things controlled by the superior. However, a mere avoidance of Tokugawa documents and reliance on daimyo house documents does not solve the problem of accuracy, because this is only one boundary among many *omote* interactions, as is evident in the examples of how the status boundaries influenced local information within Tahara domain.

The main goal of this chapter has been to suggest that one of the functions of the performances associated with the politics of *omote* and *naishō* was the enforcement of discipline and peace when the stakes of political issues were high, such as in moments of daimyo inheritance. The chapter also considered how this influenced the content of documents from the era. Finally, it touched on how these politics bound groups together and created identities through the processes of information management. The next chapter explores this last theme more thoroughly in the context of land disputes, where daimyo used these politics against each other, and villagers used them against their daimyo.

4

Territorial Border Disputes

Lord Bizen said, "Iyo's way of doing things is so ugly I'd like
to throw [the Iyo village headman] in jail." To which Lord Izu
replied, "If that's what you think, then I'd like to throw the Tosa
villager in jail for a while myself!" . . . [Bizen countered,] "Well, I
think [the Iyo village headman] Rokunoshin ought to be crucified,
and Lord Uta no kami agrees!"

—Judges discussing a boundary dispute in the Tokugawa court, 1659[1]

Land was second only to inheritance politics in its ability to excite passions
and inspire violence in Tokugawa Japan, and a chief task of the Tokugawa
government was to mediate struggles over territorial control. Formally, the
Tokugawa had land struggles adjudicated in accordance with the feudal disbursement of judicial authority. Their general goal was to contain disturbance
in the smallest possible spaces. Daimyo judged disputes within their realms,
and the Tokugawa judged in their own demesne. When territory conflicts occurred inside a single realm, and when commoners were in conflict with their
own daimyo, there was, with few exceptions, no formal right of appeal. A lord's
judgment over his subjects was final, and appealing to the Tokugawa over his
head was itself a crime. The Tokugawa courts officially took up boundary
disputes occurring in daimyo territory only when the disagreement between
two villages crossed the boundaries of two separate domains. Furthermore,
the government would not permit daimyo themselves to present territory
boundary suits. All this was the law, but the Tokugawa court broke its own
rules on these matters so regularly that informal standardized rules of behavior dominated the actual operation of the legal system.

This chapter examines three seventeenth-century boundary disputes to uncover the interplay between *omote* constraints and *naishō* activity in the Tokugawa legal system. All three cases reveal a network of constraints that encouraged settlement out of court or by court-brokered mediation, designed to preserve the appearance of peace and harmony despite the highly litigious reality. They illustrate how the political process behind the suits helped strengthen "inside" identities through the management of information. The first two disputes represent conflicts between daimyo, one resolved in court and one resolved through out-of-court settlement. The third example explores how villagers used the politics of *omote* and *naishō* to challenge and defeat their own daimyo in Tokugawa court.

Two border disputes between the Yamauchi clan and the Date clan

Between 1644 and 1659 the Yamauchi clan of Tosa domain had two closely intertwined border disputes with the neighboring Date clan of Uwajima domain. The first dispute, involving a pair of small islands in the offing between the two domains, was over rights to fishing grounds and a portion of Uwajima land rented by a Tosa village. The second dispute started a decade later, in 1656, when Yamauchi Tadayoshi, the retired lord of Tosa at that time, promised to refurbish the halls of the Sasayama temple-shrine complex that straddled the domain borders. This started a process of conflict that escalated to the point that parties ransacked the temple, assaulted villagers and samurai, and stole and destroyed goods belonging to opponents on each side of the mountain. Although the disputes began separately, their fates became closely intertwined and were resolved in rapid succession in 1659.

These incidents transformed local allegiances and created tensions between the two daimyo houses, each of which mobilized influential daimyo from throughout Japan to support their cases. One distinguishing feature of the border disputes was that, although they consumed an enormous amount of daimyo effort and expenditure of resources, they needed officially to be suits presented by villagers who lived along the borders.[2] Another aspect of the cases was that the formal legal issues involved and the clear sets of evidence did not quickly lead to solutions. Instead both cases dragged on for years, and victory was won by careful *naishō* negotiation and timely appeals to formal *omote* values.

The beginning of the Okinoshima dispute

Okinoshima is a small mountainous island located four kilometers off the west edge of mainland Tosa and sixteen kilometers south of the mainland portion of Uwajima domain. Himejima is a much smaller rocky island four kilometers to the west of Okinoshima. These two islands and their waters were the object of a boundary dispute that was sparked when the Tokugawa instructed daimyo to make maps of the provinces in 1644.[3] These provinces and their counties were defunct as administrative entities but remained a politically potent historical presence because many daimyo had been granted domains with at least one border defined along a provincial or county boundary. The mapping project led daimyo to attempt to gain firm recognition from the Tokugawa of territorial ownership along contested province boundaries and instigated a drama of widespread daimyo submission to the judicial process of the Tokugawa-dominated order.[4]

An imaginary line separating the two provinces of Tosa and Iyo snaked down the middle of both Okinoshima and Himejima island, but where this line lay came into dispute. Yamauchi Katsutoyo's grant from Tokugawa Ieyasu in 1600 had been for "the complete province of Tosa," and Date Hidemune's grant in 1614 from Tokugawa Hidetada was for "the county of Uwa in Iyo province." More fluid than one might expect to be the case for thousand-year-old entities, the provincial boundaries had been disputed by various lords in the medieval period.[5] The most recent boundary of record had been set by the previous Chōsogabe lords of Tosa. They surveyed their realm in the 1590s, and their records contained detailed verbal descriptions of the border. The 368 volumes of the Chōsogabe cadastral surveys were one of the foundation stones of Yamauchi administration in Tosa. No similar survey existed for Uwajima's realm, and this put it at a disadvantage.

The fishermen of Okinoshima had historically been adept at overcoming the division imposed by the provincial line. Descendants of the local Miura clan came to serve as headmen of the two villages on the island in the sixteenth century, but the more intrusive daimyo governments of the seventeenth century led to the intensification of local divisions. Uwajima's main village on the northern tip of the island was Mojima, well within the Iyo portion, but the Tosa village of Hirose straddled the provincial border on the west coast, divided by a creek into Iyo on the north and Tosa on the south. The main house of the Miura clan in Hirose was based on the Tosa side of the divide, and their ties were much closer to clans of Tosa than to those of Uwajima. When Toyotomi Hideyoshi defeated the leading warlord of Shikoku, Chōsogabe

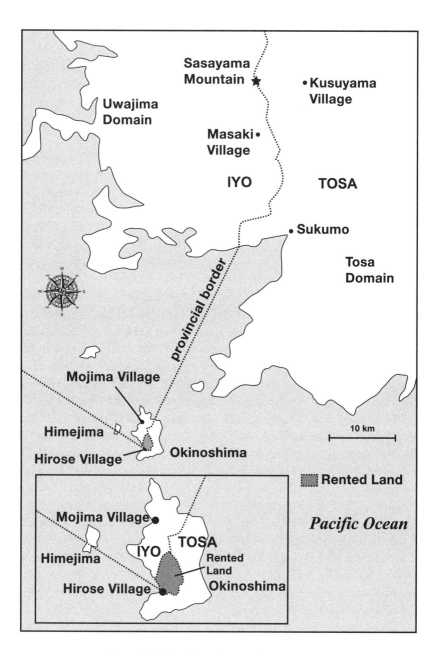

Map of the Okinoshima-Sasayama border disputes.
Produced by Andrew Roberts

Motochika, in 1585, he left Motochika in control of Tosa but took Iyo to grant to another daimyo. This politically divided the island, and the Miura of Hirose adjusted by renting a portion of Iyo land and its associated fishing rights in order to round out Hirose itself as a village. A branch family of the Miura clan served as village headmen in Mojima. Although each of the villages had its own proprietary fishing grounds, they also possessed cooperative-use rights in some of the fishing grounds on both sides of the border.[6]

With the aggressive support of the Date daimyo, the fishermen based in Mojima developed a strong fishing industry. They came to use the southern cooperative grounds around uninhabited Himejima island much more fully than the Tosa fishermen and desired to have sole use of the waters. The initial dispute was over the following issues: The headman of Mojima, Miura Rokunoshin, asserted that traditionally Iyo completely owned Himejima and its rich fishing grounds. He also disputed the boundary of the rental portion of Iyo land used by Hirose village on Okinoshima, saying that Tosa people were encroaching on unrented Iyo land by building roads and cutting wood. In response Miura Gengorō, the headman of the village of Hirose on the Tosa side, said that not only did half of Himejima and its waters traditionally belong to Tosa but that the Tosa people were using only land either recognized as part of Tosa or the portion of Iyo land that had been rented to Hirose village for over seventy years.[7] It may well have been that the start of the dispute was a truly local conflict: Miura Rokunoshin may have wished to solidify his independence from the declining but traditionally main line of the house controlled by Miura Gengorō in the south. But daimyo interests raised the stakes considerably.

As the conflict was budding locally, the Date heir wrote a polite letter to the Yamauchi heir concerning differences of opinions between the villagers of his realm and those of the Tosa realm: "Although I know it is a bother, would you send a samurai to the border to decide this? If you agree, then I shall send a samurai as well, and things will certainly be resolved."[8] Samurai officials from Uwajima and Tosa domains attempted to negotiate an agreement on their own, but things did not proceed smoothly. Tosa officials sent copies of various older legal documents describing the border, including portions of the Chōsogabe cadastral survey made in the 1590s, and requested the Date to do the same from documents within their purview.[9] The Date were unable to produce any on their side but supported the oral claims of the Mojima village headman. The Yamauchi considered the proof provided by their documents unassailable, and the Date desired a formal recognition of the fishing rights that they effectively held in the sea south of Himejima, because they wished to sustain the local dominance in fishing that Mojima had achieved. The Date

sent outside mediators to the daimyo Yamauchi Tadayoshi, but he convenient-
ly appealed to *omote* values in order to reject Date claims, saying, "The fishing
grounds around Himejima are a small thing, but to decide a provincial boundary informally would be taking lightly the command of my lord [Tokugawa],
who granted me this province."[10]

After years of fruitless negotiation, the Mojima headman Rokunoshin
departed for Edo in early 1656, with the strong support of the Date clan, to
present a suit to the Tokugawa Senior Council.[11] As was required by the law,
Rokunoshin had the Date government affix a seal and note of approval for
him to take the suit to the higher court. He wrote that in 1647 Tosa residents
began asserting ownership of the sea south of a line from their portion of
Okinoshima to the border on Himejima. Furthermore, on Okinoshima itself
Tosa villagers started cutting new roads and making new fields within border-
ing Iyo land in 1653 and were violent to Iyo people using the road. The judges
of the Senior Council heard his arguments and, following normal protocol,
affixed their seals to his suit so that Rokunoshin could summon his nominal
adversary—Gengorō, the village headman of the Tosa portion—to the Edo
court for a preliminary hearing.[12]

By this point, everyone involved, including the Tokugawa court officials,
was aware that the dispute was primarily a conflict between two lords and that
matters of lordly face and honor, although muted by the practice of villager
stand-ins, were considerable. In this instance the Date house and the Yamauchi house expended enormous resources on the effort to win, resources far
in excess of the value of the disputed portions of land and sea, but the lords
thought they were necessary to preserve their honor and reputation.[13]

Naishō arrangements were such an integral part of Tokugawa government
and law that the judges quickly tried to mediate an out-of-court settlement.
This kind of agreement was called *naisai* and, as Ōhira Yūichi's research shows,
was the court's preferred resolution for any economic conflict.[14] The judges
mobilized outside parties with connections of family and friendship to the
Date and the Yamauchi to act as middlemen in arranging such a compromise,
because if an agreement could not be reached, the court was then constrained
to give a judgment with the potential to bring shame and a loss of face to the
judges and the informal daimyo litigants. It is also clear that they regarded being forced to adjudicate a dispute to be a sign of lack of fear or awe among the
litigants for Tokugawa authority and majesty. Forcing litigation was a formal
display of disharmony, a rupturing of the peaceful order the *kubō* was supposed to maintain.

For this reason, parties in a dispute were often at pains to describe to the court their efforts to resolve things informally and with compromise. In this case, Rokunoshin said in his initial presentation to the court that the lord of Uwajima had ordered him to show forbearance by allowing Tosa suddenly to claim half of Himejima island (but not the fishing rights south of the island). For his part, Gengorō began his response by asserting that, at the express direction of the lord of Tosa, he had long attempted to resolve the difficulty through *naishō* negotiations with Uwajima, and he also made the point that it was the Mojima headman who had initiated the court case.[15] This was presented as an accusation, as if the Uwajima side's refusal to proceed with informal negotiations somehow put them in the wrong, and reflected Tosa's understanding that the Tokugawa discouraged formal suits whenever possible. Gengorō also noted that the Yamauchi clan Elders had ordered him at this time to continue to do his best to resolve the dispute by having the Tokugawa court mediate an informal *naishō* resolution, while at the same time he did his best to refute each of Rokunoshin's allegations.[16] Despite court officials' efforts to encourage compromise, neither side would give in, and a year later the Senior Council finally scheduled an official court case for the last month of 1658.

The start of the Sasayama dispute

In the same year that the Okinoshima dispute first reached the Tokugawa court, the conflict between the two domain lords broadened to other parts of the Tosa-Uwajima border. Just before the Tosa lord Tadayoshi retired due to illness in 1656, he sent a letter to the monk Yūei of Sasa Gongen Kanzeonji, a small shrine-temple complex near the peak of Sasayama Mountain, saying that he would rebuild two of the halls. Tadayoshi was an extravagant patron of religious institutions in his realm, but to choose this site right on the border just as the Okinoshima dispute was going to court in Edo must certainly have been a provocative action. Indeed the complex actually straddled the border with Uwajima domain. Perhaps Tadayoshi was surprised, but he was certainly angered when the villagers on the other side of the peak in Uwajima domain sent a message to the priest and to the Tosa villagers that the buildings could not be constructed without first asking their permission. The temple and shrine served Iyo villagers as well and was traditionally managed from both sides of the border. For generations, the headman of Masaki village in Iyo province had served as the Sasa Gongen shrine priest at festival times, and the former monk of the temple lived in retirement in Masaki village on the Iyo side of the peak. Residents of Kusuyama village on the Tosa side were likewise parishioners of the temple, and all of the seventeen villagers with hereditary duty to provide labor for the temple lived on the Tosa side. Parishioner dues and festival sponsorship were collected from people in nearby villages on both sides of the mountain. The religious and economic authority over nearby villages that the temple-shrine complex had long possessed would be put to the test under early modern politics.[17] The current monk, Yūei, who lived in the temple, did his best to mollify both sides by saying that although the temple was within the Tosa boundary, the temple had traditionally been subject to both provinces, but officials of both domains did not want to hear about compromise or mutual interest.[18]

Daimyo understanding of control was different from that of locals who, initially at least, preferred to share the site. When Tadayoshi sent in inspectors to gather information, many Tosa villagers said that one or two corner posts of the shrine were planted in Iyo land. Tadayoshi's chief adviser, the domain Elder Nonaka Kenzan, was placed in charge of managing both border disputes and sent an angry letter to the Tosa officials gathering evidence from the villagers. "What were you thinking when you let them write down such things without investigating?! . . . You had better call the monk and the villagers and tell them again and again that they should never say such senseless things. If any Iyo person ever asks, they should say that the border is from before [just as] written in the cadastral register."[19] In this way, Kenzan directed local villagers into a kind of *naishō* secrecy that instilled and enforced a sense of group membership, thereby transforming their identity to be more focused on Tosa allegiance than on their allegiance to the religious site on the mountain.

Both daimyo in this conflict possessed written records that they could use to back up their respective arguments. Tadayoshi based his claim once again on the Chōsogabe cadastral survey. The religious complex was listed in this 1590 survey, and Yamauchi Katsutoyo had followed Chōsogabe precedent by enfeoffing the Sasa Gongen shrine with some land in the village below and placed it under the management of the Tosa temple Kanzeonji. Kanzeonji was itself a branch temple of Iwami temple in the Tosa town of Nakamura, so Tadayoshi felt it natural to consider this religious site to be part of his realm. For their part the Date had found in the temple building durable older records showing that it had once been considered part of Iyo province. The inscription on the temple bell dating from 1429 and an inscription on an offering bell (*waniguchi*) dating from 1466 both describe the site as being part of Iyo. The discrepancy probably arose when the Chōsogabe daimyo of Tosa conquered that portion of Iyo in 1576. Although Chōsogabe Motochika surrendered Iyo when he was defeated in battle by Toyotomi Hideyoshi in 1585, he remained in control of Tosa, and it is likely that his cadastral survey of 1590 aggressively made the border area part of Tosa. To counter the weakness that their evidence was historically more recent, the Yamauchi asserted that the Chōsogabe survey had been acknowledged by Tokugawa Ieyasu to be the basis of the document of domain production that the Yamauchi submitted when confirmed in their possession of Tosa. Therefore, they argued, this area was legally part of Tosa under Tokugawa rules.[20]

The lords of both sides increasingly engaged local villagers and made them more invested in the outcome, thereby divesting the temple-shrine of its integrity. The immediate Date response to Tadayoshi's offer to rebuild the shrine and temple was to send some samurai along with Iyo parishioners to question the monk and search for evidence in the temple that would support Date claims to ownership. They asked Yūei for tea, and when he returned from the kitchen, he noticed that they had run off with documents from the temple and with the Buddha image itself.[21] Later some samurai came from Iyo to confiscate the two bells with inscriptions, although one was so heavy it had to be left behind. For their part, Tosa officials ordered that no documents be shown to Iyo people. The Yamauchi took a brocade altar cloth given to the temple by Chōsogabe Motochika as evidence of Tosa ownership.

As the temple was gradually emptied of its belongings, the conflicts between commoners on both sides of the mountain escalated. When Tosa assigned some villagers as border guards to prevent access, a large crowd of Iyo villagers came, beat and chased away the guards, and then broke into the locked temple. At this time they also stole some pine torches from the Tosa side of the mountain. The Tosa domain Elder Nonaka Kenzan chastised a samurai who held a large fief there along the border, telling him to organize villagers in response:

> You have asked the domain administrators to send an official to the border, but *you* have been entrusted with a large fief along that border so that you may deal with such situations as this. If we have to send someone in your stead, then you do not belong there! . . . If you had been thinking, "I will disembowel myself if there is any injury to my country on my watch," then this would never have happened! The administrators forwarded on to me your letter to them requesting assistance. I was so disgusted that I tossed it into the fire.[22]

Tosa officials soon sent out a call for support that emptied regional villages for a march on the mountain.[23] One Tosa record happily recounts how the mother of Kunii Yūtaku, who came from the town of Nakamura thirty kilometers distant, led a great crowd to the temple. She was said to have been seven feet tall, and seeing her and the accompanying crowd come up the mountain, the Iyo villagers fled in disarray, yelling, "It's a demon lady, the Great Mother of Tosa!" The Tosa villagers held the site for the day.[24] Sometime during the dispute Tosa people stole clothing and an axe from the Iyo side of the border. Eager to hide the wrongdoing on the part of Tosa people, Nonaka Kenzan ordered them to burn the clothes secretly in a distant valley, hide the axe, and admit to nothing if asked.[25] On another occasion, when a Tosa samurai went to investigate the border, he was attacked by numerous Iyo villagers on top of the hill who fired muskets into the air and tried to take the lance from one of his lackeys. Although he had been warned by senior officials to commit no violence, he brandished his sword to scare everyone away.[26] The violence was increasing, and the scale of disorder involving the mainland border regions was far greater than on the small island of Okinoshima. Tadayoshi was outraged by the violence from Iyo and began sounding out other daimyo about whether he should present a suit to the Senior Council in Edo even as he was orchestrating the defense in the Okinoshima case.[27]

The politics of conflicts in the Tokugawa court

Both daimyo clans made use of their money and their status to mobilize support from powerful allies and relatives at the Edo court. The Date realm had a formal value only half that of the Yamauchi realm, but otherwise Date status in the Tokugawa court was almost equal. Their imperial court rank, Junior Fourth, was the same as the Yamauchi's, and they sat in the same waiting room of the Tokugawa palace, the Ōhiroma. The Yamauchi were known as a province-holding (*kunimochi*) daimyo, but the Date were known as a ranking-with-province-holding (*junkunimochi*) daimyo, of only marginally lesser status. Date Hidemune, who ruled Uwajima until 1657, was the eldest son of Date Masamune, the lord of Sendai realm in the far north of Japan. The son of a concubine and therefore not in line for succession to the Sendai realm, Hidemune was nevertheless a well-connected man who in 1609 had wed a daughter of Ii Naomasa, one of the chief councillors of Tokugawa Ieyasu. The descendants of his father, Masamune, ruled Sendai, the third-largest realm in Japan, assessed at more than three times the productive value of the Yamauchi realm, and the Date were a daimyo clan of much longer lineage with a wide network of relatives. Most importantly, Hidemune and his sons were relatives by marriage to Temple and Shrine Magistrate Inoue Masatoshi and the chief of the Tokugawa Elders, Matsudaira Nobutsuna. Both sat on the Tokugawa Senior Council and lobbied for Date benefit.[28]

The Yamauchi clan were relative upstarts, common samurai first made into daimyo in 1585, but the daimyo Yamauchi Tadayoshi was also well connected. His wife was an adopted daughter (actually a niece) of Tokugawa Ieyasu, and through his wife he was uncle to Sakai Tadakiyo, an important Tokugawa Elder at the time and a politically savvy man who gradually become the most powerful individual in the Tokugawa government during the minority of the child shogun Tokugawa Ietsuna. In 1666 Sakai Tadakiyo became the *tairō*, a position akin to Regent, but at the time of Tosa's border dispute he was still on his way up.[29] Tadayoshi was also brother-in-law to Matsudaira Sadayuki, the lord of Matsuyama domain on Shikoku Island, and Matsudaira Sadafusa, the lord of Imabari domain on Shikoku. Both Sadayuki and Sadafusa were nephews of Ieyasu, and the former was a regional inspector of the Tokugawa government in charge of Shikoku.[30] Both sides mobilized their connections during the case, utilizing reason, family loyalty, and bribery in the pursuit of victory and honor.

As soon as the Iyo village headman first brought the Okinoshima case to court in 1656, the lord of Tosa wrote to his nephew Sakai Tadakiyo. Tadakiyo was not sitting on the case, but he was a Tokugawa Elder and energetically lobbied among the judges for Tosa's benefit. Tadakiyo also invited the Tosa villagers who were to appear at the court to his residence, where he had them trained on what to say and how to behave in court.[31] Tadayoshi also gained aid from the daimyo Ikeda Mitsumasa, who put Tadayoshi informally in contact with one of the judges, Sone Genzaemon, in order to gain his support.[32] The Yamauchi rushed preparations for a trial in 1656, but the case was not quickly brought to official judgment, primarily because Matsudaira Nobutsuna, the most powerful member on the Senior Council, favored his Date relatives and was encouraging an out-of-court settlement. The case was delayed for two years, until Sakai Tadakiyo and another allied daimyo, Kuze Hiroyuki, thought they had persuaded Nobutsuna to desist in his support of the Date. They then allowed the case to be formally presented in person by the litigants in the twelfth month of 1658, a delay that proved fortunate for the Yamauchi.

Tadayoshi had also solicited the advice of his brother-in-law Matsudaira Sadayuki, who advised him to present to the court a copy of the Tosa map that the domain's officials had submitted to the Tokugawa in 1644. To their chagrin, Tosa officials discovered that their copy of this map had no image of Himejima on it. They thought that if they now painted the island on their copy, comparison with the actually submitted map in Edo castle would raise doubt about the validity of all of their documents. They considered borrowing the submitted map to touch it up but decided that this would hurt their case if news leaked out. Finally Sadayuki advised them to add the island to their own copies and assert that somehow they overlooked the island when they prepared the official submitted copy. More hopefully, he said he would try to see to it that such maps would not be used in the case as evidence. This strategy was hardly without problems, and they were still somewhat worried when Tosa learned to its good fortune that the submitted maps were lost in the great Meireki fire that burnt down Edo castle in early 1657.[33] The whole exchange has further irony because back in 1654 the Tosa negotiator had self-righteously stated to the Date that the Yamauchi could not informally give land to Uwajima that had been clearly written on a map submitted to the Tokugawa.[34]

In the meantime back in Okinoshima, secret and unofficial dealings abounded in preparation for the case. The locals were coached by the Tosa officials, often under the detailed direction of the senior Elder of the domain, Nonaka Kenzan. *Naishō* arrangements were used to build a common front among all Tosa parties, and these often were strongly filled with the nuance of keeping true secrecy from Uwajima. In one instance, for example, the Uwajima village headman as part of his case had accused the Tosa villagers of cutting a new road across Uwajima territory. Uwajima requested that each domain send one samurai to the area to inspect the situation. Nonaka Kenzan, who was in Edo, then wrote to a trusted samurai official back home, Tannawa Shirōbei, to proceed beforehand to Okinoshima to inspect the situation:

> And while you are inspecting, you must get everyone to be in agreement. . . . For your part, whatever you say, you must insist on making everyone agree that this is not a new road but rather the widening of a long-used narrow road on Tosa property. Be aware that even if there were some mistakes on the part of Tosa villagers, if they say they were not starting something new and that it is an old road, then things will go well and the traditional border will be maintained. You should not allow expression of even one weak point.[35]

Senior officials in Tosa reiterated these points to Shirōbei, adding, "If people of Iyo province see you inspecting the border, they will certainly start making accusations, so you must view the border in great secrecy."[36] The essence of the meaning of *naishō* can be said to be "private arrangement." Such an arrangement could be a truly open secret that had to be excluded from expression only in ritual *omote* situations, but it also was a notion that in certain situations could facilitate true secrecy. In this case, the Yamauchi saw Uwajima's bringing the border disagreements into the *omote* situation of the Tokugawa Senior Council as ending the relations that might permit informal negotiation locally. Therefore we see examples in documents where the words *naishō* and *nainai* clearly refer to an inside unofficial agreement among Tosa people rather than an informal reaching across to Uwajima. Here the *naishō* served to tighten a consciousness of belonging to Tosa domain by bonding its members in secret agreements.

Naishō agreements also operated in Edo. As the appointed court day approached, the Tosa village headman became ill, and the parties discussed what to do. Tosa officials proposed sending an alternate person in Gengorō's place, but the Uwajima headman said he would not go if Gengorō was not present. So they decided to have Gengorō go, but accompanied by someone else to do the actual speaking due to his illness. Tadayoshi indicated he was rather glad of this, writing from his retirement in Tosa to Nonaka Kenzan in Edo:

> Gengorō's illness is fortunate for us. This man is not articulate and cannot collect and express his thoughts clearly. Let us make your retainer Ichiemon into a commoner, send him along with Jinbei of Okinoshima, and have him read out and present the petition instead of Gengorō, who cannot speak. I have informally discussed this with [the Town Magistrate and one of the judges, Kamio Motokatsu] Bizen no kami, who says this is a very good idea.[37]

The informal prearrangement with one of the judges was quite important because it was illegal for retainers to appear as litigants in such a case. As it turned out, the precaution was necessary and, even with the prearrangement, brought on ill effects. Ichiemon, speaking for Gengorō, submitted many sixteenth-century documents supporting Tosa's claims. The judges then asked Rokunoshin what he could present, and he showed a document recording that an Iyo temple had opened up new land in the disputed territory. Unfortunately, this document also recorded Tosa officials' immediate protest to the action, and a record of the proceedings relates one of the judges as saying, "This is a rather good document for Tosa's side." In response, "Rokunoshin was dumbfounded, and all of the judges laughed that Rokunoshin had presented a document so bad for his case."[38] At this point he made a desperate gambit, bringing his opponent's *naishō* arrangement into *omote* notice. He accused Ichiemon of being a Yamauchi retainer who knew nothing of Okinoshima. This was a grave accusation and, being substantially true, could have been an ugly turn for Tosa if the judges had had a desire to investigate it. Ichiemon rebutted that he had been born on Okinoshima and had lived there until he was twelve or thirteen after which he had left, but that he had later returned to live on the island during the disputes. He accused Rokunoshin of falsely making a grave accusation and, immediately following this, the complicit judge Kamio Moto-katsu reprimanded Rokunoshin for trying to bring in an argument irrelevant to the case at hand.[39] One laugh came at Tosa's expense: Ichiemon argued that an ambiguity in one of the documents was because it was written by "locals such as myself who are like simple monkeys and do not know proper writing." He added, "Why, it is good if they can write so much as the phrase '300 coppers.'" At this, Matsudaira Nobutsuna dryly replied, echoing Rokunoshin's accusation, "I've seen no monkeys as canny as you. Shikoku monkeys must be clever." The evidence seemed to clearly support the Tosa case, but the decision for the judges was not so simple, because they were split into factions.

The trial stretched out over months of occasional meetings, and the allegiances of the judges gradually hardened. Decorum vanished briefly on a number of occasions as *naishō* statements erupted into the formal proceeding of the trial and had to be contained. The Date faction was made up of the three Tokugawa Elders and the senior of the Temple and Shrine Magistrates, the Date relative Inoue Masatoshi. These four men had the highest status within the Council. At one meeting this faction, with the vocal lead of Inoue Masatoshi, was intent on deciding that the Tosa village of Hirose should return its rental rights on Iyo land and associated fishing grounds in the offing, an act that would have destroyed its economic viability. Although he was not a member of the sitting judges, Sakai Tadakiyo was a Tokugawa Elder constantly in touch with the deliberations, and he came down on them strongly, saying that the recommendation would fly in the face of the Tokugawa custom of respecting the traditions of local agreements.[40] Finally, the council called the litigants back in the third month of 1659. Gengorō again pleaded sickness and asked Ichiemon to go in his stead, to which Rokunoshin replied that he too was sick but could perhaps just make it to court if Gengorō went. As it turned out, neither showed up that day, and Ichiemon, who appeared, had to explain the situation. Some of the judges laughed that perhaps Rokunoshin hated his opponent, to which Matsudaira Nobutsuna pointedly added, "He does not want to present his case when his opponent is a retainer."[41] Ichiemon once again protested that he was indeed a commoner from Okinoshima and would later present documents attesting to this, at which Kamio Motokatsu declared his certainty that Ichiemon was a native of the island. Both litigants finally appeared on the twenty-first, but Gengorō protested in writing that he was unable to speak and that Ichiemon would present. Rokunoshin again protested that Ichiemon was a retainer and did not know the border on the island. Ichiemon denied being a retainer, offered that he should be executed if investigation proved otherwise, and demanded that Rokunoshin offer documents in proof.[42]

This was a daring move. Matsudaira Nobutsuna would not have offered his comment without strong suspicion or even clear knowledge that his accusation was valid.[43] Ichiemon's life and Tosa's defense on this point depended on no records leaking out of the Yamauchi household and ultimately on the complicity of the villagers of Okinoshima. Here, in such moments of open contest, is where *naishō,* as an informal agreement within a group, encouraged true secrecy from the outside, not only by making a common story for presentation to the outside but through its role in the promotion of group identity and loyalty. Furthermore, that Kamio Motokatsu had informally approved the use of Ichiemon meant that he would repeatedly try to suppress the accusation in council. On this occasion the council again decided that if such an accusation was formally made, then it would be treated later as a separate case, effectively discouraging the option. Such a case would have to involve the Yamauchi clan directly in a formal *omote* fashion, and this was something potentially so disruptive that few could abide the possibility.

Rokunoshin's tactic of calling attention to an incompletely arranged *naishō* reality was paying off indirectly by allowing the Uwajima allies to keep the tenor of the council from moving strongly to Tosa's side despite the strength of its written evidence for the case. On this day the litigants were told to wait out by the gate while the council continued to discuss matters. After a while the council called Ichiemon back in and declared to him that as the case was about provincial boundaries, only documents produced by provincial rulers would be accepted, and village-produced documents would not be entertained. This was a severe blow to Tosa, because although the Chōsogabe survey would be used and would confirm Tosa's notion of the land border, the key issues such as the sea boundary, fishing rights, and rental rights could not be evidenced without the village documents—all of which supported Tosa's case. Ichiemon repeatedly objected that the documents were all in accord with the Chōsogabe survey and that they reflected seventy years of local custom, but the Elder Matsudaira (Abe) Tadaaki reprimanded Ichiemon for being too assertive for a man of his status and told him be silent and leave. The vocal senior members of the council urged that the judgment should make no reference to the issue of the rental land, effectively taking Uwajima's side.[44] The threat of losing the rental would have given the

Date tremendous bargaining power with Tosa over exclusive rights to the Himejima fishing grounds.

With three Elders on their side in the court, the Date were gaining the upper hand. At this point Finance Magistrate Itami Katsunaga said that the issue should be presented to the *kubō* himself because for years local documents had been accepted in such cases, and to suddenly and innovatively declare that they would not be used here would set a precedent affecting all later cases. He also pointed out that the previous *kubō*, Tokugawa Iemitsu, had declared that any arrangements of control that had stood for more than twenty years would stand, and in this case Hirose village had controlled the rented land for seventy years. The power of Katsunaga's statement here was the threat to bring the issue to a higher *omote,* a higher level of formal relations governed by rituals and precedents, which could negate all of the informal agreements made among the council members. Three others of the nine-member council supported him, but Matsudaira Nobutsuna replied that the twenty-year rule had been applied according to the specific conditions and that even documents under Ieyasu's own seal had been revoked in the past. At this point the four members of the council supporting Tosa went to a back room to discuss issues and were soon accompanied by a fifth member, the Temple and Shrine Magistrate Itakura Shigesato, who from that point became an ally. The senior Temple and Shrine Magistrate Inoue Masatoshi then came into that room and vaguely threatened Itami Katsunaga, telling him that it was not his duty to talk so much. As one of the Finance Magistrates and a mere bannerman, he was perhaps the lowest-status member of the council. But Itami replied gamely that he was going to uphold his oath to the *kubō,* which was to speak his mind and not give in to factionalism, and that Inoue, a daimyo of middling income, was not of such consequence (*bun*) that he could stop him.[45]

At the end of the troubling day, Nonaka Kenzan, who had been orchestrating the Tosa defense behind the scenes, went to Kuze Hiroyuki, a man in charge of the current young *kubō*'s education and a Tosa ally, to learn of the inner workings of the case. Kuze, a domainal neighbor and a relative of Matsudaira Nobutsuna, thought that Nobutsuna had been persuaded to hold back on this case, but now Kuze felt tricked by him. Kenzan then visited three other related parties and was put off by one who said (without irony, it seems, although he was the only one) that there was a rule that cases in progress were not to be talked about. Even Tosa's strongest ally, Sakai Tadakiyo, said, "This case is extremely unpleasant, viewed both at its surface and from what I hear from insider discussion."[46] He noted that things looked bad and that he could not control the decisions of the Elders on the council. The only hopeful news

Kenzan received was from Itami Katsunaga, who said he would not stop raising his objections, out of duty to his oath of office in which he had sworn to speak his mind.

Sakai Tadakiyo was disturbed by Nobutsuna's attempts to negate two important precedents of Tokugawa law, but because he was not on the council and the three Elders on the council were in support of the Date, he suggested to Kenzan that perhaps the best strategy would be to delay the court's decision for three to five years and wait for the kubō, who was still only seventeen years of age and under tutelage, to reach majority and decide the case himself. Kenzan then approached one of the Grand Inspectors not at the court case, Hōjō Masafusa, and discussed the issue. Masafusa recommended that discussion of the case be held in Edo castle. This was in effect recommending bringing the discussions of the Senior Council into the omote of the kubō's space, the only location where Senior Council deliberations could be viewed as less authoritative, and would allow high officials not on the council but in charge of the young kubō's upbringing, such as Hōjō Masafusa, Kuze Hiroyuki, Sakai Tadayoshi, and Sakai Tadakiyo, a pretext to be present and bring their weight to bear. The location would likely constrain the council to deliberate according to the omote rules of the kubō, and in this regard Tokugawa Iemitsu's declaration on twenty-year precedents would clearly work in Tosa's favor. Kenzan urged this route to Sakai Tadakiyo, whose worries over the breaking of precedent during the minority of a kubō led him to agree and take a forceful line.[47] From this point they began spreading gossip in the castle about the case, highlighting that two important precedents might be done away with.

This had its intended effect, and catching the mood on the day before the meeting was to be held in the castle, Inoue Masatoshi called Nonaka Kenzan to his residence along with the two litigants to explain yet again their sides of the case. His manner seemed to be searching out a compromise.[48] On the day of the castle meeting, Matsudaira Nobutsuna queried the appropriateness of Sakai Tadakiyo's becoming involved, saying that Tadakiyo was not acquainted with the case and suggesting that he was unfairly trying to influence a case for the benefit of his Yamauchi friends. Tadakiyo responded that his concern was the breaking of precedents during the kubō's minority, which forced him to call this unconventional meeting. At this point, both sides started making threats on the villagers, as quoted in the epigraph of this chapter.[49] As the villagers' lives were being bandied about by coalitions of daimyo and government officials intent on victory, it seemed that compromise among even the judges would be impossible. In the end, the force of the location held sway, and the group agreed that they would respect local documents and Iemitsu's ruling that local arrangements of more than twenty years' standing would have legal force. This was a crucial victory for Tosa's side.

The next day, the Temple Magistrate Inoue Masatoshi was present at the Senior Council, but none of the Tokugawa Elders showed up nor did the Grand Inspector, thus leaving Inoue alone to take Uwajima's side. It was an irregular meeting time, so no final decision could be reached, but Inoue held out strongly on all of the details and took advantage of possible ambiguities in the documents to press Uwajima claims to the sea border and lessen the size of the rented land. The other parties lamented Inoue for being a "malevolent person" who, they said without ironic intent, engaged in favoritism and was supporting the Date only because they were cousins.[50]

The case carried over to a meeting in the subsequent fifth month, where Rokunoshin, aware of impending loss on the issue of Hirose's rental rights, emphasized that Mojima needed to have its traditional fishing rights to the south of Himejima island respected. He also again brought up his claim that Ichiemon was a retainer, but the members of the council rebuffed him by declaring that they would hear nothing of it. Ichiemon said that if such claims were made against him, then he would accuse Rokunoshin of being a retainer, for Rokunoshin publicly displayed all of the attributes of samurai status in Edo. He showed up at the courthouse gate riding a horse, had his things carried by a military manservant, and arrived in the company of direct retainers of the Date lord.[51] However, the councillors roundly scolded Ichiemon for raising this issue and told him to leave. It is quite clear that the council wished to preserve as much as possible the *omote* appearance that this was a case between commoners. Following further days of discussions, Matsudaira Nobutsuna announced to the litigants that a final decision would be handed down within a week.

The council debates continued intensely for a week, with Inoue and the Elders taking Uwajima's part wherever they could, pressing for Uwajima's exclusive use of the sea south of Himejima island, and defining the smallest possible size of the Tosa rented land. Sakai Tadakiyo, who had somehow made himself present at these discussions, argued strongly against this, first saying that the Yamauchi lord would "lose face" by such a decision, but when pressed on his possible favoritism, he argued that the rented border had been decided between the rulers earlier and to overturn that now would set a bad precedent, allowing the reappearance in court of numerous other cases. Sakai then stated that if the other Elders thought that favoritism was involved, it would be better to delay the judgment for five or ten years until the *kubō* could personally judge the case.[52] The Elders replied that they were now formally committed to delivering a judgment in a week and that not to do so would mean a loss of face for them. Sakai responded that because they continued to disagree, the only choice was to call a large meeting of all high officials in the castle to whom they would present their arguments. They agreed, but one of the Elders, Inaba Masanori, delivered a parting shot. Noting that Sakai Tadakiyo had been visited numerous times by Tosa's representative Nonaka Kenzan and that he had heard that Ichiemon was a Tosa retainer, he asserted that some serious crimes were being committed in the conduct of the case. Sakai denied the accusations, and all left the meeting.

Sakai Tadakiyo called Nonaka Kenzan to his residence to explain the current configuration and told him to relate to the new Tosa lord, Tadatoyo, which officials were already clearly on Tosa's side and who yet needed urgent requests for support. It is likely that these requests involved presents as well. Tadatoyo was not deeply invested in the case but was devoted to obeying the wishes of his retired father, Tadayoshi, and almost certainly carried out all "urgent requests." Nevertheless he lamented elsewhere to one of his officials the effect on domain finances, writing, "In recent years we have used extraordinary amounts of gold and silver. Due to the conflicts over Okinoshima and Sasayama, the amount of gifts to the officials involved is enormous."[53] That evening Inoue Masatoshi once again called the Tosa litigants to his residence for further questioning, perhaps hoping, fruitlessly as it turned out, to find signals that Tosa would be willing to compromise on a point or two. He then demanded that their documents be left with him so that he might inspect them further. Kenzan interpreted this as Inoue being ordered by Matsudaira Nobutsuna to find at least some problem that could be turned to Uwajima's advantage.

The next day, the various officials met at the castle. The Tosa allies spoke as expected and very strongly, so that the three Elders and Inoue found themselves pitted against the others present, including two Temple and Shrine Magistrates, one Town Magistrate, the two Finance Ministers, a Grand Inspector, and of course Sakai Tadakiyo. Accusations again grew heated, with both sides calling for the jailing or crucifixion of the other party's commoner litigants, and gradually each side began blaming each other for abusing their roles as officials to support one side of the case. Inoue was called to task for privately interviewing the litigants, and Nobutsuna accused the other side of the crime of leaking the deliberations of the Senior Council to outsiders, to which Sakai coolly responded that more than a hundred police, scribes, and monks were present at the case and that leaks in such a situation were to be expected.[54] The rules of decorum had to a large degree broken down, but the threats were so serious that they could not realistically be carried out, for, with the *kubō* in his minority, the room was filled with the most powerful men of the realm. To whom could these accusations be reported?

Finally, the Elders and Inoue were forced to accept a Tosa victory, and the officials dispersed. On the day of judgment the Supreme Council gathered to announce its decision to the litigants. Even at this point Inoue Masatoshi apparently tried to present a map with lines and names drawn favoring the Uwajima side, but the other officials noticed the issues and objected. Because of this, and to be sure of the final result, Nonaka later opened up an informal route of communication with the chief secretary recording the case and with the map artist, giving them money and gifts to make sure that they secretly communicated drafts to him and arranged things for Tosa's benefit.[55] The council then presented the village headmen with the judgment favoring Tosa and ordered the headmen to confirm the agreement on location by touring the island together. Even here at the denouement, the not-so-hidden hand of the domains was present, for Nonaka Kenzan himself accompanied their tour of confirmation "secretly" the whole time.[56] As with the case noted in Chapter 2 concerning Haramiishi and the Touring Inspectors, the "secrecy" was more likely a matter of a lack of formal awareness rather than hiding behind trees and in waters. The Tosa rulers had won the day, and they wanted to make sure that their understanding of the resolution was enforced.

It is worth noting that Tadayoshi's first response to victory was to order gifts sent to Sakai Tadakiyo and Kuze Hiroyuki, both of whom had provided assistance "that should not be forgotten for many lives and many generations," and gifts to another daimyo who "I hear had spoken in our favor."[57] At the same time he blamed the "corruption" of Matsudaira Nobutsuna and Inoue Masatoshi, who had championed Uwajima's claims.[58] This may appear hypocritical, but he believed in the correctness of Tosa's case and thought the Uwajima arguments untenable. The practices of gift giving and making fullest use of relatives were prohibited by Tokugawa *omote* rules but were so widespread a part of informal negotiation that he probably considered them to be normal and unproblematic as long as they were carried out with sufficient discretion. The support of Sakai and others was not corruption in Tadayoshi's view, because it was in the service of what appeared to him to be reason.

Before the Okinoshima dispute was even settled, Tadayoshi informally presented a document pressing his claims regarding the Sasayama dispute to two Tokugawa officials, Temple and Shrine Magistrate Matsudaira Katsutaka and Town Magistrate Kamio Motokatsu. He detailed all of the crimes of Iyo villagers and samurai against Tosa and the shrine-temple and announced his desire to formally pursue the case.[59] Their response reveals not only the importance of connections but also how deeply the maintenance of formal harmony by saving face as much as possible was part of the legal system. There was no way he could win both cases, they told him. It only stood to reason, they said, that if he won one, he would have to lose the other, as no daimyo could stand for being beaten twice, nor could the senior officials such as Inoue Masatoshi and Matsudaira Nobutsuna be expected to take another defeat. They told Tadayoshi that at any rate direct daimyo suits against another were prohibited, and urged him to accept an out-of-court agreement with mediation.[60] Various daimyo tried unsuccessfully to mediate the dispute, and both sides considered the merits and demerits of opening a formal case. The Yamauchi hoped that if a suit concerning the border had to occur, it would be initiated by their opponents, on the reasoning that the Date had already initiated one suit with the Okinoshima dispute and that "to raise two suits would be showing no fear of, and therefore a prime insult to, the Tokugawa government."[61] This is indeed what happened, and in late 1658 three commoners of Uwajima realm presented a suit concerning Sasayama to one of the Tokugawa Temple Magistrates, arguing that it was part of Iyo and that Tosa was trying to take it away.[62] The already exhausted members of the Senior Council discouraged the Date from attempting to bring this to a formal judgment and told them that to continue working for an out-of-court arrangement would be best.

Despite this pressure, a settlement could not be reached, and in the fourth month of 1659 the Temple and Shrine Magistrates formally took up the case and required the village headman of the Tosa side to appear in court. This timing was only a month before the final judgment was handed down on the Okinoshima case. It is possible that the senior Temple Magistrate Inoue Masatoshi understood that the Okinoshima case was going to be a loss and that therefore he could at least gain advantage for the Date in the Sasayama case. The Yamauchi had already begun preparing the headmen and had them travel to Edo to prepare a countersuit. They were even sent to Sakai Tadakiyo's residence to receive counsel.[63] Tadakiyo's heart was not in it this time, however, and he judged that, regardless of the merits of the case, which once again he thought looked to favor Tosa, Matsudaira Nobutsuna and Inoue Masatoshi would surely see to it that Tosa would lose. Tadakiyo told Tadayoshi that he would be unable to intervene a second time and urged an out-of-court settlement.[64] We do not have documents relating the informal negotiations on the Date side of the case, but their choice to allow another suit must have been a mistake, because various daimyo pressed more strongly for them also to accept an out-of-court settlement.[65] Tadayoshi's right-hand man, Nonaka

Kenzan, was fed up with the court process and encouraged the retired lord and the current daimyo Tadatoyo to compromise. In the sixth month of 1659, just after the Okinoshima case had been decided but before the Sasayama case had been settled, he wrote,

> I now clearly see that cases in the government's courts are all about favoritism and influence. There cannot be someone in the whole realm so stupid as to choose to go to court after seeing this case. . . . I have decided that the clan should not engage in another court case. Even though in arguing this point I must disobey my lord's will and give up my fief, it would be for the benefit of the [Yamauchi] clan . . . and would be the right way of serving the lord and fulfilling my duties as administrator.[66]

Furthermore, Tadayoshi had worries about the money needed for success, writing that, because of bruised feelings in the Okinoshima case, victory in the Sasayama case "won't happen without using an extraordinary amount of money."[67] Tadayoshi felt wronged by the Date on the Sasayama issue but justified compromise by accepting Sakai Tadakiyo's argument that his own highest duty to the Tokugawa *kubō* was to accept an informal settlement.[68] He wrote to one of the negotiators that he would agree to whatever they could arrange. Finally, in the eighth month of 1659 the Date and the Yamauchi signed an out-of-court settlement brokered by two daimyo friendly to both parties and approved by the Temple Magistrate. It acknowledged that the religious site was important to both domains and that they should cooperate equally in its rebuilding. The border was decided by an "exchange" of small parcels of land. Furthermore, in a flip of tradition, the monk would henceforth be appointed by Uwajima and the shrine priest by Tosa. This meant that losers in the case included the village headman on the Uwajima side, whose family had traditionally served as shrine priests, and the monk on top of the mountain, who suddenly found himself without a job. The former was assuaged by a promise that his family would be recognized as "first parishioner" of the shrine, and the latter was given a living stipend by the lord of Tosa and, after a few years of relative penury, finally found a place as the priest of another small temple in Tosa.[69]

The struggle thus left the Tokugawa courts in the preferred fashion of a brokered agreement, but the local tension continued throughout the Edo period. The arrangement decreed that the rebuilding would be financed equally by both parties. Debates over which side should be responsible for which portions were resolved by drawing lots on items within and for portions of all seven buildings that made up the shrine and temple complex, yet neither side was allowed to put a daimyo family crest on the architecture and both sides had to put the names of both lords on the construction plaque. This became an issue in 1721 when some Uwajima repairs to the Sasa Gongen Shrine suddenly included the Date family crest. Tosa village officials immediately reported this to the senior administrators of Tosa domain, who initiated negotiations with the Date to have the crest removed. When the building was rebuilt yet again in 1767, the building plaque was inscribed with only the Date name, which the local Tosa villagers immediately reported to Yamauchi officials.[70] Apparent in these subsequent struggles was the transformation of the allegiances of local villagers away from the religious complex as a single entity and toward their lords and domainal countries.

The Okinoshima and Sasayama cases happened relatively early in the consolidation of the conciliar government that developed in the time of the minority of Tokugawa Ietsuna. They reveal the extreme ambitions of daimyo to extend their territory by even minuscule amounts, and the potentially serious disruptive nature of these conflicts locally and among factions in Edo. *Omote* rules tamed behavior in an angry environment and could be manipulated as convenient tools of negotiation. Most importantly, the *omote* rule that daimyo not directly engage each other in litigation over territory made them operate through the management of surrogates and distanced them—if only just barely—from the dishonor of defeat in the *omote* world. Yet informal agreements were the heart of the whole process, tottering along what the participants saw as the boundary between righteous practicality and corruption.

Moving a shrine or not

A seventeenth-century border dispute between two villages inside Tahara domain demonstrates how villagers used the politics of *omote* and *naishō* against their own daimyo, Miyake Yasukatsu. These politics allowed villagers to use the threat of upsetting *hōken* forms of containment as leverage when daimyo were not supportive of their aims. The dispute began innocuously enough in 1668 when Akabane village requested permission to move its guardian deity (*ujigami*) to a shrine it wished to build on an island in a marshy lake in the Hiruwayama district. This district at the north edge of the village bordered the village of Noda. The Miyake magistrates approved the plan, but the surveyors they sent to measure out the location for the shrine were confronted by a great crowd of villagers from Noda, who demanded that the shrine not be built, because the land was theirs. After preliminary investigation determined that this area was a borderland to which both Noda and Akabane had claims, the domain relented and accepted a Noda suit forbidding construction of the shrine. The Noda villagers knew that in recent years Akabane villagers had started to develop farmland in this area, and rightly saw the creation of a guardian deity shrine as an important step in claiming that land.[71]

Noda villagers called this area Hiruwayama, but Akabane called it Ryūgahara or in later years occasionally Hiruwahara, and the essence of the conflict can be summed up in the difference between the endings *yama* and *hara*. *Yama* means mountain, and *hara* means undeveloped field. The area contained a bit of both in the geographical sense, but the two words each indicated that the area had certain kinds of economic uses, which were different. Noda called the undeveloped land *yama* because the underbrush was an important source of fertilizer and the woods were a source of pine branches and needles. Not only were these essential for sustaining the local farming and household economy, but the pine products were also an important source of outside income for the village. In 1683, for example, Noda village reported to the domain earnings of sixty-three *ryō* from sales of pine branches, giving up half of this as tax. It is likely that much went unreported and that this substantial sum represented merely a minimum amount for the real cash income earned from the area. Akabane was a village that mixed fishing and farming. Its fleet of fishing boats was the largest in the domain, but its developed farmland was half that of Noda's. In recent years fishing catches had dropped severely, and the villagers were putting energy into developing dry and wet fields in the lowlands and at the mountain edge of the Ryūgahara/Hiruwayama area. In the process they cut down brush and increased their own need for fertilizer, putting them at odds with Noda. For their part the cash-strapped Miyake were promoting land development wherever they could in order to increase production and taxes, so their instinct was to support Akabane. Noda made this difficult by its appeal to precedent: it had held foraging rights from the early seventeenth century, when the area was designated hunting ground for the Tokugawa. However, Noda harmed its own case when its leaders were punished for attempting to hide a precedent that Akabane village also had limited rights to forage in Hiruwayama and helped pay costs for maintaining a mountain guard.

Although Noda was able to prevent the shrine from being built in 1668, it was unable to stop Akabane's foraging and incremental land development. Domain officials refused to take up suits from Noda on these two points. So, early in 1673, two village headmen from Noda and seven villagers had their village temple issue them travel passes to go on a pilgrimage and travel through highway checkpoints unmolested.[72] In the guise of pilgrims, they traveled to Edo, intending to present a petition to the domain lord asking that new land development in the Hiruwayama area by Akabane villagers be stopped. Domain officials in Edo refused to accept the petition, because the villagers had not been issued a license from the domain to travel to Edo. They ordered the villagers to go back to the domain and engage in petitioning there. In this instance they were using an *omote* rule—villagers needed domain approval to travel outside—in order to refuse a petition that they really did not want to see. Unlike a modern court system, where a technicality can be the real reason for refusing a case, here it was used clearly to discourage Noda's dissent. The Noda villagers refused to return to the domain and demanded that the daimyo call representatives from Akabane and adjudicate the dispute. The Miyake clan instead called its own rural intendants up from the domain and had them face off against the Noda villagers. Unsurprisingly, the villagers lost, but they continued to press for a suit against Akabane village. The domain would not relent, and at this point the villagers made use of an illegal but unofficially tolerated action: they made a direct appeal to Tokugawa officials.

This action involved the crime of appealing over the head of one's superior, called *osso*. With a few exceptions, *osso* was clearly defined as illegal in *omote* rules. Ideally, the structure of legal petitioning followed the structure of the *hōken* politics of containment, and formal suit procedure required the plaintiff to have a seal of approval from his immediate superior in order to carry a suit to the next higher level. A common villager would have to get his village headman to approve and place his seal on a suit before being able to take it to the regional intendant. The regional intendant would have to place his seal on a suit before it could be brought to the daimyo court—or if the villager lived in Tokugawa land, the Tokugawa court. For villagers living in daimyo realms, the daimyo would have to approve any suit that would be brought to the Tokugawa—such as we have seen in the cases described above. Because all rulers, intendants, and headmen exercised both judicial and administrative authority, this system clearly made it difficult for people to appeal judgments handed down by their superiors.[73] This system thereby strengthened the authority of political heads in the feudal hierarchy, encouraged the containment of authority within discrete units, and was a major source of oppression of commoners.

However, such a system could not truly function politically because it invited—indeed necessitated—disturbances and protests, which were in themselves signs of weakness in the Great Peace. Protests were problematic because the validity of a superior's authority depended upon his displaying effective control over his assigned territory. From the vantage point of his superior, a subordinate's maintenance of peace and control over his territory was the firmest sign of the right to rule. Leaders were vulnerable to protests and attempted to suppress them through the power of their august authority (*ikō*), essentially the fear they inspired, and through earning devotion by appearing to act out of benevolence and fairness.[74] The maintenance of august authority depended ultimately on government and status system violence, but while the threat of violence loomed large in the legal system, the exercise of it was not uniform. Instead the governments frequently took the opportunity to display "benevolence" by handing out lighter punishments than the crime formally demanded.[75] Appeals over the head of a superior that were at most times and places technically illegal were nevertheless widely practiced and informally permitted in ways that adhered to the goal of suppressing and containing disturbance.

With regard to Tokugawa officials, these over-the-head appeals generally came in two forms. One was for villagers to run up to the palanquin of a senior official as he was entering Edo castle and, by forcing the appeal onto his person, succeed in getting him to accept it. Ōhira Yūichi's research reveals that this kind of suit was so common that the Edo lodging houses, which specialized in serving people presenting suits, had handbooks of advice for lodgers that included sections on how to conduct such palanquin suits. They informed potential plaintiffs of specific details of the standard protocol and gave helpful advice, such as this example: "Dress up in traveling clothes to make it look as if you are presenting the suit just as you arrived in town. This will leave the impression that you are not accustomed to petitioning."[76] For their part, high government officials also had directions on how to handle palanquin suits. One handbook for Tokugawa Elders of the 1790s instructs an accompanying retainer to receive the petition and hand it into the Elder in the palanquin, who would give it a quick read. The Elder would then decide whether (in a hierarchy of declining importance) to hold the suit himself in order to peruse it more carefully before deciding what to do; have the retainer seal the suit and take it to the Elders' meeting room in the castle to be dealt with; or have the retainer take the suit back to the Elder's residence so that one of his officials would write a summary and opinion and have it delivered to the Elder. In all cases the retainer would bind up the petitioner in rope for his crime and lead him to the Elder's residence to await preliminary judgment. From there the petitioner would likely be sent to his lord's residence along with a brief directive concerning how to treat the suit, or sometimes the petitioners were just released with directions on what to do next, such as a warning to desist under threat of punishment. The protocol was similar for the other common kind of illegal suit, the *kakekomiso,* or "barging-in suits." These began when villagers barged into the residential compound of a high Tokugawa official to present a suit. The character of the response in both cases was similar. The petitioner was treated as a criminal insofar as he was bound up and restrained for a period of time, but the petition itself might well be taken up, and the petitioner was not necessarily punished further.

With an understanding of this context, the nine Noda villagers engaged in over-the-head suits against the judgment of their domain lord. Strangely enough, they first asked the domain officials for permission to do so, perhaps as a last-minute gambit signaling that they were allowing their daimyo to save face. The domain refused, and villagers submitted a barging-in suit at the residence of the Temple and Shrine Magistrate at the beginning of the fourth month of 1673. The domain began informal negotiations with the Tokugawa officials, quickly contacting Sugiura Masatsuna, a bannerman with whom they were friendly and who was a high Tokugawa official dealing with village matters. Domain officials also reacted with punishments. By the end of the month, they had put the wives and children of the petitioners, more than forty people, in prison back in the domain. Persistence was necessary for victory, and the Noda village officials strove to make their lord lose face. They immediately responded with a series of palanquin suits to the Temple and Shrine Magistrates, again asking for the trial with Akabane villagers that their lord would not grant them.

The three Temple and Shrine Magistrates had an informal meeting (*uchi yoriai*) and decided not to accept the suit. They sent the villagers back to the domain residence, accompanied by an official messenger and a note instructing the Miyake clan to take up the Noda suit again back in the domain. Clearly hoping that the domain officials could figure out a way to keep the peace, the Magistrates were likely taken aback by the Miyake officials' subsequent militance and ineptitude. Domain officials immediately imprisoned the Noda villagers and quickly passed judgment that they should be executed. It is evident that the Tokugawa officials had not washed their hands of the matter but were hoping to influence Tahara officials to resolve the problem in a way that retained decorum, because the Temple and Shrine Magistrate Ogasawara Nagayori, who was remaining in contact, sent an unofficial message: "These farmers are not of the kind who should be executed. We think you should carefully review that decision." The Miyake certainly had the *omote* legal authority to execute the villagers. The crime of rebellion had a sentence of death, but in the interests of maintaining the peace, this was not to be. Meanwhile, villagers back in Tahara learned of the imprisonment of their representatives, and more than ninety villagers rushed to Edo in the guise of pilgrims to deliver a palanquin suit to one of the Tokugawa Elders.[77]

This threat to continue to disrupt the peace was effective. The Tokugawa Elders soon accepted the case and ordered the village representatives to appear at the high court. The consequent possibility of acquiring a bad reputation frightened the Miyake enough that they forgave and released the villagers whom they had put in prison, and they offered to allow a domain doctor to mediate the dispute. The Noda villagers assented and canceled their appearance in the Tokugawa court, in a display of their willingness to compromise. However, the mediation talks quickly fell through, and early in the sixth month Noda villagers carried out another palanquin suit. The Tokugawa Elders conducted a hearing two days later but told the villagers, "We will instruct the lord to deal with this in ways that resolve the problem, so return to your home province." Yet again we see the Tokugawa government attempting to return the villagers to the management of the domain lord, along with giving informal advice to the lord on how to handle it. This recurring tension between shoring up the lord's authority and intrusively directing him was mediated by the Tokugawa government interest in keeping the peace. It is likely in this interest that they accepted illegal suits from villagers regularly and for the most part did not punish them severely. In this case the astounding number of ninety villagers showing up to present a suit also broke the law against "forming bands for political activity," a crime that invited capital punishment, but the Tokugawa officials also ignored this.

The villagers returned to Tahara domain and held a meeting at which village unity was reaffirmed, and all signed a document stating that, no matter what the cost or the punishment, they would struggle until the village succeeded. Soon after this, domain officials passed down a judgment: Noda had rights to the mountain and foraging, and Akabane had rights to continue field development. This was a defeat for Noda, but when the seven village leaders protested the judgment, the domain directly confiscated their homes and property and banished them and their families from the domain and Edo.[78] Rebuffed but not defeated, five hundred Noda villagers gathered at the village Hachiman shrine to pray for victory and decide on a plan. Thereupon fifty of them again traveled to Edo, departing by boat to avoid domain forces, and opened up a campaign of illegal petitioning. They again requested that the Senior Council take up Noda village's petition against Akabane village. Formally this was not a suit against their domain lord, which would have been unthinkable in *omote* activity, but the reality was clear to everyone. In terms of keeping the peace, the Miyake had misjudged the case, because the Noda villagers were not going to back down. The senior Tokugawa officials tried to back up the Miyake and repeatedly refused to take up the case, calling the villagers, "despicable people who do not obey their lord!" and they had the guards chase the villagers away. But over the next three months the villagers initiated thirty-two palanquin suits and twenty-two barging-in suits, sometimes as many as six a day and targeting all three of the Tokugawa Elders and all three of the Shrine and Temple Magistrates.

They were threatened with punishments for the crimes of forming political groups, disobeying one's lord, and bringing palanquin and barging-in suits, but the threats were not carried out. The villagers wrote, "You can throw eighty of us in prison, or you can crucify each one of us at the Shinagawa execution grounds," but they would not relent without a trial against Akabane in the Tokugawa high court. Tokugawa officials finally yielded and agreed to adjudicate a court case early the following year in 1674. The Temple Magistrate Ogasawara Nagayori tried one last maneuver to give advantage to the Miyake. He ordered the villagers to come to a brief trial between the villagers and their lord first, before Noda village would face the Akabane villagers. The Noda villagers refused, rightly seeing that this would put them in jeopardy of resisting their lord in the courtroom itself, and said that their only opponent in this case was Akabane village. However, the Tokugawa Elders interpreted this refusal as insubordination against themselves, so they again refused to take up the case, but further palanquin suits finally achieved Noda's desire. In the second month of 1674 each village sent representatives laden with documents as evidence for the rightness of their claims. The case spread over four sessions, and finally in the fourth month the Senior Council handed down a judgment that largely supported Noda village. Noda had exclusive control of foraging rights in the mountain and the wild field area, and no new field development would be allowed, although Akabane could keep the fields that it had developed up to this point. Because the dispute took place wholly within Miyake territory, the judgment used the curious expression "the territory head [*jitō*] orders" this and that, rather than "the Tokugawa government orders," still trying to keep a seemly image of the daimyo's full authority over his fief. To further emphasize the lord's authority, the judgment also said that of the seven new leaders, six were to be banished for the crime of disobeying their lord and one was to be handed over to the daimyo. Eventually that one man was executed and his head displayed back in the domain.

Thus, at a monetary cost of over 600 *ryō* for expenses, the tragedy of the banishment of thirteen leading members of the village and their associated families, and the execution of one of their members, Noda village won its suit. At every step of the way greater power was in the hands of the samurai government, but the Noda villagers were not powerless against their domain lord. They could hold the lord hostage to the ideology of lordly competence, because the Tokugawa officials systematically informally accepted and processed suits that were not tolerated in *omote* legal discourse. By manipulating the politics of *omote* and *naishō* and possessing a willingness for substantial self-sacrifice, the Noda villagers were able to defeat the intentions of their domain lord and protect the long-term interests of the village. In the end the Noda villagers paid a heavy price, but they continued a local degree of "inside" autonomy. It was illegal to bury someone after such an execution, an act that was supposed to cut the criminal's spirit off from prayers and divine assistance, but the united villagers of Noda set up a memorial stone declaring him the Buddha Shaka Dōnen, with the assistance of the village priest who had helped them on their "pilgrimage" at the beginning of the conflict with their daimyo. They had shamed their lord who was under threat for a while of disenfeoffment for his mismanagement of the case. Only the support of one of the Shrine and Temple Magistrates who happened to be the previous ruler of Tahara domain, Toda Tadamasa, prevented the Miyake from punishment. Toda argued that because the Miyake clan had a distinguished lineage that went back to the famous medieval warrior Kojima Takanori, it should not be erased.[79] As stability of tenure became the norm, such claims to lineage and ancestry, fictitious or not, became increasingly powerful.

The Hiruwayama case was comparatively extreme, due to the intransigence of the Miyake lord and the Noda villagers. More often in such cases one or both sides were willing to compromise, with villagers under the threat of government violence and rulers under the threat of embarrassment and being perceived as incompetent. Quick defeat or compromise was the ideal resolution rather than strict observance of the rules of law.[80] Viewed from the perspective of modernity, this illegal appeal process might be viewed as an undeveloped legal system, but in the Tokugawa days this was a relatively effective form of containment and maintenance of the Great Peace. It constantly encouraged subjects to act in accord with *omote* feudal principles, even while it somewhat restrained authoritarian abuse by allowing subjects to carry out illegal suits in an orderly fashion. Some suits might be permitted to go against the hierarchy of authority, but only a protest so important that the petitioner would carry it out with such resolve that he would likely be punished could appear in higher courts. Because the ultimate goal was the retention of the hierarchy of authority, this required punishment of the villagers even if they were judged correct in their suit. Usually punishment was light, sometimes only involving a period of being tied up with rope at the time of the over-the-head suit, and other times involving house arrest or jail time that might be rescinded after a few weeks, but it could end in banishments and even, as we have seen, executions for leaders. These punishments not only served to discourage all but the most committed protestors, but also restored the hierarchy at the conclusion of the case where "disorder" had been informally allowed in the legal process. A respect for the feudal hierarchy was reinscribed even into judgments that themselves highlighted flaws in the system, such as in the Hiruwayama case.

In all cases of adjudication described in this chapter there were repeated measures to limit engagement with the courts and to prevent an appearance of disorder. Where samurai were the true plaintiffs in territorial disputes, they had to engage the courts through commoner proxies. This served to encourage civility on both sides and prevented a very public loss of face for the defeated. The incivilities and true losses of position and face happened to various commoners involved, who were the more steady victims of the feudal hierarchy. This was most evident in contests where villagers' defiance of the lord's authority was as stake. Yet because *omote* and *naishō* shaped politics and the legal system in the interests of maintaining peace, villagers with enough desire, resources, and understanding made "illegal" over-the-head suits standard practice from early in the Tokugawa period.

In the chapters up to this point in the book, the focus has been on aspects of politics according to the rules of *omote* and *naishō* without an emphasis on change over time. The purpose has been to display the power of this schema to explain a wide range of political interaction in the Edo period and to show that rather than being a symptom of governmental decline, these politics were part of the manufacture of the government in its heyday. One more point to be covered is how these politics accommodated broad changes of deep historical significance. Contained within the uncommon stability of the formal face of the Tokugawa regime were broad spaces of change and innovation, some of which in time played a role in the Meiji national polity. The next chapter analyzes changing relationships between the political order and religion over the Tokugawa period as an example.

5

Daimyo Gods

The festival of Fujinami Myōjin is to be held on the twenty-fifth
and twenty-sixth of the third month. All men and women in this
country [of Tosa] may freely enter the north gate of the castle
between dawn and the hour before dusk between the twelfth
and the twenty-sixth days of the third month in order to worship.
Although we should prescribe seating arrangements according to
status in this country, the lord has ordered that there will be no
distinction between high and low.

—On the 1807 inauguration of the shrine to Yamauchi Katsutoyo in Kōchi[1]

The Yamauchi clan of Tosa domain inaugurated three new deities in 1807,
placing them in a new shrine in the castle and creating a major new festival for
their realm. At the time, the Tokugawa government had laws prohibiting the
creation of new deities, new shrines, and new festivals, but the Yamauchi wanted to develop a more populist form of religiosity to strengthen the position
of their government in Tosa's changing society and economy. Domain officials learned in their preliminary research that many daimyo had done similar
things before them, and they learned how to create illegal shrines and festivals
with enough deference that they caused no offense to the Tokugawa *omote*.
This chapter explores these deifications in terms of how they benefited from
and strengthened the feudal spaces of political organization and behavior and
how, by doing so, they participated in major changes in political and religious
thought that strongly influenced the shape of the subsequent nationalist Meiji
government.

The relations of government and religions

There was a wide variety of coexisting philosophical and ritual Teachings (*kyō*) and Ways (*dō*) in the Tokugawa period, which have come down to us as the philosophies and religions of Buddhism, Confucianism, Shinto, and Daoism. Mutually integrated to a substantial degree, these bodies of knowledge and their institutions and rituals gave shape and meaning to people's lives. People participated in worship and rites, in part to recognize and re-create signs of the political spaces and the hierarchies that shaped their lives. The knowledge that people gained from the various teachings and their rituals invested their community arrangements with deeper meaning and also gave meaning to the grander hierarchies into which their communities fit. Government-sponsored religious rituals made people enact the hierarchies of power, the boundaries of political space, the duties of subjects, and the obligations of rulers. Although these teachings were for the most part a combined, mutually supporting net-work of knowledge and practice in people's lives, they also had varying de-grees of competition and separate institutional and ideological identities that shaped various struggles during the Edo period. The Tokugawa and daimyo authorities forced all of these systems of thought to be integrated into the hi-erarchy, and the leaders of these institutions to be supportive of government, obedient, and mutually tolerant in *omote* activities. However, away from *omote* the government permitted much individual religious freedom and substantial degrees of freedom within the feudal spaces.[2]

The key to the hierarchic integration of religion into politics was the Tokugawa strengthening of the long tradition of Buddhist dominance on the islands, while making the religion and its institutions more subservient to the interests of warrior government. Buddhism's leanings for combination—creating identity by association rather than by exclusion—was a philosophical base that the Tokugawa could use to make hierarchic integration and mutual tolerance be the *omote* law that governed religious interaction. The govern-ment furthered the combinatory urges in Buddhism, Shinto, Daoism, and even Confucianism to such a degree that many rituals, deities, and ideas are impossible to pin to any one tradition. The Tokugawa bound everyone to per-form a relatively steady and strong integration of religious traditions and to accept the high place of Buddhist institutions in *omote* activity. Religious ex-perimentation and conflict happened more often in *uchi* spaces than in *omote*, because in its pursuit of accommodation and combination, the government suppressed the phenomenon of religious exclusivity. Buddhism could be said to be the state religion in the sense that everyone became required to affiliate with a Buddhist temple; but unlike common patterns of relations between religion and government in western Eurasia, the goal was not exclusion of other religions in favor of a "one true religion."

This combinatory *omote* was the main reason that the Fujufuse branch of Nichiren Buddhism, which taught its adherents neither to receive offerings from nor to provide them to nonbelievers, was suppressed in the Tokugawa period.[3] In 1599 when Ieyasu invited monks of many sects to read sutras in Osaka castle, the Fujufuse monk refused on religious grounds and was promptly banished. In 1630 the monk's heir condemned a more moderate Nichiren monk, saying that anyone who followed that monk was going straight to hell. This successor had held and expressed these views for years, but choosing on this occasion to declaim them in Edo castle, he ended up banished like his teacher. When the temple registration system took shape between the 1630s and 1660s, Fujufuse sect temples were banned along with Christianity, which was the system's main target. There were many reasons for the prohibition of Christianity throughout Japan that have been well studied elsewhere, but included among them was Christianity's penchant for an exclusivist form of religiosity that promoted conflict with nonbelievers. Christianity was, in short, not amenable to the Tokugawa's ideal politics of *omote* and *naishō*.[4]

Although the *omote* of the Buddhist-dominated religious hierarchy of combination was relatively stable until the Meiji period, religious organization on the islands was anything but static. Dispute, defiance, and change were far more common in *uchi* spaces of authority but were managed relatively peacefully throughout the Tokugawa era.[5] The multifaceted and compartmented religious order paralleled and provided teachings for a political order that encouraged subservience to the overall hierarchy but nevertheless, through its structured maintenance of diversity in *naibun* realms, also evolved in ways portending a revolutionary imperial order.

Changing Shinto understandings

Beginning in the latter half of the eighteenth century, some daimyo clans created significant new strategies of manipulating the religious realm that involved a shift in emphasis from Buddhist-dominated ritual to Shinto-dominated ritual in state rites. Shinto deifications, the making of individuals into *kami* deities, happened from the beginning to the end of the Edo period, but they became much more common in the latter half. More important than the growing quantity of deifications was a shift in their character. In the seventeenth century, such deifications were generally integrated into the management of samurai households and focused on making deities out of living and recently deceased daimyo. They were personal cults of devotion appropriate to the strongly emotional bonds tying lord and retainer that were prominent in the seventeenth century.[6] Deifications in the latter half of the Tokugawa period involved the creation of cultic centers devoted to the ruling house itself. They focused on promoting among retainers a sense of membership in the daimyo household through the deification of "founding ancestors" and the creation of a Shinto cult of dynasty. Some domains also used these sites to create popular worship among commoners of their domains. Furthermore, the deifications tied the daimyo houses more closely to the imperial clan and its history and therefore served as a politically useful link to the nativism that was rapidly spreading in the last century of Tokugawa rule.[7]

Because Tokugawa policy encouraged combinatory religion with Buddhism at the core, and because it encouraged maintenance of traditional privileges and practices, the trend of daimyo *kami* deification was not an attempt at clear replacement of one "religion" by another. Extremism was suppressed, and change more often was revealed in incremental innovations—a shift in balance. Buddhism and Shinto had from long before the Tokugawa era traditionally been highly integrated in sacred sites and ritual and were only situationally distinct or competing entities. Notions of difference and distinction existed from ancient times: a building might be identified as a *jinja* (Shinto shrine) or a *tera* (Buddhist temple), but the two religions most commonly could be found together on the same sacred site, each building might very likely contain deities from both religious traditions, and the (Shinto) priest and the (Buddhist) monk might very well be the selfsame person, who additionally used Confucian and Daoist texts in his rituals and instruction. Indeed, it was common for a single deity to be simultaneously identified as both a *kami* and a *buddha*.[8] "Pure" Buddhism and "pure" Shinto are largely the inventions of modernity, of a policy and a spirit most clearly enacted in the violent moment known as *haibutsu kishaku* of the early 1870s, when most aspects of the hitherto normative religious integration were forcibly destroyed and "distinct" traditions were invented.[9]

Nevertheless, this revolutionary moment of shift toward distinction and exclusive religion was not without antecedent thought and action. There were politicized movements to create separation and distinction in various daimyo domains in the mid-seventeenth century, and—existing within the broader field of combinatory religion—an ideology of Shinto exclusivity went back to the fifteenth-century priest Yoshida Kanetomo's creation of One and Only Shinto. His claim of Japanese sui generis religiosity, and of a separate Shinto existing free from impure foreign influence, was, of course, ideology rather than fact. Indeed, the actual content of Yoshida's One and Only Shinto (and indeed of modern state Shinto) owed much to Buddhist, Daoist, and Confucian thought. The exclusive Shinto movement that occurred in some domains in the seventeenth century was also heavily dependent on the incorporation of beliefs of Confucianism and its anti-Buddhist discourse that had roots going back many centuries in China.[10] When some daimyo tried to force some or all of the people under their rule to adhere to an exclusivist Yoshida Shinto and to suppress other forms of Shinto *kami* worship and Buddhism by defining them as "superstition," these actions were actually the jockeying for greater consequence by self-styled Shinto and Confucian representatives. Such elite initiatives did not succeed, in part because they did not have deep roots and support in the broader society, which mostly preferred combinatory religious practice and thought. They also failed because the Tokugawa government actively discouraged them for causing disruptions of the peace.

Major changes in this situation happened because of the spread of print culture and literacy in popular society. Knowledge of the imperial past, interpreted in terms of the *kami* traditions, spread because of the publication of the earliest surviving written myths and histories, such as the *Kojiki* (Record of Ancient Matters) and the *Nihon shoki* (The Chronicles of Japan). New understandings of history and identity were transforming the religious and political landscapes of the archipelago in the latter half of the Edo period.[11] A growing interest in historicizing the landscape with sacred objects and new shrines rooted in *kami* textual traditions provided spiritual confirmation of local identity, as well as increasingly binding that identity to the imperial tradition.[12] Some of the growing desire for an imperial Japanese religiosity was related to the disruptions and opportunities created by the expansion of commercial economic networks across the islands. Inoue Tomokatsu's research has shown that deities from the imperial story began replacing the local deities of community shrines throughout the Osaka region at the end of the eighteenth century.[13] He sees some locals attempting to tie into the broad system of authority represented by the historical imperial clan, as a means to fend off the progressively more troubled social, economic, and political climate and also to attract devotion and support for shrines from outside the local community in a more commercialized and mobile world. This search for alternative forms of order contributed to the growing cultural authority of the imperial house itself.[14] Finally, with regard specifically to deity creation and shrine practice, much credit for this transformation must be given to the vigorous efforts of the Yoshida sacerdotal house itself, which energetically increased its own income through the sale of priest licenses, grants of rank to shrines, and the creation of new *kami*.[15]

The final century of Tokugawa and daimyo rule saw a wave of daimyo creating *kami* out of their ancestors. Here I argue that some of these new forms of devotion were daimyo state Shinto, a kind of religious devotion to the domainal country. There was a shift from forms of worship that emphasized status and house membership to forms of worship based on membership in the realm ruled by the daimyo. This paralleled and was somewhat integrated with similar changes in other aspects of the political economy. In my earlier book I explored the economic and fiscal dimension of the origins of the eighteenth-century decline in governmental authority, and the response in terms of the new mercantilist political economic thought of *kokueki*. This new territorial form of political economy supplemented the dominant traditional economy of service that was organized along the structure of a samurai household polity. The use of *kokueki* as a political economic ideology by domains in *uchi* spaces permitted a gradual shift away from a political economy of service organized around samurai household polities and the appearance of a less status-oriented and more territorially defined political economy with populist dimensions.[16] The trend of daimyo deification can likewise be seen to have populist tendencies involving a downplaying of the organization of society by status, even as it paradoxically shored up daimyo clan rule. This religious change happened within the context of the dominant combinatory religiosity tied to the status-based polity, but as was the case with *kokueki* thought, the new religiosity continued to play out more fully in the Meiji Restoration, influencing the development of Meiji State Shinto. Revolutionary from the perspective of Tokugawa rule and authority, this domain state *kami* worship nevertheless was fostered within the Tokugawa's ideal form of politics. Daimyo continued to perform all of the *omote* requirements to support Buddhist institutions, and combinatory religion remained dominant throughout the islands until the Tokugawa order collapsed.

Seventeenth-century deifications of the hegemons

The seventeenth-century daimyo religious order in general focused on Buddhist memorial services and shrine deifications that emphasized both the feudal household and the feudal rulers themselves. During this time the Tokugawa worked to suppress what they saw as the exclusivist, disruptive, and tendentious bent of some Shinto-Confucian religious activity. They forced a powerful group of activists, including many leading daimyo of the Tokugawa

house itself, to participate in an *omote* of Buddhist dominance and mutual toleration among Shinto and Confucian traditions, even while setting up a tradition that, in the *uchi* space of domains, daimyo could pursue individual religious trends as long as they did so with enough circumspection and reserve to
maintain the peace.

The seventeenth-century samurai order had important uses for Shinto divinity, and from the very start a certain amount of struggle occurred over the
proper place of Shinto in the new order. The Tokugawa overlord tried to dominate this religious realm by suppressing *omote* competition and making the
shogunal house a focal point of warlord *kami* worship. This was the main function of creating the Tōshōgū shrine-temple complex at Nikkō, where Ieyasu
was deified in 1617 as the *kami* Tōshō Daigongen, and his son and grandson were thereafter enshrined as Reijin deities to be cared for by monks and
priests alike according to a Tendai Buddhist–inflected form of Shinto called
Sannō Shinto. Daimyo were required on various occasions to worship at this
shrine in ways that marked their places in hierarchies of service.[17]

The creation of this site owed much to the influence of the somewhat
novel deification of the previous hegemon Toyotomi Hideyoshi as Toyokuni
Daimyōjin upon his death in 1598.[18] The imperial decree recognizing Hideyoshi as a Daimyōjin deity carried great power for the surviving Toyotomi clan.
Along with the neighboring Hōkōji temple created by Hideyoshi, Toyokuni
shrine was the grandest site in Kyoto at the beginning of the seventeenth century. Daimyo and others who felt indebted to Hideyoshi for their success built
branch shrines in locations around Japan.[19] Ieyasu became hegemon after the
Battle of Sekigahara in 1600, but the continuing existence of the Toyotomi
clan and its budding religious order was a threat to the stability of his regime.
So he destroyed the Toyotomi in the siege of Osaka in 1615, and he confiscated the fief and most of the buildings of Toyokuni shrine and moved the *kami*
emblem (*shintai*) to a small, rather inaccessible location. In 1620 his successor,
Tokugawa Hidetada, confiscated the remaining shrine buildings and left behind only a small covered grave site.[20] They had the known Toyotomi shrines
destroyed throughout Japan, and Tōshōgū shrines quickly began springing up
in castle towns and elsewhere. Shrine worship of Hideyoshi disappeared or
in some cases went underground, such as at the site of his first castle town in
Nagahama, where the townspeople held a festival that formally was devoted to
the fishermen's god Ebisu but involved "inner rituals" devoted to Hideyoshi.[21]
The Tokugawa government also worked to protect its monopoly by gaining
oversight and rights of approval over all subsequent imperial declarations of
divinity. The imperial clan could not disburse Myōjin titles or Gongen titles

without Tokugawa permission, and the Tokugawa did not permit this to occur after Ieyasu's own deification.[22]

The one key surviving influential aspect of the Toyotomi shrine was that the Yoshida lineage/school of Shinto priests that had created it continued to flourish in the Edo period. Other lineages of priests, such as the Shirakawa lineage/school, remained important, but the Yoshida lineage's Yuitsu (One and Only) Shinto came to play the most significant role in the spread of shrines.[23] Most pertinent to the subject of this book is that much of its activity was carried out in *uchi* spaces, invisible to official Tokugawa knowledge. Partly because of its temporary loss of prestige and power with the fall of the Toyotomi, Yoshida Shinto began spreading its influence at lower levels of political and social authority. It asserted the authority to make people into *kami* and to grant titles of high court rank to preexisting *kami,* and would do so for a nice fee. The documents that it produced were called *senge,* a type of document that implied issuance on behalf of imperial authority. Although they were not actually transmissions of imperial will and were usually called *sōgen senge* to distinguish them, the distinction was likely unclear to many people. In this way the Yoshida house was a key element in the proliferation of shrines and deities at all levels of society in the Edo period.[24]

Seventeenth-century deifications of daimyo— the case of Hoshina Masayuki

In addition to hegemons, many daimyo of the era became enshrined as *kami* as well. Mase Kumiko's research reveals that, beginning with the daimyo Maeda Toshiie in 1599, at least fifteen lords were deified upon death and had shrines built in the seventeenth century. The enshrinements were carried out without formal notification to the Tokugawa. Maeda Toshiie's enshrinement was done with what seems to have been true secrecy, in the guise of moving a Hachiman shrine to inside Kanazawa castle.[25] Because daimyo enshrinement posed problems to the formal structure of Tokugawa authority, notice of them had to be kept from the Tokugawa *omote,* but mostly they were not truly secret.

The case of Hoshina Masayuki, lord of Aizu domain, illustrates many of the problems that emerged from these deifications and how such problems were managed politically. Masayuki had written in his will that he desired a Shinto burial enshrined as the *kami* Hanitsu. Masayuki was a half brother of Iemitsu, a natural son of Hidetada, and a grandson of Ieyasu, all three by this time enshrined at Nikkō. He was also adviser to the current *kubō* Tokugawa Ietsuna and had been for many years one of the most powerful men in the

Tokugawa government. Because of this, his Shinto burial did not need to be kept truly secret, but despite his power, most aspects of his enshrinement had to be dealt with informally. Masayuki had a strong interest in Shinto, thanks largely to his advisers Yamazaki Ansai and Yoshikawa Koretaru. Koretaru was a leading priest trained in the Yoshida house and had learned its "most secret teachings." He became one of the people responsible for returning the Yoshida house to Tokugawa favor in 1665, when it was granted authority to grant ranks to most of the priests in Japan.[26] As a priest he taught Masayuki and Ansai the "inner secrets" of Yoshida Shinto and in 1671 gave Masayuki the deification name "Hanitsu" in preparation for the creation of a shrine.[27]

However, Masayuki's request for a "purely Shinto" burial and enshrinement was problematic to the Tokugawa government, of which he himself had been a key member, because of recent conflicts over religious policy. As part of its anti-Christian policies the government required everyone under its extended authority to be registered with a Buddhist temple and to be buried with Buddhist rites. This system had roots in western Japan as part of the vigorous Christian suppression of the 1630s, but by the 1660s it was taking shape for all of the realm under Tokugawa hegemony. Despite an expressed Tokugawa preference for Buddhism, some domains tried to make Shinto registration be the basis of anti-Christian policies. These included Mito domain, ruled by Tokugawa Mitsukuni, and Okayama domain, ruled by Ikeda Mitsumasa, who was influenced by the anti-Buddhist thought of an exclusivist, highly Confucianized form of Shinto. In 1666 Mitsumasa began to force all domain people to use Shinto registration at shrines of the type that he approved. Hostile to religious views unlike his own, he also ordered destroyed more than ten thousand small shrines, and more than half of the thousand temples in the domain, and he reduced the number of monks by more than half.[28] This latter set of acts provoked a powerful backlash in 1667, led by temple organizations that claimed he was trying to remove all priests from the domain. The Tokugawa Elders reprimanded Mitsumasa and ultimately forced him into retirement in 1672. Under continued government pressure, his heir Tsunamasa quickly ended the anti-Buddhist policies and allowed people to choose registration at either shrines or temples, but by 1687 Tsunamasa forced everyone in his domain to register with temples only.[29] Buddhism had become the required *omote* religion.

Hoshina Masayuki also had encouraged in his domain religious registration in shrines rather than in temples, albeit in a way less hostile to Buddhist institutions. The year he died in Edo, 1672, was the same year that Mitsumasa was forced to retire. Despite his written will, Masayuki's retainers decided to have Buddhist rites before sending his body home to Aizu, so as to perform compliance with Tokugawa law. After they reported this to the Tokugawa Elders, the priest Yoshikawa Koretaru persuaded the domain officials to change their decision, saying that Masayuki had wanted a "purely Shinto" burial. The domain Elder Tomomatsu Kanjūrō, the man Masayuki had appointed to be in charge of the burial, then attempted informal negotiations with the Tokugawa government. He approached Inaba Masamichi, who had married Hoshina Masayuki's daughter and whose father, Inaba Masanori, was a leading Tokugawa Elder. Kanjūrō enlisted Masamichi's help, saying, "Recent popular customs have misled us into asking for Buddhist rites, but this goes against the will of our deceased lord and is indeed a travesty polluting the way of our imperial land." Masamichi agreed to take Yoshikawa Koretaru to his father to make an informal bid to get approval to change the plans. The lively discussion between Koretaru and Masanori is worth quoting at length because it reveals much about the religious issues and government policy.

> After Koretaru explained everything to Mino no kami [Inaba Masanori], Mino no kami said, "I cannot change things now. Just today I informed my fellow Elders [about your earlier report that you would do Buddhist services]. You may have reasons to dislike having Buddhist rites carried out within your lord's mansion, but there should be no problem with having Buddhist rites carried out in temples outside the mansion. It is against the basic laws of the realm to hold to things too strongly and not be willing to recant. Shinto is an inappropriate, narrow way of thinking."
>
> Koretaru replied, "Buddhist rites read in any province or indeed anywhere on behalf of our former lord would not be One and Only Shinto."
>
> On hearing this, Mino became very angry and said, "This is not something to be decided on your authority! Kanjūrō is the one to say this. Kanjūrō is outspoken, like a wild horse, and only Masayuki could rein him in. But—now you listen well!—even so, his is a character fully faithful to Masayuki, and he is a person who thinks about everything so as not to harm the government. He would never think of trying to carry out his own ideas in a way that went against the laws of the day. Now, the lord of Owari [the daimyo of Nagoya domain] carried out his father's burial rites in the Confucian way according to his father's will, but he also carried out Buddhist rites. So if you can think of an example [like what you propose], then tell me!"

Koretaru replied, "Well, there is the example of the Regent Toyotomi, but as he is a person who ended badly with the current ruling house, perhaps I should not mention it."

Mino became even angrier, saying, "That would be a very poor precedent!"

Seeing this, Koretaru replied, "Well, fighting would not be good for the Way or for myself. I see it is unavoidable. The only way for me to repay my debt to lord Hanitsu is to carry out One and Only rites for him in my own residence. I will take it as heaven's will that I quit without achieving my stated aims. It is the law of the land that one may not refrain from using all [of the beliefs], but such is nothing compared with a world where Buddhism flourished and Shinto were eradicated. As using all beliefs is the law of the land, and as Shinto is the Way of this imperial land, I think it not too difficult to have both ways accommodate to the other.

Still, insofar as these include the Way of our land and the law of a foreign region, it is not my inner desire. Although I do not need to go on saying this, this imperial land was created by the *kami,* and all of its people are descended from these deities. You yourself are one of these. Although the Way was taught to us by [the Shinto sun goddess] Amaterasu, the Way has naturally become less clear with the passing years, and we have adopted the Way of a foreign region. In the end, this is because although we have had many enlightened kings and wise generals, we have not had people who excelled in Shinto. In spite of this, there suddenly appeared someone as excellent and talented as Lord Masayuki, who revived the true Way of Shinto, and I desired for you to hear this and inform the ruler of the land, hoping that he would straighten the law in accord with this request. Then everyone's abilities would be made clear and the abandoned Way would be revived, and this great work would be written in histories for later ages. If this request is not approved now, then perhaps never will the old ways be revived in this imperial land. Or maybe now is not the time for the flower to bloom."

Lord Mino saw Koretaru's deep pain and sadness, and his anger dispersed. He asked, "What is in the box that you brought?" Koretaru replied, "This is a certificate showing the ranks that lord Masayuki has passed in Shinto. Kanjūrō wished that you see this." After looking at the document, Mino said, expressing his deep feeling, "What a man Masayuki is! Without doubt he has mastered numerous arts and skills. And that he has mastered Shinto into its deepest secrets! He is certainly not an average man. I will accept your request completely. Do just as you wish, but without informing us. And be sure to do things quietly!" Koretaru received this with thanks. Mino then said to Tango [nephew Inaba Masamichi] not to mention his anger and confusion, and he praised Koretaru after he left.

Well, Koretaru returned to the Aizu residence and explained in detail how Mino had accepted the request. Everyone was very happy. Especially Izawa Shigeemon, who said with deep thanks, "Only someone with your talents could have made this happen!"[30]

One notable issue in this exchange is the political spatial consciousness. For Koretaru the ideal space is the Japanese imperial realm (*honchō*). He attempted to politicize this space through appeal to a nationalistic and exclusivist form of religiosity that he imagined was rooted in an originary and essential moment of ancient history that created that space. By contrast, Masanori saw this consciousness as an "inappropriate, narrow way of thinking," and he encouraged an eclectic religious attitude, and an understanding of political space as compartmented into households. He was quick to concede domain control over the space of the Aizu mansion, saying they could do what they liked there, but he required conciliatory and subservient integration of that space into the Tokugawa order. Therefore he said that Aizu should still request Buddhist services at some outside temples. When Koretaru announced acceptance of defeat for his plan, he also relied on this Tokugawa-style political spatial structure when he said, "The only way for me to repay my debt to lord Hanitsu is to carry out One and Only rites for him in my own residence." Of course, in the end Koretaru won his argument, and Aizu was allowed not to request outside Buddhist services, but in a way appropriate to the politics of *omote* and *naishō*.

This is evident in the shape of the resolution. Masanori accepted Aizu's plan for purely Shinto rites, but he made it clear that the approval was not a formal acceptance when he added that it should be done "without informing us." Since he was just informed and gave his approval, such a statement makes sense only in a world of compartmented politics structured into formal and informal interactions. Then by adding the admonition "Do things quietly!" he encouraged circumspection and left an excuse for punishment should things go wrong. Domain officials were slow to catch on to this point. Pleased by what Koretaru told them, they then tried to get a formal recognition for Masayuki's divinity. They sent an informal request to the Tokugawa Elders sounding out the possibility of getting the Tokugawa *kubō* himself to pronounce Masayuki to be a Myōjin deity and grant it high court rank. However, this did not even elicit an answer. As Masanori had said, the Elders were not to be informed.[31] Myōjin was a title with status lower than Ieyasu's divine rank of Daigongen, but it was higher than Reijin, and Masayuki's own father, Hidetada, and half brother Iemitsu were enshrined as Reijin in Nikkō. It is a surprising testament to Koretaru's influence that Aizu officials thought they ever could have gained Tokugawa formal recognition for such a request to raise the posthumous status of a daimyo higher than that of his father, the former *kubō*.

Domain officials sent Masayuki's body back to Aizu, and over the subsequent two years they held a burial and constructed Hanitsu shrine. The Tokugawa Elders repeatedly sent orders that the whole thing be carried out without excess, so as not to cause peasants undue hardship and especially so as "not to be heard outside the domain." This phrase was repeated again and again in many missives of informal negotiation back and forth between Edo and Aizu, and even within the domain there was debate over scale and propriety. Various formally Buddhist elements also eventually entered into the mourning. Masayuki's widow took the Buddhist title of Seikō-in and shaved her head to become a lay nun. Tokugawa officials and relatives sent "incense money," a Buddhist-styled standard form of condolence that Aizu officials formally had to accept, in a sense wrapping the space of Aizu in Buddhist ritual so as to integrate it with the Tokugawa polity.[32]

As Inaba Masanori noted in his response to Koretaru quoted above, the Tokugawa daimyo ruler of Nagoya castle at that time had been buried with Confucian rites rather than Buddhist rites. The Tokugawa lords of Mito castle were from this time also buried with Confucian-infused Shinto rites as well. These were two of the three main collateral houses of the Tokugawa, and when one remembers that Hoshina Masayuki was Tokugawa Hidetada's son, it becomes clear that the Tokugawa clan's ties to Shinto were deep and did not end with the enshrinements of the first three *kubō* at Nikkō. The containment of the daimyo religious activity to inside domains operated in a manner similar to the way their other ambitions were controlled. As we shall see, when activities crossed the vague boundary of circumspection and entered the field of brash disrespect, then the informal toleration could be denied and the formal law could be applied.

Many years later, in 1732, the domain requested and received the most prestigious Daimyōjin title from the Yoshida house based in Kyoto, making Hanitsu equivalent in rank to Ieyasu's own deity. This was done without official Tokugawa approval, and the domain went beyond the bounds of propriety when it had the head of the Yoshida house make a placard that would be hung on the outer gate of the shrine, proclaiming Masayuki a Daimyōjin. Overestimating the value of their domain's consequence, they even initiated informal negotiations with the Tokugawa Elders to try to get formal acknowledgment. However, in 1735 they received a rather stiff informal response from the Tokugawa Elders saying that this action was selfish and showed disrespect to Tōshōgū shrine and that the placard should be taken down immediately. They also added, "You can call him Daimyōjin within your realm and among your house retainers, but you should know that in formal relations [with the Tokugawa] and in all communications with other provinces you should write 'Hanitsu Reisha.'"[33] This response reveals that the Tokugawa Elders envisioned the Hanitsu shrine precincts to be a religious spatial metaphor for the ruling authority of the daimyo. There is a clear consciousness that the space of "independent" daimyo authority involved the samurai house and the realm of people, but even within the domainal space the Hoshina clan could not display on the *outside* of the shrine a placard with a statement at variance with formal *omote* relations. Requiring the outside of the shrine to be obedient to the Tokugawa formal order served to architecturally manifest the way that daimyo authority itself fit within the Tokugawa order. As the Elder's statement makes clear about the integration of the various compartments of authority, formal relations with the "outside" had to be carried out on Tokugawa terms.[34]

It is natural that Tokugawa dominance was successfully asserted in these negotiations, but if the Tokugawa government at this time clearly prohibited the kind of exclusivist religious extremism propounded by Koretaru, why did Masanori and the other Elders give their informal approval? Confucianism and Shinto could both be cantankerous (in part precisely because of their jockeying to be of greater consequence), and the enthusiasm of some devoted daimyo, such as Ikeda Mitsumasa, created problems for the Tokugawa Great Peace. Yet, as we saw in Chapter 3, harming daimyo houses engendered its own conflicts that led to greater instability, so the Tokugawa government was willing informally to permit deviation in subcompartments of authority, as long as this deviation "knew its place," or, in the language of the day, *bun o shiru* (to recognize one's status or consequence).

This culture of knowing the limits of one's consequence played throughout the layers of the polity, working both ways and producing complex results. In Mimasaka Katsuyama domain the Miura daimyo had laws forbidding Yoshida Shinto to exist in their domain, and they did not allow shrine priests to have Shinto burials. The latter prohibition was in accordance with Tokugawa policy that required everyone to have Buddhist rites, but the former was out of place insofar as the Tokugawa granted to the Yoshida house a near monopoly of the right to give shrine priests rank and status. A history by a former village headman shows that as late as 1835 shrine priests who were unofficially One and Only adherents were still petitioning for the right to be buried according to Shinto rites but were refused. However, the headman noted that "although there were shrine families who buried themselves according to shrine rites, officially [*omotedatte*] this did not happen."[35] The daimyo informally permitted deviation from its *omote* orders, and the exclusivist religious traditions were more accommodating to authority than their theology preached. The Yoshida sacerdotal clan was itself quite accommodating to Tokugawa and daimyo demands and publicly participated in many Buddhist-dominated environments, despite the "pure" pretensions of its belief system. Even Christians in Japan gradually became quietly tolerated to the degree that Tokugawa officials would regularly turn a blind eye to "hidden Christians," as long as the believers would obediently perform Buddhist rites in public and accept a very low "consequence" in the world.[36]

Deifications of the late Tokugawa period

Kami deification was somewhat common among the overlords and some daimyo in the seventeenth century, but daimyo deifications became much more common in the last century of Tokugawa rule and they often had a different character. One change was a shift away from deifying a recently living warlord to deifying the ancestral founders of daimyo houses. Another change was the markedly increased populism of the rituals associated with many of the latter deifications. The earlier shrines were largely limited to organizing worship by samurai retainers.[37] Worship at Nikkō, for example, was open only to daimyo, bannermen, and some foreign emissaries. Lesser samurai and all commoners were forbidden to worship there.[38] Commoners participated outside the center in these rituals as servants and suppliers of goods. It seems clear that the religious organization of the seventeenth century primarily encoded participation of the samurai household community, even when it was strongly Shinto inflected, and all the more so when it was strongly Buddhist. However, from the latter half of the eighteenth century forward, the Shinto deifications were less likely to be forms of burial and memorial for living or recently deceased lords and more likely to be the deifications of daimyo house founders. Shrine buildings and precincts were built for these new deities, and worship and festivals tended to emphasize involving the population of the ruled territory.

The growing daimyo interest in deification and Shinto was itself part of a broader interest in *kami* spirituality and the imperial tradition that was spreading in the late Edo period along with new understandings of local history. As Haga Shōji has argued, *kami* had become in the nineteenth century an integral part of "a movement locating historical value in all corners of society" and "a mode of social activity that used the new objects of historical value it created to influence others."[39] The creation of local histories, memorial steles, and new religious spaces was popular in part because they were vehicles for imparting to communities a history of holding common values.[40] Inoue Tomokatsu has shown in his research that newly popular deities among commoners in the eighteenth century often reflected a bonding of their religious life with the imperial tradition.[41] Hiromi Maeda's studies reveal that the Yoshida house licensed increasingly large numbers of priests and granted ranks to local deities throughout commoner society in regions all over Japan.[42]

The desire to establish control over a changing religious and ideological landscape lay behind the transformation of many daimyo ancestors into *kami* in the late eighteenth and early nineteenth centuries. The deifications spiritually linked daimyo authority to the new forms of *kami* worship and attempted to assert a continuing position of high daimyo status in that expanding religious realm. Just as many village *kami* and clan *kami* of commoners asserted significance and meaning through linkage to the ancient historical texts and imperial story, so too did many daimyo seek to tie their memories to the imperial clan and its servants. The Yamauchi clan of Tosa declared that they had descended from the seventh-century imperial minister Fujiwara Kamatari. The Mōri of Hagi domain linked their house with the ninth-century imperial prince Abo and with the twelfth-century Ōe no Hiromoto, who had the double distinction of being an imperial court servant and one of the founders of the Kamakura samurai government. These and other houses highlighted such identities in shrines they created, and for some of them the goal was to enlist domain residents in rites of political belonging.[43]

The shrines had to be created within the *hōken* order dominated by the Tokugawa, so the politics of these deifications were not merely local. By the late Tokugawa period the creation of new temples, shrines, and deities was clearly prohibited by law. The first prohibition of new temples was issued as early as 1630, although when the Tokugawa reissued this law in 1692, they permitted "new temples" that had been built up to that time to continue. In 1685 they also issued a law prohibiting the creation of any new Buddhist or Shinto festivals or rites or of new shrines.[44] The Tokugawa even forbade the enlargement of older festivals, out of suspicion of the corrupting influence of luxury.[45] So, with all of these prohibitions, how did these shrines get created, and how did they become the festive centers of daimyo countries without being an affront to Tokugawa dominance and order? The remainder of this chapter examines these events of creation and ritual.

Tosa domain's Fujinami shrine

In 1805 the officials of Tosa domain had the priestly Yoshida house of Kyoto invoke the new deity Fujinami Myōjin, after which they installed it in the Fujinami shrine created in the grounds of Kōchi castle.[46] Fujinami Myōjin was the *kami* deification of Yamauchi Katsutoyo, the founder of the Tosa Yamauchi clan. He had lived in the tumultuous unification era and rose in status from a fatherless teenage *rōnin* with no prospects to become the lord of the province-sized realm of Tosa. Also enshrined at Fujinami as *reijin*, understood to be auxiliary and lesser-status deities, were two other figures. One was Katsutoyo's wife, Kenshō-inden, a woman whose story was celebrated by Arai Hakuseki in his *Hankanfu* (Records and Lineages of Daimyo) and who was by the early nineteenth century famous throughout Japan as a model wife and savvy agent directly responsible for engineering many of Katsutoyo's political successes. The other deity was Katsutoyo's nephew and adopted heir, Tadayoshi (Chikugan-inden), whose bloodline sustained the Yamauchi house. The deification of a woman was quite uncommon, but the choice of a main and two auxiliary deities was reminiscent of Nikkō shrine, where Ieyasu was main deity and his inheriting son and grandson were *reijin*. Yet the functioning of Fujinami shrine had more populist goals than that of Nikkō.

Fujinami shrine notably refashioned and adjusted local politico-religious practices by a general shift in emphasis from lineage to space, or from control of the household to territorial control. Household religiosity in Tosa had up to this point been built on the ceremonial worship of deceased members of the Yamauchi house at the grave sites and family temples of the Yamauchi clan. These primarily Buddhist rituals had long been a means of spiritually incorporating retainers into the Yamauchi clan. The novel aspects of Fujinami shrine were its emphasis on Shinto and its vastly increased inclusion of Tosa commoners in its rituals. The Tosa domain rulers created their Fujinami shrine as part of an attempt to have people regard Katsutoyo's time as the days when things were good because people were frugal and dutiful. At the core of the message was a story that Katsutoyo's personal sacrifices and privations during the tumultuous Warring States era were the source of the peace and the well-being of all people in present-day Tosa. This vision was purveyed to counteract what domain rulers perceived to be the disintegrating effects of those very benefits of peace and wealth.[47] Fujinami Myōjin became styled as a deity responsible for maintaining the fertility of the land of Tosa, and its calendar of worship was designed to keep all classes of people mindful of their duties and obligations to the Yamauchi household and the domainal country of Tosa. The creation of the shrine then led to a process of the domain's encouraging villages and towns to alter the dates of some of their festivals to accord with the ritual calendar of Fujinami shrine, constructing a religious time and space of Tosa centered upon and presided over by the Yamauchi house.[48] The rulers intended the worship to become the living center of a Tosa state Shinto.

When the Yamauchi set to deifying the house founders, they were well aware of the Tokugawa prohibitions and feared making a misstep in the enshrinement process. At each new stage, they looked into precedents among the Sō of Tsushima, the Makino of Nagaoka, the Hoshina of Aizu, and the Nabeshima of Saga, by having their Edo ambassadors informally contact and consult with the ambassadors of these houses.[49] They learned that because of the interdiction the deifications must be carried out discreetly and without reporting them to the Tokugawa government.

The Hoshina and Makino clans were *fudai* daimyo who served in key offices in the Tokugawa government, so its officials not only would have been aware of daimyo deifications but indeed would have been participating themselves within their own domains. We have already looked at the Hoshina example. As for the Makino, in 1722 the lord of Nagaoka castle, Makino Tadatoki, died and was buried with Buddhist rites, but he was also deified as Aoshi Reijin, and a small shrine was built within the castle. The clan had the deity's status raised to Aoshi Myōjin in 1733. Because this was the deification of a recently living lord and the shrine was within the castle for worship by house samurai, this fit the earlier pattern of deifications. However, in 1781 Makino Tadakiyo moved Aoshi shrine to a park at the edge of the castle town and enlarged it so that popular festivals could be carried out. He did this at the very time he was serving as Master of Ceremony in the Tokugawa court. In 1787 he became Temple and Shrine Magistrate and presumably held a straight face as he told daimyo that it was the firm law of the Tokugawa ever since 1685 that no new shrines or festivals be created, nor could any shrine be relocated.[50] His close colleague and the chief Tokugawa official of his era, Matsudaira Sadanobu, deified and created a shrine for his (adoptive) ancestor Matsudaira Sadatsuna as Chinkoku Reijin in 1784 in Shirakawa domain, and later he arranged to have himself enshrined as Kokushu Reijin following his own death, which occurred in 1833.[51] Because the Tokugawa officials were themselves complicit, Tosa's informal communications preparing for the enshrinement clearly did not require true secrecy from the Tokugawa, nor did the forms of hiding from the Tokugawa *omote* prevent Tosa from using the enshrinement to forge new bonds with powers outside the domain.

Not only was there cooperation of daimyo in assisting each other with information concerning the process of deification, but the deification was also a way by which the imperial house in Kyoto was quietly expanding its authority over the ritual space of Japan and making links to daimyo.[52] The Tokugawa forbade the emperor to create new deities without Tokugawa permission, but the imperial clan kept its hand in by claiming in 1738 the right to grant court rank to shrine priests, and they did so even for priests of newly created *kami* at these new "illegal" shrines.[53] The Yoshida house invoked *kami* on its own authority but served as intermediary to the imperial house in the process of acquiring rank for deities and their priests. So at the beginning of 1805 the domain sent the priest of the Kōchi castle Hachiman shrine, Miyaji Buzen, and the priest of Jinmeigu shrine, Miyaji Wakasa, to Kyoto to approach the head of the clan Yoshida Yoshitsura with the request for the three deifications, as well as a request for court rank for Miyaji Buzen. The granting of court rank for Buzen was forthcoming, and the Yoshida elders soon led him to make the rounds of all of the aristocratic houses to present gifts of thanks.[54] The acquisition of Junior Fifth imperial court rank for Miyaji Buzen increased his own authority and the prestige of the shrine itself within the domain. This may be seen as curious in that his master, Tosa lord Yamauchi Toyokazu, along with all samurai in the employ of the Tokugawa, was unable to directly receive court rank from the emperor but rather received his rank (Junior Fourth) via the parallel Tokugawa-controlled system of warrior house ranking. The policy had the dual aims to limit daimyo interactions with the imperial order and to give the Tokugawa government control over competition for status among the daimyo. Yet daimyo gradually devised other ties to the imperial clan, many of which had to remain officially unnoticed by the Tokugawa. This resulted in a network of integration into the imperial order that was incongruous with, but coexisted alongside, the formal Tokugawa order of relations.

The Tokugawa's main interest was to preserve the peace through the maintenance of the various privileges that accrued from tradition and the status order, and Buddhist institutions had a large place in this order. Yamauchi officials were quick to determine that local Buddhist priests might be the most upset by the creation of Fujinami shrine. To prevent difficulty from arising, they checked with the head priests of two of the most powerful local Shingon sect temples and early on co-opted the priest, Henmeiin, of the Tendai sect temple that had traditionally had control of Kasuga shrine in Kōchi. They checked with him for the name of the deity and later rewarded him for his cooperation. Ultimately he was appointed *bettō* (Buddhist administrator of a shrine) of Fujinami and given a large portion of the shrine's income—more indeed than the income the two priests would receive. He was allowed to perform at his own expense a ceremony that made Fujinami Myōjin a local manifestation of a buddha—although what buddha Fujinami became is not recorded in the domain documents or announced in subsequent festival notifications. Following the installation ceremony in Kōchi, Henmeiin and other priests were rewarded with gifts of money.[55] These facts and consideration of the rituals that are described below suggest that the Buddhist identity was superfluous—more an exercise in preventing dissent from powerful players than an original intent of the shrine. The Yoshida clan and its priests in Tosa would hardly have been happy with this kind of treatment of a *kami*, but they were certainly used to such accommodations. In their residence in Kyoto, they could do what they wanted and practice their notion of a "pure" invocation unsullied by other beliefs.

The domain had sent Buzen unofficially in a private capacity to request the deifications. They also had him check out the payments necessary for each deification, and he returned to Tosa's Finance Magistrate in Osaka with a price list detailing roughly two *ryō* to call forth a *reijin*, four for a *reisha*, nine for a *myōjin*, and on top of these charges a base fee of about eleven *ryō* for the invocation ceremony itself.[56] Buzen also informed them that the Yoshida head priest happened to have already performed all of his personal purifications, and therefore he could carry out the invocation soon if the Yamauchi wished. Within a few days two Tosa officials in Osaka traveled to Kyoto unofficially to further discuss and express domain approval. The negotiations proceeded so rapidly that the domain had to ask the Yoshida to keep the deities at the Yoshida residence while Tosa prepared the appropriate procession to Kōchi. The two Tosa officials also informed other domain officials that the deification was being done without informing the Tokugawa, so they would have to behave accordingly.[57]

Tosa officials checked with other domains about what was appropriate for the procession from Kyoto to the domain. Representatives of the daimyo of Saga, who had already gone through the process, counseled Tosa to have a small entourage for the deity as far as the border of the domain and from there to have a procession as large as they wished. This was explicitly "for fear that Kantō [meaning the Tokugawa] would hear of it."[58] However, Tosa opted for a slightly larger entourage than Saga's (which was two priests and two foot soldiers), perhaps striving for status and testing the limits of what might be safely heard in Edo. The portable shrine carrying the deity was accompanied to the domain's Osaka residence by two high-ranking officials of the domain, two priests, one samurai, two foot soldiers, two servants, and four porters. Rather than hiring a private boat as Saga had done, Tosa used the lord's own boat that was commonly engaged on the alternate attendance voyage, one medium-sized war vessel, and four assisting boats to carry a much larger procession to Kannoura, the easternmost port of Tosa. From there, safely within the realm, the procession grew to more than fifty retainers and servants participating in a miniature version of the alternate attendance procession to Kōchi through the major towns and villages of the eastern half of the domain. They followed the seventeenth-century route that Katsutoyo, Kenshōin, and Tadayoshi had themselves used, and each night they had the portable shrine set in the lord's room of the various traditional resting houses. Commoners and retainers along the way made obeisances to the *kami* as for their daimyo, bringing them into patterns of obedience to the founders of the Yamauchi clan. The increasing numbers of the procession from Kyoto to Kōchi mapped out in a sense the informal geography of the Yamauchi clan's power.[59]

When the portable shrine and the deities arrived at the castle, they had to be placed in a palace room because of the difficulties concerning building a new shrine. Only a few years earlier, the domain had directly received from the Tokugawa a reminder of the prohibition on building any new shrines. This worried the Tosa officials considerably, and it took them over a year to even decide on a location and build a temporary shrine. They needed a large shrine with ample space for festivals, but the officials noted, "It is prohibited by the [Tokugawa] government, and formally we cannot build it."[60] As they debated the best course of action, they decided to unofficially ask the relevant Tokugawa officials themselves how best to solve the dilemma. The Edo ambassador thus contacted a monk to relay a query to the Temple and Shrine Magistrate Ōkubo Tadazane and also contacted the Tokugawa Elder Mizuno Tadatomo via one of his representatives. They asked off the record if they could move the Kasuga Daimyōjin shrine from its current location in Hijima, which was east of the castle town, into the middle of the city near the riding grounds and simultaneously install the ancestral *kami* in the new precincts. However, the correspondents came back with the same discouraging answer that there was little hope of approval. They had both been told that another daimyo had earlier asked permission to move the location of a certain shrine because a landslide had destroyed it, and even that request was not approved. On this occasion the Tokugawa officials could not be helpful, for their hands were tied by precedent. So the Tosa officials looked to how other domains had handled the problem. The Nabeshima of Saga and the Tōdō of Tsu had both enlarged small existing shrines and at that time added on buildings devoted to the new ancestral deities. This, they reasoned, was neither creating a new shrine nor moving one, so therefore it need not be reported to the Tokugawa. However, the Tosa officials felt that they had no appropriately located shrine to use in this way, and they were in a bind.

Finally, officials at the domain held a council and decided to build a new shrine within the castle grounds, reasoning that "since therefore there would be no need to hang the shrine name plaque [*kakefuda*] outside the castle boundary, then there would be no problem."[61] Exactly why this logic persuaded them that it was therefore somehow legitimate to build a new shrine despite formal illegality is not clear, but they probably felt that a Tokugawa official would recognize the *hōken* sanctity of the castle itself and would not officially notice the existence of the shrine.

However, this new plan came up against another problem, because the *kubō* had from long ago forbidden any new construction work on castles without first receiving permission. This seventeenth-century law was intended to discourage rebellion by preventing lords from strengthening their defenses, but the letter of the law was clear, even in the peaceful early nineteenth century, and needed to be shown respect. Faces surely brightened in the Tosa council when someone pointed out that they had asked the Tokugawa permission for extensive repairs when the castle had burned down in 1727 and that they had not yet—in 1806!—sent the Tokugawa a notice saying that repairs had been completed, whereupon they decided that construction of the shrine could certainly fit under the old request. After deciding that this was the best option available, the committee sent a query to the Edo residence asking for the lord's approval of the plan. Within three months of the approval they constructed a temporary shrine building and installed the embodied *kami*.

The amount of anxiety and informal querying concerning the shrine location reveals that making a shrine was not an "anything goes" situation even though Tokugawa officials were informally in the know. We can see herein the continued power of Tokugawa authority to inspire fear and to require cooperation and interaction with government officials even when daimyo were clearly breaking laws. The nature of these politics is probably not best understood by the notions of Tokugawa "decline" and "hidebound tradition" that many scholars have provided. This very form of "disobedience" and innovation was happening at the peak of Tokugawa authority in the 1660s and in itself was not a symptom of decline but rather an expression of the government's ideal form of operation. This is not to say that there were not worries over decline among the rulers, but *uchi* disobedience per se was not necessarily evidence of that.

One problem that the deifications were designed to address locally was a perceived decline in the martial, dutiful, and frugal nature of the samurai themselves. The *kami* and the shrine were created in the hope that worshipping the founders of the Yamauchi house would make samurai recall their debt to the lord and work more dutifully. Such an idea had been common in the domain for a long time, but up to this point worship had been promoted at Buddhist temples and through the Buddhist hierarchy. As an example of this, the diary of samurai Mori Yoshiki shows that he regularly participated in observances of his own family ancestors at Shōmyōji and observances for his lord's clan variously at Shinmyōji and Yōhōji temples. The latter observances happened once or twice a month, tied to the anniversary of the death of some lord or near family member. Yoshiki was especially dutiful in observance of the anniversary of the death of lord Toyochika, whom he had personally served in his youth as a page but who died suddenly in 1789.[62] The Buddhist rituals of worship had been carried out for each lord, wife, and other key family members according to a calendar of declining frequency of observance for each memory. The most important characters, such as the founders, had much more staying power in comparison with later lords and ladies, but they were just a few among many and always competed with the ritual observances of the more recent lords and ladies. The latter observances strengthened the personal bonds of retainer to individual master, which was at the core of a house-based political imagination and religiosity.

The Fujinami shrine and festival were different in important ways. The festival, which happened once a year, was devoted to the Yamauchi household founders rather than to all of the various ancestors or the specific lord that one had served, and it was an appeal to return to an imagined original moral character of the samurai supposed to have existed at the time of the domain beginnings. Such a message was doubtless attractive to Yoshiki, an amateur historian who collected numerous documents from the clan's seventeenth-century past. Years earlier, in the 1790s, the domain had even sent Yoshiki to the Owari region to carry out research on Katsutoyo's personal history. So when Fujinami shrine was finally created, he took his eldest son to make obeisance at dawn four days before the inaugural festival in 1807. On the festival day he watched the offering of archery that samurai performed for the deity.[63] The message of restoration of the samurai's military roots was clear enough that Yoshiki, who had lapsed in his archery practice, returned to his teacher's school, and on another day of an offering of archery to the *kami* he went again to the school, where he was surprised to find forty people practicing. He then went daily for the following month. The festival had clearly achieved one of its aims. However, holding a pure heart and living in the past can last for only so long. A month later a number of the students left for a different teacher, and Yoshiki noted, "The remainder were a bunch of complaining kids, so I quit."[64] A couple of weeks later a friend invited him over to a party, about which he wrote, "There were many men and women there. . . . I haven't gotten so drunk in years!"[65]

In addition to its efforts to influence samurai, the shrine signaled a domain attempt to forge in ritual new types of bonds with its retainers and the commoner subjects by creating a loyalty with a stronger territorial dimension. This is most evident in that from the first festival in 1807 not only samurai but all commoners were invited to the observances. The order for the festival was sent to all villages in the domain and proclaimed, "All men and women in this country [of Tosa] may freely enter the north gate of the castle between dawn and the hour before dusk between the twelfth and the twenty-sixth days of the third month in order to worship. Although we should prescribe seating arrangements according to status in this country, the lord has ordered that there will be no distinction between high and low."[66] This permission for random commoners to come inside the castle itself for fourteen days of the observances and to worship at the shrine without any regard for differences in status, gender, or household connections is a key distinctive element of the new populist state religiosity promoted at Fujinami.

Efforts to include all residents of the domain in the ceremonies of Fujinami increased throughout the remainder of Yamauchi rule. In 1836 domain officials had the Yoshida clan raise the status of the Fujinami Myōjin deity to Fujinami Daimyōjin, and they aggressively pursued more active involvement of villages throughout the domain. Becoming a Daimyōjin bestowed on Fujinami a ritual parity with Kasuga Daimyōjin, the deification of the purported distant ancestor of the Yamauchi house and imperial minister, Fujiwara Kamatari, and made it possible to have joint festivals without an apparent second-tier status accorded to the Yamauchi clan. In practice, the Yamauchi procession took the lead while the Kasuga held up the rear. In this way the domain was taking advantage of the link with a traditional deity and the Fujiwara name to increase Yamauchi prestige.

All people of Tosa continued to be invited into the castle grounds to visit the shrine for the sixteen days around the annual festival, but the actual festival was moved to a more spacious location where thousands could participate. The domain built a special temporary resting house for the deity in the great open area along the river just south of the castle, so that it might hold a grand three-day festival in 1836. It began with a procession of the deity from its home, traveling along a route through the town and ending at the resting house at the river plain. All villages and shrine keepers were invited to "freely make offerings and enter troupes" into the procession, but perhaps the response was too large, because they soon instead created an annual rotation system allowing various Kōchi wards, four villages, and three ports each year to enter procession troupes. In a curious mixture of old values and a new inclusiveness less tied to status, these processions included many villagers carrying swords, lances, bows, and other arms who put on displays of their martial skills in sword dances and the like as their offerings to the deity, as if they gauged their membership in the domain by their ability to serve militarily. As procession participants the commoners were combinatory in their expression: the parades and floats were not limited to martial and historical themes, with many commoners dressing as the Tengu deity or as *yamabushi* (mountain ascetic) spiritualists. More than fifty shrine keepers from around the realm also participated in the procession, which contrasted with only one Buddhist monk, the *bettō* Henmeiin, who was put in a palanquin at the tail end of the procession, a power to be recognized if not given familiarity. During the days of offering, all temples were ordered not to ring their bells, out of respect for the festival, suggesting that the domain's intent was to keep the focus on the *kami*.[67]

The festival was designed to get many people participating as spectators, and at this the domain succeeded. One participant wrote that a hundred thousand people, equal to a fourth of the realm population, had attended the 1838 ceremony. The price of ferry crossings skyrocketed, and commerce in the city flourished "enormously," he noted, citing the example of "the granny of the confectionary Hisakichiya, who sold 400 *monme* worth of sweets on the first day alone."[68] This general experience must have made many townspeople grateful for the benefits the new deity. The participation of all residents of Tosa was deemed important enough that the domain also constructed a special temporary shrine in Hata county, which was in the distant west and from which travel to Kōchi was difficult, so that its people might simultaneously participate in a parallel celebration as well.[69]

Commoner participation was not free, however. This new shape of integrating religion and politics came with its own new costs and regulations for commoners. In 1837 every household in Tosa was required to give money for the festival.[70] There was also an aspect of taking over the roles of other shrines and temples in the domain and incorporating them into

Fujinami religious time. In 1837 the priests of the traditional leading eight shrines of Tosa were all ordered to carry out three days of prayers at the Fujinami shrine for the pacification of the deities of mountain, river, and sea, the fruition of crops, and success in commerce. Buddhist priests were not required to come to the shrine but were required to offer these prayers on the same days. These rituals predated Fujinami shrine itself but were a recent trend. Since the 1780s the domain had frequently ordered shrines throughout the realm to carry out rites to increase the productivity of the land and sea as a "general festival of our country." Officials intended the rites to convey this message: "The misery of the people and that of the lord is the same; the happiness of the people and that of the lord is the same. High and low are a single body." Not surprisingly, these rites too were usually supported by levies on all villages. As the frequency of the rites rose, so did the costs, and in time village headmen were asking domain officials to have all rites for productivity of the land happen on the same day, bringing the domain into one ritual calendar and reducing costs.[71]

These changes were a form of worship with many similarities to Japanese State Shinto of the Meiji period but were formed to shore up the Tosa territorial state with the lord's dynasty as its imagined holy center. To point out this similarity is to suggest that instead of a simple top-down schema whereby government officials instrumentally used religion to control commoners, government actions were trying to appropriate grassroots-level conditions that allowed the production of a state Shinto. These conditions operative in Meiji were also operative in many large domains, and their rulers were making similar attempts to harness these trends.[72]

The key local ideological trend was the spread of *kokugaku* learning, which increasingly centered the imperial mythic traditions rooted in *kami* devotion. Tosa was among the many domains where this ideology spread and heightened a historical consciousness of an imperially centered history.[73]

This had manifestations in the political world. For example, from the 1830s on, village headmen of Tosa were mobilizing their own political activities by forming a secret league with the following stated vision of Japan: "This land's overlord is without doubt the Revered Emperor. Its Intendant is the Shogun. Its group headmen are the daimyo. . . . Its headmen are the *shōya* (village headmen), to whom is entrusted the full management of land and people." The headmen were positioning themselves in an "imperial" Japan so that they could mobilize in their conflicts with the domain, and it made sense for domain leaders to incorporate themselves into this informally expanding imperial order.[74] Thus, as part of the feudal politics of the era it was possible for a domainal country consciousness and a Japanese imperial country consciousness to grow simultaneously and in mutual support.

Daimyo deification for the Miyake clan

Many domains had other purposes for deifications than fashioning a domain territorial state. When the Miyake daimyo of Tahara domain created a *kami* out of their founding ancestor, Miyake Yasusada (1544–1615), in 1814, they used his deification mainly to mobilize retainers of the household rather than as a device of populist management. This deification was timed to commemorate the two hundredth anniversary of Yasusada's death.[75] Up to this point the Miyake had had *kami* worship for the putative house ancestor Kojima Takanori, a samurai who, according to the widely read *Taiheiki,* a chronicle of the fourteenth century, had fought on behalf of Emperor Godaigo during the civil wars between the northern and southern imperial lines, thereby becoming legendary for imperial loyalism. These ceremonies were held within the castle's first enceinte and at the domain's main Edo residence and involved the Miyake clan and elite samurai of the domain rather than all retainers. Yasusada had served as a page of Tokugawa Ieyasu and was close enough to Ieyasu to have been granted the *yasu* character for his name when he moved into adulthood. He ended up a minor daimyo and lord of Koromo castle, and his descendants were transferred through a number of domains until they came to rule Tahara from 1664 on. He came to be regarded as the "restorer of the house" that had begun with Kojima Takanori long before. The 1814 deification of Yasusada involved constructing a shrine in the second enceinte of the castle and creating festivals for the full range of Miyake retainers. This was an expansion of the community of ritual observances to include the whole house, which suggests that new needs were being filled, but, unlike Tosa, the Miyake did not extend that community to incorporate the territorial domain. House hierarchies were reinforced by regulations that indicated the different times when various ranks of retainers could show up and specified their seating arrangements.[76]

Haga Shōji's research on Watanabe Kazan, who was an elder of Tahara domain, puts the deification of Yasusada in the larger context of a movement to bolster daimyo authority through the production of histories that re-created the past glories of the house and set the agenda for rule.[77] The deification certainly happened at a time when the domain was producing a historical memory focused on the lord's household. In 1810 the domain created the Seishōkan school in front of the main castle gate in order to foster learning and devotion. Then, in 1813, the domain held a special celebration commemorating the 150th anniversary of being granted the castle. They placed the *kubō*'s letter that granted the realm to them in a prominent position in the reception room of the castle, where they then provided an unusually lavish feast to all retainers of the house.[78] The next year, when the elder retainer Muramatsu Rokurōzaemon returned from the Yoshida house in Kyoto in possession of the document of divinity and the portable shrine, domain officials set it up in the castle reception room along with the letter of grant and one newly acquired historical document. This was a letter written in Yasusada's own hand that the domain had obtained especially for this occasion from Miyake Rihei, a samurai of Okazaki domain whose ancestors were close to Yasusada. This letter was shown, as a memento or talisman of the original glory of the Miyake house, to all domain retainers as they came to pay respects to the Yasusada Myōjin deity.[79] By the sixth month of 1815, they built a shrine to house the deity and held even grander celebrations for all retainers, after which it became a site of worship and annual festivities. The importance of the site as religiously embodying the history of house origins is evident in that soon after its creation seven samurai, whose ancestors had served the house all the way back to Yasusada's time, were given especial permission to make offerings of sake and items to become part of the shrine's collection of holy implements.[80] The emphasis on the household and its hierarchies was somewhat different from the aims of the Tosa deifications, but just the same was that the whole creation of deity, shrine, and festival had to be kept from Tokugawa *omote* notice.

Testing the limits of one's consequence

The rules and boundaries of acceptable *uchi* deification and protocol had developed a long tradition by the second quarter of the nineteenth century, and the Tokugawa government could articulate a clear idea of what it wanted. In the 1830s the Date clan of Sendai sent an informal query to the Temple and Shrine Magistrate, asking if they could deify an ancestor who had made particularly important contributions to "the country." The informal response is a clear summation of the Tokugawa stance:

> Although descendants may choose on their own accord to worship
> as *kami* ancestors who made a particular contribution to the ruling
> house, it has been the law of the government for generations that all
> houses have Buddhist funerals. If people have Shinto worship after
> receiving permission from the government, then naturally before
> long they will start requesting court rank for the deities, and even

for recognition by imperial order, and other such undesirable effects will accrue. . . . Thus if it is the worship as *kami* of one individual and strictly limited to within the household, you may do as you wish, but you are directed to know that nothing is to be arranged with our [formal] approval.[81]

This reveals that the Edo government had become quite comfortable with allowing private deification to occur (avoiding mention of the problematic issues of shrine construction and festivals), but they could not allow any formal recognition, because it could become the occasion to promote *omote* linkages between daimyo and the imperial clan. There was a fine line here; the imperial clan had the general right to grant court rank to *kami* with Tokugawa approval but could not grant these ranks to daimyo "private" deities. Although the court did grant court ranks to the priests who served these *kami,* some daimyo clearly wanted closer ties to the imperial clan in its role as high priest of the realm.

The remark "They will start requesting court rank for the deities, and even for recognition by imperial order" was not made lightly, for such attempts had already happened. Mase Kumiko notes that the Hosokawa clan of Kumamoto domain made a shrine for Hosokawa Fujitaka (1534–1610) and other ancestors in 1782, and they soon opened up informal negotiations directly with the imperial house, hoping to get an imperial deification for Fujitaka. The response was clear and negative. Only Hideyoshi and Kakimoto Hitomaro had ever been granted the Myōjin title by imperial decree. Myōjin was a first-rank deity equivalent in status to the emperor himself. Instead all the Hosokawa had to do was go to the Yoshida or Shirakawa house and pay a little money, and they could get a Myōjin title easily. Perhaps hoping that this was only an initial refusal, the Hosokawa continued negotiations until 1801 when they received the following response from the Imperial Regent: "The shogun's house might have objections. Without approval from the Kantō it will not happen." Following this refusal, they tried to obtain an imperial decree of higher court rank for Fujitaka but were likewise refused. The Hosokawa knew they had the option of a "private" deification, and they were well aware of acceptable *uchi* behavior for shrines and deifications. But they wanted a shrine that could be built anew and whose plaque at the front gate could not be ordered taken down by the Tokugawa. So it is clear that they were going for a change in *omote* rules by first gaining an end run around the Tokugawa by going directly to the imperial house. However, changing *omote* rules was extremely difficult in the Tokugawa order, for it implied a lack of respect for and fear of the regime. In the case of the rules for shrines and deifications, they did not change until the government itself was torn apart.[82]

Following the collapse of the Tokugawa in 1868, the new Meiji government started approving shrines and organizing them into hierarchies serving the new state's interest. As with the Tokugawa management of religion, this too was a complicated process, reflecting numerous struggles in the social and political world.[83] Many of the "private" daimyo deities founded in the Tokugawa era pursued imperial recognition. The creation of daimyo deities flourished in the Meiji period, both before domains were abolished and even afterward, as their descendants became nobility in the new regime. Grants of court rank and affirmation of deity names proceeded rapidly, and Fujinami Daimyōjin and Yasusada Reijin, who had existed only in *uchi* spaces of the Tokugawa world, found an official place in the new pantheon of the Meiji state.[84]

Meiji State Shinto co-opted numerous shrines and destroyed a large number of other shrines in the name of orthodoxy, not unlike what happened in Okayama in the seventeenth century. Similar events occurred in nineteenth-century domainal state Shinto as well, and the case of Mito domain is famous. Likewise Chōshū domain not only harnessed support from existing sites but also destroyed the majority of shrine and *kami* sites that neither dated from before the Genroku period nor were distinctly related to domain policy. They stigmatized these shrines as *inshi,* "depraved sites of worship."[85] Tosa domain's policies were less bent on destroying "depraved sites" than on binding shrines and rites to the calendar of Fujinami. All of these domainal state activities were carried out by officials responding to the problems of their own times, but these activities remained meaningful resources for the creators of Meiji Japan.

This chapter has shown how the politics of *omote* and *uchi* worked in an area of religious politics. As we have seen in earlier chapters, disobedience was not necessarily a sign of decline or lack of Tokugawa authority. This chapter has supplied further evidence that the separation of *omote* rituals of obedience and *uchi* activities of difference was operating from the mid-seventeenth-century peak of government power and maturity. The emphasis here has been to highlight that this form of politics not only promoted stability but also permitted political evolution. The Tokugawa order may look stagnant, hidebound, or in decline when we assume that *omote* laws and rituals functioned as they do in modernity, but when they are understood as half the story of politics that must occur in conjunction with *uchi* activity, we can recognize the potential for change and adaptation in the political culture of the Tokugawa order.

The Meiji regime was created to respond to and fit in with the vigorous imperialism and nationalism of the West, and ideal forms of politics therefore changed in Japan. *Omote* and *uchi* were phased out as ideals of political behavior and were replaced with a centralized form of bureaucratic rule. The Meiji government had to promote freedom of religion in order to be perceived as "civilized" and achieve higher status among the Western imperialist nations. By the 1890s freedom of religion was ensconced as a right in the new constitution, although limited, as were all rights, by state interest. This was to impress Western countries, which in their own lands had hammered out the separation of church and state as a way to escape the violence endemic to their own early modern experiences of religious civil war and oppression. Nevertheless, the leaders of the Japanese state hoped to promote nationalism by inculcating and indeed requiring worship of the imperial clan, which historically had functioned as the highest *kami* of the realm. Because of its constitution, the Meiji government had to argue that Shinto was not a religion but a civic rite, in order use its knowledge and ritual as a tool of nationalization.

By treating Shinto as something qualitatively different from religion, the Meiji government set up what is surprisingly an interesting parallel with the Tokugawa order, but centered around Shinto rather than Buddhism. It demanded that everyone participate in government Shinto rites as the normal duty of a subject of the emperor. Subjects might pursue "religion" in private life but not bring it into sites of "civic ritual." The problems that the Christian Uchimura Kanzo faced, because he would not bow to the emperor's rescript on education, arose because he would not participate in a ritual of submission. He found himself fired as an instructor and vilified in the press.[86] If he had bowed, as most Christians in this era did, then he would have had no trouble. His type of religiosity taught him to disdain other religions as idolatry and prevented him from combinatory practice. This made him heroic in the eyes of his type of faith, but as an imperial subject he became a person who lacked civic consciousness.

The creation of historical narrative is, like the creation of religion, deeply political. Its stories translate pasts into contemporary identities for its consumers and set agendas for future action. The next chapter takes up the Edo-Meiji divide in history writing, first analyzing feudal patterns of history production in the Edo period and then contrasting these patterns with historical writing in the modern national era so as to highlight how the preoccupations of modernity shape our historical understanding of prenational pasts.

6

Histories

[This lineage of the Hisamatsu clan] is largely based on the lineage
of the Bunka era [1818–1829]. However, as the Bunka-era lineage
was submitted to the Tokugawa government, it contains not a
few matters involving discretion. Regarding some of these I have
written the truth.

—From the preface of a daimyo lineage composed by Tsuda Masatada
in 1844[1]

A school of historiography called Mitogaku flourished in the castle town of
Mito, the heart of a daimyo realm ruled by one of the three main collateral
houses of the Tokugawa clan. Mitogaku is best known for crafting a history of
Japan, the *Dai Nihon shi.* Modeled on Chinese imperial dynastic histories, the
Dai Nihon shi's narrative centered on the Japanese imperial line. Its vision of
the place of the emperor and the warrior governments of Japan was not created with any revolutionary intent, but because it made the imperial line the
organizing principle of the history, it became highly influential among the activists of the 1860s who emphasized the ideal of service to the imperial line in
their vision of a new Japan. They propounded the notion that warrior government, then represented by the Tokugawa clan, had usurped the authority of
the emperor, and they used this idea to justify the overthrow of the Tokugawa
and to "restore" the emperor as the rightful center and ruler of the country of
Japan. This political movement became the nationalist revolution known as
the Meiji Restoration, and its leaders immediately began rewriting the past of
the archipelago. They reinvented the Tokugawa past so that it could be duly
discarded (The Tokugawa failed to carry out their duty to serve the emperor's

will!) and narratives for future action could be created (Serve the emperor!). This influential vision made the emperors' will over a unified and expanding Japan the prime context in which to organize the narration of the entire past of the archipelago.[2]

The historian Watanabe Hiroshi has critically discussed the importance of Mitogaku's role in popularizing a broad slate of modern Japanese historiographical terms to describe the Edo period. He has advanced the argument that the terms *bakufu, tennō, chōtei,* and *han* have been commonly used by modern historians in ways that do not accurately reflect the Edo-period past.[3] Watanabe notes that Mitogaku scholars encouraged the popularization of the first three of these terms, and this practice became normalized by the history writing produced under the ideology of the Meiji Restoration. He questions whether historians should continue to use them to describe the Edo past. He himself made a decision to rewrite most of the previously published chapters of his 1997 book, *Higashi Ajia no ōken to shisō* (East Asian kingly authority and ideologies), changing the terminology to be, as he argues, more faithful to the Edo past, using such Edo-period terms as *kōgi* (government) for *bakufu* (military government), *tenshi* (child of heaven) for *tennō* (heavenly sovereign), and *kinri* (forbidden quarter) for *chōtei* (court). There is much truth to his stimulating argument, and although it is not entirely without problems in the context of *omote* and *uchi* politics, it has been a prime inspiration for my current analysis.

Using the actual Edo-period terms raises the prestige of the Tokugawa vis-à-vis the imperial clan, which is more true to the era than is represented in modern narratives. Watanabe's method allows more sensitive exploration of Edo-era history because he employs narratives emanating from Tokugawa authority, but I suggest that because this uses the space of Japan as an unspoken frame of reference, the replacement of terms alone does not provide a method for understanding the feudal arrangement of political space into *omote* and *uchi* and its political culture. Feudal spaces become translated into "regions" of the nation, rather than spaces with *naibun* identities.[4]

This chapter analyzes a variety of official histories composed by samurai in the Tokugawa period for what they tell us about how the politics of *omote* and *uchi* shaped their narratives. As was discussed in earlier chapters, many "facts" recorded in past history are not easily translated into present standards of "fact" and can inadvertently be misread as modern-style history. This chapter explores some of the intentions embedded in many types of Edo-era history writings and suggests some guidelines for interpreting their information for present uses. Another particular interest of this chapter is to consider how some historical narratives created in the Edo period relate to Mitogaku's emperor-centered vision and to other modern narratives about Tokugawa-era history. The Meiji Restoration was not merely a political revolution but also a historiographical revolution, and this chapter clarifies some of the major changes that continue to influence the way that we narrate Tokugawa history. The place of the emperor is central to Meiji-era historiography, so this chapter begins by comparing how the emperor was presented in histories formally presentable to the Kyoto court and in those presentable to the Tokugawa.

The feudal nature of Tokugawa-period historiography requires that we understand for which *omote* a history was composed. Here I analyze issues beginning with the imperial *omote* and descending the hierarchy through the Tokugawa and daimyo in order to understand the differences between their various historiographical discourses and also to compare their narratives with modern national historiography. After introducing the terminology and political assumptions of Mito's *Dai Nihon shi,* I analyze similar issues in two histories commissioned by the ruling Tokugawa clan, *Honchō tsugan* (A Complete Mirror of Our Dynasty) and *Tokugawa jikki* (A True Record of the Tokugawa). I then compare those to two histories written by and for the Yamauchi clan of Tosa, "Otōke nendai ryakki" (An Abridged Chronology of Our Honored House) and "Hanshi naihen" (An Internal History of Our *Han*), and conclude with a brief discussion of *Tosa hansei roku* (A Record of Tosa Domain Government), a Tosa domain history written for presentation to the early Meiji court, to look at the transformation of Tosa from a domainal country to a *han* and then ultimately to a region in historical discourse.

Politicizing the *tennō* suffix

A key issue in this historiography is how to name individual emperors and how to name their office or position. One of Watanabe's main goals is to reflect what he regards as actual Edo-period consciousness. He chooses to call the position of the emperor *tenshi* rather than the now ubiquitous *tennō* because, in fact, *tenshi* was a much more common Edo-period term—although there were many other commonly used terms as well. Watanabe also approaches the issue from an analysis of posthumous titles and argues that the custom of granting the posthumous title *tennō* to emperors had ended in the thirteenth century. This practice was revived only at the death of the strong-willed emperor Kōkaku in 1840. Watanabe therefore chooses to append the suffix *-in* rather than *-tennō* to the names of earlier Edo-period emperors. *In* identifies the emperor as a Buddhist lay monk or nun, and *tennō* as "heavenly sovereign."

Modern historiography uses only *tennō* for all emperors of the Edo period, but Watanabe's choice to use *-in* for all emperors up to Kōkaku accords with Edo-period usage, and he attributes the origins of modern historiographical practice to the emperor-centered discourse of which Mito scholars were the foremost proponents.[5]

Watanabe bases this claim on the research of Fujita Satoru, who examined the circumstances of the posthumous naming of the man we now call "Emperor Kōkaku." The Kyoto court made a special request to the Tokugawa at the death of this emperor, named in life Tomohito, for permission to give him the honorific posthumous name "Kōkaku" and the suffix *-tennō* (a name that meant Heavenly Sovereign of Shining Qualities).[6] The ostensible grounds for this appeal were that this emperor was particularly great. Clearly, however, the court's request was a move to increase the authority of Kyoto vis-à-vis the Tokugawa, actually the last gambit from the grave of this emperor who had spent most of his reign trying to augment imperial court power. It was Kōkaku who much earlier, in 1789, had tried to get for his father, a prince who never actually reigned, the title of retired emperor (*dajōtennō*). The chief Tokugawa Elder, Matsudaira Sadanobu, successfully resisted this unprecedented move, but it became an incident, known as the *songō jiken,* that was a key factor in forcing Sadanobu's early retirement from office.[7] Although Kōkaku did not have the power to attain his objective in 1789, perhaps the difficulties caused by the incident led the Tokugawa government, which at any rate in 1840 was facing many more serious problems, to be more compliant upon Kōkaku's death. Thus the Tokugawa granted the request for what they thought would be a single-occasion revival of using an honorific name (*shigō*) and the *-tennō* suffix. The incident was significant enough to be greeted with surprise by many people in Japan; a few went so far as to write graffiti making fun of the problems caused by this break with tradition.[8] It was then commonly understood that for well over half a millennium the Buddhist suffix *-in* had been attached to the posthumous names of deceased emperors, and those posthumous names were generally chosen by identifying the location of a favorite retirement palace. It had been sufficient to give the emperor Tōhito the posthumous name Momozono-in (meaning Retired in the Peach Garden Palace). Warriors commonly received the very same *-in* suffix for their posthumous names, as did many well-off commoners, thereby emphasizing a religious identity more than a status identity. This troubled some people in the Edo period and earlier, and such anxieties ultimately led to the modern ubiquity of the moniker *tennō.*[9]

Some loyalists interpreted the use of the moniker for Kōkaku in 1840 as a revival of a practice that had been consciously discontinued, a restoration, as it were, of the emperor's rightful place at the pinnacle of a government that he had entrusted to the care of the Tokugawa. The mid-fourteenth-century scholar Kitabatake Chikafusa lamented in his history, the *Jinnō shōtōki* (Chronicles of the Authentic Lineage of the Divine Emperors), that the emperor Reizei (950–1011, r. 967–969) had ordered that he not be assigned the title *tennō* after his death:

> From the time of this *mikado,* use of the title *tennō* was discontinued. Bestowal of the honorific posthumous name had earlier ceased at the time of Uda-tennō. Reizei's will said that the anniversary of his death should not be observed and also that no mausoleum should be built for him. He did this out of consideration for the people and to encourage frugality. This was thoughtful, but to dispense with the honorific title makes it impossible for subjects and children to do their righteous duty. The imperial Sinitic posthumous names for sovereigns from the time of Jinmu-tennō on were picked in later ages. Beginning with Jitō and Genmei, *tennō* honorific titles were given to each sovereign after he retired or entered holy orders. Indeed, they should all be called *tennō*. The decision to abandon the *tennō* title was made by wise men of the middle age, but I absolutely cannot agree.[10]

Chikafusa lived and wrote during a troubled age of civil war when there were two competing branches of the imperial line, the era of Northern and Southern Courts (1336–1392). The Northern Court was dominated by the Ashikaga warrior clan and gave the Ashikaga the rank of shogun. The Southern Court fled the capital and ineffectively strove to reassert its control over the land. Chikafusa mainly blamed the imperial clan for slowly letting go of power, thus leading to the conflicts and disorder of his day. For him the issue of naming was politically consequential, as naming should frame the rituals of relations between ruler and ruled and thereby inculcate obedience.

In his history Chikafusa appended the *-tennō* suffix to the names of all emperors before Reizei and the *-in* suffix to Reizei and his successors, a technique he employed in his agenda to highlight imperial decline. From today's vantage point on the surviving records, it is clear that Chikafusa was wrong in his facts concerning when naming practices changed.[11] It seems impossible to identify with any certainty a moment when the suffix *-tennō* stopped being consistently used. It most likely began to decline in frequency with the emperor who was named in life Nariakira (926–967). His posthumous name,

Murakami, by which we know him today, was the location of his grave site, and in some records he is the last emperor with the title *tenno.* However, the whole issue of the posthumous title *tennō* seems to be related to a general decline in use of the honorific posthumous names. This decline seems to have begun soon after the capital was moved from Heijō (Nara) to Heian (Kyoto). The first examples of naming an emperor by his site of retirement are the second and third emperors of the Heian era: Heizei (786–842) and his brother Saga (774–824).[12] Subsequently, more emperors were given the honorific names, but following Murakami less than a century later, most emperors were known by the name of retirement villas or by the location of where they lived out their lives after being banished. The only emperors granted posthumous honorific names were those who had died before retiring, as well as a few who had suffered the pain of banishment and therefore needed posthumous appeasement to prevent them from becoming vengeful spirits. Along with the increasing use of retirement villa names, it gradually became more common than not to use the suffix *-in,* but practice was not at all uniform. Another medieval example, the *Gukanshō,* written circa 1219 by the well-connected aristocratic monk Jien, does not remark on any change and continues calling all sovereigns with the suffix *-tennō*—for example, Reizei-tennō and Ichijō-tennō (980–1011).[13] Many medieval court records and histories show an indiscriminate use of *-in,* *-tennō,* and even the compound *-intennō* for emperors both before and after Ichijō, which suggests that "a moment of discontinuance" did not exist for many of the authors. In a similar fashion, the naming of the office or position of the living emperor was highly varied and complex in medieval and Tokugawa times. People used such terms as *tenshi, mikado, tōgin,* and *kinri* much more commonly than the term *tennō,* which is uniform today.[14]

Anxieties over the normative absence of the *-tennō* suffix for emperors existed in some circles in the Edo period, perhaps under the influence of Chikafusa's history. The idea that there had been a moment of abandonment of the *tennō* title caught hold, but the moments of "discontinuance" that such people identified varied, ranging from events of the tenth century to those of the thirteenth century, because the original records, likely through an original lack of concern with the issue, are unrevealing. Some histories of the Edo period list Emperor Murakami as the last sovereign with the *-tennō* suffix.[15] Others follow Chikafusa's lead, and yet others list Juntoku (1197–1242), who was deposed by the Kamakura warrior government following defeat of the emperor's "rebellion" against Kamakura.[16] The issue of the "discontinuance" of the title *tennō* is more accurately seen as arising from the rhetoric of Edo-period politics concerning the position of the emperor. Some scholars of the Edo period made attachment of *-tennō* to names an issue symbolic of the proper hierarchy of loyalty in politics, an idea that peaked in the linkage of late Edo-era imperial loyalism and the early Meiji-era negation of the warrior *hōken* order. With this as a background, let us move to Edo-period historical writing, beginning with the *Dai Nihon shi* of the Mito school.

Mito's *Dai Nihon shi* for the imperial *omote*

It is a curious thing that although *Dai Nihon shi* became influential in the early eighteenth century, it was not completed until long after the Edo period was over. Indeed the final published product represents two and a half centuries of writing and editing.[17] The project was begun in 1657 at the order of the lord of Mito domain, Tokugawa Mitsukuni, and was overseen by a Chinese historian who had fled to Japan when the Manchus conquered the Ming dynasty. It arranged history as a succession of reigns of emperors, with added chapters on relatives, loyal subjects, and traitorous subjects, and it achieved a complete draft status good enough to be presented to the Tokugawa *kubō* in 1720. Although initially presented to the Tokugawa, *Dai Nihon shi* can be considered an emperor-*omote* history because it was written with all of the facts arranged around the imperial order and with an eye toward making the work formally presentable to the emperor. A woodblock print edition was presented to the imperial court in 1851.[18] From early on, it possessed the distinctive vision that it would impart to modern readers and writers. But the history continued to go through revisions of interpretation and structure and consumed the energies of Mito historians until 1906. Portions of its eighteenth-century manuscript version nevertheless had significant influence on other historical writing in the Edo period. The *Dai Nihon shi sansō* (also known as *Dai Nihon shi ronsan*) was written by Asaka Tanpaku, one of the chief editor-compilers of the 1720 draft.[19] It was a commentary that evaluated the actions of various historical people appearing in the main text of the history. Although removed from the official *Dai Nihon shi* by the Fujita Yūkoku group in the early nineteenth century, *Dai Nihon shi sansō* circulated in manuscript form from the eighteenth century onward and influenced such works as Rai San'yō's tremendously popular *Nihon gaishi* (Unofficial History of Japan), published in 1827.[20]

The period covered by *Dai Nihon shi* ranges from the historic origins of the dynasty through the end of the reign of Southern Court emperor Go-Kameyama (r. 1383–1392), who retired without an heir in order to resolve the dynastic split that eighty years earlier had created the two competing imperial lines known as the Northern Court and the Southern Court. The authors of *Dai Nihon shi* considered the Southern Court the more legitimate of the two lines, and the ending of this line's claims was significant enough to finish the history.[21] The narrative thus does not continue into the Edo period but ends with the demise of the Southern Court at the height of Ashikaga power. However, certain issues of political terminology and ideology have direct relevance to modern description of the Edo period, such as the way the narrative deals with the relations between what we now commonly term the shogun and the emperor. The *Dai Nihon shi* refers to all of the heads of the imperial line with the *-tennō* suffix regardless of era, just as in modern practice, but the general appellations for the emperors are more varied and are modeled on premodern Chinese practice; these include *tei* (emperor, also read *mikado*), *tenshi* (son of heaven), and, in compound words, *ō* (king), suggesting a strong use of Confucian standards of authority.[22] *Dai Nihon shi* is also consistent with modern practice in that it consistently identifies the emperor's government as the court (*chōtei*) of Japan, while the Minamoto and the Ashikaga are referred to as *shōgun* and their government is occasionally referred to as *bakufu, fu* (government administrative office), or *gunsei* (military government).[23] These basic terms were used by many Restoration-era activists and also appear generally as they do in modern work on Japanese history. Even the word *han* appears briefly in a usage meaning daimyo, if not domain. In modern writing about history, *han* is not applied to daimyo domains earlier than those of the Tokugawa era, so the term would not likely have been used in *Dai Nihon shi*, because its story ends in the fourteenth century. However, there is one location in a later version of *Dai Nihon shi* that does refer to the daimyo of the Edo period. The 1851 woodblock print version has a preface written by the Mito domain lord in 1810 wherein he refers to his position as *hanpei*, a word that literally means "bulwarks" and is a classical allusion to the daimyo's role as protector of the Tokugawa overlord.[24] Such usage of the word *han* to mean the person of the daimyo had begun to appear sporadically in histories from the time of Ogyū Sorai and Arai Hakuseki in the early eighteenth century.[25] Allowing for a subsequent shift in the meaning of *han* from daimyo to his domanial government or the domain itself, this also reveals a connection between Mitogaku historiographical discourse and modern writing.

The overall design of the history has all public authority emanate from the position of the emperor, and it studiously defines the warrior rule as a military government deriving its authority through appointment by the emperor. As seen with the example of Jien's *Gukanshō*, and as we shall see with *Honchō tsugan,* it might be wrong to overemphasize the singularity of *Dai Nihon shi* in this vision, but without doubt it played the most direct role in creating the language of the Restoration, and the way by which Meiji leaders would interpret the recent Edo past. With this in mind, one can see Restoration historiography as the temporal extension of Edo-era emperor-*omote* history modified to fit modern national space.

Honchō tsugan for the Tokugawa *omote*

The Tokugawa were the supreme power holders of the Edo period, and therefore it is worth looking at the kinds of histories that were composed for formal presentation to them. Two histories commissioned by the ruling Tokugawa house were the seventeenth-century *Honchō tsugan* and the nineteenth-century *Tokugawa jikki.* Written for the most part by scholars of the Hayashi school, who were retainers of the Tokugawa, these were official histories, designed for the edification of, and use by, the Tokugawa overlords. *Honchō tsugan* covers the history of Japan from the imperial origins up to 1611 and so allows easy comparison with *Dai Nihon shi.* Because it extends into the early seventeenth century, it also allows us to explore its narration of Edo-period history. *Tokugawa jikki* spans the history of the Tokugawa house from 1603 to 1786 and thus is properly a description of the Edo polity. Because both histories were written for presentation to the warrior hegemon and not the Kyoto court, their terminology reflects aspects of the feudal nature of politics. Although they record clearly that the Tokugawa recognized the sovereignty of the imperial court and were incorporated into its hierarchy, these histories also portray the Tokugawa in ways that make them equal to, or in certain respects superior to, that court and also reveal sources of ruling authority separate from those derived by integration into imperial authority. These were elements that they could not formally present directly to the court, and indeed they do not appear in *Dai Nihon shi.*

Completed in 1670, *Honchō tsugan* was the final product of a project begun by Hayashi Razan in the 1640s, carried on by his son Gahō, and finally finished by his grandson Hōkō.[26] Gahō's workplace was designated the Kokushikan (Government Building for the History of the Country), reflecting the Hayashi family's ambitions for their project to produce an authoritative history of the country of Japan from the "first human" emperor, Jinmu, up through Emperor Go-Yōzei, whose reign ended in 1611. The organization of the book into chapters named for each successive emperor shows that the country the Hayashi had in mind centered on the imperial dynasty. The terminology regarding the emperor and his or her court in *Honchō tsugan* is in basic agreement with subsequent Mito school work and modern histories. The suffix -*tennō*, not -*in*, is used for all emperors. Similarly, the term *chōtei* in *Honchō tsugan* consistently refers to the Kyoto court and not the Tokugawa court, even though, as Watanabe points out, quite a few scholars of the Edo period did refer to the Tokugawa court as the *chōtei*. It is worth noting, with reference to Watanabe's argument, that the emperor-centered terminology is not necessarily just the product of Mitogaku historiographical discourse. Rather it has much broader and older roots; Mitogaku scholarship nourished those roots and shaped the branches that grew from them. Watanabe's decision to eschew the terms *tennō* and *chōtei* and instead use *tenshi* and *kinri* is certainly a legitimate one, reflecting the most common usage in the Edo period, and it suggests to us a profitable new way of understanding political consciousness of the day. However, we should also realize that he is rejecting a deep strand of historiography on these points, a strand that was also strong within Tokugawa circles.

On the other hand, *Honchō tsugan* is a Tokugawa *omote* product that significantly differed in many respects from *Dai Nihon shi*. Mito scholars criticized it and its Hayashi school authors for expressing forms of disrespect to the imperial clan.[27] One area of difference concerned the relative status of the emperor and the Tokugawa ruler, which can be seen in the formatting of sentences. It was customary in history writing of the day to mark respect for one's sovereign by leaving a blank space open in the line before mention of his name, thereby highlighting it. In some writings particularly given to this form, two blank spaces showed more respect, and the highest respect was shown by starting a new line whenever the name was mentioned. Although *Dai Nihon shi* did not treat the Tokugawa period itself, in the preface that the ruler of Mito, Tokugawa Harutoshi, wrote in 1810 for presentation to the imperial house, he refers to the Tokugawa as the *daishōgun no ie* (the great general's house) and does not leave any honorific open spaces before this term. This term in itself treats the Tokugawa overlord in a manner identical to the way that *Dai Nihon shi* treated the Minamoto and Ashikaga houses in the text. Mention of the emperor in the preface leads to the starting of a new line and even goes to the extreme of having his name start one space higher than the normal level of a regular line of text, elevating his name above the bounds of normal prose to indicate that the emperor was sovereign.[28] By contrast *Honchō tsugan* had no open spaces before either emperors' names or the names of members of the previous military dynasties such as the Minamoto or the Ashikaga, but in the portion that deals with the Tokugawa, it employs honorific open spaces before the names of the first three Tokugawa rulers where they appear in the text.[29]

This elevation of the Tokugawa to sovereign status helps us identify the work as written for the Tokugawa *omote*.

Furthermore, in *Honchō tsugan* the Tokugawa rulers are identified by their posthumous holy identities rather than common names. Ieyasu is referred to as Jinkun (divine lord) or Daijinkun (great divine lord), deriving from his deification as Tōshō Daigongen at Nikkō. The next two Tokugawa heirs are referred to by their posthumous deification names—Hidetada as Daitokukun, and Iemitsu as Daiyū'inden. The respect expressed by these forms of naming is superior to that expressed by the ways of naming of the emperor, who is called by a posthumous *-in* name, and his sons, who are referred to by their names in life. Although the Tokugawa acknowledged the ritual superiority of the emperor, *Honchō tsugan* displays a discourse emphasizing the holiness and centrality of the Tokugawa that existed alongside this recognition. This pattern had an exact parallel in daimyo-*omote* histories expressing their relationship with the Tokugawa. Such was fundamentally unacceptable in the emperor-centered Mito scholarship, which consistently subordinated the identity and status of the warriors to those of the emperor.

While identifying the authority of the Tokugawa through a form of divine naming independent of Kyoto authority, *Honchō tsugan*'s narrative reveals a significant emperor-centered dimension to Tokugawa authority, by portraying it as held by virtue of Tokugawa appointment to posts of Minister of State by the emperor. With regard to the Kamakura and Muromachi governments, the *Honchō tsugan*'s terminology is quite similar to that of *Dai Nihon shi,* indicating a "military government" headed by a shogun.[30] This changes with regard to the Tokugawa era, where *Honchō tsugan* does not use the term *bakufu* for the Tokugawa government, nor does it place particular emphasis on the term or rank of *shōgun*. In this sense it is distinct from Mitogaku writing and most writing about Japanese history since the nineteenth century, a trait that can be cited in support of Watanabe's claim that use of the term *bakufu* does not represent the preference of the ruling Tokugawa. When Ieyasu is not called Divine Lord, he is referred to by such imperial court posts as Minister of the Interior or Minister of the Right. The promotion of Ieyasu to Minister of the Right in 1603 is an important event in the narrative, and the clause "to which was augmented appointment to *seiitaishōgun*" is a brief addendum to the description.[31] The importance placed on the various imperial ministerial ranks indicates that, in the historical vision of *Honchō tsugan*, Tokugawa rule operated largely within the framework of imperial government. It placed limited importance on the post of shogun or the idea of military government. One senses in the pattern of differentiation from the Minamoto and Ashikaga houses that usage of *bakufu* and *shōgun* might have been regarded as somehow diminishing, as missing the full dimensions of Tokugawa authority. Yet the treatment of the Minamoto and the Ashikaga internalizes for "military houses" a historical discourse that is essentially similar to that found in *Dai Nihon shi,* suggesting that Mito scholarship was part of a broader field of imperial imagination.

The idea of military houses and rule was important in this history. Hayashi Gahō set down the following moralizing generalization in the final lines of the section dealing with "imperial fortunes": "The imperial court depends upon the military houses and so is all the more revered. The military houses look up to the imperial house, and they increasingly flourish."[32] So far as it goes, this view is consistent with the Mitogaku ideal, but the integration of the imperial order and the military order is subtler and more multifaceted than the simple court/*bakufu* dichotomy that was emphasized by the Restoration. What the imperial house contributes to warrior authority in the *Honchō tsugan* is integration into the imperial hierarchy by making the Tokugawa into high-ranking aristocrats and ministers of imperial government.

The Tokugawa government was also built upon the military and household authority of warriors themselves and had its own traditions of legitimation separate from those of the imperial order. This is also expressed in *Honchō tsugan.* When it names the government of the military rulers subsequent to the collapse of the Ashikaga, including Nobunaga and Hideyoshi, it refers to that government as a *kokka,* which could mean state and/or ruling household. One instance records Ieyasu's appointment to the Council of Five Regents at Hideyoshi's deathbed so that he would help with the governance of the "military country/countries" (*gunkoku no sei*) and deal with important matters of state (*kokka daiji*).[33] A later appearance of the term also confirms *Honchō tsugan's* vision of the limited role of the post of shogun in authorizing control of the Tokugawa government. *Honchō tsugan* confirms that not long after Ieyasu's retiring from the post of shogun and giving it to his son Hidetada, Ieyasu continued to govern: "The Divine Lord surrendered the office of general over the military to Taitoku-kō, but he continued to decide important matters of the *kokka* from Sunpu."[34] In this sense it seems that *Honchō tsugan* regarded the post of shogun to be an important one of Tokugawa generalship, but the post was not presented as essential to the authority to rule the country. Here one can see that Mitogaku usage of the terms *bakufu* and *shōgun* did not reflect the Tokugawa image of itself as created in this seventeenth-century history. The same point holds true, although not as strongly, for the nineteenth-century *Tokugawa jikki* as well.

Tokugawa jikki, a house history
for the Tokugawa *omote*

The *Ojikki,* now known as *Tokugawa jikki* (which I will hereafter shorten to *Jikki*), was commissioned by the Tokugawa in the early nineteenth century (comp. 1809–1849) and narrates a relationship between the emperor and the Tokugawa that is similar to that described in *Honchō tsugan.* But it is different in character from *Honchō tsugan* in a number of important ways. The *Jikki* is a dynastic house history rather than a history of the country of Japan at that time. A reading of the preface shows that the authors certainly saw the Tokugawa as a dynasty and a court (*chō*) worthy of treatment along the lines of Chinese imperial lineages, albeit their Tokugawa dynasty coexisted with a Japanese imperial dynasty (*kōchō*).[35] Reflecting this choice to emphasize the household, the volumes of the *Jikki* are organized around Tokugawa reigns rather than imperial reigns. In this respect it more fully expresses some forms of feudal narrative, especially with regard to the way it narrates descriptions of Tokugawa subordinates.

When the Tokugawa relationship with the emperor is mentioned in the *Jikki,* the Kyoto emperor is clearly superior in rank and is the lord who bestows appointments on the Tokugawa. The emperor is referred to as lord (*shujō*) and his location as the court. Furthermore, the aristocratic Regents have the suffix -*kō* attached to their names when they appear, equivalent to the way the head of the Tokugawa himself is named. Receiving the rank of shogun has more importance in *Jikki* than it does in *Honchō tsugan.* It is an event necessitating the beginning of a new chapter, and the history details the week of extensive rituals involved. This perhaps indicates a changing self-image in the Tokugawa government. The *Jikki* shows an acceptance of the Kyoto court's formal superiority and provides a framework of understanding that links all of Japan under Kyoto authority at that time.

In addition to various appointments in the imperial court, however, the *Jikki* covers other events in the Tokugawa acquisition of ruling authority. For example, Tokugawa Ienobu ordered that he be referred to as *uesama* (ruler; this can also be read as *kami-sama*) from three days after the burial of Tsunayoshi, but well before his appointment to the rank of shogun. This title was based on his patrimonial authority as head of the Tokugawa clan, an independent form of warrior public identity. On occasions when the generalized role of the Tokugawa hegemon is specified, the term given is not *shōgun* or *kubō,* as one might expect from actual daily usage, but *kō* (ruler), a more literary word to describe head of the government.[36]

Other inconsistencies with narration of imperial superiority also exist in the *Jikki*. Despite the above evidence based on office and rank, the relative status of the emperor and the Tokugawa ruler as expressed by patterns of naming and verb usage indicates equality rather than subordination. For example, no family name is used when referring to the ruling Tokugawa, a convention that is a sign of deference and puts them and the imperial clan on equal footing. Ieyasu is referred to as the deity Tōshōgū. The other heads of the Tokugawa house and their wives and mothers are referred to without family name and with their posthumous names and the suffix *-inden*. The emperor is referred to by the posthumous title and the less grandiose suffix *-in*.[37] The verbs that indicate social relationship are those used for equals. A gift from the Tokugawa to the head of the Kyoto court is described using the verb *susumeru*, which implies polite equality on the part of the Tokugawa. Imperial princes are a step below the Tokugawa, referred to by name and the honorific suffix meaning son of the king (*-shin'nō*), a form comparable in level to that of the daughters of the Tokugawa, who are referred to by name and the suffix *-hime* (princess). With regard to the princes, the verbs used, such as *fusetamau* (bestow) when the Tokugawa give gifts to them, and *kenzu* (proffer up) when they give to the Tokugawa, clearly indicate the princes' status inferiority.[38] This kind of language is not seen in *Dai Nihon shi*, which is consistently at pains to stress the superiority of the imperial house. Viewed from the emperor's perspective, these Tokugawa *omote* narratives, which elevated the status of the Tokugawa house vis-à-vis the emperor, can be described as a Tokugawa *naibun* history writing.

Because politics was largely organized metaphorically along the dimensions of a household, house history was the natural choice to fully express the feudal political vision of the Tokugawa. Events of family history such as births, deaths, marriages, and the like took on a governmental or political aspect in the *Jikki*. For example, the death of the mother of Tokugawa Ietsugu in 1752 occasioned a ten-day mourning period in which no music could be played, all daimyo in Edo had to report to their assigned rooms in the Tokugawa castle, and those not able to be present were required to send messengers. All people living in the direct and indirect dominion of the Tokugawa were ordered to show respect by refraining from various pleasurable activities.[39] Well recorded in the *Jikki* are the names of which parties contributed what presents, who sent messengers of congratulation or condolence, and similar details about such "family" events. Listings of participation by those with right of audience and similar minutiae can be tedious to modern readers whose notions of government are different, but they are a precious resource on the structure of subordination necessary to Tokugawa hegemony.

The way people are named in the *Jikki* reveals messages about status and loyalty throughout the Tokugawa order. When not referred to by posthumous names and -*inden,* the head of the Tokugawa house is referred to by his formal personal name followed by the suffix -*kō* or by *kō* used as a pronoun indicating his lordly position and leadership of government. The heads of the three Tokugawa collateral houses are distinguished from all other retainers through their incorporation in the imperial order. Instead of being referred to by family name, they are denoted more respectfully by their fief name (Kii, Owari, and Mito), their imperial court office as middle-rank councillors (*chūnagon*), and then the honorific suffix -*kyō,* indicating their status as councillors to the Kyoto court. The remainder of retainers are more fully subsumed within a Tokugawa identity. Daimyo and others with right of audience such as bannermen are referred to by office in the Tokugawa government (if they have any), then family name, court rank, and formal personal name (*jitsumyō*), which indicates a lower level of respect. Another dimension of personal naming that expresses house organization in the *Jikki* is the Matsudaira family name applied to many daimyo. As discussed in Chapter 1, the Tokugawa employed a version of a common samurai practice of bestowing the clan name upon chief retainers, which the retainers then had to use in all formal dealings with the lord. Acceptance of the Matsudaira surname had the effect of suppressing independent daimyo clan identities in certain ritual interactions and incorporating daimyo into the household while reminding them of their dependent status. Many daimyo houses such as the Ikeda, the Shimazu, and the Yamauchi appear in the *Jikki* only as Matsudaira. Likewise, a daimyo realm is called personal income (*shiryō*), personal territory (*shiryō*), or fief (*hō, fu,* or *hōchi*), which are ways of naming that deny the independently based authority of the lords over their realms. Daimyo are distinguished from bannermen by being called *daimyō, ryōshu, jōshu* (lord of a castle), or *mangokuijō* ([holders of] more than 10,000 *koku*), but with no use of the language they might employ in their *uchi* spaces.

The essential character of the information contained in these histories needs to be understood as the performance of *omote* demands at two levels. One is the imperial *omote* that the Tokugawa were answerable to, and the other is the Tokugawa *omote* that the Tokugawa retainers were answerable to. The Tokugawa acknowledged their dependence on the emperor and, at the same time, presented their equality to the emperor in certain ways. They also presented their independent forms of authority that they used to control daimyo and other inferiors. As we saw earlier with the birth dates, the death dates, the blood relations, and even the number of lives of various daimyo in the

Tokugawa *omote* histories, this order means that the content of *Tokugawa jikki* and the history of retainer houses that is the *Kansei chōshū shokafu* are quite different from daimyo inside histories.

Histories for a daimyo *omote*

Much as histories written for the Tokugawa contain narratives that could not be formally presented to the emperor, histories written for a daimyo expressed distinctive political visions that could not be formally submitted to the Tokugawa. The historiographical discourses of the Tokugawa and daimyo are recognizably different, but the distinctions are mild in comparison with the distinctions in the language used within domain politics and that used in relations with the Tokugawa in actual practice. This circumstance is similar to the way in which the *Jikki* reveals less independence from the emperor than the actually used Tokugawa discourses of politics, which tend to emphasize authority emanating directly from the Tokugawa. Such differences may result from the broader view that history writing takes (presenting the whole context of one's relations and authority) relative to specific proclamations and statements that express narrower contexts of relations in political action.

This section examines two official histories of the Yamauchi daimyo household of Tosa and then briefly comments on a third history produced immediately after the abolition of the domain in 1871, following the Meiji Restoration. The first of these histories was completed in the early nineteenth century, and the second was written just as Tokugawa authority was collapsing and the new Meiji government was being created. These two alone indicate important shifts in terminology and political imagination as the old order disintegrated and a new order quickly replaced it. The third history, written within a few years after the abolition of domains, reflects an essentially modern discourse of domainal history that marks the end of feudal historiography and the adoption of a unitary vision of an imperial Japan.

The "Otōke nendai ryakki" (An abridged chronology of our honored house; hereafter "Nendai ryakki") was completed in 1812 by the domain scholar and retainer Miyaji Nakae. It was never published, but manuscript copies were kept in the domain lord's house and the domain school and also circulated among Tosa samurai, with each holder tending to make updates of the history as late as the 1850s.[40] The "Nendai ryakki" mostly treats the two higher external authorities, imperial and Tokugawa, with the terminology actually used at that time in the domain, terms proper for *omote* interaction with them. The head of the Tokugawa house is generally called *kubō-sama*. The title *kubō* denotes his position of highest authority within the warrior order of things, rather than the direct affective relationship to the Tokugawa authority that the *Jikki* terms *kō* and *uesama* (my lord) express. The loyalty of Yamauchi house subjects belonged to the Yamauchi lord, so use of *uesama* for the Tokugawa would likely have seemed discordant. It is also noteworthy that the primary title of Tokugawa authority in the "Nendai ryakki" is the more expansive *kubō* rather than *shōgun,* reflecting an important distancing from Mito-style terminology.[41] Likewise, the "Nendai ryakki" does not use the term *bakufu* but calls the Edo government the *kōgi;* and the Kyoto court is called the forbidden quarter (*kinri*) rather than the court (*chōtei*), both of which implied the central position of the Tokugawa as the government.

Where the "Nendai ryakki" diverges from either an imperial or a Tokugawa vision is in the way that it centers and makes holy the daimyo clan itself. Specific *kubō* are referred to by posthumous names followed by *-insama* (revered retired), just as specific emperors are called by their posthumous names and *-insama.* The Yamauchi lords are not identified by family name, and they and their wives and mothers are called by their posthumous names with *-insama,* in the same way as for the emperor and the Tokugawa. Likewise, Yamauchi daughters are called by their personal name with *-himesama* (revered princess), which in the dimension of naming puts their status on par with that of the Tokugawa daughters. Noninheriting sons are identified by their childhood names and the high honorific *-sama,* which puts them below the inheriting son but above all nonfamily members of the domain. The "Nendai ryakki" uses no honorific open spaces for either lord, Tokugawa, or emperor. In these various ways, it effectively puts the Yamauchi on the same plane as the Tokugawa and the emperor within its discourse, reflecting its character as a document for use within Tosa and the Yamauchi household.

The "Nendai ryakki" treats the Yamauchi realm differently as well, calling it a domainal country (*ryōgoku, kuni*) rather than a territory (*ryō*) and the other common forms used in the *Jikki.* The meaning within the Yamauchi discourse is that the realm is an entity of government rather than mere private property to be managed. The term for government in the text is *seiji* (the modern term for government), indicating local governance in a way inexpressible at the Tokugawa *omote,* but the term *kōgi* is used to mean the Tokugawa government. This is somewhat different from actual usage at the time, in which *kōgi* could be used to refer to domain government. The word *han* is not utilized at all, either to identify the domain lord, as seen in the preface of *Dai Nihon shi,* or the domain itself, as has become common in modern historiography. Nor is it used to refer to other lords and domains. Other daimyo are described as *daimyō* or are individually named by their Tokugawa *omote* family name (for many, Matsudaira), their nominal imperial court post (such as Oki no kami), and the high honorific suffix *-sama*. This way of naming reveals respect and identifies them in Tokugawa terms rather than their own internal-use terms, suggesting that the framework of interaction with outside lords is always mediated by Tokugawa-dictated norms—just as in actual political practice. Bannermen are named in the same way as daimyo but with the less honorific *-dono* suffix, suggesting awareness that the Yamauchi daimyo are higher in status.

A daimyo's *uchi* is an *omote* to his own samurai and commoner subjects. The ways of naming people of the realm in the "Nendai ryakki" reveal their clear subordination to the Yamauchi house and are used to distinguish the graded hierarchy of status within the house. This naming system parallels the forms in the *Jikki*, but with the Yamauchi at the center of its own sphere. The ruling Yamauchi house members are called only by their personal or posthumous names, distinguished from retainers by the absence of a family name. Retainers of the highest status, such as House Elders, are called by family name, "court title," and formal personal name, without any honorific suffix. "Court titles" such as Wakasa and Mondo were not granted by either the imperial court or the Tokugawa court and could not have been used publicly outside of the domain or in external historical discourses. They were merely a holdover from the Warring States era when people commonly called themselves by various court ranks taken on by themselves or issued by a local lord. Yamauchi custom permitted the hereditary usage of such titles by certain senior clans of Tosa as marks of status, but the titles could not be used outside the domain. The independence of many of these senior houses was rhetorically bound to the clan by use of "Yamauchi" as the family name in lieu of the original name. For example, the *karō* Inui Hikosaku is called Yamauchi Hikosaku in the "Nendai ryakki." Samurai retainers of lesser status than House Elder are called by their family name and their daily-use name (*yobina*), marking a lower degree of respect. In general terms, samurai are identified as house members (*gokachū*) or servants (*hōkōnin*) or as "all samurai" (*shoshi*). Merchants, farmers, and other nonsamurai are not mentioned by name at all and, if they appear, are called "someone" (*nanigashi*), a way of indicating that they are of no importance. This is similar to usage in the *Jikki*, wherein neither commoners nor daimyo retainers are normally identified by name. These patterns reflect the intense status consciousness of the samurai world. Historians can look to these various naming patterns as messages about status and belonging and as clues to identify the specific *omote* of any given history of the Edo period.

Facts about the daimyo household in internal-use histories such as the "Nendai ryakki" are often different than those that appear in Tokugawa histories such as the *Jikki*. For example, in the "Nendai ryakki" the lord Toyotsune's birth is in the year 1711 and he dies in 1725 at the age of fifteen, too young to name an heir. Because his Tokugawa *omote* birth was reported as 1707, he was officially nineteen, and the domain was able to arrange an adopted heir. The death and adoption are reported without incident in the *Jikki,* and his age is of course given as nineteen in the Tokugawa official lineages.[42] Similar discrepancies exist throughout, although the degree to which inside facts and outside facts are presented is sometimes inconsistent. For example, in both the "Nendai ryakki" and the Tokugawa histories Toyofusa's death in 1705 and Toyotsune's death in 1725 are each reported as occurring a suspicious one day after their requests to adopt an heir.[43] The Yamauchi must have considered actual death date information too sensitive even for local consumption, but other daimyo—the Miyake, for instance, as we have seen—were less concerned about this. Even the Yamauchi changed policy in the following history to be discussed, "Hanshi naihen," which records Toyofusa's actual death as one day earlier than his reported death.[44]

Tokugawa authorities ordered the fifteenth Tosa domain lord, Yamauchi Yōdō, into enforced retirement in 1862 because of the role he had played on the losing side of a Tokugawa inheritance dispute. From his retirement villa Yōdō ordered his scholars to begin writing a new domain history. Actual work did not begin until 1866. Numerous volumes of the envisioned history were finished, mostly those pertaining to the seventeenth century, but all work on the project ceased in 1869 during the tumult of the Meiji Restoration, and the history was never completed.[45] A key point in understanding the discourse of the history is that it was largely written between the collapse of Tokugawa authority in 1868 and the end of Yamauchi lordly authority with the abolition of domains in 1871. Initially the work was entitled "Kokushi naihen," with reference to the domain as a *koku* rather than as a *han,* but the government reorganization of the Meiji Restoration in 1868 included changing the official term for domains to *han* in an attempt to promote unity under the emperor and to foster a consciousness of Japan as the sole country. This political change was reflected in the removal of the term *koku* and the insertion of *han* in the renaming of this historical work.[46] That this change occurred in mid-composition is seen, for example, in the near-final draft of the governmental history "Seitai enkaku" volume devoted to the years 1700–1703. The outer cover and the inner cover have the title "Hanshi naihen" while the first page of the actual text begins with the title "Okokushi naihen."[47] In another rough-draft volume the title on the first page is "Okokushi naihen," with a line neatly drawn through "Okokushi" and, to the right, the word "Hanshi" inscribed in red.[48] The linguistically unsettled transitional period influenced a number of word choices in the "Hanshi naihen," and they are not always internally consistent. Title change aside, within even the final version the word *han* remains very rarely used and the Yamauchi realm remains predominantly a *kuni* (or *koku*). The common pronoun for the lord is *kō* and on occasion *kimi* (ruler), and government of the realm is called *kokusei*, all terms that could not be used in histories presented to either the Tokugawa or the emperor. The Yamauchi lords and immediate family are referred to without the family name and with the posthumous -*in* names and the -*sama* suffix. Heads of branch houses are referred to by formal name or title with the -*sama* suffix and without the family name. Beneath them are the chief retainers, who are referred to by family name (for many of them, the granted Yamauchi name) and either hereditary title name or formal name. Regular retainers are referred to by family name and informal personal name. On the whole, descriptions of internal domainal realities are consistent with the "Nendai ryakki" and incongruous with both Mito history and Tokugawa history and reflect the continuing feudal authority of the Yamauchi ruler in the first years of the Restoration.

Despite the similarities with the "Nendai ryakki" in terms of descriptions of internal realities, descriptions of the Tokugawa and imperial clan in the "Hanshi naihen" make it seem closer to the historical vision of the Mito style of historiography as seen in the *Dai Nihon shi*. A "general guidelines" volume, probably written in 1866, describes the organization projected for the complete work that includes a "Gaihen" external history component as well.[49] The "Gaihen" section deals with important events in Japan that, although not directly connected with the domain, occurred after 1600 when the Yamauchi clan entered into rule of Tosa. This organization situates the later event as the anchor of the political history of the whole project and indicates the centrality of Yamauchi concerns to the history itself, but the terminology proposed for the "Gaihen" generally is congruent with the imperial vision and certainly reflects the ending of the Tokugawa order of things. The external history includes a projected section called "Tenchō" (Imperial Court) and reveals that the suffix for all emperors would be -*tennō*. Their history was to be treated simply, mainly with notice of succession, and there was also to be a record of appointments of officials to high ranks within the imperial court. This envisioned volume was never written, but the finished volumes of the "Hanshi naihen" have occasional mention of the emperor and use the -*tennō* suffix for all emperors.

The next section of the external history was to be called the "Bakufu." Furthermore, in the surviving portions of the history itself, the Tokugawa government was called the *bakufu*. Frequently the name of this government is written with characters that would normally be read as *hakufu* but in this case were probably intended to be read *bakufu* as well. There is no explanation of this word choice, which is not in the dictionaries and which I have not seen anywhere else. The *haku* character meant someone who had the status of councillor in the Chinese imperial government, and came to be used to identify an aristocratic rank in the Meiji aristocracy. Its use in the "Hanshi naihen" likely was intended to connote the high rank of the Tokugawa within the imperial court. Thus it may have been subordinating the Tokugawa to imperial authority, but as a noble government rather than as a military government, and may have reflected lingering Tokugawa discourse. At any rate, the use of both *bakufu* and *hakufu* in this work, and the use of neither in the earlier "Nendai ryakki," suggests the relative novelty of this way of naming the Tokugawa government—part of a newly accepted vision within the domain of political relations resulting from the Tokugawa collapse. Likewise, the Tokugawa overlord himself is frequently referred to as *shōgun* rather than as *kubō*, and his house as *shōgunke*, also in line with Mito terminology. Thus it seems that this history written during and after the fall of the Tokugawa by a domain that played a key role in creating the new Meiji government was heavily influenced by the imperial vision propounded in Mitogaku.

For the first few years of its existence, the fledgling Meiji government chose not to do away with the feudal order and continued to have daimyo rule their own domains. This feudal arrangement is reflected in the "Hanshi naihen," which continued an internal discourse inherited from the Tokugawa period but used a new discourse in external relations. Attempts to decrease domainal independence by modifying this emperor-centered feudal system failed, and the new government, fearing a resurgence of civil war, abolished domains in 1871 and took rule away from the daimyo. At nearly the same time the Imperial Ministry ordered the newly created Kōchi prefecture to write a history of the role the Yamauchi played in the Meiji Restoration from the time of the 1853 arrival of Commodore Perry to the present. The ministry's ultimate goal was to create a history celebrating the Restoration and providing participants an investment in the revolution. The product of this order in Kōchi was the history called *Tosa hansei roku*, completed in the mid-1870s by a number of former Yamauchi retainers, some of whom had worked on the "Hanshi naihen."[50] They finished *Tosa hansei roku* within just a few years of abandoning work on the "Hanshi naihen" project, yet regarding the Yamauchi clan, the domain, and the larger Tokugawa order, the discourses of the two works are a revolution apart.

Only the emperor receives special respect in *Tosa hansei roku*. The lord of the domain and the Tokugawa shogun are identified by family name and formal name with no suffix. No open spaces appear before their names, and their actions are described with common verbs in plain form. It as if the aura of heightened respect or numinous feeling that upheld the old order had dissipated. The new history had its own aura, one that suited Japan's imperial modernity: the Tokugawa government is called *bakufu*, the domain government is called *han*, and the imperial court is called the Court (*chōtei*)—and only the last of these is preceded by an open space in the sentence indicative of special respect. The emperor is referred to by posthumous title plus *-tennō*, and with an open space before each appearance. The verbs for imperial actions are in plain form, but the narrative uses polite vocabulary peculiar to the imperial station, such as *chokumei* (imperial order) and *hōzuru* (to die), and these words are preceded by open spaces. The diction of history writing reflected that the new divine polity was that of an imperially ruled Japan exerting its power directly into the lower spaces of rule such as Kōchi prefecture.

As evidenced in the changes that occurred over the period of composition of the three Tosa histories, Watanabe is clearly correct in identifying the importance of an emperor-centered political vision in forming much of Meiji-era historiographical discourse. The vocabulary and rhetoric of imperial loyalism employed in the imperial *omote* narrative negated much of the ideology of the Tokugawa and its feudal order. Mito historical scholarship played a significant role in this formulation, in part because it resonated with and appropriated elements of other styles of imperial narrative present in Japanese writing about history, before and during the Tokugawa era. These other elements defined a written cultural tradition that had ever greater influence thanks to the spread of print culture.[51] The needs of the revolution continued to transform the imperial *omote* discourse into an appropriate imperial national discourse, ultimately destroying the forms of narration meaningful to the feudal order.

Historiography in Japan and elsewhere has changed greatly since the late nineteenth century. It would be unacceptable, for example, in scholarly writing today to use open spaces before an emperor's name in order to express reverence. Yet prewar and postwar writing styles share a number of common elements that characterize them both as distinctly modern. As Watanabe points out, the basic terms that we continue to use to describe government of the Edo period were made hegemonic at the start of Meiji. Some would say that we have thereby escaped the ideology of the Tokugawa period, which is certainly true, but this is not simply a shift from ideology to objectivity. It is the replacement of one ideology with another. While most markers of holiness have largely disappeared from modern scholarship, many writers continue to employ terms peculiar to the imperial station such as *chokumei* and *hōgyo* (the latter meaning "to die," used only of the emperor). The use of era names as posthumous names in modern Japanese historiography such as Meiji-tennō for the man named in life Mutsuhito is also a form of making the emperor numinous, and this usage remains nearly ubiquitous. The emperor remains in some sense holy for his position and also for his role in symbolizing the nation-state of Japan. Because modernity is no less ideological than premodernity, we can resist the desire to claim that we are now achieving true impartiality and are therefore free to ignore the ideological structure of past histories. The emic deconstruction of either is made possible by translating their discourses into each other.

The *hōken,* or compartmentalized, nature of authority in the Edo period led to diverse historiographical discourses, each representing different levels of politics. It is worthy to question with Watanabe how using an imperial historiographical vocabulary to interpret Tokugawa politics may obscure certain issues better understood using the Tokugawa's own language. Likewise, it is worthy to question how the historiographical language of the Tokugawa *omote* might obscure elements useful in understanding the histories of lordly domains and events of interaction with the emperor. The *hōken* order of things permitted a proliferation of historiographical discourses appropriate to different realms of political power, only a fraction of which have been explored here. There are a great variety of house histories, temple histories, and village histories, for example, many of which were protected by *naibun* spaces of authority, and we could learn much by exploring how they crafted meaningful visions of themselves. Furthermore, non-government-sponsored histories such as those written by individuals for printing by publishing houses, and with a view to selling to a broad readership, crafted yet other historical narrative styles worthy of our understanding and analysis. The national narrative of modernity and the imperial narrative of Mito scholarship are not wrong, but their spheres of competence do not include helping us understand how most people of the Tokugawa period saw themselves and understood their own politics.

Conclusion

The Tokugawa *kubō* suffered a great loss of face with Commodore Perry's arrival and the subsequent interactions with Western powers. The "august glory" of the Tokugawa clan and their Great Peace crumbled midcentury when their inability to persuade foreigners to play prescribed roles became publicly evident.[1] The old regime soon collapsed, but it initially broke apart along feudal lines of power. All the daimyo, who for centuries had performed rites of obedience to the Tokugawa in *omote* interaction, proved in the event to make their own choice as to whether to be an ally or an enemy of the Tokugawa. When civil war arrived, even those daimyo who continued to profess obedience to the Tokugawa included many who hedged their bets by indefinitely delaying troops on such acceptable grounds as "the lord's illness."[2] In the end a rebel/imperial army, led and primarily staffed by members of the four domains of Chōshū, Satsuma, Tosa, and Hizen, proceeded eastward under an imperial banner. They occupied Edo and then marched northward to defeat in battle the remaining Tokugawa forces and its allied daimyo. In this conclusion we will briefly consider, with particular reference to Tosa domain, the process by which the Meiji revolution destroyed the institutions and ideals of feudal politics and political spaces that have been described in this book.

The first few years after the Tokugawa fall saw feudal arrangements continue, with the emperor as nominal head of the new government. A debate ensued over the relative merits of a *hōken* feudal order and an imperial bureaucratic order of counties and prefectures.[3] This ambivalence was already built into the new government because most of the lands confiscated from the

Tokugawa and its allied daimyo were put under direct imperial control and reclassified as prefectures (*ken*) and urban prefectures (*fu*) rather than as territories (*ryō*). Daimyo were allowed to continue to be rulers of their domains, but the oft-used phrase "the unity of *fu, ken,* and *han*" reflected the aspiration of the new leaders for unity. On the side of unity, the renaming of daimyo houses and their domains as *han* in the spring of 1868 was accompanied by an order limiting their autonomy. Daimyo were told to "give up all laws that disturbed the imperial equanimity, even if those laws had stood since the beginning if the Tokugawa era," because "the holy enterprise of renewing Japan will be made manifest only if all the *han* and the imperial court put their full efforts into one unified path."[4]

The domains began various reforms under the auspices of this order, but they separately chose which of their laws to actually alter. The rules of interaction had changed greatly in the world exterior to the domain, but the inner operations of domains such as Tosa continued to have their own logic and vocabulary that contradicted the outside order from the very start: When the lord of Tosa domain conveyed the new government's order to his chief retainers, he referred to the domain as a *kuni* rather than a *han,* and his government ignored many new imperial policies.[5] For example, in 1869 the domain prohibited the circulation of imperial government currency within Tosa so as to force the circulation of domain-issued currency. This must have been a common problem, because the imperial government issued a reprimand to all domains concerning the disregard of its previous orders: "We hear that quite a number of *han* are still not allowing the circulation of imperial currency. This is outrageous! The currency is to circulate freely throughout the imperial country." Tosa officials were in no rush to reply to this reminder, and only in the following year did they permit circulation of imperial currency.[6] Such continuation of the political spatial consciousness of the Edo period had to be destroyed before a unified imperial nation could be created. Administratively, 1868 was a mere coup d'etat, placing the emperor in the position of the Tokugawa *kubō* as nominal head of a continuing Japanese feudal government.

Many domain retainers became leaders in the new government, however, and engineered the destruction of the feudal. Key players such as Kido Kōin and Ito Hirobumi from Hagi domain, Ōkubo Toshimichi and Mori Arinori from Kagoshima domain, Sasaki Takayuki and Itagaki Taisuke from Tosa domain, and many others very early on advanced various proposals for the return of domains to the emperor and their reconstitution as prefectures.[7] They worried about the danger of feudal arrangements leading the country to fall back into civil war and desired a stronger imperial government so that Japan might not succumb to a predatory world of Western powers. Some, such as Itagaki Taisuke, ironically made use of the continuing domainal independence to implement policies to destroy feudalism from within their own domains, because they thought that the new imperial government was not yet strong enough to enact a revolution. Itagaki described his thinking in his memoirs:

> I went for a period as a councillor in the imperial court in 1869. Since then, I observed how the affairs of state were mediated in the imperial government, and I saw that even when it was called "public opinion" or "public consensus," almost all aspects of government were left up to discretion of each domain. There was no truth to the notion of a unified government, and it had no autonomous power. Its officials merely queried the opinions of the strong domains. I thought over the matter privately and decided that if we did not cease doing things in this manner, then at some point some strong unbeatable domain would carry out things to its own selfish advantage and at some point just steal the government's authority. . . . Desiring to break this government by domain factions and instead carry out a policy of uniformity, I thought that first we should reform Tosa domain government, take away retainer stipends, prohibit the right of samurai to summarily execute commoners, permit commoners to ride horses [in the presence of samurai], etc., so as to give the ability to participate in government to all people and to give equal rank to samurai and commoners. Indeed Tosa's reforms in this direction preceded those of the rest of Japan.[8]

Itagaki saw the relationship between the social and economic system and the feudal political order, and he had more confidence in the power of his domain than in the imperial government to carry out the necessary changes. Yet the imperial government did destroy feudal spaces in 1871 and soon began to erase the status system. It abolished the 302 *han* and replaced them with an equivalent number of prefectures in the seventh month of that year. People other than daimyo, mostly former chief retainers of each domain, were chosen to be governors of these prefectures in a sign that feudal loyalties were no longer operative. The former lords were ordered to live in Tokyo, to prevent them from mobilizing resistance from their domains. Samurai were given government bonds in place of their fiefs and stipends, which were taken away, and they and commoners were told to pursue any occupation that they might wish. Because at the start of this process domains continued as *ken* with retainers staffed in their old posts, there was an initial continuity in the division of political space.

But the replacement of domains with prefectures was immediately recognized by locals as a fundamental change in the shape of government. Officials of Tosa domain relayed the order, prefacing it with a comment noting the end of feudal politics: "Hitherto there has been private possession of state authority, . . . but this can no longer be allowed to continue."[9] Within a year, the government amalgamated these 302 early prefectures into 69 prefectures whose staff was transferred hither and thither, thereby abolishing most domainal spaces and households. These prefectures were further reduced in number to 35 by 1876 in the name of government efficiency. Even when the number of prefectures rebounded to 43 in 1889, not a single one ended up having exactly the same boundary as a former domain realm. Their new shapes had a greater affinity for the old imperial provinces than for daimyo territories—suggesting an appropriation of the imperial *omote* of Tokugawa days for modern national use.[10]

The worlds of commoners changed rapidly as well, and many naturally were not pleased. In 1873 the villagers of Nanokawa in Tosa protested the removal of the daimyo to Tokyo, the abolition of the domain, and the implementation of the army conscript system. They demanded that the lord and retired lord be allowed to return to Tosa, writing, "The governor is off at Tokyo. This is deeply upsetting to villagers, and they take no pleasure in their livelihood. Indeed, when the two lords do not preserve righteousness in this country [of Tosa], it makes it very difficult for farmers to carry out their work. Please, we request that you take care of this problem." The protest soon expanded to include neighboring villages, and the demands extended to a restoration of the status system, freedom from the new system of military conscription, and other novelties. They summed up their argument as follows: "Until all of the government laws are returned to what they were ten years ago, we will neither pay taxes nor fulfill our duties to the government."[11] Although the language of this protest began by highlighting the demand to return the lord, such villagers were antirevolutionary because at lower levels in the administrative hierarchy their own hierarchies and positions were threatened. Most Tokugawa-era villages and towns underwent amalgamation and erasure of traditional institutional identity, as well as losing traditions of self-management and *naibun* competence. By the end of the 1880s local governments reduced the number of villages and towns from more than 70,000 to near 15,000, in a process that reconfigured local identities and their relationships to their Tokugawa-era pasts. The new government ended the corporate village responsibility for taxation when it initiated a land survey in 1873 and made the landowners individually responsible for the property tax.[12] This was in line with a new policy that made households and, to much a greater degree than before, individuals directly responsible to the state for their duties as subjects. It thus took three years from the Restoration to begin the abolition of the feudal order in 1871. However, from 1868 the Tokugawa-era past was being officially recast into the terms by which modernity would recognize it. The emperor's initial announcement of the restoration of imperial rule defined the Tokugawa government as the *bakufu*, ironically making the first official use of this term the declaration of its own abolition.[13] Likewise, the first official use of the word *han* to describe daimyo and their domains occurred a few months later when the emperor's new government issued an order to daimyo, requiring them to reform their administrations and laws.[14] Modern students of Japanese history now learn that the *bakufu* was abolished in 1868, but how many learn of the singularity of that moment in which it existed only for the purpose of being destroyed, a black hole of history obscuring the nature of its origins? Similarly, the abolition of the *han* in 1871 is well known, but how many regard the abolition of daimyo *ryōbun* and their replacement by *han* in early 1868 as a moment of significance? Few things can press our attention to the political importance of historical narration than that the radicals at the head of a fledgling government, still busy fighting the armies of the old regime, so quickly created a vision of the past that the new government was going to replace. The major policies of the actual nationalist revolution—beyond the coup's initial idea of imperial sovereignty and the pursuit of equality in the international arena—took longer to articulate and put into effect. Yet it was a profound revolution, and the interplay between the imperial visions of the future and the new narration of the past is a fascinating coda to the era of performing the Tokugawa Great Peace.

In the end, the revolution destroyed the status system and replaced it with an ideology of an equality of subjecthood to the emperor and the Japanese state. The new government abolished feudal privileges and enshrined the rights of private property and capital, reshaping the space of the political world into, as the activist Itagaki Taisuke wrote, "a policy of uniformity." Distinctly new hierarchies were created on this national foundation, and new paths of advancement into positions of power opened up before ambitious young men. The language and basis of government were reformulated to take on immediate meaning within the new political space of an imperial Japan, both for its present and by reformulating the past. This revolution was an indigenous response to an outside Western threat. Although the influences of the Western powers helped shape the revolution in crucial ways, many of the changes had numerous deep roots in the islands' own past. Old frustrations became manifest in the vastly widened opportunities to express dissatisfactions with the traditional feudal politics. The feudal divisions themselves rapidly lost administrative legitimacy and were increasingly understood as having been corrupt, selfish, and obstructionist. The nationalist revolution brought about an associated decline in the ideology of the politics of *omote* and *naishō* and replaced it with a new discourse of individual, popular, and state rights that by 1890 had become enshrined in law and constitution.

Reconfiguring *omote* and *naibun* in modernity

People changed in the Meiji era from feudal subjects to imperial subjects who came to argue politically in the language of individual rights, but where did the concepts of *omote* and *naibun* go in modernity? The cultural bases of the old politics continued in many common patterns of social interaction, and they informally influenced governmental practice, but the old politics was no longer an ideal by which to structure the disbursement of authority. Changes in language tell of a shift in the nuances of meaning. On occasions when I have proposed to Japanese scholars the usefulness of the notions of *omote* and *naibun* for analyzing Edo politics, many have quickly responded with a modern polarity, "Ah! *Omote* and *ura.*" *Ura* generally means "behind" or "behind a front" and has a nuance of "hidden from view." To this degree, *ura* has much in common with *uchi*. However, the differences are also significant. At the simplest level of spatial meaning, *ura* indicates the backside of something within a larger unitary space, whereas *uchi* and *naibun* indicate a separated enclosed space. The shift from *uchi* to *ura* parallels the transition from feudal to national politics and their various associated discourses. In its political usage, *uchi* enclosed space was, as we have seen, a space of tacitly acknowledged control that gained legitimacy through its leaders' participation in *omote* rituals of subservience, whereas in modern politics, *ura* quickly—if not necessarily—gained a nuance of corrupt maneuvering. The word *ura* did exist in the Edo period, and in political discourse it also could express a negative nuance of dishonesty, whereas *uchi* was morally neutral. The modern use of *ura* as a replacement for *naibun* is a product of the trend toward the delegitimization of *omote* and *naishō* politics that occurs within a discourse of constitutionality and individual rights, and in which transparency in government has become an ideal and a legitimate issue of political contestation. This is not to say that behavior based on a separateness between exterior promises and inner realities has disappeared from politics. Not by a long stretch. Government in modern Japan, the United States, and seemingly everywhere involves a great degree of covert agreements and duplicity. However, such behavior is recurrently the subject of debate. The point is that *omote* and *naishō* is no longer an ideal form of politics and, by becoming *omote* and *ura,* has been disassociated from the feudal apportioning of *naibun* inner spaces of authority.

Another modern linguistic link to Edo political culture is the polarity of *uchi* (inside) and *soto* (outside), terms that have been used analytically in the field of cultural linguistics.[15] *Omote* and *soto* are similar to each other because both reference in spatial terms the different social norms of behavior one should perform when away from one's insider group. They differ slightly, in that in its Tokugawa political context, *omote* was closely tied to the politics of face, honor, and submission, whereas *soto* refers to an undifferentiated outside and to general rules of social civility in an implicitly national society.

A similar pair of terms that have been used in modern cultural analysis are *honne* and *tatemae. Honne* refers to one's "real" intentions, and *tatemae* refers to the front that one presents to meet societal expectations. These two words were created in the Meiji period, likely out of a need to reconfigure understandings of traditional *naibun* and *omote* practices in a way more suited to a unitary space. Whereas neither *naibun* nor *omote* was any more "real" than the other, *honne* refers nonspatially to an individual's "real" intentions as if its opposite, the *tatemae,* were sham or a mask to those intentions. Culturalist understandings based on the concepts of *tatemae* and *honne* have been deployed in nationalistic fashion to highlight a Japanese peculiar identity, as part of what is often called Nihonjinron, a discourse that identifies Japanese as different from an undifferentiated community of all other people in the world. However, I believe that the terms *tatemae* and *honne* express a condition common to other people in the modern world: the tensions that an individual faces when integrated into national society by framing issues in terms of one's inner self and one's social self. I could explain much of my life as a child growing up in a preacher's home in West Virginia in terms of *honne* and *tatemae,* for example, whereas it would be quite a stretch to use *naibun* and *omote* to explain those experiences.

Likewise, although *naibun* and *omote* are terms of political culture appropriate to a premodern *hōken* order in the Japanese archipelago, they express behaviors that have appeared elsewhere in premodern world history, and they easily could be used to analyze and create a dialogue with the premodern histories of some non-Japanese places as well. *Omote* can be roughly translated as rituals of subservience, and *omote* behavior can, for example, be compared to the peacemaking and integrating role of rituals in Renaissance Venice. There would naturally be similarities and differences, and the ensuing dialogue would inspire new perspectives on the place of ritual in government.[16] My presumption is, because language is imprecise and rough, that translation is possible, and a cultural approach to politics does not preclude possibilities of comparison and dialogue.

This book intends to create a space of acceptance for a certain cultural approach to interpreting the politics of the Tokugawa world primarily and, by extension, those of other prenational worlds. Consciously setting up a dialogue between the discourses of the past and those of the present permits us to structure knowledge in a nonexclusive fashion. This book is not making the argument that because this method is right, then other methods are therefore wrong. Nationalizing the past has been dominant over the last century precisely because it is so useful to nationals. Its framework of understanding is easier for the modern reader because the past is thereby more fully translated into present concerns and ways of thinking or of organizing information. Furthermore, it can better highlight aspects of the past that specifically were appropriated to create the present, a topic that I and many others find interesting, and it is a method that I have employed in parts of this book. Yet any methodology will configure its own limitations, and I have used Tokugawa-period discourses of political space to highlight some of the limitations inherent to a nationalizing perspective on history.

This book's specific approach of analyzing spatial politics in Tokugawa-period terms should be particularly useful to understanding why people of the Tokugawa period chose to behave in the way they did as they dealt with conflicts of interest. I have found this approach useful when addressing the following topics: the coexistence of seemingly incongruous discourses of political authority and legitimacy; the operation of the legal system; the seemingly incongruous discourses of life, death, and identity among political figures; the seemingly endless decline of the extraordinarily stable Tokugawa authority; and the problem of ideological rigidity versus creativity. One could equally apply this method to such other issues as relations between villagers and their seigneurs, which I have explored only tangentially in this book, and gender relations, which I have only nominally touched upon.

Distinct from these issues of interpretation, this approach also raises a question about the nature of documents that needs to be addressed even when producing history under other methodologies, such as a nationalizing history. The Tokugawa political culture that produced primary sources and such secondary sources as histories produced them for its own needs and uses. Because it is dangerous to assume that the standards or meanings of truth and factuality were the same in the past as they are in the present, it seems necessary to first analyze the particular political discourses of a document's production before one can recover meanings useful for the present. With regard to the Tokugawa world, identifying for which *omote* a document was composed seems to be an essential first step to analyzing the meaning of its narrative.

Notes

Introduction

1. Tahara-chō Bunkazai Hogo Shingikai, ed., *Tahara-han nikki,* vol. 8 (Aichi Pref., Tahara-chō, 1995), pp. 124–125, 142–143; Tahara-chō Bunkazai Chōsakai, ed., *Tahara-chō shi, chūkan* (Aichi Pref., Tahara-chō, 1975), pp. 1194–1195.

2. *Tokugawa jikki,* ed. Kuroita Katsumi, 9 vols., in *Shintei zōhō Kokushi taikei* series, vols. 38–47 (Tokyo: Yoshikawa Kōbunkan, 1964); *Shintei Kansei chōshū shokafu,* 26 vols. (Tokyo: Zoku Gunsho Ruijū Kanseikai, 1964–1967).

3. The ending date of the Warring States era varies considerably in historiography, ranging from Oda Nobunaga's entry into Kyoto in 1568, through Hideyoshi's 1590 defeat of the last lords in Japan willing to resist him, and Ieyasu's 1600 defeat of partisans of Hideyoshi's son, on up to the 1615 defeat of Hideyoshi's son Hideyori by Ieyasu. Each date has a logic to it, but for the purposes of this book the 1590 creation of an order incorporating all daimyo seems most appropriate.

4. Ozawa Eiichi, "Bakuhanseika ni okeru hōken, gunken ron josetsu," *Tōkyō Gakugeidai kiyō,* 3 *bumon shakai kagaku* 24 (1972): 111–128. A good summary of this understanding of the early modern order is laid out in Fujii Jōji, "Jūnana seiki no Nihon: Buke no kokka no keisei," in vol. 12 of *Iwanami kōza Nihon tsūshi,* ed. Asao Naohiro et al. (Tokyo: Iwanami Shoten, 1994), pp. 1–64. Also see Mizubayashi Takeshi, *Hōkensei no saihen to Nihonteki shakai no kakuritsu* (Tokyo: Yamakawa Shuppan, 1987), which has been influential in my own thought.

5. The classics in the field are Fujino Tamotsu, *Bakuhan taisei shi no kenkyū,* 3rd ed. (Tokyo: Yoshikawa Kōbunkan, 1967); Kitajima Masamoto, *Edo bakufu no kenryōku kōzō* (Tokyo: Iwanami Shoten, 1964); and Conrad Totman, *Politics in the Tokugawa Bakufu, 1600–1843* (Cambridge, MA: Harvard University Press, 1967).

6. Takagi Shōsaku has explored the division of *omote* and *naishō* communication routes between daimyo and the Tokugawa as they were being created in the early to mid-seventeenth century in chapter 3 of his *Edo bakufu no seido to dentatsu monjo* (Tokyo:

Kadokawa Shoten, 1999). Kasaya Kazuhiko has described information networks between daimyo in his *Edo orusuiyaku: Kinsei no gaikōkan* (Tokyo: Yoshikawa Kōbunkan, 2000).

7. I am influenced here strongly by Watanabe Hiroshi's essay "Goikō to shōchō" in his *Higashi Ajia no ōken to shisō* (Tokyo: Tōkyō Daigaku Shuppankai, 1997).

8. Anne Walthall, "Japanese *Gimin:* Peasant Martyrs in Popular Memory," *American Historical Review* 91, no. 5 (December 1986): 1076–1102; Irwin Scheiner, "Benevolent Lords and Honorable Peasants," in *Japanese Thought in the Tokugawa Period, 1600–1868: Methods and Metaphors,* ed. Tetsuo Najita and Irwin Scheiner (Chicago: University of Chicago Press, 1978), pp. 39–62.

9. Ernest Renan, *Oeuvres complètes de Ernest Renan,* vol. 1 (Paris: Calmann-Lévy, 1947); Benedict Anderson, *Imagined Communities: Reflections on the Origins and Spread of Nationalism,* rev. ed. (London: Verso, 1991); Eric Hobsbawm, *Nations and Nationalism since 1780: Programme, Myth, Reality,* 2nd ed. (Cambridge: Cambridge University Press, 1992); Prasenjit Duara, *Rescuing History from the Nation: Questioning Narratives of Modern China* (Chicago: University of Chicago Press, 1995).

10. Mary Elizabeth Berry, *Japan in Print: Information and Nation in the Early Modern Period* (Berkeley: University of California Press, 2007).

11. Luke Roberts, *Mercantilism in a Japanese Domain: The Merchant Origins of Economic Nationalism in 18th-Century Tosa* (Cambridge: Cambridge University Press, 1998).

12. David Lowenthal, *The Past Is a Foreign Country* (Cambridge: Cambridge University Press, 1985).

13. These points are made by Watanabe Hiroshi in the introduction of his *Higashi Ajia no ōken to shisō.* For an English translation of Watanabe's introduction, see his "About Some Japanese Historical Terms," trans. Luke Roberts, *Sino-Japanese Studies* 10, no. 2 (1998): 32–42.

14. Margaret Mehl, *History and the State in Nineteenth-Century Japan* (New York: St. Martin's Press, 1998), pp. 1–6. For a thoughtful and fascinating exploration of how nationalism has transformed the modes and content of history in Jordan, see Andrew Shryock, *Nationalism and the Genealogical Imagination: Oral History and Textual Authority in Tribal Jordan* (Berkeley: University of California Press, 1997).

15. Kanai Madoka, *Hansei* (Tokyo: Shibundō, 1962), pp. 74–75.

16. David Howell, *Geographies of Identity in Nineteenth-Century Japan* (Berkeley: University of California Press, 2005).

17. Katsumata Shizuo with Martin Collcutt, "The Development of Sengoku Law," in *Japan before Tokugawa: Political Consolidation and Economic Growth, 1500–1650,* ed. John W. Hall, Nagahara Keiji, and Kōzō Yamamura (Princeton, NJ: Princeton University Press, 1981).

18. Fujita Teiichirō, *Kinsei keizai shisō no kenkyū—kokueki shisō to bakuhan taisei* (Tokyo: Yoshikawa Kōbunkan, 1966). See Miyamoto's insightful commentary

in Miyoshi Tsunenori, *Kokka kanjō roku,* ed. Miyamoto Mataji (Osaka: Seibundō, 1971).

19. Ronald Toby, "Rescuing the Nation from History: The State of the State in Early Modern Japan," *Monumenta Nipponica* 56, no. 2 (Summer 2001): 197–237.

20. Ibid., p. 200.

21. Mizumoto Kunihiko, *Tokugawa no kokka dezain* (Tokyo: Shōgakukan, 2008), pp. 10–11. I translate Mizumoto's use of *kokka* as "nation-state" because of his emphasis on a unitary vision of country membership and a single government to the exclusion of other possibilities.

22. As for the distinction between "early modern" and "premodern" to describe Tokugawa Japan, I regard both terms as applicable, depending on the topic the historian is highlighting. In an economic sense and a cultural sense the realm is profitably understandable as early modern, but in a formal political sense it was to my mind more clearly premodern.

23. Philip Brown, *Central Authority and Local Autonomy in the Formation of Early Modern Japan: The Case of Kaga Domain* (Stanford, CA: Stanford University Press, 1993); Kären Wigen, *The Making of a Japanese Periphery, 1750–1920* (Berkeley: University of California Press, 1995); David Howell, *Capitalism from Within: Economy, Society and the State in a Japanese Fishery* (Berkeley: University of California Press, 1995); Edward Pratt, *Japan's Protoindustrial Elite: The Economic Foundations of the Gōnō* (Cambridge, MA: Harvard University Press, 1999); Mark Ravina, *Land and Lordship in Early Modern Japan* (Stanford, CA: Stanford University Press, 1999).

24. Brown, *Central Authority,* pp. 25–27, 229–233.

1: The Geography of Politics

1. J. F. van Overmeer Fisscher, *Nihon fūzoku bikō,* trans. Shōji Mitsuo and Numata Jirō, vol. 1 (Tokyo: Nihon Hyōronsha, 1978), p. 52. The original 1833 book is entitled *Bijdrage tot de kennis van het Japansche rijk.* Thanks to Watanabe Hiroshi for this reference.

2. Ravina, *Land and Lordship,* pp. 27–28; Mizubayashi, *Hōkensei no saihen,* pp. 141–142, 279–281.

3. Makino Seiichi, *Uchi to soto no gengobunkagaku* (Tokyo: Aruku, 1996); Jane Bachnik and Charles Quinn Jr., eds., *Situated Meaning: Inside and Outside in Japanese Self, Society, and Language* (Princeton, NJ: Princeton University Press, 1994).

4. Lee Butler, *Emperor and Aristocracy in Japan, 1467–1680: Resilience and Renewal* (Cambridge, MA: Harvard University East Asia Center, 2002).

5. For the complex historical process leading to a stability in the new relationship between the imperial court and the hegemons, see the middle chapters of Butler, *Emperor and Aristocracy.*

6. George Elison, "Hideyoshi: The Bountiful Minister," in *Warlords, Artists*

and Commoners: Japan in the Sixteenth Century, ed. George Elison and Bardwell L. Smith (Honolulu: University of Hawaiʻi Press, 1981), pp. 223–244; Mary Elizabeth Berry, *Hideyoshi* (Cambridge, MA: Harvard University Press, 1982), pp. 168–205.

7. Ieyasu held appointment in the increasing ranks of Minister of the Interior, Minister of the Right, and Minister of the Left, and, upon his retirement from the shogunal post, Grand Minister of State. His heir Tokugawa Hidetada, who also retired, followed the same course. Subsequent heads of the clan followed this pattern, but most gained the Grand Minister title posthumously. All received the first Minister of State title simultaneously with appointment as shogun.

8. Totman, *Politics in The Tokugawa Bakufu,* pp. 38–39.

9. Hashimoto Masanobu, ed., *Kinsei buke kanʼi no kenkyū* (Tokyo: Zoku Gunsho Ruijū Kanseikai, 1999), pp. 1–56.

10. Katsumata with Collcutt, "Development of Sengoku Law."

11. Ishii Ryōsuke, ed., *Tokugawa kinreikō* (Tokyo: Sōbunsha, 1959), vol. 1, pp. 63–65.

12. Roberts, *Mercantilism.* Also see Ravina, *Land and Lordship.*

13. MS "Yamauchi-ke shiryō: Toyochika-kō ki," vol. 58, fols. 24–29, in Yamauchi-ke Hōmotsu Shiryōkan, Kōchi. This incident was part of a larger pattern in samurai society of using "personal" reasons to avoid duty to one's superior. The need to care for an ill family member was another commonly acceptable reason in samurai society for not performing duty. See Yanagiya Keiko, *Kinsei no josei sōzoku to kaigo* (Tokyo: Yoshikawa Kōbunkan, 2007), pp. 259–282.

14. Michael Birt, "Samurai in Passage: Transformation of the Sixteenth-Century Kanto," *Journal of Japanese Studies* 11, no. 2 (Summer 1985): 369–399.

15. John Hall, "The Castle Town and Japan's Modern Urbanization," in *Studies in the Institutional History of Early Modern Japan,* ed. John Hall and Marius B. Jansen (Princeton, NJ: Princeton University Press, 1968).

16. The territorial authority of bannermen went through many vicissitudes and overall was increasingly circumscribed over the Tokugawa period. Kitajima, *Edo bakufu no kenryoku kōzō;* Fujino Tamotsu, ed., *Hatamoto to chigyōsei* (Tokyo: Yūzankaku, 1995).

17. Relative ruling autonomy existed for the Andō over their fief in Sukumo, the Fukao over their fief in Sakawa, and the Gotō over their fief in Aki. The Fukao case is well discussed in Sakawa-chō Shi Hensan Iinkai, ed., *Sakawa-chō shi, jōkan* (Kōchi Pref., Sakawa-chō, 1982), pp. 355–451. The reduction of fief autonomy for other samurai is discussed in Marius B. Jansen, "Tosa in the Seventeenth Century: The Establishment of Yamauchi Rule," in Hall and Jansen, *Studies in the Institutional History of Early Modern Japan,* pp. 115–129. Despite the reduction, many enfeoffed retainers in Tosa had social bonds with people of their fiefs and exercised authority by local custom and consent in ways not officially supported by the domain government. John Morris explores the continuing significance of fiefs in early modern Sendai in his *Kinsei Nihon chigyōsei no kenkyū* (Osaka: Seibundō, 1988).

18. Kanai, *Hansei,* pp. 37–43.

19. Brown, *Central Authority,* p. 24.

20. Fujino Tamotsu, ed., *On'eiroku, Haizetsuroku* (Tokyo: Kondō Shuppansha, 1970), pp. 267, 279–280, 287.

21. Examples of daimyo cited for this offense can be found in Fujino Tamotsu, ed., *Tokugawa kajofū roku* (Tokyo: Kondō Shuppansha, 1972), pp. 334, 339, 341 passim. Examples of samurai of Tosa punished for the offenses of household members can be found in "Okachū hengi," part 2, *Tosa shidan,* no. 55 (June 1936), pp. 209–232 passim; quotations from pp. 216 and 225.

22. Fukuda Chizuru, *Oie sōdō: Daimyō-ke o yurugashita kenryoku tōsō* (Tokyo: Chūōkōronsha, 2005).

23. Kasaya Kazuhiko, *Shukun "oshikome" no kōzō: Kinsei daimyō to kashindan* (Tokyo: Heibonsha, 1988).

24. Ishii Ryōsuke, ed., *Hanpōshū,* vol. 5, *Shohan* (Tokyo: Sōbunsha, 1964), p. 16, for Yoshida; and for Okayama, vol. 1:1, *Okayama-han* (Tokyo: Sōbunsha, 1959), p. 400.

25. Vol. 5 of MS "Yōsha zuihitsu," authored by Yamauchi (Maeno) Akinari, a junior elder of the domain, held in the personal collection of Kattō Isamu of Kōchi city. The relative severity of the punishment was because the domain was unofficially aware that Shō had been having an affair with the man she killed. If it had been officially aware, however, then the punishment would have been even more severe.

26. Eiko Ikegami, *The Taming of the Samurai* (Cambridge, MA: Harvard University Press, 1995), pp. 228–230.

27. Matsura Seizan, *Kasshi yawa,* ed. Nakamura Yukihiko and Nakano Mitsutoshi (Tokyo: Heibonsha, 1977–1978), vol. 1, p. 16.

28. Kate Nakai, *Shogunal Politics: Arai Hakuseki and the Premises of Tokugawa Rule* (Cambridge, MA: Council on East Asian Studies, 1988), pp. 131–135.

29. Kasaya Kazuhiko, *Kinsei buke shakai no seiji kōzō* (Tokyo: Yoshikawa Kōbunkan, 1993), pp. 103–136.

30. Harold Bolitho in his *Treasures among Men: The Fudai Daimyo in Tokugawa Japan* (New Haven, CT: Yale University Press, 1974) has shown that the *fudai/tozama* distinction did not generally reflect differing patterns of loyalty or behavior as daimyo. *Fudai* were self-interested daimyo first and Tokugawa loyalists second, but the presumption of difference remains strong.

31. Philip Brown points out this generalization but also highlights the actual variety of local organization in *Central Authority,* pp. 133–134, 223–225.

32. Hitomi Tonomura, *Community and Commerce in Late Medieval Japan: The Corporate Villages of Tokuchin-ho* (Stanford, CA: Stanford University Press, 1992); Birt, "Samurai in Passage."

33. Mary Elizabeth Berry, *The Culture of Civil War in Kyoto* (Berkeley: University of California Press, 1994).

34. Igeta Ryōji, *Kinsei sonraku no mibun kōzō* (Tokyo: Kokusho Kankōkai, 1984).

35. Herman Ooms, *Tokugawa Village Practice* (Berkeley: University of California Press, 1996), p. 312.

36. Ibid., pp. 203–216. For more detail on this case, see chapter 3 of Igeta, *Kinsei sonraku no mibun kōzō*.

37. Saitō Yōichi and Ōishi Shinzaburō, *Mibunsabetsu shakai no shinjitsu* (Tokyo: Kōdansha, 1995).

38. David Howell succinctly and admirably explores the relations between status and feudal territory—with an emphasis on status—in "Territoriality and Collective Identity in Tokugawa Japan," in *Public Spheres and Collective Identities*, ed. Shmuel N. Eisenstadt, Wolfgang Schluchter, and Björn Wittrock (New Brunswick, NJ: Transaction Publishers, 2001), pp. 105–132, and more extensively in *Geographies of Identity*, where he is working in dialogue with such scholars as Tsukamoto Takashi and Yoshida Nobuyuki, who have spearheaded recent trends in Tokugawa-era status studies.

39. Wakita Osamu provides a good general exposition of the relation between women and the polity in the Tokugawa period in "Bakuhan taisei to josei," in *Nihon josei shi*, vol. 3, *Kinsei*, ed. Joseishi Sōgō Kenkyūkai (Tokyo: Tōkyō Daigaku Shuppankai, 1982), pp. 1–30.

40. Yanagiya, *Kinsei no josei sōzoku to kaigo*, pp. 32–85.

41. Ishii, *Hanpōshū*, vol. 1:1, *Okayama-han*, p. 343.

42. As quoted in my "Tosa to ishin: 'Kokka' no sōshitsu to 'chihō' no tanjō," *Nenpō kindai Nihon kenkyū* 20 (1997): 216. Original in MS "Yamauchi-ke shiryō: Toyonobu-kō ki," vol. 121, fol. 61, Yamauchi-ke Hōmotsu Shiryōkan, Kōchi.

43. Roberts, "Tosa to ishin," p. 216.

44. Kōchi Kenritsu Toshokan, ed., *Tosanokuni gunsho ruijū*, vol. 3 (Tokyo: Kōchi Kenritsu Toshokan, 2000), pp. 60–105, 266–281.

45. Roberts, "Tosa to ishin," pp. 215–217.

46. *Yamauchi-ke shiryō: Tadayoshi-kō ki* (Kōchi: Yamauchi Jinja Hōmotsu Shiryōkan, 1982), vol. 3, p. 472.

47. Partly due to Katsutoyo's wife's taking the tonsure and the name "Kenshōin" upon Katsutoyo's early death in 1603, and a relative lack of inside documents, we are not sure of her personal name. Judging from one signature in a surviving document, her name might have been Chiyo, but this Chiyo may have been one of her servants.

48. For example, see the compilations of such submissions in *Shintei Kansei chōshū shokafu*.

49. Anne Walthall in *The Weak Body of a Useless Woman* (Chicago: University of Chicago Press, 1998), p. 64, notes how modern naming practices have similar functions of subordinating women to male authority. The main subject of this biography variously used the name "Tase" and the diminutive "Taseko" in her own life but is uniformly known as Taseko in modernity. It might be possible to distinguish her two uses in terms of the *omote* that she was addressing at the time.

50. Yamamoto Hirofumi, *Bakuhansei no seiritsu to kinsei no kokusei* (Tokyo: Azekura Shobō, 1990), p. 323.

51. Toby, "Rescuing the Nation from History."

52. Ravina, *Land and Lordship*; Roberts, *Mercantilism*.

53. Katsura Yoshiki, ed., *Iwakuni-han kengen roku* (Yamaguchi Pref., Iwakuni: Iwakuni Chōkokan, 1979), p. 30.

54. Kokushi Daijiten Hensan Iinkai, ed., *Kokushi daijiten* (Tokyo: Yoshikawa Kōbunkan, 1979–1997), vol. 1, p. 841.

55. *Kagawa-ken shi*, vol. 9, *Shiryō hen, Kinsei shiryō 1* (Takamatsu: Kagawa-ken, 1987), pp. 498–501.

56. Ozawa Kōichi and Haga Noboru, eds., *Watanabe Kazan shū* (Tokyo: Nihon Tosho Sentaa, 1999), vol. 1, pp. 293–294. *Bōfū* refers to many varieties of a parsleylike, coastal flowering plant in Japan.

57. This point is made based on a review of Ishii, *Hanpōshū*, vol. 5, *Shohan*, which contains laws from numerous such domains.

58. Mutō Yoshikazu, *Nanroshi*, ed. Yorimitsu Kanji, Akizawa Shigeru, et al., vol. 8 (Kōchi: Kōchi Kenritsu Toshokan, 1990–1998), pp. 536, 539.

59. Saiki Kazuma, Okayama Taiji, and Sagara Tōru, eds., *Mikawa monogatari, Hagakure* (Tokyo: Iwanami Shoten, 1974), pp. 216–579. The terms mentioned can be found in the first few pages.

60. Both usages are shown within a single document on p. 5 of Ishii Ryōsuke, ed., *Hanpōshū*, vol. 2, *Tottori-han* (Tokyo: Sōbunsha, 1961).

61. Examples can be found throughout Kindai Shi Bunko Kenkyūkai, ed., *Kiroku kakinuki Date-ke orekidai jiki* (Uwajima: Kindai Shi Bunko Kenkyūkai, 1981), vol. 1, for example, on pp. 153, 207, 311, and 313.

62. Moriya Yoshimi, "Kokueki shuhō o meguru shomondai: Morioka-han no baai," *Tōhoku Daigaku Tōhoku Bunka Kenkyūjo kiyō*, no. 17 (1985): 125–126.

63. Yokoyama Toshio, "'Han' kokka e no michi—shokoku fūkyō fure to tabinin," in *Kasei bunka no kenkyū*, ed. Hayashiya Tatsusaburō (Tokyo: Iwanami Shoten, 1976), pp. 113–120.

64. Ishii Ryōsuke, ed., *Hanpōshū*, vol. 9:1, *Morioka-han* (Tokyo: Sōbunsha, 1970), p. 827.

65. Ibid. Early eighteenth-century examples can be found on pp. 14, 17, 33, 58, 82, and 103 passim. From the late eighteenth century, usage of *kuni* increases.

66. Ibid., p. 75. For similar proclamations, see p. 90 and vol. 9:2, p. 334.

67. Constantine Vaporis explores the role of the system in transmitting culture throughout Japan in his *Tour of Duty: Samurai, Military Service in Edo and the Culture of Early Modern Japan* (Honolulu: University of Hawai'i Press, 2008).

68. Ishii, *Hanpōshū*, vol. 9:1, *Morioka-han*, p. 766.

69. Moriya, "Kokueki shuhō," p. 129.

70. See Roberts, *Mercantilism*, chaps. 6–8; and J. F. Morisu (John Morris), *Kinsei bushi no "ōyake" to "watakushi": Sendai hanshi Tamamushi Jūzō no kyaria to zasetsu* (Osaka: Seibundō, 2009), pp. 299–308.

71. Ravina, *Land and Lordship*, pp. 155–176.

72. For example, Ishii, *Hanpōshū*, vol. 9:1, *Morioka-han*, p. 826; Moriya, "Kokueki shuhō," p. 126. In *Mercantilism*, pp. 1, 5–7, 12, 200–202, I explore the significance of *kokueki* thought primarily with reference to Tosa domain but introduce its use in many other domainal contexts as well. See references in that work to the broad Japanese scholarship on this topic.

73. Fujita Teiichirō, *Kinsei keizai shisō no kenkyū*, p. 37.

2: Performing the Tokugawa Right to Know

1. Akizawa Shigeru, "Keichō jūnen Tokugawa gozenchō ni tsuite," *Kainan shigaku*, part 1 in no. 30 (August 1992): 33.

2. Brown, *Central Authority*, pp. 14–19, 58–88; Howell, *Capitalism from Within*, pp. 28–29, 34–35.

3. Akizawa provides a masterful discussion on pp. 44–55 of "Keichō jūnen," *Kainan shigaku*, part 2 in no. 31 (August 1993).

4. Fredrik Barth, "Boundaries and Connections," in *Signifying Identities: Anthropological Perspectives on Boundaries and Contested Values*, ed. A. P. Cohen (London: Routledge, 2000), pp. 17–36; Barth, *Ethnic Groups and Boundaries* (London: Allen and Unwin, 1969).

5. Thomas C. Smith, "The Land Tax in the Tokugawa Period," *Journal of Asian Studies* 18, no. 1 (November 1958): 3–19.

6. Brown, *Central Authority*, chap. 3.

7. *Yamauchi-ke shiryō: Tadatoyo-kō ki* (Kōchi: Yamauchi Jinja Hōmotsu Shiryōkan, 1980–1981), vol. 2, pp. 617–618. The one express limitation on these Inspectors was that they were not to accept any petitions or legal suits, a point to which I will return later in this chapter.

8. The literature on these tours is extensive. An excellent consideration of the important Japanese research is Ōhira Yūichi, "Edo bakufu junkenshi kō," in *Hō to kenryoku no shiteki kōsatsu*, ed. Harafuji Hiroshi and Oyama Sadao (Tokyo: Sōbunsha, 1977), pp. 569–603.

9. See, for example, the entry on *junkenshi* in Kokushi Daijiten Hensan Iinkai, comp., *Kokushi daijiten* (Tokyo: Yoshikawa Kōbunkan, 1979–1997), vol. 7, p. 414, which says, "They directly observed conditions of the people in Tokugawa territory as well as private [daimyo and lesser retainer] territory and put most effort into observing the good and bad of a lord's management. However, gradually local seigneurs prepared formalistic responses, and the quality of real observance gradually deteriorated and the whole process became ever more an empty ritual"; or the comments of Harold Bolitho, who writes in "The Han," in *The Cambridge History of Japan*, vol. 4, *Early Modern Japan*, ed. John Whitney Hall (Cambridge: Cambridge University Press, 1991), p. 206, "The Tokugawa bakufu's inspection scheme, too, lost its early vigor, with surprise visits from parties of *junkenshi*, charged with ferreting out any misgovernment, giving way to formal and perfunctory tours, all announced

well ahead of time (even down to the details of their itinerary), all asking predictable questions, and all—inspectors and inspected alike—hoping earnestly that they might be spared the necessity of presenting a critical report."

10. Ōhira, "Edo bakufu junkenshi"; Takano Nobuharu, "Kyūnin chigyōchi ni okeru junkenshi geisetsu o meguru ikkōsatsu: Saga-han o sozai ni," in *Kinsei Nihon no shakai to ryūtsū,* ed. Fujino Tamotsu Sensei Kanreki Kinen Kai (Tokyo: Yūzankaku, 1993), p. 166.

11. *Yamauchi-ke shiryō: Tadatoyo-kō ki,* vol. 2, p. 602.

12. *Yamauchi-ke shiryō: Tadayoshi-kō ki,* vol. 2, pp. 488–489.

13. Ibid., vol. 2, p. 494.

14. Ibid., vol. 2, p. 502.

15. Ibid., vol. 2, pp. 483–484.

16. Ibid., vol. 2, pp. 498–502.

17. Roberts, *Mercantilism,* pp. 52–55, 98.

18. Kōchi-ken Shi Hensan Iinkai, *Kōchi-ken shi, Kinsei* (Kōchi-ken, 1968), pp. 86–99, 108–110; Jansen, "Tosa in the Seventeenth Century."

19. *Yamauchi-ke shiryō: Tadayoshi-kō ki,* vol. 2, pp. 486, 489.

20. Ibid., vol. 2, pp. 487–488, 495.

21. Ibid., vol. 2, p. 408.

22. Ibid., vol. 2, p. 489.

23. Ibid., vol. 2, pp. 485, 502.

24. Ibid., vol. 2, p. 503.

25. Handa Takao, "Bakufu junkenshi taisei to saigoku keiei," in *Kinsei Nihon no seiji to gaikō,* ed. Fujino Tamotsu Sensei Kanreki Kinenkai (Tokyo: Yūzankaku Shuppan, 1993).

26. *Shintei Kansei chōshū shokafu,* entries for the three inspectors: Koide Yoshichika, vol. 15, p. 15; Jō Nobumochi, vol. 8, p. 351; and Nose Yoritaka, vol. 5, p. 103.

27. The series of documents related to this tour are in *Yamauchi-ke shiryō: Tadatoyo-kō ki,* vol. 2, pp. 591–618.

28. Ibid., vol. 2, pp. 593–597.

29. Ibid., vol. 2, p. 610.

30. Ibid., vol. 2, pp. 612–613; *Shintei Kansei chōshū shokafu,* vol. 13, p. 377; MS "Kanbun hachinen bugenchō, jōkan," in Kōchi Prefecture Library. The entry for Kuwayama Hanzaemon (Sadakatsu) listed in Teramura Awaji's unit says he was hired by Tadayoshi in 1650. He appears in the 1660 retainer register with 500 *koku,* as printed in Kōchi-ken Bunkyō Kyōkai, *Nonaka Kenzan kankei monjo* (Kōchi: Kōchi-ken Bunkyō Kyōkai, 1965), p. 555. For a more general discussion of how such connections worked, see Takagi, *Edo bakufu no seido.*

31. *Yamauchi-ke shiryō: Tadatoyo-kō ki,* vol. 2, p. 605.

32. Ibid., vol. 2, pp. 602–605. This same pattern can also be seen in 1746, when villagers were instructed to describe all samurai homes as commoner homes. Kōchi-ken Shi Hensan Iinkai, *Kōchi-ken shi,* p. 31.

33. *Yamauchi-ke shiryō: Tadatoyo-kō ki,* vol. 2, pp. 612, 616.

34. Ibid., vol. 2, pp. 604–605.

35. Ibid., vol. 2, p. 616.

36. Ibid., vol. 2, p. 594.

37. Ibid., vol. 2, p. 618.

38. Kasei Jikki Kanpon Hensan Iinkai, ed., *Aizu-han kasei jikki,* vol. 2 (Tokyo: Yoshikawa Kōbunkan, 1976), pp. 300–301, 309, 310–316.

39. Tahara-chō Bunkazai Hogo Shingikai, *Tahara-han nikki,* vol. 1, p. 76.

40. Ibid., vol. 1, pp. 79–82.

41. Ibid., vol. 1, pp. 45–46, 79, 84.

42. Ōhira, "Edo bakufu junkenshi," p. 589, p. 598 n. 6.

43. John Hall, "The *Bakuhan* System," in *The Cambridge History of Japan,* vol. 4, *Early Modern Japan,* ed. John Whitney Hall (Cambridge: Cambridge University Press, 1991), p. 152.

44. The resurgence of attainders during Tsunayoshi's reign may have been due to the lack of appreciation for the politics of *uchi* and *omote* that emerged from his idealistic approach to government.

45. Kokushi Daijiten Hensan Iinkai, *Kokushi daijiten,* vol. 2, pp. 284–285; Beatrice Bodart-Bailey, *The Dog Shogun: The Personality and Policies of Tokugawa Tsunayoshi* (Honolulu: University of Hawai'i Press, 2006), pp. 82–89.

46. Fujino, *On'eiroku, Haizetsuroku,* p. 288; *Tokugawa jikki,* vol. 5, p. 437.

47. Akabane-chō Shi Hensan Iinkai, ed., *Akabane-chō shi* (Aichi-ken Akabane-chō, 1968), pp. 256, 270.

48. MS "Sendai gyōjō," biography by Mori Shirō, fols. 73–74, original held in Kōchi Museum of History and Culture. I used a copy held in Kōchi Prefecture Library.

49. The known figures are from sources cited in my *Mercantilism* for chart 3.1, pp. 61, 214–215. Amounts reported to the Tokugawa can be found in Susan Hanley and Kozo Yamamura, *Economic and Demographic Change in Preindustrial Japan, 1600–1868* (Princeton, NJ: Princeton University Press, 1977), pp. 71–73. The *koku* amounts are based on a Tosa government conversion known as *jidaka,* created by calculating one *tan* of land to be one *koku* of rice.

50. This document can be found in the collection of a domain retainer held in microfilm at Kōchi Prefecture Library as "Shibuya-ke monjo," vol. 3 (call no. kenshi 124-3).

51. For a detailed set of such reports from 1727–1731, see MS "Hanshi nai-hen" (Kōchi University Library, special collections, call no. 001.2/Han/2), in the volume entitled "Seitai enkaku, Daishōin-sama odai Kyōhō jūshichinen mizunoe shougatsu yori dō nijūnen kinoetora jūichigatsu no kan," entry for 1732.

52. Kawamura Hirotada, *Edo bakufu sen kuniezu no kenkyū* (Tokyo: Kokon Shoin, 1984), pp. 247–249.

53. Kokushi Daijiten Hensan Iinkai, *Kokushi daijiten,* vol. 5, p. 450. Many

economic historians have naturally relied on these figures, such as myself in chapter 3 of *Mercantilism;* Nishikawa Shunsaku in his *Nihon keizai no seichōshi* (Tokyo: Tōyōkeizai Shinpōsha, 1985), p. 22; and Hanley and Yamamura, *Economic and Demographic Change,* pp. 69–78.

54. Kawamura, *Edo bakufu sen kuniezu,* p. 251.

55. Ibid.

56. Ibid., pp. 253–257, 259–264.

57. Kokushi Daijiten Hensan Iinkai, *Kokushi daijiten,* vol. 3, p. 234.

58. Kawamura, *Edo bakufu sen kuniezu,* p. 264.

59. These figures can be found in Hanley and Yamamura, *Economic and Demographic Change,* pp. 69–90. The authors give a date of 1829 for the figures submitted in 1834, but otherwise the data are identical to the chart I relied on from *Nihon rekishi daijiten,* vol. 4 (Tokyo: Shōgakukan, 2001), p. 303, prepared by Fujii Jōji.

60. Tahara-chō Bunkazai Chōsakai, *Tahara-chō shi, chūkan,* pp. 95–98.

3: Politics of the Living Dead

1. Katsu Kokichi, *Musui's Story: The Autobiography of a Tokugawa Samurai,* trans. Teruko Craig (Tucson: University of Arizona Press, 1988), p. 12.

2. Tahara-chō Bunkazai Hogo Shingikai, ed., *Tahara-han nikki,* vol. 10, p. 353.

3. Nakada Kaoru provides a well-organized survey of the laws of samurai adoption and inheritance in *Hōsei-shi ronshū,* vol. 1 (Tokyo: Iwanami Shoten, 1970), pp. 375–466, 492–539.

4. Fukuda Chizuru, *Oie sōdō: Daimyō-ke o yurugashita kenryoku tōsō* (Tokyo: Chūōkōronsha, 2005), p. 8.

5. Fujino, *Bakuhan taisei shi no kenkyū,* pp. 192–194. Note that I use "age" in the Japanese reckoning as a stand-in for *sai,* which means the number of calendrical years that one has lived in. This tends to be one year greater than Western notions of age.

6. Hozumi Nobushige, "Yui Shōsetsu jiken to Tokugawa bakufu no yōshi hō," in his *Hozumi Nobushige ibunshū,* vol. 3 (Tokyo: Iwanami Shoten, 1934), pp. 626–632.

7. Berry, *Hideyoshi,* pp. 218–223, 227.

8. Fujino, *Bakuhan taisei shi no kenkyū,* pp. 192–217, 250–252, 327–332; Hozumi, "Yui Shōsetsu." The number sixty-one accounts for daimyo attainders only. If Tokugawa bannermen and housemen (*gokenin*) were included, the number would be much greater.

9. *Kanmei nikki,* ed. Minami Kazuo, vol. 2, *Naikakubunko shozō shiseki sōkan* series, vol. 67 (Tokyo: Gyūko Shoin, 1986), pp. 225–227.

10. Ikeda Mitsumasa notes that some of his retainers and those of Kii, Owari, Takada, Fukuoka, and Odawara, all domains of powerful lords, were suspect. Not

incidentally, they were outside the group in charge of the Tokugawa government during Ietsuna's reign. Ikeda Mitsumasa, *Ikeda Mitsumasa nikki,* ed. Fujii Shun et al. (Okayama: San'yō Tosho Shuppan, 1967), p. 176.

11. *Kanmei nikki,* vol. 2, pp. 237–238.

12. Hozumi, "Yui Shōsetsu," pp. 643–644.

13. Ibid., pp. 626–632.

14. Fujino, *On'eiroku, Haizetsuroku,* pp. 270–271. For the official statements of policy in 1683 and thereafter, see Nakada, *Hōsei-shi ronshū,* vol. 1, pp. 426–427.

15. Ōmori Eiko, *Oie sōzoku: Daimyōke no kutō* (Tokyo: Kadokawa Shoten, 2004).

16. Nakada, *Hōsei-shi ronshū,* vol. 1, pp. 375–466, 492–539. Harafuji Hiroshi notes in his *Sōzokuhō no tokushitsu* (Tokyo: Sōbunsha, 1982), p. 323, that Nakada's research on this point has stood the test of time against later historians of law.

17. Based on a reading of Fujino, *On'eiroku, Haizetsuroku.* Each instance had a special backstory. The first instance happened in 1653 when a lord who himself had arrived at his position due to a special dispensation then quickly died without heir. The other two were the 1664 fief reduction of Uesugi clan of Yonezawa domain, who for unknown reasons apparently did not even attempt to carry out a last-minute adoption, and the 1669 attainder of a branch domain of a daimyo that was refolded into the main domain. For the Uesugi case, see Hansei shi kenkyūkai, ed., *Hansei seiritsu shi no sōgō kenkyū: Yonezawa-han* (Tokyo: Yoshikawa Kōbunkan, 1963), pp. 333–337.

18. Kyūji Shimon Kai, ed., *Kyūji shimonroku,* annotated by Shinji Yoshimoto (Tokyo: Iwanami Shoten, 1986), vol. 1, pp. 256–257. A generally good translation can be found in Anna Beerens, "Interview with a *Bakumatsu* Official: A Translation from *Kyūji Shimonroku,*" *Monumenta Nipponica* 55, no. 3 (Autumn 2000): 369–398.

19. Matsura, *Kasshi yawa,* vol. 1, pp. 5–6. This concerned Tsuchiya Yasunao, lord of Tsuchiura, who official Tokugawa records say fell ill in the fourth month of 1790 and died on the twelfth day of the fifth month.

20. Haruko Iwasaki has perceptive comments on this issue in her essay "Portrait of a Daimyo: Comic Fiction by Matsudaira Sadanobu," *Monumenta Nipponica* 38, no. 1 (Spring 1983): 1–19.

21. Mutō, *Nanroshi,* vol. 7, pp. 95–96.

22. MS "Ohanmoto omitodoke no setsu ozashiki ezu," in Yamauchi-ke Hōmotsu Shiryōkan, Kōchi, along with other documents relating to these two incidents.

23. Hoya Tōru, "Daimyo monjo no teishutsu: Juri shisutemu to rōjū no kaitō: Ueda Matsudaira-ke monjo 'nichijō' no bunseki kara," in *Kinsei bakufu monjo no komonjogakuteki kenkyū,* ed. Katō Hideyuki (Tokyo: Tokyo Daigaku Shiryōhensanjo, 1992).

24. *Yamauchi-ke shiryō: Bakumatsu Ishin hen,* vol. 2:1 (Kōchi: Yamauchi Jinja Hōmotsu Shiryōkan, 2002), pp. 4–5.

25. Matsura, *Kasshi yawa,* vol. 1, p. 14.

26. I have found for another house, that of the Miura daimyo of Katsuyama domain, a record indicating that secret arrangements were made with a temple to give the lord a posthumous name on the day following his actual death, which was kept from *omote* notice for more than two months. This might suggest an early cremation process, but I have found no explicit documents. Okayama-ken Shi Hensan Iinkai, *Okayama-ken shi,* vol. 26, *Shohan monjo* (Okayama: Okayama-ken, 1983), p. 1101.

27. The "will" is quite vague on the matter, merely asking everyone to be obedient and listing the names of his *ichimon* relatives. The two-day delay in taking the request to the Elders may also indicate a period of discussion among the survivors. *Sōma-han seiki,* vol. 1 (Tokyo: Zoku Gunsho Ruijū Kanseikai, 1999), pp. 113–121; *Sōma-shi shi,* vol. 5 (Fukushima Pref., Sōma-shi, 1971), pp. 405–406.

28. *Sōma-shi shi,* vol. 5, p. 47.

29. Ibid., vol. 5, p. 52.

30. Ibid., vol. 5, pp. 49–53.

31. Fujino, *On'eiroku, Haizetsuroku,* p. 281.

32. Fukuda, *Oie sōdō,* pp. 70–73.

33. Okayama-ken Shi Hensan Iinkai, *Okayama-ken shi,* vol. 5, *Kinsei 1* (Okayama: Okayama-ken, 1984), pp. 106–115, and vol. 25, *Tsuyama-han monjo* (1981), pp. 238–245, 276–279; Tsuyama-shi Shi Hensan Iinkai, ed., *Tsuyama-shi shi,* vol. 3, *Kinsei 1* (Okayama Pref., Tsuyama shi, 1973), pp. 100–115.

34. Okayama-ken Shi Hensan Iinkai, *Okayama-ken shi,* vol. 26, *Shohan monjo,* pp. 30–33.

35. Ōmori, *Oie sōzoku.*

36. Honma Shūhei, ed., *Shokokoroedome, shokokoroetoiawase aisatsudome, shomuki kikiawasegaki, shomuki toiawase otsukefudazumi no utsushi* (Tokyo: Sōbunsha, 2006), p. 67.

37. Ōmori, *Oie sōzoku,* p. 203.

38. Ibid., pp. 39–40.

39. Matsunoo Shōkō, comp., *Kaizanshū,* ed. Hirao Michio et al., vol. 3 (Kōchi: Kōchi Kenritsu Toshokan, 1976), pp. 405, 426.

40. Ōmori, *Oie sōzoku,* pp. 72–85.

41. Ibid., pp. 116–140. For the Nanbu clan, see Morioka-shi Shi Hensan Iinkai, ed., *Morioka-shi shi,* vol. 3:2 (Morioka: Morioka-shi, 1968), pp. 59–60.

42. Matsura, *Kasshi yawa,* vol. 1, p. 74.

43. The internal-use lineage for the Miyake clan has an entry for the younger brother Kōzō, which notes that his time with his brother in Tahara had been without notification to the Tokugawa government. Tahara-chō Bunkazai Chōsakai, *Tahara-chō shi, chūkan,* p. 1197.

44. Tahara-chō Bunkazai Hogo Shingikai, *Tahara-han nikki,* vol. 10. The events described are based on the relevant portions of four diaries for 1823, pp. 348–431. Quotations come from pp. 357 and 373.

45. Tahara-chō Bunkazai Chōsakai, *Tahara-chō shi, chūkan,* pp. 56–57. As was

the case in most domains in this era, the fiefs were fictive, but the title remained an important matter of status distinction putting them above stipendiaries.

46. Tahara-chō Bunkazai Hogo Shingikai, *Tahara-han nikki,* vol. 10, pp. 437–438, 491–493.

47. Ibid., vol. 10, p. 414.

48. Ibid., vol. 8, p. 123.

49. Tahara-chō Bunkazai Hogo Shingikai, *Tahara-han nikki,* vol. 8, pp. 120–125, 141–144. The quotation is from p. 143.

50. Ozawa Kōichi, *Watanabe Kazan kenkyū* (Tokyo: Nihon Tosho Sentaa, 1988), pp. 66–98; Tahara-chō Bunkazai Chōsakai, *Tahara-chō shi, chūkan,* pp. 166–169, 1065–1070, 1103–1110.

51. *Yamauchi-ke shiryō: Bakumatsu Ishin hen,* vol. 1, pp. 424–428, 433. The news arrived on the twenty-seventh, and the son died on the twenty-eighth, but he officially died on the twenty-ninth.

52. Matsunoo, *Kaizanshū,* vol. 3, pp. 449–453.

53. *Yamauchi-ke shiryō: Bakumatsu Ishin hen,* vol. 1, pp. 447–455; Sasaki Takayuki, *Hogohiroi: Sasaki Takayuki nikki,* vol. 1 (Tokyo: Tōkyō Daigaku Shuppankai, 1970), p. 39.

54. Ōmori, *Oie sōzoku,* p. 19.

55. Kusunose Ōe, *Hiuchi bukuro,* ed. Kōchi Chihōshi Kenkyūkai, vol. 1 (Kōchi: Kōchi Shimin Toshokan, 1966), in *Tosa gunsho shūsei* series, p. 2; Marius Jansen, *Sakamoto Ryōma and the Meiji Restoration* (Princeton, NJ: Princeton University Press, 1961), pp. 40, 121.

56. Matsunoo, *Kaizanshū,* vol. 3, p. 454.

57. The letters are copied in a memorandum fragment that is filed together with a similar-looking memorandum fragment from Toyoteru's death. The latter is called "Kaei gan sarudoshi Toyoteru-sama obyōchū oenkō ikkan te hikae, ni," a manuscript held in Yamauchi-ke Hōmotsu Shiryōkan, Kōchi, and listed in the archive catalogue on p. 222.

58. *Yamauchi-ke shiryō: Bakumatsu Ishin hen,* vol. 2:1, pp. 10–17. The source for this information, Date Munenari's memorandum, does not provide details, but at this time the Shimazu clan was defending itself against accusations of carrying on illegal foreign trade. For a brief narrative of the inheritance, see Hirao Michio, *Yamauchi Yōdō* (Tokyo: Yoshikawa Kōbunkan, 1961), pp. 12–17.

59. *Yamauchi-ke shiryō: Bakumatsu Ishin hen,* vol. 2:1, p. 11.

60. Itō Seirō et al., *Abe Masahiro no subete* (Tokyo: Shin Jinbutsu Ōraisha, 1997).

61. Yamamoto Takeshi et al., eds., *Kenshōbo* (Kōchi: Kōchi Kenritsu Toshokan, 1982–1986), vol. 1, p. 342.

62. Both Conrad Totman, "Political Reconciliation in the Tokugawa Bakufu: Abe Masahiro and Tokugawa Nariaki, 1844–1852," and Robert Sakai, "Shimazu Nariakira and the Emergence of National Leadership in Satsuma," in *Personality in*

Japanese History, ed. Albert Craig and Donald Shively (Berkeley: University of California Press, 1970), pp. 180–208, 209-233, describe the importance of *naishō* politics among this group. See also Nagae Shinzō, *Ansei no taigoku: Ii Naosuke to Yoshida Shōin* (Tokyo: Nihon Kyōbunsha, 1966).

63. Based on my visit to the Miyake clan graves at Reiganji temple in Tahara.

64. Wakabayashi Kisaburō, *Kyū Ise Kanbe-hanshu Honda-ke shiryō* (Nishinomiya: Ōtemae Joshi Daigaku Shigaku Kenkyūsho, 1988), pp. 7, 144.

65. The Yamauchi graves are not open to the public, but photographs are in the slim volume *Tosa hanshu Yamauchi-ke bosho,* produced by the Yamauchi-ke Hōmotsu Shiryōkan, n.d. The stele inscriptions are recorded in Takeichi Saichirō, *Takeichi Saichirō shū,* vol. 9 (Kōchi: Kōchi Shimin Toshokan, 1996), pp. 483, 656–657, 664–665.

66. *Yamauchi-ke shiryō: Bakumatsu Ishin hen,* vol. 2:1, p. 94.

67. Takeichi, *Takeichi Saichirō shū,* vol. 9, culls from various histories, each with attribution, in a chronologically arranged history, and comparison of these data confirms the above argument.

68. Tokushima-ken Shi Hensan Iinkai, ed., *Tokushima-ken shiryō,* vol. 1 (Tokushima: Tokushima-ken, 1964), pp. 379, 443.

69. These facts are presented identically in "Hisamatsu kafu" and in "Matsuyama okafu" in *Matsuyama-shi shiryōshū,* ed. Matsuyama-shi Shiryōshū Henshū Iinkai, vol. 2 (Matsuyama: Matsuyama-shi Shiyakusho, 1987), pp. 918–984.

70. This document is called "Matsuyama joshu Hisamatsu-shi keifu ryaku" and is on pp. 985–998 of Matsuyama-shi Shiryōshū Henshū Iinkai, *Matsuyama-shi shiryōshū,* vol. 2.

71. *Shintei Kansei chōshū shokafu,* vol. 16, p. 15; Tahara-chō Bunkazai Chōsakai, *Tahara-chō shi, chūkan,* p. 1195.

4: Territorial Border Disputes

1. *Yamauchi-ke shiryō: Tadayoshi-kō ki,* vol. 3, p. 677.

2. There are numerous references to this made by various parties in the cases: *Yamauchi-ke shiryō: Tadayoshi-kō ki,* vol. 3, p. 739, and vol. 4, pp. 655, 684, 691. Nevertheless the daimyo Tadayoshi once hoped to make a direct suit concerning the second case, based on the violence inflicted on Tosa parties rather than on the border dispute itself; vol. 4, p. 687.

3. The relation between the mapping project and border disputes is discussed in Marcia Yonemoto, "Silence without Secrecy? What Is Left Unsaid in Early Modern Japanese Maps," *Early Modern Japan* 14 (2006): 27–39. The fullest treatments of the subjects are Kawamura, *Edo bakufu sen kuniezu* (note especially pp. 127–128 for border disputes), and his newer but less expansive *Kuniezu* (Tokyo: Yoshikawa Kōbunkan, 1990).

4. Kawamura, *Kuniezu,* pp. 87–89.

5. Yokogawa Suekichi, "'Okinoshima chikai ron' no kenkyū," *Tosa shidan,* no. 88 (May 1956): 1–10.

6. Fishing grounds were considered part of the territory of lordly realms and part of village property as well. For a detailed discussion, see Arne Kalland, *Fishing Villages in Tokugawa Japan* (Richmond, UK: Curzon Press, 1995), chap. 9; and Yokogawa, "Okinoshima," p. 4.

7. Yokogawa in "Okinoshima" emphasizes how external lordly interests worked to politically divide the island. Rokunoshin's written accusations and Gengorō's response are included in pp. 615–621 of *Yamauchi-ke shiryō: Tadayoshi-kō ki,* vol. 3. Additional documents produced by various people on the Iyo side can be found in Ehime Kenshi Hensan Iinkai, ed., *Ehime kenshi, Shiryō-hen, Kinsei, ge* (Matsuyama: Ehime-ken, 1988), pp. 227–253.

8. *Yamauchi-ke shiryō: Tadayoshi-kō ki,* vol. 3, p. 607. The use of heirs in this case was probably to save face for the daimyo themselves.

9. Ibid., vol. 3, p. 610; some early letters of negotiation are on pp. 607, 711–718.

10. Ibid., vol. 3, pp. 698–699.

11. Rokunoshin's first suit is in ibid., vol. 3, pp. 615–618. The Senior Council (*hyōjōsho*) was the highest court and administrative decision-making body in the land, and only the Tokugawa *kubō* himself, whose authority the council represented, had higher judicial authority. The council membership (*hyōjōshū*) at this time was made up of three Tokugawa Elders, three Shrine and Temple Magistrates, two Town Magistrates, two Finance Magistrates, and one of the Grand Inspectors.

12. The seals on the reverse are listed in ibid., vol. 3, p. 708.

13. This point is made in pp. (33)–(38) of Kamiya Masaji, "Jidai to Nonaka Kenzan ron," in the front matter of *Yamauchi-ke shiryō: Tadayoshi-kō ki,* vol. 4.

14. Ōhira Yūichi, "Naisai to saiban," in *Kinsei hō no saikentō: Rekishigaku to hōshigaku to no taiwa,* ed. Fujita Satoru (Tokyo: Yamakawa Shuppan, 2005).

15. *Yamauchi-ke shiryō: Tadayoshi-kō ki,* vol. 3, pp. 618, 630.

16. Gengorō's statement can be found in ibid., vol. 3, pp. 618–621, and his more detailed restatement at the time of the actual trial in pp. 630–641.

17. Because many religious sites were built upon peaks, and mountain ridges were commonly used to mark boundaries, this may have been a relatively common situation. A border dispute between Sendai and Morioka domains began in 1631 when Sendai domain repaired on its own initiative a shrine with two posts in each domain. Iwate Kenritsu Toshokan, ed., *Naishi ryaku* (3), in *Iwate shisō* series (Morioka: Iwate-ken Bunkazai Aigo Kyōkai, 1974), p. 459. Mention of a shrine whose torii gate had one post in each province and whose space between marked the boundary can be found in pp. 225–226 of Sugimoto Fumiko, "Kuniezu sakusei jigyō to kinsei kokka," in *Kinsei kokka,* ed. Fukaya Katsumi and Hori Shin, vol. 13 of *Tenbō Nihon rekishi* series (Tokyo: Tōkyōdō Shuppan, 2000). For a study that deals with competing "religious space" and "governmental space," see Laura Nenzi, *Excursions*

in Identity: Travel and the Intersection of Place, Gender, and Status in Edo Japan (Hono-lulu: University of Hawai'i Press, 2008), chap. 1.

18. This interpretation is that of Yokogawa Suekichi, "'Sasayama kokkyō ron sadame' no kenkyū: Nonaka Kenzan kankei no ichi shiryō," *Tosa shidan,* no. 99 (October 1960): 1–12, which is the main research on this dispute. See also the excel-lent account by Takagi Shōsaku on pp. 625–632 in Ehime Kenshi Hensan Iinkai, ed., *Ehime kenshi, Kinsei, jō,* (Matsuyama: Ehime-ken, 1986).

19. *Yamauchi-ke shiryō: Tadayoshi-kō ki,* vol. 4, pp. 634–635.

20. Yokogawa, "Sasayama," pp. 1–2.

21. Although in Yūei's account this incident happened in 1655, all other evidence points to 1656. Yūei's account is in *Yamauchi-ke shiryō: Tadayoshi-kō ki,* vol. 4, pp. 619–624. Insofar as we do not hear of the Buddha image again, it is likely that the evidence supposed to be carved on the base either did not exist or did not favor the Iyo side.

22. *Yamauchi-ke shiryō: Tadayoshi-kō ki,* vol. 4, p. 638.

23. Ibid., vol. 4, pp. 637–678.

24. Ibid., vol. 4, p. 632.

25. Yokogawa, "Sasayama," p. 6.

26. *Yamauchi-ke shiryō: Tadayoshi-kō ki,* vol. 4, pp. 616–617.

27. Ibid., vol. 4, pp. 605–613.

28. Ibid., vol. 3, p. 663.

29. For a diagram of the marriage connections, see Ehime Kenshi Hensan Iinkai, *Ehime kenshi, Kinsei, jō,* p. 631.

30. Kamiya, "Jidai to Nonaka Kenzan ron," discusses the importance of family connections in this dispute.

31. *Yamauchi-ke shiryō: Tadayoshi-kō ki,* vol. 3, p. 622; Yokogawa, "Sasayama," pp. 11–12.

32. *Yamauchi-ke shiryō: Tadayoshi-kō ki,* vol. 3, pp. 644–645.

33. Ibid., vol. 3, pp. 729–735.

34. Ehime Kenshi Hensan Iinkai, *Ehime kenshi, Shiryō-hen, Kinsei, ge,* p. 246.

35. *Yamauchi-ke shiryō: Tadayoshi-kō ki,* vol. 3, p. 628.

36. Ibid., vol. 3, p. 630.

37. Ibid., vol. 3, p. 644. This man was almost certainly Doi Ichiemon, a retainer of Nonaka Kenzan's who was later made a direct samurai retainer. He was placed in the domain home guard (*rusuikumi*) in 1660 and granted a fief of 100 *koku*. One record of his employment says, "He was a retainer of Nonaka Den'emon [Kenzan], who received this post for his services in the Okinoshima border dispute" (ibid., vol. 1, p. 327; this source gives the year of employment incorrectly as 1659). Two other records have him being employed directly by Tadatoyo in 1660 and also note that he had been a retainer of Nonaka's and had served in the border dispute (ibid., vol. 1, pp. 398–399). The Ichiemon at court had certainly been Nonaka's retainer (ibid., vol. 3, p. 744), and the rise in his status to a full-fledged samurai in 1660 was likely a reward for his services.

38. Ibid., vol. 3, p. 655.

39. Ibid., vol. 3. pp. 654–655.

40. Ibid., vol. 3, p. 662.

41. Ibid., vol. 3, p. 664.

42. Ibid., vol. 3, pp. 665–666.

43. How he knew this is not in the records. A likely scenario is that he had been informally approached by Kamio Motokatsu for understanding on the issue before his animosity toward Tosa had become clear.

44. *Yamauchi-ke shiryō: Tadayoshi-kō ki,* vol. 3, pp. 667, 673.

45. Ibid., vol. 3, p. 668.

46. Ibid., vol. 3, p. 669.

47. Ibid., vol. 3, p. 672.

48. Ibid., vol. 3, p. 675.

49. Ibid., vol. 3, p. 677.

50. Ibid., vol. 3, p. 682.

51. Although Rokunoshin was without doubt the traditional headman of the Uwajima half of the island, the Date had given him these accouterments of status as reward for representing their interests.

52. *Yamauchi-ke shiryō: Tadayoshi-kō ki,* vol. 3, p. 686.

53. Ibid., vol. 4, p. 712.

54. Ibid., vol. 3, p. 694.

55. Ibid., vol. 3, pp. 696, 751. Also noted in Ehime Kenshi Hensan Iinkai, *Ehime kenshi, Kinsei, jō,* p. 632.

56. Yokogawa, "Sasayama," p. 11.

57. *Yamauchi-ke shiryō: Tadayoshi-kō ki,* vol. 3, p. 755.

58. Ibid., vol. 3, pp. 642–643.

59. Ibid., vol. 4, pp. 605–610.

60. Ibid., vol. 4, pp. 610–613, 649.

61. Ibid., vol. 4, p. 685.

62. Ibid., vol. 4, pp. 653, 684.

63. Yokoyama, "Sasayama," p. 11.

64. *Yamauchi-ke shiryō: Tadayoshi-kō ki,* vol. 4, p. 715.

65. Ibid., vol. 4, p. 710.

66. Ibid., vol. 4, p. 642.

67. Ibid., vol. 3, p. 644.

68. Ibid., vol. 4, pp. 612, 722.

69. Ibid., vol. 4, pp. 629–630, 719.

70. Hashida Kokin, "Nonaka Kenzan Sasayama ronsō no ichi ketsumatsu: Dōji kyōyū no jittai," *Tosa shidan,* no. 132 (July 1972): 1–4.

71. Unless otherwise noted, the following discussion is based on Fujii Tomozuru, "Mikawa Hiruwayama sanron no tenkai: Shiryō sanron no kōgi osso o megutte," *Shien* 51, no. 1 (January 1991): 5–23; Akabane-chō Shi Hensan Iinkai, ed., *Akabane*

no komonjo: Kinsei shiryō hen (Aichi-ken: Tahara-shi Kyōiku Iinkai, 2005), pp. 443, 454–456; and Tahara-chō Bunkazai Chōsakai, *Tahara-chō shi, chūkan,* pp. 927–935.

72. Tahara-chō Bunkazai Chōsakai, *Tahara-chō shi, chūkan,* p. 928.

73. Ōhira Yūichi, "Kinsei no higōhōteki soshō: Kagoso, kakekomiso o sozai to shite, (1)," *Ritsumeikan hōgaku,* no. 183–184 (May–June 1985): 750–766. Here and below I depend on Ōhira's research on illegal suits.

74. Fukaya Katsumi, "Hyakushō ikki no shisō," *Shisō,* no. 584 (February 1973): 206–227.

75. Dani Botsman, *Punishment and Power in the Making of Modern Japan* (Princeton, NJ: Princeton University Press, 2005). Chapters 1 and 2 explore the role of the ideology of benevolence in the irregular application of punishments.

76. Ōhira, "Kinsei no higōhōteki soshō," p. 751.

77. Fujii Tomozuru, "Mikawa Hiruwayama sanron no tenkai," p. 11.

78. Tahara-chō Bunkazai Chōsakai, *Tahara-chō shi, chūkan,* p. 929.

79. Ibid., p. 934.

80. Ōhira Yūichi, in "Naisai" and "Kinsei no higōhōteki soshō" (1)–(7), explores this issue in depth. Tahara-chō Bunkazai Chōsakai, *Tahara-chō shi, chūkan,* pp. 939–940, describes a case from 1725 where the domain quickly followed directions from the Senior Council on a water dispute and rescinded punishments of villagers for insubordination. See also Scheiner, "Benevolent Lords."

5: Daimyo Gods

1. Yamamoto Takeshi, *Kenshōbo,* vol. 7, p. 48.

2. Peter Nosco, "Keeping the Faith: Bakuhan Policy towards Religions in Seventeenth-Century Japan," in *Religion in Japan,* ed. Peter Kornicki and I. J. McMullen (Cambridge: Cambridge University Press, 1996), pp. 135–155. This is a stimulating and succinct account of the creation of this order in terms of the distinction between formal claims and actual practice in religious policy, and in terms of the place of privacy and secrecy in power relations. Nosco contrasts individual freedom with "the state." I think one can apply his understandings of the individual's place in power relations to feudal spaces as well. Despite this small difference, Nosco's argument guides my approach in this chapter.

3. Ibid.

4. Tamamuro Fumio, *Edo bakufu no shūkyō tōsei* (Tokyo: Hyōronsha, 1971), pp. 62–74. For the temple registration system and Christianity, see Nam-lin Hur, *Death and the Social Order in Tokugawa Japan: Buddhism, Anti-Christianity, and the Danka System* (Cambridge, MA: Harvard University Asia Center, 2007), pp. 37–106. Nosco, in "Keeping the Faith," discusses how both Christianity and Fujufuse Buddhism developed amid the mid-seventeenth century practices that made it possible for officials to turn a blind eye to their continued presence.

5. The variety of local manifestations of social competition and religious

institutional arrangements is described in Helen Hardacre, *Religion and Society in Nineteenth-Century Japan: A Study of the Southern Kantō Region, Using Late Edo and Early Meiji Gazetteers* (Ann Arbor: University of Michigan Center for Japanese Studies, 2002), especially chaps. 2 and 4.

6. Ikegami, *Taming of the Samurai*, pp. 218–222.

7. Walthall, *Weak Body*, pp. 100–139.

8. Helen Hardacre, *Shinto and the State, 1868–1988* (Princeton, NJ: Princeton University Press, 1990), pp. 3–19.

9. Allan Grapard, "Japan's Ignored Cultural Revolution: The Separation of Shinto and Buddhist Divinities in Meiji (*shimbutsu bunri*) and a Case Study; Tōnomine," *History of Religions* 23, no. 3 (February 1984): 240–265; James Ketelaar, *Of Heretics and Martyrs in Meiji Japan: Buddhism and Its Persecution* (Princeton, NJ: Princeton University Press, 1990).

10. Allan Grapard, "The Shinto of Yoshida Kanetomo," *Monumenta Nipponica* 47, no. 1 (Spring 1992): 27–58.

11. Harry Harootunian, *Things Seen and Unseen: Discourse and Ideology in Tokugawa Nativism* (Chicago: University of Chicago Press, 1988); Berry, *Japan in Print*; Richard Rubinger, *Popular Literacy in Early Modern Japan* (Honolulu: University of Hawai'i Press, 2007).

12. Haga Shōji, *Shisekiron: 19 seiki Nihon no chiiki shakai to rekishi ishiki* (Nagoya: Nagoya Daigaku Shuppankai, 1998).

13. Inoue Tomokatsu, "Kansei ki ni okeru ujigami, ryūkōgami to chōtei," *Nihonshi kenkyū*, no. 365 (1993): 1–26.

14. Fujita Satoru, *Bakumatsu no tennō* (Tokyo: Kōdansha, 1994).

15. Hiromi Maeda, "Imperial Authority and Local Shrines: The Yoshida House and the Creation of a Countrywide Shinto Institution in Early Modern Japan" (PhD dissertation, Harvard University, May 1993).

16. Roberts, *Mercantilism*, chap. 7.

17. Herman Ooms, *Tokugawa Ideology: Early Constructs, 1570–1680* (Princeton, NJ: Princeton University Press, 1985), pp. 50–62; W. J. Boot, "The Death of a Shogun: Deification in Early Modern Japan," in *Shinto in History: Ways of the Kami*, ed. John Breen and Mark Teeuwen (Honolulu: University of Hawai'i Press, 2000), pp. 144–166.

18. Andrew Watsky, *Chikubushima: Deploying the Sacred Arts of Momoyama Japan* (Seattle: University of Washington Press, 2004), pp. 204–208, 227–230; Kurachi Katsunao, *Kinsei minshū to shihai shisō* (Tokyo: Kashiwashobō, 1996), pp. 172–196.

19. Kondō Yoshihiro, "Toyokuni Daimyōjin no bunpai ni tsuite," in *Kokushigaku ronshū*, ed. Ueki Hakase Kanreki Kinen Shukugakai (Tokyo: Ueki Hakase Kanreki Kinen Shukugakai, 1938), pp. 357–377.

20. Tōkyō Daigaku Shiryō Hensanjo, ed., *Dai Nihon shiryō* (Tokyo: Tōkyō Daigaku Shuppankai, 1968–), vol. 12:22, pp. 67–121, and vol. 12:31, pp. 425–440.

21. Nagahama-shi Hensan Iinkai, *Nagahama-shi shi,* vol. 6, *Matsuri to gyōji* (Shiga Pref., Nagahama-shi, 2004), pp. 116–128; Shiritsu Nagahama-jō Rekishi Hakubutsukan, ed., *Kami ni natta Hideyoshi: Hideyoshi ninki no himitsu o saguru* (Nagahama: Shiritsu Nagahama-jō Rekishi Hakubutsukan, 2004). In the latter book, Tsuda Saburō writes that Hideyoshi's divine title (*shingō*) was taken away by Ieyasu. Because the title was granted by the emperor, such an act would likely have generated a large paper trail, but I have seen no documents. The Toyokuni Shrine was revived in 1868 by the imperial court.

22. Mase Kumiko, "Jinja to tennō," in *Tennō to shakai shoshūdan,* vol. 3 of *Kōza zenkindai no tennō,* ed. Nagahara Keiji et al. (Tokyo: Aoki Shoten, 1993), p. 230.

23. Maeda, "Imperial Authority and Local Shrines"; Grapard, "Shinto of Yoshida Kanetomo," pp. 46–47, 56–57.

24. Maeda, "Imperial Authority and Local Shrines."

25. Mase, "Jinja to tennō," chart on pp. 231–232. Furthermore, Takano Nobuharu has researched hundreds of *kami* made from warriors, including daimyo, retainers, and warriors from tales and earlier eras, which he reads as part of changing the image of warriors into divine protectors of the region. See his *Bushi shinkakuka ichiran, kō,* 2 vols., *Kyūshū bunkashi kenkyū kiyō* series, no. 47 (March 2003) and no. 48 (March 2005). Also see his "Edo jidai bushi no imeeji," *Rekishi chiri kyōiku,* no. 711 (March 2007): 66–71.

26. Ooms, *Tokugawa Ideology,* pp. 194–198, 221–232; Maeda, "Imperial Authority and Local Shrines," pp. 80–82. Ultimately Yoshikawa developed an uneasy relationship with the Yoshida clan and came to be regarded as starting his own school of Yoshikawa Shinto in Aizu domain.

27. Kasei Jikki Kanpon Hensan Iinkai, *Aizu-han kasei jikki,* vol. 2, pp. 578–579.

28. James McMullen, *Idealism, Protest, and "The Tale of Genji": The Confucianism of Kumazawa Banzan, 1619–91* (Oxford: Oxford University Press, 1999), pp. 131–135. Beatrice Bodart-Bailey argues in *The Dog Shogun,* pp. 60–66, that Mitsumasa allowed people to choose either Buddhist or Shinto affiliation and that he "intended to have Buddhism, Shinto and Confucianism equally revered," but this interpretation is not borne out by the evidence. Tamamuro Fumio shows in "Okayama-han no Shintō uke seido," in *Shintō no tenkai,* ed. Shimode Sekiyo and Tamamuro Fumio (Tokyo: Ōfūsha, 1991), that 98% of people were registered Shinto by 1669. See also Mase, "Jinja to tennō," pp. 102–105, for more on disputes between Yoshida Shinto adherents and Buddhists.

29. Tamamuro, "Okayama-han no Shintō uke seido," and Ikeda, *Ikeda Mitsumasa nikki,* pp. 576–578.

30. Kasei Jikki Kanpon Hensan Iinkai, *Aizu-han kasei jikki,* vol. 2, pp. 650–651.

31. Ibid., vol. 2, pp. 651–652.

32. Ibid., vol. 2, p. 656.

33. Ibid., vol. 8, pp. 14–15.

34. There is much good research on Hoshina Masayuki and his deification.

Those interested in Yoshikawa Koretaru's role in the deification should consult Taira Shigemichi, *Yoshikawa shintō no kisoteki kenkyū* (Tokyo: Yoshikawa Kōbunkan, 1966), pp. 25–40, 353–355.

35. Sano Tokutarō, *Mimasaka Katsuyama-han shikō* (Okayama: Okayama-ken Chihōshi Kenkyū Renraku Kyōgikai, 1965), pp. 142–143, 147. Shrine priests could manage this by paying for an empty casket to go through Buddhist rites at their registered temple and separately arranging for their burials by Shinto rites.

36. Nosco, "Keeping the Faith," pp. 147–150.

37. Most limited the grave sites and shrines to scheduled rites and visits by retainers. However, Hanitsu shrine was an exception that did encourage forms of popular participation.

38. Ooms, *Tokugawa Ideology*, pp. 50–62.

39. Haga, *Shisekiron*, as highlighted on p. 1 of Kishimoto Satoru, "Chōshū-han hansobyō no keisei," *Nihon rekishi kenkyū*, no. 438 (February 1999): 1–25.

40. This topic is explored in both Haga, *Shisekiron*; and Harootunian, *Things Seen and Unseen*, chap. 5.

41. Inoue, "Kansei ki ni okeru ujigami, ryūkōgami to chōtei."

42. Maeda, "Imperial Authority and Local Shrines."

43. Haga, *Shisekiron*, pp. 217, 226; and Yui Katsumasa, "Tosa-han ni okeru hanso shinkakuka no dōkō," *Kainan shigaku*, no. 42 (August 2004): 46; Kishimoto, "Chōshū-han hansobyō no keisei."

44. For the orders, see Umeda Yoshihiko, *Kaitei Zōhō Nihon shūkyō seido shi, kinsei hen* (Tokyo: Tōsen Shuppan, 1972), pp. 274, 452; and Yui, "Tosa-han," p. 52.

45. Ishii Ryōsuke and Harafuji Hiroshi, eds., *Mondōshū 5: Sanchō hiroku* (Tokyo: Sōbunsha, 2005), p. 505. This collection of Tokugawa government responses to requests from daimyo and *hatamoto* shows clearly that there were policies in the 1790s and early 1800s that forbade the rebuilding, expanding, or moving of temples and shrines (pp. 496, 507, 521 passim).

46. Unless otherwise noted, most of the information presented here on Fujinami shrine is based on the research of Yui, "Tosa-han."

47. Ibid., pp. 45–46.

48. Noted in commentary by Takahashi Shirō in Yamamoto Takeshi, *Kenshōbo*, vol. 7, p. 409; and Ogi Shin'ichirō et al., *Kōchi-ken no rekishi* (Tokyo: Yamakawa Shuppansha, 2001), p. 210.

49. Yui, "Tosa-han," p. 47; MS "Oboe, Seki Yasoemon yori sashikosu shimen obugyōchū yori shakuyō itasu utsushi" and MS "Fujinami Myōjin okanjō ikkan sōan," in Yamauchi-ke Hōmotsu Shiryōkan, Kōchi; Kishimoto Satoru, "Chōshū-han no hanso kenshō to hansei kaikaku," *Nihon rekishi kenkyū*, no. 464 (April 2001): 106–128.

50. For details on the shrine, see Nagaoka-shi, "Aoshi jinja," http://www.city. nagaoka.niigata.jp/kankou/rekishi/jinjya/aoshi.html (accessed 8/2/10). For Tadatoki's career, see Kokushi Daijiten Hensan Iinkai, *Kokushi daijiten*, vol. 13, p. 35.

51. Herman Ooms, *Charismatic Bureaucrat: A Political Biography of Matsudaira Sadanobu, 1758–1829* (Chicago: University of Chicago Press, 1975), pp. 43–48, 152; Kuwana City, "Chinkokusyukoku," http://kanko.city.kuwana.mie.jp/history/chinkokusyukoku/index.html (accessed 2010/8/2).

52. This point is made by Yui, "Tosa-han," pp. 48–49, developing from the research of Inoue Tomokatsu, "Kansei ki ni okeru ujigami, ryūkōgami to chōtei," and his "Kinsei chūki ni okeru Yoshida-ke hihan no genjitsuka," in *Chūkinsei no shūkyo to kokka,* ed. Imatani Akira and Takano Toshihiko (Tokyo: Iwata Shōin, 1998).

53. Inoue, "Kinsei chūki ni okeru Yoshida-ke hihan no genjitsuka."

54. MS "Miya no in, Kiroku, okirokukata," in Yamauchi-ke Hōmotsu Shiryōkan, Kōchi. This document is Buzen's report to the domain regarding his activities. The amounts of gifts and payments are not recorded. Yui, "Tosa-han," p. 48, describes the deification as being ordered by imperial edict, but this is not correct, at least formally.

55. This was part of a long tradition of Buddhist appropriation of local *kami* deities according to *honjisuijaku* theology, which argued that local deities were manifestations of buddhas. This religious accommodation and appropriation was tied to institutional and economic control over shrines and deities that was the dominant pattern in Japan until the Meiji period. Information on Henmeiin is gleaned from MS "Fujinami Myōjin okanjō ikkan sōan" (see dates 4/16, 9/18, 9/27); MS "Fujinami Myōjin okanjō omiya ozōei osengu ikkan kiroku" (see fol. 2); and MS "Yamauchi-ke shiryō: Toyokazu-kō ki," vol. 70, pp. 38–44, all held in Yamauchi-ke Hōmotsu Shiryōkan, Kōchi. An 1814 document from a local samurai notes that the buddha manifestation was Aizen Myōō, as printed in Yoshimura Yoshiho, *Tenpō shichinen Fujinamigū otabisho ojinkō kiroku* (Kōchi: Kōchi Shimin Toshokan, 1988), p. 9.

56. MS "Bunka ni ushi doshi, Osanreisama myōjingō okanjō goyō ikkan" and "Fujinami Myōjin okanjō ikkan sōan," held in Yamauchi-ke Hōmotsu Shiryōkan, Kōchi. I calculated *gin ichi mai* (a special unit for wrapped gifts of silver, with one piece of silver equaling about forty-three *monme*) as a bit more than two-thirds of a *ryō*. In addition to this the domain also presented the Yoshida with twenty-seven pieces of silver (about nine *ryō*) and a sword after the ceremony was completed, by way of thanks. So the Yoshida house's total take was about thirty-five *ryō*.

57. Mutō, *Nanroshi*, vol. 5, p. 244.

58. Yui, "Tosa-han," p. 50.

59. MS "Fujinami Myōjin okanjō ikkan sōan."

60. Yui, "Tosa-han," p. 52.

61. Ibid., p. 54.

62. MS "Nichiroku," diary by Mori Yoshiki, 12 vols., held in Kōchi Prefecture Library. The memorial observances happened on 8/23 and 8/24 of each year.

63. Ibid., vol. 12, 1807/3/26. For details of the ceremonies, see Mutō, *Nanroshi,* vol. 5, pp. 246–256.

64. From his diary, MS "Nichiroku," vol. 12, 1807/3/22–4/22.

65. Ibid., vol. 12, 1807/5/5.

66. Yamamoto Takeshi, *Kenshōbo,* vol. 7, p. 48; Mutō, *Nanroshi,* vol. 5, pp. 245–246. Ogi et al., *Kōchi-ken no rekishi,* makes this argument on p. 210.

67. Yoshimura, *Tenpō shichinen Fujinamigū,* pp. 45–90. For research on the lordly use of festivals as rites that connected lords and commoners, see Kurushima Hiroshi, "Kinsei ni okeru matsuri no 'shūhen'," *Rekishi hyōron,* no. 439 (1986): 12–24.

68. Ibid., pp. 118–119.

69. Yamamoto, *Kenshōbo,* vol. 7, pp. 90–95.

70. Ibid., vol. 7, pp. 89–93.

71. Ibid., vol. 7, pp. 56, 60, 88, and generally 37–136 passim.

72. Haga, *Shisekiron,* pp. 217, 226; Kishimoto, "Chōshū-han hansobyō no keisei" and "Chōshū-han no hanso kenshō"; Takano Nobuharu, "Edo Jidai no bushi," pp. 69–70.

73. Anne Walthall's research on the spread of Hirata Atsutane–style *kokugaku* in the countryside around Japan is germane here; see her *Weak Body,* pp. 100–139. For Tosa, see Kōchi-ken Shi Hensan Iinkai, *Kōchi-ken shi, Kinsei,* pp. 947–956; and Teraishi Masaji (Masamichi), *Nangakushi* (Tokyo: Fuzanbō, 1934).

74. Takahashi Shirō, "Tosa-han 'shōya dōmei' kenkyū no ichi zentei," *Kainan shigaku,* no. 3 (January 1965): 18.

75. Tahara-chō Bunkazai Hogo Shingikai, *Tahara-han nikki,* vol. 9, p. 343.

76. This judgment is based on records relating to the annual festival in Tahara-chō Bunkazai Hogo Shingikai, *Tahara-han nikki,* vols. 9 and 10.

77. Haga, *Shisekiron,* pp. 216–217.

78. Tahara-chō Bunkazai Hogo Shingikai, *Tahara-han nikki,* vol. 9, p. 324.

79. Ibid., vol. 9, pp. 344–345, 358.

80. Ibid., vol. 9, p. 393. The first annual festival was actually not held until the following year. This was probably because the shrine completion festival was held in the sixth month, and in the subsequent year at the time of the annual festival (10/23) that commemorated Yasusada's death, the current lord would be in the domain for the first time.

81. Shiseki Kenkyūkai, ed., *Naikakubunko shozō shiseki sōkan* series, vol. 9, *Shisō zasshiki* (Tokyo: Kyūko Shoin, 1981), vol. 3, pp. 179–182.

82. Mase, "Jinja to tennō," pp. 229–232.

83. Hardacre, *Shinto and the State.*

84. Mase, "Jinja to tennō," pp. 234–235. See Hardacre, *Shinto and the State,* chap. 4, for the rearrangement of shrines into the imperial order. Haga, *Shisekiron,* deals with many local cases of pursuit of status and name for deities in the new Meiji order; see especially chap. 7.

85. Kishimoto, "Chōshū-han no hanso kenshō," pp. 120–126.

86. Hardacre, *Shinto and the State,* pp. 121–124.

6: Histories

An earlier version of portions of this chapter was originally published as "The Diverse Political Languages of Edo Histories," in *Writing Histories in Japan: Texts and Their Transformations from Ancient Times through the Meiji Era*, ed. James C. Baxter and Joshua A. Fogel (Kyoto: International Research Center for Japanese Studies, 2007), pp. 223–252.

1. "Matsuyama jōshu Hisamatsu shi keifuryaku," in Matsuyama-shi Shiryōshū Henshū Iinkai, *Matsuyama-shi shiryōshū*, vol. 2, pp. 985–988.

2. There is an extensive English-language literature focusing on Mito historiography, which is well known for its key role in an imperial-centered vision of Japan, most importantly J. Victor Koschmann, *The Mito Ideology: Discourse Reform and Insurrection in Late Tokugawa Japan, 1790–1864* (Berkeley: University of California Press, 1987).

3. Watanabe, *Higashi Ajia*, pp. 1–13.

4. I address this issue and its relationship to the writing of regional history in "Cultivating Non-National Historical Understandings in Local History," in *The Teleology of the Modern Nation-State: Japan and China*, ed. Joshua A. Fogel (Philadelphia: University of Pennsylvania Press, 2004), pp. 161–173.

5. Watanabe, *Higashi Ajia*, p. 7.

6. Fujita Satoru, *Bakumatsu no tennō*. A good summary of posthumous titles and suffixes can be found in Yamaguchi Osamu, "'Tennō' shō no keifu," special issue, *Bukkyō Daigaku Sōgō Kenkyūjo kiyō*, no. 2 (March 1995): 96–118. The best discussion in English of the position of the emperor in the Edo period is Bob Wakabayashi, "In Name Only: Imperial Sovereignty in Early Modern Japan," *Journal of Japanese Studies* 17, no. 1 (1991): 25–57.

7. For a nice discussion of the incident, see Conrad Totman, *Early Modern Japan* (Berkeley: University of California Press, 1993), pp. 473–476.

8. As noted in Fujita Satoru, *Bakumatsu*, p. 129.

9. See, for example, the scholar Nakai Chikuzan's 1789 lament of the use of *-in* and proposal to revive calling emperors by era names after the Chinese fashion and to use *-tennō* suffixes. Nakai Chikuzan, *Sōbō kigen*, in *Nihon keizai taiten*, ed. Takimoto Seiichi (Tokyo: Meiji Bunken, 1969), vol. 23, pp. 324–327.

10. In Nagahara Keiji, ed., *Jien, Kitabatake Chikafusa*, in *Nihon no Meicho* series, vol. 9 (Tokyo: Chūōkōronsha, 1971), p. 412. I have adapted H. Paul Varley's translation of this passage, found in his *A Chronicle of Gods and Sovereigns: Jinnō Shōtōki of Kitabatake Chikafusa* (New York: Columbia University Press, 1980), p. 191.

11. For the evidence and more details on this issue, see pp. 225–230 of my "Diverse Political Languages."

12. The name "Heizei" is written with the characters for Heijō capital, where he retired in unofficial banishment. The capital itself was likely called Heizei in its day, but Heijō is now customary.

13. Nagahara, *Jien, Kitabatake,* pp. 104–132.

14. Butler, *Emperor and Aristocracy,* pp. 12–13.

15. Fujita Satoru, *Bakumatsu,* pp. 130–133.

16. Watanabe, *Higashi Ajia,* p. 7, cites an Edo-period compendium.

17. Herschel Webb, "What Is the *Dai Nihon Shi*?" *Journal of Asian Studies* 19, no. 2 (1960): 135.

18. I consulted the 1851 woodblock print version of *Dai Nihon shi* held in Osaka City University Main Library. I have not consulted the final 1906 version of the *Dai Nihon shi,* in order to avoid the problem of Meiji-era editing.

19. My references to Mitogaku usage here are based primarily on readings of *Dai Nihon shi sansō* (circa 1720), in *Kinsei shi ronshū,* ed. Matsumoto Sannosuke and Ogura Yoshihiko, vol. 48 of *Nihon shisōshi taikei* (Tokyo: Iwanami Shoten, 1974), but also on perusal of the 1851 version.

20. On the *Dai Nihon shi sansō,* see the essay by modern historians Matsumoto Sannosuke and Ogura Yoshihiko, in *Dai Nihon shi sansō,* p. 560. The reason for the removal was that the Fujita group felt that historians should not presume to evaluate a dynasty that had not changed and that therefore continued to hold heaven's mandate. For Rai San'yō, see Thomas Keirstead, "San'yō, Bakin, and the Reanimation of Japan's Past," in *Writing Histories in Japan: Texts and Their Transformations from Ancient Times through the Meiji Era,* ed. James C. Baxter and Joshua A. Fogel (Kyoto: International Research Center for Japanese Studies, 2007).

21. This followed accepted Chinese practice, in which a new dynasty writes the history of the previous dynasty.

22. *Dai Nihon shi sansō,* especially p. 61.

23. As noted above, *Dai Nihon shi sansō* frequently uses the term *shōgun* to identify heads of the Kamakura and Muromachi military governments (pp. 172–213 passim) and the term *bakufu* to denote those governments (pp. 176, 178, 190, 192), although it sometimes uses other terms such as *gunsei* and *fu* (p. 185), and once describes the ideal role of the *shōgun*'s government as being the *hanpei,* or bulwark of protection for the imperial house (p. 180).

24. *Dai Nihon shi,* vol. 1, sec. *jōhyō,* fol. 2.

25. Watanabe Hiroshi, *Kinsei Nihon shakai to Sōgaku* (Tokyo: Tōkyō Daigaku Shuppankai, 1985), pp. 34–40.

26. Yasukawa Minoru, *Honchō tsugan no kenkyū: Hayashi-ke shigaku no tenkai to sono eikyō* (Tokyo: Gensōsha, 1980); Hanami Sakumi, "Honchō tsugan kō," in *Honpō shigaku shi ronsō,* ed. Shigakkai (Tokyo: Fuzanbō, 1939), pp. 793–834. Yasukawa's work is especially interesting for its tracing of the many commonalities between *Honchō tsugan* and *Dai Nihon shi.* Also see the discussion of both in Kate Nakai, *Shogunal Politics,* pp. 267–275.

27. One story goes that an early draft of the *Honchō tsugan* presented the possibility of tracing the origins of Japan's imperial line to an immigrant descended from a duke of the Zhou Dynasty of China. Tokugawa Mitsukuni, the patron of the

Dai Nihon shi, saw this story, and declaring that to describe Japan's own dynasty as having foreign origins was impertinent, he ordered its authors to revise it. Hanami, "Honchō tsugan kō," pp. 1–2.

28. *Dai Nihon shi,* vol. 1, sec. *jōhyō.*

29. See for example Hayashi Razan, *Honchō tsugan* (Tokyo: Kokusho Kankōkai, 1918), vol. 2, pp. 684–685, where Ieyasu and Hidetada both receive honorific open spaces while the emperor does not. This is consistent throughout in my survey of pp. 578–707.

30. Note, for example, Hayashi, *Honchō tsugan,* vol. 1, pp. 290–291, 438, and vol. 2, p. 504, where the terms *shōgun* and *bakufu* are used and the shoguns are called by their formal personal names such as Sanetomo and Yoshimitsu.

31. Hayashi, *Honchō tsugan,* vol. 2, p. 702.

32. Ibid., vol. 2, p. 751.

33. Ibid., vol. 2, p. 683.

34. Ibid., vol. 2, p. 706.

35. *Tokugawa jikki,* vol. 1, pp. 1–5.

36. For example, *Tokugawa jikki,* vol. 7, pp. 29–30, and vol. 10, pp. 1–16.

37. The *Tokugawa jikki* does not treat the pre-Tokugawa period extensively, but in one location Montoku and Seiwa are given the *-tennō* suffix and Reizei and some subsequent emperors are given the *-in* suffix (vol. 1, p. 15), thus following Kitabatake Chikafusa's lead.

38. For example, *Tokugawa jikki,* vol. 7, pp. 38, 67–68.

39. Ibid., vol. 9, pp. 574–575. There was a complex ritual and legal system of mourning throughout Japan that inculcated a consciousness of the feudal hierarchies. See Hayashi Yukiko, *Kinsei bukkiryō no kenkyū: Bakuhansei kokka no mo to kegare* (Osaka: Seibundō, 1998).

40. Versions of this history exist in manuscript in many places, some of which are cited in the final notations of the second volume of the manuscript in held at Princeton University, Gest Library. The Gest manuscript continues the history to 1846. Alternate names for this history include "Okuni nendai ryakki," where *kuni* refers to Tosa domain.

41. Nevertheless, the moment of appointment to the rank of shogun is highlighted and is one of the few Tokugawa events not directly related to some domain action that appears in this history. In this treatment the "Nendai ryakki" differs from *Honchō tsugan,* but the trend is similar to that seen in *Tokugawa jikki,* which was written in the same era as the "Nendai ryakki." Perhaps by the early nineteenth century a historiographical consensus was growing that was beginning to accord more value to the rank of shogun than had been the case in the seventeenth century.

42. *Tokugawa jikki,* vol. 8, pp. 383, 392; *Shintei Kansei chōshū,* vol. 13, p. 307.

43. Although specific dates are not provided, the circumstances of the secrecy surrounding Toyofusa's death are well described in a memorandum of one of his personal servants, in MS "Ikuta Oboegaki," held in Kōchi Prefecture Library, fols. 10–13.

44. MS "Hanshi naihen," held in Kōchi University Library, vol. "ichi," fols. 72–73, entries for third year of Hōei era, seventh month, sixth and seventh days.

45. Sekita Komakichi, *Sekita Komakichi rekishi ronbunshū* (Kōchi: Kōchi Shimin Toshokan, 1981), vol. 2, pp. 293–298; Kōchi-ken Rekishi Jiten Hensan Iinkai, comp., *Kōchi-ken rekishi jiten* (Kōchi: Kōchi Shimin Toshokan, 1980), pp. 626–627. This history has never been published, but near-final-draft versions of many volumes are held in the Kōchi University Library, and many rough-draft volumes and related correspondence and notes are held separately in the Miyaji collection in the Kōchi Prefecture Library and the Hirao collection of Kōchi City Library.

46. Roberts, "Tosa to ishin."

47. MS "Hanshi naihen," "Seitai enkaku," "Tenyōin-sama odai," held in Kōchi University Library, call no. 001.2/Han/2.

48. MS "Hanshi naihen," "Ichi," held in Kōchi Prefecture Library, call no. K250/25/1 Miyaji.

49. MS "Kokushi gaihen hanrei," held in Kōchi City Library, Hirao Bunkō doc. no. 465. The title is the library's title of convenience for this document, but the document includes the guidelines for the *naihen* volumes as well. This document is undated, but a separate document of copies of various memoranda related to the writing of the history contains an outline of a *hanrei* submitted to the retired lord Yamauchi Yōdō in the fourth month of 1866 that is the same in all essentials as the complete *hanrei* cited above. MS "Hanshi hensan toriatsukai hikae," held in Miyaji Bunko, Kōchi Prefecture Library, K250/25/Miyaji, fols. 8–9.

50. I used the manuscript held in the Kōchi University Library, and this is in print as Kōchi Chihōshi Kenkyūkai, ed., *Tosa hansei roku*, 2 vols. (Kōchi: Kōchi Shimin Toshokan, 1969–1970). Another, slightly different manuscript is discussed in Ishio Yoshihisa, "'Tosa hansei roku' no genpon ni tsuite," *Kansai Daigaku hōgaku ronshū* 31, nos. 2–4 (1981): 459–472.

51. Mary Elizabeth Berry, "Was Early Modern Japan Culturally Integrated?" *Modern Asian Studies* 31, no. 3 (1997): 547–581.

Conclusion

1. Watanabe, *Higashi Ajia,* chap. 1.

2. Jansen, *Sakamoto Ryōma,* p. 213; Conrad Totman, *The Collapse of the Tokugawa Bakufu, 1862–1868* (Honolulu: University of Hawai'i Press, 1980), pp. 156, 231.

3. Matsuo Masahito, *Haihan chiken: Kindai tōitsu kokka e no kutō* (Tokyo: Chūōkōronsha, 1986), pp. 27–33.

4. *Yamauchi-ke shiryō: Bakumatsu Ishin hen,* vol. 9, p. 392.

5. For more details and examples, see Roberts, "Tosa to ishin," pp. 222–229.

6. *Yamauchi-ke shiryō: Bakumatsu Ishin hen,* vol. 12, pp. 403–406, 707; Shihara Yasuzō, *Meiji seishi,* vol. 2, reprinted in *Meiji bunka zenshū,* vol. 9, ed. Meiji Bunka

Kenkyūkai (Tokyo: Nihon Hyōronsha, 1956 [1928]), pp. 67–73; Hirao Michio, *Tosa han shōgyō keizai shi* (Kōchi: Kōchi Shimin Toshokan, 1958), pp. 227–228.

7. Matsuo, *Haihan chiken,* pp. 28–33.

8. Shihara, *Meiji seishi,* vol. 2, pp. 91–92.

9. *Yamauchi-ke shiryō: Bakumatsu Ishin hen,* vol. 14, pp. 126–129.

10. Kären Wigen, *A Malleable Map: Geographies of Restoration in Central Japan, 1600–1912* (Berkeley: University of California Press, 2010), pp. 12–13. Of all the domains, Tosa remained the closest to its former boundary as Kōchi prefecture, but it gained full ownership of the divided Okinoshima Island, which had cost the Yamauchi so much in the Tokugawa courts in the 1650s.

11. Hirao Michio, *Tosa nōmin ikki shi kō* (Kōchi: Kōchi Shimin Toshokan, 1953), p. 101.

12. Fukushima Masao, *Chiso kaisei no kenkyū* (Tokyo: Yūhikaku, 1970), pp. 211–216.

13. *Yamauchi-ke shiryō: Bakumatsu Ishin hen,* vol. 7, pp. 317–372. Only five months later the lord of Tosa was using the term *bakufu* in an official pronouncement (ibid., vol. 9, pp. 743–744).

14. Aoyama Tadamasa, *Meiji ishin no gengo to shiryō* (Osaka: Seibundō, 2006). pp. 1–5.

15. Makino, *Uchi to soto no gengobunkagaku;* Bachnik and Quinn, *Situated Meaning.*

16. Indeed, Edward Muir's *Civic Ritual in Renaissance Venice* (Princeton, NJ: Princeton University Press, 1981) has provided me with some inspiration on the connections between ritual and political structure, integration, and pacification.

Glossary

bakufu 幕府	Tokugawa government. In the Edo period it was an uncommonly used scholarly term.
bettō 別当	Buddhist monk administrator of a shrine.
bun 分	One's portion, consequence, or status.
bun o shiru 分を知る	To know and keep to one's consequence or status.
chigyō 知行	Fief.
chiji 知事	Prefectural governor.
chō 朝	The court; usually refers to the imperial court, sometimes to the Tokugawa court.
chokumei 勅命	An imperial order.
chōtei 朝廷	The court; usually refers to the imperial court, sometimes to the Tokugawa court.
chūnagon 中納権	Middle-rank councilor in the imperial court.
daijinkun 大神君	"Great divine lord"; one posthumous term for Tokugawa Ieyasu.
daikan 代官	Intendants; rural administrators.
daimyō 大名	Daimyo, a samurai lord of the Muromachi and Edo periods. In the Edo period the term was defined as a lord holding a fief with an *omote* value of at least 10,000 *koku*.
daimyōjin 大明神	The highest-ranked *kami* created by the Yoshida house.
daishōgun no ie 大将軍の家	The shogunal house.
dajōtennō 太上天皇	Retired emperor.

fu 府 — Government headquarters, usually regional; in the modern period, an urban prefecture.

fudai 譜代 — A hereditary vassal or servant. Among Tokugawa daimyo it referred to daimyo lineages descended from people who were vassals before 1600.

fusetamau 布施たまう — To bestow; a polite way of referring to a social superior's giving to an inferior.

ganso 元祖 — Founder of a house or lineage.

gōchō 郷帳 — Cadastral registers summarizing village productivity totals by imperial county.

gokachū, okachū 御家中 — The members of a samurai house.

gokenin 御家人 — Tokugawa housemen, samurai of lesser status than bannermen.

gunkoku no sei 軍国之政 — Government of the military country or countries.

gunsei 軍政 — Military government.

haibutsu kishaku 廃仏毀釈 — The early Meiji-era separation of Buddhism and Shinto that involved a large degree of destruction of Buddhist sites.

hakufu 伯府 — A word used in an early Meiji history written in Tosa to identify the *bakufu*.

han 藩 — Domain, in modern discourse. In the Edo period the term was used by Sinitic learning scholars to mean daimyo.

hanpei 藩屏 — Bulwarks. In the Edo period the term was used by Sinitic learning scholars to mean daimyo and, less often, the Tokugawa shogun.

hatamoto 旗本 — Bannermen, samurai retainers of the Tokugawa shogun whose *omote* fief amount was less than 10,000 *koku* and generally more than 500 *koku*.

hatto 法度 — Law code; ordinances.

-hime 姫 — Name suffix meaning princess.

hō 封 — Fief.

hōchi 封地 — Fief.

hōgyo 崩御 — A word meaning for the emperor to die.

hōken 封建 — Polity of sealed-off spaces; feudal.

hōkōnin 奉公人 — Retainers or commoner servants of a household.

honchō 本朝 — "This dynasty"; a way for Japanese to refer to the imperial realm of Japan or, less commonly, to the Tokugawa dynasty.

honne 本音	One's true intention or desire.
hōzuru 崩ずる	A verb meaning for the emperor to die.
hyakushōmae 百姓前	A full-status villager's respected sphere of competence.
hyōjōsho 評定所	The high court of the Tokugawa government.
hyōjōshū 評定衆	The membership of the Tokugawa high court, often consisting of three Tokugawa Elders, three Shrine and Temple Magistrates, two Town Magistrates, two Finance Magistrates, and one of the Grand Inspectors.
ichimon 一門	Collateral houses; daimyo houses that were considered descendants of Tokugawa Ieyasu; Tokugawa collateral houses. The term was used in similar fashion within daimyo houses.
ie 家	House or clan; in the Edo period, a political unit for samurai and a unit of corporate authority among many status groups.
iesōdō 家騒動	A violent conflict within a daimyo house.
ikō 威光	August authority.
-in 院	Name suffix indicating that the person has retired and taken Buddhist orders.
-inden 院殿	Name suffix reserved for elite warriors, indicating that the person has retired and taken Buddhist orders.
jibun shioki 自分仕置	A lord's right to manage his domain as identified by an overlord.
jingi 神祇	The deities of heaven and earth.
jinja 神社	A Shinto shrine.
jinkun 神君	"Divine lord"; one posthumous term for Tokugawa Ieyasu; sometimes also used to identify deified founders of daimyo houses.
jitsumyō, jitsumei 実名	One's formal personal name.
jōbutodoke 丈夫届	A daimyo's notification to the Tokugawa that a sickly born child had unexpectedly lived and therefore the birth should be formally recorded.
kahō 家法	House law.
kakekomiso 駆込み訴	An illegal suit made by barging into the residence of a judicial official.
kakushi metsuke 隠し目付	Secret investigators.
kami 神	Shinto deity.
karō 家老	House Elder in a domain government.

231

ken 県	Prefecture.
kenzu 献ず	To proffer to a social superior.
kimi 君	Prince or ruler.
kinri 禁裏	"The forbidden quarter"; the residence of the emperor in premodern times, occasionally applied to the Tokugawa residence.
kō, ōyake 公	Ruler, governmental authority, ruling authority, ruler, lord; also a name suffix for imperial regents.
kōchō 皇朝	Japanese imperial dynasty.
kōgi 公義 or 公儀	Government.
kōgi-sama 公義様	The ruler.
kōhen 公辺	Governmental; the government as identified by an inferior.
kōhen naibun sōzoku 公辺内分相続	An inheritance unreported to one's lord.
kokka 国家	State, or ruling household of a domain or country; in modern discourse, nation-state.
kokka daiji 国家大事	Important matters of state.
koku 石	A measurement of rice volume equal to 180 liters or 5.1 bushels.
kokueki 国益	Prosperity of the (domainal) country; a mercantilist ideology.
kokufu 国府	Government office of a *kuni*.
kokugaku 国学	Study about one's domainal country; study about Japan.
kokuhō 国法	The laws of "province-holding" daimyo generally as named from within; laws of Japan.
kokusei 国政	Government of a country; government of a domainal country.
kokushu 国守	Imperial provincial governor.
kokushu 国主	Ruler of a domainal country, or imperial provincial master.
kokuyaku, kuniyaku 国役	An occasional tax assessed on provinces in the Tokugawa period.
kubō 公方	Ruler; a term the Tokugawa overlords commonly used to identify themselves.
kuni 国	Country, domainal country, imperial province, or home region.
kunimiyako 国都	Capital city of a *kuni*.
kunimochi daimyō 国持大名	"Province-holding" daimyo.
kyō 卿	A person of councilor status in the imperial court.

mae 前	Front or in front of; one's acknowledged respectable identity; one's portion.
mikado 御門	"The august gate"; one common premodern name for the emperor.
monogashira 物頭	A samurai rank usually indicating a captain of musketeers.
mura-uke sei 村請制	System of subcontracting local management to villages.
myōjin 明神	Second-highest-ranked *kami* created by the Yoshida house.
nai 内	Inside, informal.
naibun 内分	Inside portion of competence and authority.
naijitsu 内実	The inside truth; the collective truth that functioned within a group but could not be expressed at the higher *omote*.
nainai 内々	Between a select group of parties and away from *omote* interaction.
naisai 内済	Mediated resolution to a court case.
naishō 内証	Informal agreement, inside agreement.
nanigashi 某	"Someone."
omote 表	Surface or interface; ritual relations of subservience to superior.
omote 面	Face, honor.
omotedaka 表高	Formal assessed production of a fief or domain.
omotedatte 表立って	Officially, formally, or publicly.
omotemuki 表向	Proper for *omote* relations; involved in *omote* relations.
osso 越訴	Illegally appealing over the head of one's feudal superior.
ōyake 公	Lord, government, or public.
reijin 霊神	Lowest-ranked *kami* created by the Yoshida house.
reisha 霊社	Second-lowest-ranked *kami* created by the Yoshida house.
rōjū 老中	Tokugawa Elder.
rōnin 牢人 or 浪人	Masterless samurai.
ryō 両	The basic unit of gold currency, usually about eighteen grams, but at times debased in size and quality.
ryō 領	Feudal territory; fief.
ryōbun 領分	Feudal territory; fief and associated competence of rule.

ryōgoku 領国	Domainal country.
ryōgoku 両国	Two provinces; both provinces.
sakite hatamoto 先手旗本	Bannermen who serve as mediators and messengers between the Tokugawa government and daimyo.
seiitaishōgun 征夷大将軍	Shogun; full title of imperial appointment as chief general of samurai in Japan.
seiji 政事	Government; governmental affairs.
seikun 聖君	Divine prince or ruler.
senge 宣下	Document transmitting an imperial order.
shi or *watakushi* 私	Personal, private, or selfish.
shigō 諡号	Posthumous names that describe some aspect of the greatness of the emperor.
shingō 神号	Title of divinity.
shinkoku 神国	Country of the gods; a way to refer to Japan.
-shin'nō 親王	Name suffix for an imperial prince.
shinobi 忍び	Formally unacknowledged; secretly.
shiryō 私領	Feudal territory identified as the subordinate's "private" possession by the overlord.
shiryō 私料	Personal income; a name for fief used by a superior for the retainer's income source.
shōgun 将軍	Shogun; imperial appointment as chief general of samurai in Japan.
shujō 主上	"One's lord"; used variously for emperor, shogun, or daimyo.
sōgen senge 宗源宣下	A document issued by the Yoshida house that conferred court rank or divinity.
songō jiken 尊号事件	The name of a late eighteenth-century political incident that revolved around granting the title of "retired emperor" to the father of Emperor Kōkaku.
soto 外	Outside; public.
susumeru 進める	To give; a verb used to suggest polite equality.
taiju 大樹	Alternate name meaning the Tokugawa ruler, sometimes used of daimyo.
taikun 大君	Title used by the Tokugawa ruler in foreign diplomacy.
tairō 大老	A regent of the Tokugawa *kubō*.
tatemae 建前	The image that one presents to meet social expectations.
tei 帝	Sinitic-rooted term for emperor.
tennō 天皇	A posthumous title of emperors of Japan that

	had fallen into relative disuse in the early Heian and was revived in 1840, but historians made some use of this term in the intervening years for all emperors; also a name suffix.
tenryō 天領	Term first used in the early Meiji era to identify Tokugawa demesne.
tenshi 天子	"Child of heaven"; one common premodern term for the emperor.
tera 寺	A Buddhist temple.
tōgin 当今	The current emperor.
tono-sama 殿様	"My lord."
toshiyori 年寄	An elder; usually indicating an advisory role in houses and villages.
tozama 外様	Lords who descended from those who submitted to the Tokugawa only near or after the time of his decisive victory at the Battle of Sekigahara in 1600.
uchi 内	Inside; inner portion; informal.
uchidaka 内高	Internally assessed production of a fief or domain.
uchi yoriai 内寄合	An off-the-record insider meeting.
uesama, kami-sama 上様	"My lord."
ujigami 氏神	Guardian deity of a village or clan.
ura 裏	Behind; the backside; hidden.
watakushi 私	Personal, private, or selfish; often used in contrast with *ōyake*.
yobina 呼び名	Daily use name.

Works Cited

Unpublished sources

"Bunka ni ushi doshi, Osanreisama myōjingō okanjō goyō ikkan" 文化二丑年　御三霊様明神号御勧請御用一巻. In Yamauchi-ke Hōmotsu Shiryōkan, Kōchi 山内家宝物資料館. Listed in archive catalogue on p. 222.

"Fujinami Myōjin okanjō ikkan, sōan" 藤並御勧請一巻　草案. In Yamauchi-ke Hōmotsu Shiryōkan, Kōchi 山内家宝物資料館. Listed in archive catalogue on p. 223.

"Fujinami Myōjin okanjō omiya ozōei osengu ikkan kiroku" 藤並明神御勧請御宮御造営御遷宮一巻記録. In Yamauchi-ke Hōmotsu Shiryōkan, Kōchi 山内家宝物資料館. Listed in archive catalogue on p. 222.

"Hanshi hensan toriatsukai hikae" 藩史編纂取扱控. In Miyaji Bunko 宮地文庫, Kōchi Prefecture Library, call no. K250/25/Miyaji.

"Hanshi naihen" 藩史内篇. Multivolume. In Kōchi University Library, call no. 001.2/Han/2.

"Hanshi naihen" 藩史内篇. Multivolume. In Miyaji Bunko, Kōchi Prefecture Library, call no. K250/25/1 Miyaji.

"Ikuta Oboegaki" 生田覚書. In Kōchi Prefecture Library, call no. K275/3.

"Kaei gan sarudoshi Toyoteru-sama obyōchū oenkō ikkan te hikae, ni" 嘉永元申年豊熙様御病中御遠行一巻手扣、二. In Yamauchi-ke Hōmotsu Shiryōkan, Kōchi 山内家宝物資料館. Listed in archive catalogue on p. 217.

"Kanbun hachinen bugenchō" 寛文八年分限帳. 2 vols. In Kōchi Prefecture Library.

"Kokushi gaihen hanrei" 国史外篇凡例. In Kōchi City Library, Hirao Bunkō 平尾文庫 doc. no. 465.

"Miya no in, Kiroku, Okirokukata" 宮ノ印、記録、御記録方. In Yamauchi-ke Hōmotsu Shiryōkan, Kōchi 山内家宝物資料館. Listed in archive catalogue on p. 223.

"Nichiroku" 日録. Diary by Mori Yoshiki, 森芳材. 12 vols. In Kōchi Prefecture Library, call no. K289 Mori.

"Oboe, Seki Yasoemon yori sashikosu shimen obugyōchū yori shakuyō itasu utsushi" 覚、関八十右衛門より指越紙面御奉行中より致借用写. In Yamauchi-ke Hōmotsu Shiryōkan, Kōchi 山内家宝物資料館. Listed in archive catalogue on p. 223.

"Ohanmoto omitodoke no setsu ozashiki ezu" 御判元御見届之節御座鋪繪圖. In Yamauchi-ke Hōmotsu Shiryōkan, Kōchi 山内家宝物資料館. Listed in archive catalogue on p. 218.

"Otōke nendai ryakki" 御当家年代略記. Miyaji Nakae 宮地仲枝. In Princeton University, Gest Library.

"Sendai gyōjō" 先代行状. Biography by Mori Shirō 森四郎. Original held in Kōchi Museum of History and Culture. I used a photocopy held in Kōchi Prefecture Library.

"Shibuya-ke monjo" 渋谷家文書. Vol. 3. Print copy from microfilm held in Kōchi Prefecture Library, call no. kenshi 124-3.

"Tosa hansei roku" 土佐藩政録. In Kōchi University Library, call no. 001.2/tos.

"Yamauchi-ke shiryō: Toyochika-kō ki" 山内家史料：豊雍公紀. Multivolume. In Yamauchi-ke Hōmotsu Shiryōkan, Kōchi 山内家宝物資料館.

"Yamauchi-ke shiryō: Toyokazu-kō ki" 山内家史料：豊策公紀. Multivolume. In Yamauchi-ke Hōmotsu Shiryōkan, Kōchi 山内家宝物資料館.

"Yamauchi-ke shiryō: Toyonobu-kō ki" 山内家史料：豊敷公紀. Multivolume. In Yamauchi-ke Hōmotsu Shiryōkan, Kōchi 山内家宝物資料館.

"Yōsha zuihitsu" 湧舎随筆. Miscellany authored by Yamauchi (Maeno) Akinari 山内（前野）顯成, a junior elder of the domain. 6 vols. Held in the personal collection of Kattō Isamu 甲藤勇 of Kōchi city.

Published works

Akabane-chō Shi Hensan Iinkai 赤羽根町史編纂委員会, ed. *Akabane-chō shi* 赤羽根町史. Aichi-ken Akabane chō 愛知県赤羽根町, 1968.

———. *Akabane no komonjo: Kinsei shiryō hen* 赤羽根の古文書　近世史料編. Aichi-ken: Tahara-shi kyōiku iinkai 愛知県田原市教育委員会, 2005.

Akizawa Shigeru 秋沢繁. "Keichō jūnen Tokugawa gozenchō ni tsuite" 慶長10年徳川御前帳について. *Kainan shigaku* 海南史学, part 1 in no. 30 (August 1992): 28–46, and part 2 in no. 31 (August 1993): 25–80.

Anderson, Benedict. *Imagined Communities: Reflections on the Origins and Spread of Nationalism*. Rev. ed. London: Verso, 1991.

Aoyama Tadamasa 青山忠正. *Meiji ishin no gengo to shiryō* 明治維新の言語と史料. Osaka: Seibundō 清文堂, 2006.

Bachnik, Jane, and Charles Quinn Jr., eds. *Situated Meaning: Inside and Outside in Japanese Self, Society, and Language*. Princeton, NJ: Princeton University Press, 1994.

Barth, Fredrik. "Boundaries and Connections." In *Signifying Identities: Anthropological Perspectives on Boundaries and Contested Values,* edited by A. P. Cohen, pp. 17–36. London: Routledge, 2000.

———. *Ethnic Groups and Boundaries.* London: Allen and Unwin, 1969.

Beerens, Anna. "Interview with a *Bakumatsu* Official: A Translation from *Kyūji Shimonroku.*" *Monumenta Nipponica* 55, no. 3 (Autumn 2000): 369–398.

Berry, Mary Elizabeth. *The Culture of Civil War in Kyoto.* Berkeley: University of California Press, 1994.

———. *Hideyoshi.* Cambridge, MA: Harvard University Press, 1982.

———. *Japan in Print: Information and Nation in the Early Modern Period.* Berkeley: University of California Press, 2007.

———. "Was Early Modern Japan Culturally Integrated?" *Modern Asian Studies* 31, no. 3 (1997): 547–581.

Birt, Michael. "Samurai in Passage: Transformation of the Sixteenth-Century Kanto." *Journal of Japanese Studies* 11, no. 2 (Summer 1985): 369–399.

Bodart-Bailey, Beatrice. *The Dog Shogun: The Personality and Policies of Tokugawa Tsunayoshi.* Honolulu: University of Hawai'i Press, 2006.

Bolitho, Harold. "The Han." In *The Cambridge History of Japan,* vol. 4, *Early Modern Japan,* edited by John Whitney Hall, pp. 183–234. Cambridge: Cambridge University Press, 1991.

———. *Treasures among Men: The Fudai Daimyo in Tokugawa Japan.* New Haven, CT: Yale University Press, 1974.

Boot, W. J. "The Death of a Shogun: Deification in Early Modern Japan." In *Shinto in History: Ways of the Kami,* edited by John Breen and Mark Teeuwen, pp. 144–166. Honolulu: University of Hawai'i Press, 2000.

Botsman, Dani. *Punishment and Power in the Making of Modern Japan.* Princeton, NJ: Princeton University Press, 2005.

Brown, Philip. *Central Authority and Local Autonomy in the Formation of Early Modern Japan: The Case of Kaga Domain.* Stanford, CA: Stanford University Press, 1993.

Butler, Lee. *Emperor and Aristocracy in Japan, 1467–1680: Resilience and Renewal.* Cambridge, MA: Harvard University East Asia Center, 2002.

Dai Nihon shi 大日本史. 243 vols. [Minamoto Mitsukuni 源光圀 listed as author, publisher Mito domain, not listed], 1851. Woodblock printing, copy held in Osaka City University Main Library.

Dai Nihon shi sansō 大日本史賛藪. In *Kinsei shi ronshū* 近世史論集, edited by Matsumoto Sannosuke 松本三之介 and Ogura Yoshihiko 小倉芳彦, vol. 48 of *Nihon shisōshi taikei* 日本思想史体系. Tokyo: Iwanami Shoten 岩波書店, 1974.

Duara, Prasenjit. *Rescuing History from the Nation: Questioning Narratives of Modern China.* Chicago: University of Chicago Press, 1995.

Ehime Kenshi Hensan Iinkai 愛媛県史編纂委員会, ed. *Ehime kenshi, Kinsei, jō* 愛媛県史, 近世, 上. Matsuyama: Ehime-ken 愛媛県, 1986.

———, ed. *Ehime kenshi, Shiryō-hen, Kinsei, ge* 愛媛県史, 資料編, 近世, 下. Matsuyama: Ehime-ken 愛媛県, 1988.

Elison, George. "Hideyoshi: The Bountiful Minister." In *Warlords, Artists and Commoners: Japan in the Sixteenth Century,* edited by George Elison and Bardwell L. Smith, pp. 223–244. Honolulu: University of Hawai'i Press, 1981.

Fujii Jōji 藤井讓治. "Jūnana seiki no Nihon: Buke no kokka no keisei" 一七世紀の日本：武家の国家の形成. In vol. 12 of *Iwanami kōza Nihon tsūshi* 岩波講座日本通史, edited by Asao Naohiro 朝尾直弘 et al., pp. 1–64. Tokyo: Iwanami Shoten 岩波書店, 1994.

Fujii Tomozuru 藤井智鶴. "Mikawa Hiruwayama sanron no tenkai: Shiryō sanron no kōgi osso o megutte" 三河ひるわ山山論の公儀越訴をめぐって. *Shien* 史苑 51, no. 1 (January 1991): 5–23.

Fujino Tamotsu 藤野保. *Bakuhan taisei shi no kenkyū* 幕藩体制史の研究. 3rd ed. Tokyo: Yoshikawa Kōbunkan 吉川弘文館, 1967.

———, ed. *Hatamoto to chigyōsei* 旗本と知行制. Tokyo: Yūzankaku 雄山閣, 1995.

———, ed. *On'eiroku, Haizetsuroku* 恩栄録・廃絶録. Tokyo: Kondō Shuppansha 近藤出版社, 1970.

———, ed. *Tokugawa kajofu roku* 徳川加除封録. Tokyo: Kondō Shuppansha 近藤出版社, 1972.

Fujita Satoru 藤田覚. *Bakumatsu no tennō* 幕末の天皇. Tokyo: Kōdansha 講談社, 1994.

Fujita Teiichirō 藤田貞一郎. *Kinsei keizai shisō no kenkyū: Kokueki shisō to bakuhan taisei* 近世経済思想の研究—国益思想と幕藩体制. Tokyo: Yoshikawa Kōbunkan 吉川弘文館, 1966.

Fukaya Katsumi 深谷克巳. "Hyakushō ikki no shisō" 百姓一揆の思想. *Shisō* 思想, no. 584 (February 1973): 206–227.

Fukuda Chizuru 福田千鶴. *Oie sōdō: Daimyō-ke o yurugashita kenryoku tōsō* 御家騒動—大名家を揺るがした権力闘争. Tokyo: Chūōkōronsha 中央公論社, 2005.

Fukushima Masao 福島正夫. *Chiso kaisei no kenkyū* 地租改正の研究. Tokyo: Yūhikaku 有斐閣, 1970.

Grapard, Allan. "Japan's Ignored Cultural Revolution: The Separation of Shinto and Buddhist Divinities in Meiji (*shimbutsu bunri*) and a Case Study; Tōnomine." *History of Religions* 23, no. 3 (February 1984): 240–265.

———. "The Shinto of Yoshida Kanetomo." *Monumenta Nipponica* 47, no. 1 (Spring 1992): 27–58.

Haga Shōji 羽賀祥二. *Shisekiron: 19 seiki Nihon no chiiki shakai to rekishi ishiki* 史蹟論— １９世紀日本の地域社会と歴史意識. Nagoya: Nagoya Daigaku Shuppankai 名古屋大学出版会, 1998.

Hall, John. "The *Bakuhan* System." In *The Cambridge History of Japan,* vol. 4, *Early Modern Japan,* edited by John Whitney Hall, pp. 128–182. Cambridge: Cambridge University Press, 1991.

———. "The Castle Town and Japan's Modern Urbanization." In *Studies in the Institutional History of Early Modern Japan,* edited by John Hall and Marius B. Jansen, pp. 169–188. Princeton, NJ: Princeton University Press, 1968.

———. "Rule by Status in Tokugawa Japan." *Journal of Japanese Studies* 1, no. 1 (Autumn 1974): 39–49.

Hanami Sakumi 花見朔巳. "Honchō tsugan kō" 本朝通鑑考. In *Honpō shigaku shi ronsō* 本邦史学史論叢, edited by Shigakkai 史学会, pp. 793–834. Tokyo: Fuzanbō 富山房, 1939.

Handa Takao 半田高夫. "Bakufu junkenshi taisei to saigoku keiei" 幕府巡見使体制と西国経営. In *Kinsei Nihon no seiji to gaikō* 近世日本の政治と外交, edited by Fujino Tamotsu Sensei Kanreki Kinenkai 藤野保先生還暦記念会, pp. 161–186. Tokyo: Yūzankaku Shuppan 雄山閣出版, 1993.

Hanley, Susan, and Kozo Yamamura. *Economic and Demographic Change in Preindustrial Japan, 1600–1868.* Princeton, NJ: Princeton University Press, 1977.

Hansei shi kenkyūkai 藩政史研究会, ed. *Hansei seiritsu shi no sōgō kenkyū: Yonezawa-han* 藩政成立史の綜合研究—米沢藩. Tokyo: Yoshikawa Kōbunkan 吉川弘文館, 1963.

Harafuji Hiroshi. *Sōzokuhō no tokushitsu.* Tokyo: Sōbunsha, 1982.

Hardacre, Helen. *Religion and Society in Nineteenth-Century Japan: A Study of the Southern Kantō Region, Using Late Edo and Early Meiji Gazetteers.* Ann Arbor: University of Michigan Center for Japanese Studies, 2002.

———. *Shinto and the State, 1868–1988.* Princeton, NJ: Princeton University Press, 1990.

Harootunian, Harry. *Things Seen and Unseen: Discourse and Ideology in Tokugawa Nativism.* Chicago: University of Chicago Press, 1988.

Hashida Kokin 橋田庫欣. "Nonaka Kenzan Sasayama ronsō no ichi ketsumatsu: Dōji kyōyū no jittai" 野中兼山篠山論争の一結末—堂寺共有の実態. *Tosa Shidan* 土佐史談, no. 132 (July 1972): 1–4.

Hashimoto Masanobu 橋本政宣, ed. *Kinsei buke kan'i no kenkyū* 近世武家官位の研究. Tokyo: Zoku Gunsho Ruijū Kanseikai 続群書類従完成会, 1999.

Hayashi Razan 林羅山. *Honchō tsugan* 本朝通鑑. 17 vols. Tokyo: Kokusho Kankōkai 国書刊行会, 1918–1920.

Hayashi Yukiko 林由紀子. *Kinsei bukkiryo no kenkyu: Bakuhansei kokka no mo to kegare* 近世服忌令の研究: 幕藩制国家の喪と穢. Osaka: Seibundō, 1998.

Hirao Michio 平尾道雄. *Tosa han shōgyō keizai shi* 土佐藩商業経済史. Kōchi: Kōchi Shimin Toshokan 高知市民図書館, 1958.

———. *Tosa nōmin ikki shi kō* 土佐農民一揆史考. Kōchi: Kōchi Shimin Toshokan 高知市民図書館, 1953.

———. *Yamauchi Yōdō* 山内容堂. Tokyo: Yoshikawa Kōbunkan 吉川弘文館, 1961.

Hobsbawm, Eric. *Nations and Nationalism since 1780: Programme, Myth, Reality.* 2nd ed. Cambridge: Cambridge University Press, 1992.

Honma Shūhei 本間修平, ed. *Shokokoroedome, shokokoroetoiawase aisatsudome, shomuki kikiawasegaki, shomuki toiawase otsukefudazumi no utsushi* 諸心得留・諸心得問合挨拶留・諸向聞合書・諸向問合御附札済之写. Tokyo: Sōbunsha 創文社, 2006.

Howell, David. *Capitalism from Within: Economy, Society and the State in a Japanese Fishery.* Berkeley: University of California Press, 1995.

———. *Geographies of Identity in Nineteenth-Century Japan.* Berkeley: University of California Press, 2005.

———. "Territoriality and Collective Identity in Tokugawa Japan." In *Public Spheres and Collective Identities,* edited by Shmuel N. Eisenstadt, Wolfgang Schluchter, and Björn Wittrock, pp. 105–132. New Brunswick, NJ: Transaction Publishers, 2001.

Hoya Tōru 保谷徹. "Daimyo monjo no teishutsu: Juri shisutemu to rōjū no kaitō; Ueda Matsudaira-ke monjo "nichijō" no bunseki kara 「大名文書の提出—受理システムと老中の回答—上田松平家文書「日乗」の分析から. In *Kinsei bakufu monjo no komonjogakuteki kenkyū* 近世幕府文書の古文書学的研究, edited by Katō Hideyuki 加藤秀幸, pp. 65–85. Tokyo: Tokyo Daigaku Shiryōhensanjo 東京大学史料編纂所, 1992.

Hozumi Nobushige 穂積陳遠. "Yui Shōsetsu jiken to Tokugawa bakufu no yōshi hō" 由比正雪事件と徳川幕府の養子法. In *Hozumi Nobushige ibunshū* 穂積陳遠遺文集, vol. 3, pp. 625–673. Tokyo: Iwanami Shoten 岩波書店, 1934.

Hur, Nam-lin. *Death and the Social Order in Tokugawa Japan: Buddhism, Anti-Christianity, and the Danka System.* Cambridge, MA: Harvard University Asia Center, 2007.

Igeta Ryōji 井ヶ田良治. *Kinsei sonraku no mibun kōzō* 近世村落の身分構造. Tokyo: Kokusho Kankōkai 国書刊行会, 1984.

Ikeda Mitsumasa 池田光政. *Ikeda Mitsumasa nikki* 池田光政日記. Edited by Fujii Shun 藤井駿 et al. Okayama: San'yō Tosho Shuppan 山陽図書出版, 1967.

Ikegami, Eiko. *The Taming of the Samurai.* Cambridge, MA: Harvard University Press, 1995.

Inoue Tomokatsu 井上智勝. "Kansei ki ni okeru ujigami, ryūkōgami to chōtei" 寛政期における氏神・流行神と朝廷. *Nihonshi kenkyū* 日本史研究, no. 365 (1993): 1–26.

———. "Kinsei chūki ni okeru Yoshida-ke hihan no genjitsuka" 近世中期における吉田家批判の現実化. In *Chūkinsei no shūkyō to kokka* 中近世の宗教と国家, edited by Imatani Akira 今谷明 and Takano Toshihiko 高埜利彦, pp. 343–372. Tokyo: Iwata Shoin 岩田書院, 1998.

Ishii Ryōsuke 石井良助, ed. *Hanpōshū* 藩法集. Vols. 1:1 and 1:2, *Okayama-han* 岡山藩. Tokyo: Sōbunsha 創文社, 1959.

———, ed. *Hanpōshū* 藩法集. Vol. 2, *Tottori-han* 鳥取藩. Tokyo: Sōbunsha 創文社, 1961.

———, ed. *Hanpōshū* 藩法集. Vol. 5, *Shohan* 諸藩. Tokyo: Sōbunsha 創文社, 1964.

———, ed. *Hanpōshū* 藩法集. Vols. 9:1 and 9:2, *Morioka-han* 盛岡藩. Tokyo: Sōbunsha 創文社, 1970.

———, ed. *Tokugawa kinreikō* 徳川禁令考. Vol. 1. Tokyo: Sōbunsha 創文社, 1959.

Ishii Ryōsuke and Harafuji Hiroshi 腹藤弘司, eds. *Mondōshū 5: Sanchō hiroku* 問答集 5・三聴秘録. Tokyo: Sōbunsha 創文社, 2005.

Ishio Yoshihisa 石尾芳久. "'Tosa hansei roku' no genpon ni tsuite" 土佐藩政録の原本について. *Kansai Daigaku hōgaku ronshū* 関西大学法学論集 31, no. 2–4 (1981): 459–472.

Itō Seirō 伊東成郎 et al. *Abe Masahiro no subete* 阿部正弘のすべて. Tokyo: Shin Jinbutsu Ōraisha 新人物往来社, 1997.

Iwasaki, Haruko. "Portrait of a Daimyo: Comic Fiction by Matsudaira Sadanobu." *Monumenta Nipponica* 38, no. 1 (Spring 1983): 1–19.

Iwate Kenritsu Toshokan 岩手県立図書館, ed. *Naishi ryaku.* 内史略 (3). In *Iwate shisō* 岩手史叢 series. Morioka: Iwate-ken Bunkazai Aigo Kyōkai 岩手県文化財愛護協会, 1974.

Jansen, Marius B. *Sakamoto Ryōma and the Meiji Restoration.* Princeton, NJ: Princeton University Press, 1961.

———. "Tosa in the Seventeenth Century: The Establishment of Yamauchi Rule." In *Studies in the Institutional History of Early Modern Japan,* edited by John Hall and Marius B. Jansen, pp. 115–129. Princeton, NJ: Princeton University Press, 1968.

Kagawa-ken shi 香川県史. Vol. 9, *Shiryō hen, Kinsei shiryō 1* 史料編, 近世史料. Takamatsu: Kagawa-ken 香川県, 1987.

Kalland, Arne. *Fishing Villages in Tokugawa Japan.* Richmond, UK: Curzon Press, 1995.

Kamiya Masaji 神谷正司. "Jidai to Nonaka Kenzan ron" 時代と野中兼山論. In *Yamauchi-ke shiryō: Tadayoshi-kō ki* 山内家史料—忠義公紀, vol. 4, pp. (3)–(51) in front matter. Kōchi: Yamauchi Jinja Hōmotsu Shiryōkan 高知：山内神社宝物資料館, 1982.

Kanai Madoka 金井圓. *Hansei* 藩政. Tokyo: Shibundō 至文堂, 1962.

Kanmei nikki 寛明日記. Edited by Minami Kazuo 南和男. 2 vols. Vols. 66–67 of *Naikakubunko shozō shiseki sōkan* 内閣文庫史籍叢刊 series. Tokyo: Gyūko Shoin 汲古書院, 1986.

Kasaya Kazuhiko 笠谷和比古. *Edo orusuiyaku: Kinsei no gaikōkan* 江戸御留守居役—近世の外交官. Tokyo: Yoshikawa Kōbunkan 吉川弘文館, 2000.

———. *Kinsei buke shakai no seiji kōzō* 近世武家社会の政治構造. Tokyo: Yoshikawa Kōbunkan 吉川弘文館, 1993.

―――. *Shukun "oshikome" no kōzō: Kinsei daimyō to kashindan* 主君「押し込め」の構造―近世大名と家臣団. Tokyo: Heibonsha 平凡社, 1988.

Kasei Jikki Kanpon Hensan Iinkai 家世実記刊本編纂委員会, ed. *Aizu-han kasei jikki* 会津藩家世実紀. 15 vols. Tokyo: Yoshikawa Kōbunkan 吉川弘文館, 1975–1989.

Katsu Kokichi. *Musui's Story: The Autobiography of a Tokugawa Samurai.* Translated by Teruko Craig. Tucson: University of Arizona Press, 1988.

Katsumata Shizuo with Martin Collcutt. "The Development of Sengoku Law." In *Japan before Tokugawa: Political Consolidation and Economic Growth, 1500–1650,* edited by John W. Hall, Nagahara Keiji, and Kōzō Yamamura, 101–124. Princeton, NJ: Princeton University Press, 1981.

Katsura Yoshiki 桂芳樹, ed. *Iwakuni-han kengen roku* 岩国藩建言録. Yamaguchi Pref., Iwakuni: Iwakuni Chōkokan 岩国徴古館, 1979.

Kawamura Hirotada 川村博忠. *Edo bakufu sen kuniezu no kenkyū* 江戸幕府撰国絵図の研究. Tokyo: Kokon Shoin 古今書院, 1984.

―――. *Kuniezu* 国絵図. Tokyo: Yoshikawa Kōbunkan 吉川弘文館, 1990.

Keirstead, Thomas. "San'yō, Bakin, and the Reanimation of Japan's Past." In *Writing Histories in Japan: Texts and Their Transformations from Ancient Times through the Meiji Era,* edited by James C. Baxter and Joshua A. Fogel, pp. 201–222. Kyoto: International Research Center for Japanese Studies, 2007.

Ketelaar, James. *Of Heretics and Martyrs in Meiji Japan: Buddhism and Its Persecution.* Princeton, NJ: Princeton University Press, 1990.

Kindai Shi Bunko Kenkyūkai 近代史文庫研究会, ed. *Kiroku kakinuki: Date-ke orekidai jiki* 記録書抜―伊達家御歴代事記. Vol. 1. Uwajima: Kindai Shi Bunko Kenkyūkai 近代史文庫研究会, 1981.

Kishimoto Satoru 岸本覚. "Chōshū-han hansobyō no keisei" 長州藩藩祖廟の形成. *Nihon rekishi kenkyū* 日本歴史研究, no. 438 (February 1999): 1–25.

―――. "Chōshū-han no hanso kenshō to hansei kaikaku" 長州藩の藩祖顕彰と藩政改革. *Nihon rekishi kenkyū* 日本歴史研究, no. 464 (April 2001): 106–128.

Kitajima Masamoto 北島正元. *Edo bakufu no kenryoku kōzō* 江戸幕府の権力構造. Tokyo: Iwanami Shoten 岩波書店, 1964.

Kōchi Chihōshi Kenkyūkai 高知地方史研究会, ed. *Tosa hansei roku* 土佐藩政録. 2 vols. Kōchi: Kōchi Shimin Toshokan 高知市民図書館, 1969–1970.

Kōchi Kenritsu Toshokan 高知県立図書館, ed. *Tosanokuni gunsho ruijū* 土佐国群書類従. 12 vols. Kōchi: Kōchi Kenritsu Toshokan 高知県立図書館, 1998–2009.

Kōchi-ken Bunkyō Kyōkai 高知県文教協会. *Nonaka Kenzan kankei monjo* 野中兼山関係文書. Kōchi: Kōchi-ken Bunkyō Kyōkai 高知県文教協会, 1965.

Kōchi-ken Rekishi Jiten Hensan Iinkai 高知県歴史辞典編纂委員会, comp. *Kōchi-ken rekishi jiten* 高知県歴史辞典. Kōchi: Kōchi Shimin Toshokan 高知市民図書館, 1980.

Kōchi-ken Shi Hensan Iinkai 高知県史編纂委員会. *Kōchi-ken shi* 高知県史. 10 vols. Kōchi: Kōchi-ken 高知県, 1968–1978.

Kokushi Daijiten Hensan Iinkai 国史大辞典編纂委員会, comp. *Kokushi daijiten* 国史大辞典. 16 vols. Tokyo: Yoshikawa Kōbunkan 吉川弘文館, 1979–1997.

Kondō Yoshihiro 近藤喜博. "Toyokuni Daimyōjin no bunpai ni tsuite" 豊国大明神の分配に就いて. In *Kokushigaku ronshū* 国史学論集, edited by Ueki Hakase Kanreki Kinen Shukugakai 植木博士還暦記念祝賀会, pp. 357–377. Tokyo: Ueki Hakase Kanreki Kinen Shukugakai 植木博士還暦記念祝賀会, 1938.

Koschmann, J. Victor. *The Mito Ideology: Discourse Reform and Insurrection in Late Tokugawa Japan, 1790–1864*. Berkeley: University of California Press, 1987.

Kurachi Katsunao 倉地克直. *Kinsei minshū to shihai shisō* 近世民衆と支配思想. Tokyo: Kashiwashobō 柏書房, 1996.

Kurushima Hiroshi 久留島浩. "Kinsei ni okeru matsuri no 'shūhen'" 近世における祭りの「周辺」. *Rekishi hyōron* 歴史評論, no. 439 (1986): 12–24.

Kusunose Ōe 楠瀬大枝. *Hiuchi bukuro* 燧袋. Edited by Kōchi Chihōshi Kenkyūkai 高知地方史研究会. 16 vols. In *Tosa gunsho shūsei* 土佐群書集成 series. Kōchi: Kōchi Shimin Toshokan 高知市民図書館, 1966–1987.

Kyūji Shimon Kai 旧事諮問会, ed. *Kyūji shimonroku* 旧事諮問録. Annotated by Shinji Yoshimoto 進士慶幹. 2 vols. Tokyo: Iwanami Shoten, 1986.

Lowenthal, David. *The Past Is a Foreign Country*. Cambridge: Cambridge University Press, 1985.

Maeda, Hiromi. "Imperial Authority and Local Shrines: The Yoshida House and the Creation of a Countrywide Shinto Institution in Early Modern Japan." PhD dissertation, Harvard University, May 2003.

Makino Seichi 牧野成一. *Uchi to soto no gengobunkagaku* ウチとソトの言語文化学. Tokyo: Aruku アルク, 1996.

Mase Kumiko 間瀬久美子. "Jinja to tennō" 神社と天皇. In *Tennō to shakai shoshūdan* 天皇と社会集団, vol. 3 of *Kōza zenkindai no tennō* 講座前近代の天皇, edited by Nagahara Keiji 永原慶二 et al., pp. 217–246. Tokyo: Aoki Shoten 青木書店, 1993.

Matsunoo Shōkō 松野尾章行, comp. *Kaizanshū* 皆山集. Edited by Hirao Michio 平尾道雄 et al. 10 vols. Kōchi: Kōchi Kenritsu Toshokan 高知県立図書館, 1973–1978.

Matsuo Masahito 松尾正人. *Haihan chiken: Kindai tōitsu kokka e no kutō* 廃藩置県近代統一国家への苦闘. Tokyo: Chūōkōronsha 中央公論社, 1986.

Matsura Seizan 松浦静山. *Kasshi yawa* 甲子夜話. Edited by Nakamura Yukihiko 中村幸彦 and Nakano Mitsutoshi 中野三敏. 6 vols. Tokyo: Heibonsha 平凡社, 1977–1978.

Matsuyama-shi Shiryōshū Henshū Iinkai 松山市史料集編集委員会, ed. *Matsuyama-shi shiryōshū* 松山市史料集. Vol. 2. Matsuyama: Matsuyama-shi Shiyakusho 松山市市役所, 1987.

McMullen, James. *Idealism, Protest, and "The Tale of Genji": The Confucianism of Kumazawa Banzan, 1619–91.* Oxford: Oxford University Press, 1999.

Mehl, Margaret. *History and the State in Nineteenth-Century Japan.* New York: St. Martin's Press, 1998.

Miyoshi Tsunenori 三善庸礼. *Kokka kanjō roku* 国家勘定録. Edited by Miyamoto Mataji 宮本又次. Osaka: Seibundō 清文堂, 1971.

Mizubayashi Takeshi 水林彪. *Hōkensei no saihen to Nihonteki shakai no kakuritsu* 封建制の再編と日本的社会の確立. Tokyo: Yamakawa Shuppan 山川出版, 1987.

Mizumoto Kunihiko 水本邦彦. *Tokugawa no kokka dezain* 徳川の国家デザイン. Tokyo: Shōgakukan 小学館, 2008.

Morioka-shi Shi Hensan Iinkai 盛岡市史編纂委員会, ed. *Morioka-shi shi* 盛岡市史. Vol. 3:2. Morioka: Morioka-shi 盛岡市, 1968.

Morisu, J. F. (John Morris). *Kinsei bushi no "ōyake" to "watakushi": Sendai hanshi Tamamushi Jūzō no kyaria to zasetsu* 近世武士の「公」と「私」―玉蟲十蔵のキャリアと挫折. Osaka: Seibundō 清文堂, 2009.

―――. *Kinsei Nihon chigyōsei no kenkyū* 近世日本知行制の研究. Osaka: Seibundō 清文堂, 1988.

Moriya Yoshimi 守屋嘉美. "Kokueki shuhō o meguru shomondai: Morioka-han no baai" 国益主法をめぐる諸問題―盛岡藩の場合. *Tōhoku Daigaku Tōhoku Bunka Kenkyūjo kiyō* 東北大学東北文化研究所紀要, no. 17 (1985): 123–151.

Muir, Edward. *Civic Ritual in Renaissance Venice.* Princeton, NJ: Princeton University Press, 1981.

Mutō Yoshikazu 武藤致和. *Nanroshi* 南路志. Edited by Yorimitsu Kanji 依光貫之, Akizawa Shigeru 秋沢繁, et al. 10 vols. Kōchi: Kōchi Kenritsu Toshokan 高知県立図書館, 1990–1998.

Nagae Shinzō 永江新三. *Ansei no taigoku: Ii Naosuke to Yoshida Shōin* 安政の大獄―井伊直弼と吉田松陰. Tokyo: Nihon Kyōbunsha 日本教文社, 1966.

Nagahama-shi Hensan Iinkai 長浜市史編纂委員会. *Nagahama-shi shi* 長浜市史. Vol. 6, *Matsuri to gyōji* 祭りと行事. Shiga Pref., Nagahama-shi 長浜市, 2004.

Nagahara Keiji 永原慶二, ed. *Jien, Kitabatake Chikafusa* 慈円・北畠親房. In *Nihon no Meicho* 日本の名著 series, vol. 9. Tokyo: Chūōkōronsha 中央公論社, 1971.

Nakada Kaoru 中田薫. *Hōsei-shi ronshū* 法制史論集. Vol. 1. Tokyo: Iwanami Shoten 岩波書店, 1970.

Nakai, Kate. *Shogunal Politics: Arai Hakuseki and the Premises of Tokugawa Rule.* Cambridge, MA: Council on East Asian Studies, 1988.

Nakai Chikuzan 中井竹山. *Sōbō kigen* 草茅危言. In *Nihon keizai taiten* 日本経済大典 series, vol. 23, edited by Takimoto Seiichi 滝本誠一. Tokyo: Meiji Bunken 明治文献, 1969.

Nenzi, Laura. *Excursions in Identity: Travel and the Intersection of Place, Gender, and Status in Edo Japan.* Honolulu: University of Hawai'i Press, 2008.

Nihon rekishi daijiten 日本歴史大事典. 4 vols. Tokyo: Shōgakukan 小学館, 2000–2001.

Nishikawa Shunsaku 西川俊作. *Nihon keizai no seichōshi* 日本経済の成長史. Tokyo: Tōyōkeizai Shinpōsha 東洋経済新報社, 1985.

Nosco, Peter. "Keeping the Faith: *Bakuhan* Policy towards Religions in Seventeenth-Century Japan." In *Religion in Japan,* edited by Peter Kornicki and I. J. McMullen, pp. 135–155. Cambridge: Cambridge University Press, 1996.

Ogi Shin'ichirō 荻慎一郎 et al. *Kōchi-ken no rekishi* 高知県の歴史. Tokyo: Yamakawa Shuppan 山川出版, 2001.

Ōhira Yūichi 大平祐一. "Edo bakufu junkenshi kō" 江戸幕府巡見使考. In *Hō to kenryoku no shiteki kōsatsu* 法と権力の史的考察, edited by Harafuji Hiroshi 服藤弘司 and Oyama Sadao 小山貞夫, pp. 569–603. Tokyo: Sōbunsha 創文社, 1977.

———. "Kinsei no higōhōteki soshō: Kagoso, kakekomiso wo sozai to shite" 近世の非合法的訴訟—駕籠訴・駆込訴を素材として. *Ritsumeikan hōgaku* 立命館法学, in seven parts: 183–184 (1985): 750–766; 194 (1987): 509–532; 211 (1990): 263–277; 243–244 (1996): 1275–1313; 250 (1996): 1495–1525; 254 (1997): 685–722; 265 (1999): 541–562.

———. "Naisai to saiban" 内済と裁判. In *Kinsei hō no saikentō: Rekishigaku to hōshigaku to no taiwa* 近世法の再検討—歴史学と法史学の対話, edited by Fujita Satoru 藤田覚, pp. 5–32. Tokyo: Yamakawa Shuppan 山川出版, 2005.

"Okachū hengi" 御家中変義. *Tosa shidan* 土佐史談, in eight parts: no. 54 (March 1936): 152–163; no. 55 (June 1936): 209–232; no. 57 (December 1936): 123–132; no. 59 (June 1937): 131–140; no. 62 (March 1938): 140–148; no. 64 (September 1938): addendum 65–74; no. 66 (March 1939): addendum 75–84; no. 68 (September 1939): addendum 85–100.

Okayama-ken Shi Hensan Iinkai 岡山県史編纂委員会. *Okayama-ken shi* 岡山県史. Vol. 5, *Kinsei 1* 近世 1. Okayama: Okayama-ken 岡山県, 1984.

———. *Okayama-ken shi* 岡山県史. Vol. 25, *Tsuyama-han monjo* 津山藩文書. Okayama: Okayama-ken 岡山県, 1981.

———. *Okayama-ken shi* 岡山県史. Vol. 26, *Shohan monjo* 諸藩文書. Okayama: Okayama-ken 岡山県, 1983.

Ōmori Eiko 大森英子. *Oie sōzoku: Daimyōke no kutō* お家相続大名家の苦闘. Tokyo: Kadokawa Shoten 角川書店, 2004.

Ooms, Herman. *Charismatic Bureaucrat: A Political Biography of Matsudaira Sadanobu, 1758–1829.* Chicago: University of Chicago Press, 1975.

———. *Tokugawa Ideology: Early Constructs, 1570–1680*. Princeton, NJ: Princeton University Press, 1985.

———. *Tokugawa Village Practice*. Berkeley: University of California Press, 1996.

Overmeer Fisscher, J. F. van. *Nihon fūzoku bikō* 日本風俗備考. Translated by Shōji Mitsuo 庄司三男 and Numata Jirō 沼田次郎. 2 vols. Tokyo: Nihon Hyōronsha 日本評論社, 1978.

Ozawa Eiichi 小沢栄一. "Bakuhanseika ni okeru hōken, gunken ron josetsu" 幕藩制下における封建・郡県論序説. *Tōkyō Gakugeidai kiyō* 東京学芸大紀要, 3 *bumon shakai kagaku* 3 部門社会科学 24 (1972): 111–128.

Ozawa Kōichi 小澤耕一. *Watanabe Kazan kenkyū* 渡辺華山研究. Tokyo: Nihon Tosho Sentaa 日本図書センター, 1988.

Ozawa Kōichi 小澤耕一 and Haga Noboru 芳賀登, eds. *Watanabe Kazan shū* 渡辺華山集. Vol. 1. Tokyo: Nihon Tosho Sentaa 日本図書センター, 1999.

Pratt, Edward. *Japan's Protoindustrial Elite: The Economic Foundations of the Gōnō*. Cambridge, MA: Harvard University Press, 1999.

Ravina, Mark. *Land and Lordship in Early Modern Japan*. Stanford, CA: Stanford University Press, 1999.

Renan, Ernest. *Oeuvres complètes de Ernest Renan*. Vol. 1. Paris: Calmann-Lévy, 1947.

Roberts, Luke. "Cultivating Non-National Historical Understandings in Local History." In *The Teleology of the Modern Nation-State: Japan and China,* edited by Joshua A. Fogel, pp. 161–173. Philadelphia: University of Pennsylvania Press, 2004.

———. "The Diverse Political Languages of Edo Histories." In *Writing Histories in Japan: Texts and Their Transformations from Ancient Times through the Meiji Era,* edited by James C. Baxter and Joshua A. Fogel, pp. 223–252. Kyoto: International Research Center for Japanese Studies, 2007.

———. *Mercantilism in a Japanese Domain: The Merchant Origins of Economic Nationalism in 18th-Century Tosa*. Cambridge: Cambridge University Press, 1998.

———. "Tosa to ishin: 'Kokka' no sōshitsu to 'chihō' no tanjō" 土佐と維新—「国家」の喪失, と「地方」の誕生. *Nenpō kindai Nihon kenkyū* 年報近代日本研究 20 (1997): 211–235.

Rubinger, Richard. *Popular Literacy in Early Modern Japan*. Honolulu: University of Hawai'i Press, 2007.

Saiki Kazuma 斎木一馬, Okayama Taiji 岡山泰四, and Sagara Tōru 相良亨, eds. *Mikawa monogatari, Hagakure* 三河物語・葉隠. Tokyo: Iwanami Shoten, 1974.

Saitō Yōichi 斉藤洋一 and Ōishi Shinzaburō 大石慎三郎. *Mibunsabetsu shakai no shinjitsu* 身分差別社会の真実. Tokyo: Kōdansha 講談社, 1995.

Sakai, Robert. "Shimazu Nariakira and the Emergence of National Leadership in Satsuma." In *Personality in Japanese History,* edited by Albert Craig and Donald Shively, pp. 209–233. Berkeley: University of California Press, 1970.

Sakawa-chō Shi Hensan Iinkai 佐川町史編さん委員会, ed. *Sakawa-chō shi* 佐川 町史, *jōkan* 上巻. Kōchi Pref., Sakawa-chō 佐川町, 1982.

Sano Tokutarō 佐野篤太郎. *Mimasaka Katsuyama-han shikō* 美作勝山藩志稿. Okayama: Okayama-ken Chihōshi Kenkyū Renraku Kyōgikai 岡山県地 方史研究連絡協議会, 1965.

Sasaki Takayuki 佐々木高行. *Hogohiroi: Sasaki Takayuki nikki* 保古飛呂比—佐 佐木高行日記. Vol. 1. Tokyo: Tōkyō Daigaku Shuppankai 東京大学出 版会, 1970.

Scheiner, Irwin. "Benevolent Lords and Honorable Peasants." In *Japanese Thought in the Tokugawa Period, 1600–1868: Methods and Metaphors,* edited by Tetsuo Na-jita and Irwin Scheiner, 39–62. Chicago: University of Chicago Press, 1978.

Sekita Komakichi 関田駒吉. *Sekita Komakichi rekishi ronbunshū* 関田駒吉歴史論 文集. 2 vols. Kōchi: Kōchi Shimin Toshokan 高知市民図書館, 1981.

Shihara Yasuzō 指原安三, ed. *Meiji seishi* 明治政史. Vol. 2 (1892). Reprinted in *Meiji bunka zenshū* 明治文化全集, vol. 9, edited by Meiji Bunka Kenkyūkai 明治文化研究会. Tokyo: Nihon Hyōronsha 日本評論社, 1956 (1928).

Shintei Kansei chōshū shokafu 新訂寛政重修諸家譜. 26 vols. Tokyo: Zoku Gun-sho Ruijū Kanseikai 続群書類従完成会, 1964–1967.

Shiritsu Nagahama-jō Rekishi Hakubutsukan 市立長浜城歴史博物館, ed. *Kami ni natta Hideyoshi: Hideyoshi ninki no himitsu o saguru* 神になった秀 吉—秀吉人気の秘密を探る. Nagahama: Shiritsu Nagahama-jō Rekishi Hakubutsukan 市立長浜城歴史博物館, 2004.

Shiseki Kenkyūkai 史籍研究会, ed. *Naikakubunko shozō shiseki sōkan* 内閣文庫 所蔵史籍叢刊 series. Vol. 9, *Shisō zasshiki* 祠曹雑識. Tokyo: Kyūko Shoin 汲古書院, 1981.

Shryock, Andrew. *Nationalism and the Genealogical Imagination: Oral History and Textual Authority in Tribal Jordan.* Berkeley: University of California Press, 1997.

Smith, Thomas. "The Land Tax in the Tokugawa Period." *Journal of Asian Studies* 18, no. 1 (November 1958): 3–19.

Sōma-han seiki 相馬藩世紀. Vol. 1. Tokyo: Zoku Gunsho Ruijū Kanseikai 続群書 類従完成会, 1999.

Sōma-shi shi 相馬市史. Vol. 5. Fukushima Pref., Sōma-shi 相馬市, 1971.

Sugimoto Fumiko 杉本史子. "Kuniezu sakusei jigyō to kinsei kokka" 国絵図作成 事業と近世国家. In *Kinsei kokka* 近世国家, edited by Fukaya Katsumi 深谷克己 and Hori Shin 堀新, vol. 13 of *Tenbō Nihon rekishi* 展望日本 歴史 series, pp. 217–233. Tokyo: Tōkyōdō Shuppan 東京堂出版, 2000.

Tahara-chō Bunka Hogo Shingikai 田原町文化保護審議会, ed. *Tahara-han okachū bugenchō sono hoka* 田原藩御家中分限帳その他. *Tahara no bunka* 田原の文化 series, no. 11. Aichi Pref., Tahara-chō: Tahara-chō Kyōiku Iinkai 田原町教育委員会, 1984.

Tahara-chō Bunkazai Chōsakai 田原町文化財調査会, ed. *Tahara-chō shi, chūkan* 田原町史　中巻. Aichi Pref., Tahara-chō 田原町, 1975.

Tahara-chō Bunkazai Hogo Shingikai 田原町文化財保護審議会, ed. *Tahara-han nikki* 田原藩日記. 10 vols. Aichi Pref., Tahara-chō 田原町, 1987–1997.

Taira Shigemichi 平重道. *Yoshikawa shintō no kisoteki kenkyū* 吉川神道の基礎的研究. Tokyo: Yoshikawa Kōbunkan 吉川弘文館, 1966.

Takagi Shōsaku 高木昭作. *Edo bakufu no seido to dentatsu monjo* 江戸幕府の制度と伝達文書. Tokyo: Kadokawa Shoten 角川書店, 1999.

Takahashi Shirō 高橋四朗. "Tosa-han 'shōya dōmei' kenkyū no ichi zentei" 土佐藩「庄屋同盟」研究の一前提. *Kainan shigaku* 海南史学, no. 3 (January 1965): 1–19.

Takano Nobuharu 高野信治. *Bushi shinkakuka ichiran, kō* 武士神格化一覧・稿. 2 vols. *Kyūshū bunkashi kenkyū kiyō* 九州文化史研究所紀要 series, no. 47 (March 2003) and no. 48 (March 2005).

———. "Edo jidai no bushi no imeeji" 江戸時代の武士のイメージ. *Rekishi chiri kyōiku* 歴史地理教育, no. 711 (March 2007): 66–71.

———. "Kyūnin chigyōchi ni okeru junkenshi geisetsu o meguru ikkōsatsu: Saga-han o sozai ni" 給人知行地における巡見使迎接をめぐる一考察—佐賀藩を素材に. In *Kinsei Nihon no shakai to ryūtsū* 近世日本の社会と流通, edited by Fujino Tamotsu Sensei Kanreki Kinen Kai 藤野保先生還暦記念会, pp. 153–172. Tokyo: Yūzankaku 雄山閣, 1993.

Takeichi Saichirō 武市佐一郎. *Takeichi Saichirō shū* 武市佐一郎集. Vol. 9. Kōchi: Kōchi Shimin Toshokan 高知市民図書館, 1996.

Tamamuro Fumio 圭室文雄. *Edo bakufu no shūkyō tōsei* 江戸幕府の宗教統制. Hyōronsha 評論社, 1971.

———. "Okayama-han no Shintō uke seido" 岡山藩の神道請制度. In *Shintō no tenkai* 神道の展開, edited by Shimode Sekiyo 下出積與 and Tamamuro Fumio 圭室文雄, pp. 125–139. Tokyo: Ōfūsha 桜楓社, 1991.

Teraishi Masaji (Masamichi) 寺石正路. *Nangakushi* 南学史. Tokyo: Fuzanbō 冨山房, 1934.

Toby, Ronald. "Rescuing the Nation from History: The State of the State in Early Modern Japan." *Monumenta Nipponica* 56, no. 2 (Summer 2001): 197–237.

Tokugawa jikki 徳川実紀. Edited by Kuroita Katsumi 黒板勝美. 9 vols. In *Shintei zōhō Kokushi taikei* 新訂増補国史体系 series, vols. 38–47. Tokyo: Yoshikawa Kōbunkan 吉川弘文館, 1964.

Tokushima-ken Shi Hensan Iinkai 徳島県史編纂委員会, ed. *Tokushima-ken shiryō* 徳島県史料. Vol. 1. Tokushima: Tokushima-ken 徳島県, 1964.

Tōkyō Daigaku Shiryō Hensanjo 東京大学史料編纂所, ed. *Dai Nihon shiryō* 大日本史料. Multivolume. Tokyo: Tōkyō Daigaku Shuppankai 東京大学出版会, 1968–.

Tonomura, Hitomi. *Community and Commerce in Late Medieval Japan: The Corporate Villages of Tokuchin-ho.* Stanford, CA: Stanford University Press, 1992.

Totman, Conrad. *The Collapse of the Tokugawa Bakufu, 1862–1868*. Honolulu: University of Hawai‘i Press, 1980.

———. *Early Modern Japan*. Berkeley: University of California Press, 1993.

———. "Political Reconciliation in the Tokugawa Bakufu: Abe Masahiro and Tokugawa Nariaki, 1844–1852." In *Personality in Japanese History*, edited by Albert Craig and Donald Shively, pp. 180–208. Berkeley: University of California Press, 1970.

———. *Politics in the Tokugawa Bakufu, 1600–1843*. Cambridge, MA: Harvard University Press, 1967.

Tsuyama-shi Shi Hensan Iinkai 津山市史編纂委員会. *Tsuyama-shi shi* 津山市史. Vol. 3, *Kinsei 1* 近世 1. Okayama Pref., Tsuyama shi 津山市, 1973.

Umeda Yoshihiko 梅田義彦. *Kaitei Zōhō Nihon shūkyō seido shi, kinsei hen* 改訂増補日本宗教制度史 近世篇. Tokyo: Tōsen Shuppan 東宣出版, 1972.

Vaporis, Constantine. *Tour of Duty: Samurai, Military Service in Edo and the Culture of Early Modern Japan*. Honolulu: University of Hawai‘i Press, 2008.

Varley, H. Paul. *A Chronicle of Gods and Sovereigns: Jinnō Shōtōki of Kitabatake Chikafusa*. New York: Columbia University Press, 1980.

Wakabayashi, Bob. "In Name Only: Imperial Sovereignty in Early Modern Japan." *Journal of Japanese Studies* 17, no. 1 (1991): 25–57.

Wakabayashi Kisaburō 若林喜三郎. *Kyū Ise Kanbe-hanshu Honda-ke shiryō* 旧伊勢神戸藩主本多家史料. Hyōgo Pref., Nishinomiya: Ōtemae Joshi Daigaku Shigaku Kenkyūsho 大手前女子大学史学研究所, 1988.

Wakita Osamu 脇田修. "Bakuhan taisei to josei" 幕藩体制と女性. In *Nihon josei shi* 日本女性史, vol. 3, *Kinsei* 近世, edited by Joseishi Sōgō Kenkyūkai 女性史総合研究会, pp. 1–30. Tokyo: Tōkyō Daigaku Shuppankai 東京大学出版会, 1982.

Walthall, Anne. "Japanese *Gimin*: Peasant Martyrs in Popular Memory." *American Historical Review* 91, no. 5 (December 1986): 1076–1102.

———. *The Weak Body of a Useless Woman*. Chicago: University of Chicago Press, 1998.

Watanabe Hiroshi 渡辺浩. "About Some Japanese Historical Terms." Translated by Luke Roberts. *Sino-Japanese Studies* 10, no. 2 (1998): 32–42.

———. *Higashi Ajia no ōken to shisō* 東アジアの王権と思想. Tokyo: Tōkyō Daigaku Shuppankai 東京大学出版会, 1997.

———. *Kinsei Nihon shakai to Sōgaku* 近世日本社会と宋学. Tokyo: Tōkyō Daigaku Shuppankai 東京大学出版会, 1985.

Watsky, Andrew. *Chikubushima: Deploying the Sacred Arts of Momoyama Japan*. Seattle: University of Washington Press, 2004.

Webb, Herschel. "What Is the *Dai Nihon Shi*?" *Journal of Asian Studies* 19, no. 2 (1960): 135–149.

Wigen, Kären. *The Making of a Japanese Periphery, 1750–1920*. Berkeley: University of California Press, 1995.

———. *A Malleable Map: Geographies of Restoration in Central Japan, 1600–1912.* Berkeley: University of California Press, 2010.

Yamaguchi Osamu 山口修. "'Tennō' shō no keifu"「天皇」称の系譜. Special issue, *Bukkyō Daigaku Sōgō Kenkyūjo kiyō* 仏教大学総合研究所紀要, no. 2 (March 1995): 96–118.

Yamamoto Hirofumi 山本博文. *Bakuhansei no seiritsu to kinsei no kokusei* 幕藩制の成立と近世の国制. Tokyo: Azekura Shobō 校倉書房, 1990.

Yamamoto Takeshi 山本大 et al., eds. *Kenshōbo* 憲章簿. 7 vols. Kōchi: Kōchi Kenritsu Toshokan 高知県立図書館, 1982–1986.

Yamauchi-ke Hōmotsu Shiryōkan 山内家宝物資料館, ed. *Tosa hanshu Yamauchi-ke bosho* 土佐藩主山内家墓所. Pamphlet. Kōchi: Yamauchi-ke Hōmotsu Shiryōkan 山内家宝物資料館, n.d.

Yamauchi-ke shiryō: Bakumatsu Ishin hen 山内家史料—幕末維新編. 15 vols. Kōchi: Yamauchi Jinja Hōmotsu Shiryōkan 山内神社宝物資料館, 1983–2003.

Yamauchi-ke shiryō: Tadatoyo-kō ki 山内家史料—忠豊公紀. 3 vols. Kōchi: Yamauchi Jinja Hōmotsu Shiryōkan 山内神社宝物資料館, 1980–1981.

Yamauchi-ke shiryō: Tadayoshi-kō ki 山内家史料—忠義公紀. 4 vols. Kōchi: Yamauchi Jinja Hōmotsu Shiryōkan 山内神社宝物資料館, 1982.

Yanagiya Keiko 柳谷慶子. *Kinsei no josei sōzoku to kaigo* 近世の女性相続と介護. Tokyo: Yoshikawa Kōbunkan 吉川弘文館, 2007.

Yasukawa Minoru 安川実. *Honchō tsugan no kenkyū: Hayashi-ke shigaku no tenkai to sono eikyō* 本朝通鑑の研究—林家史学の展開とその影響. Tokyo: Gensōsha 言叢社, 1980.

Yokogawa Suekichi 横川末吉. "'Okinoshima chikai ron' no kenkyū"「沖の島地堺論」の研究. *Tosa shidan* 土佐史談, no. 88 (May 1956): 1–10.

———. "'Sasayama kokkyō ron sadame' no kenkyū: Nonaka Kenzan kankei no ichi shiryō"「篠山国境論定」の研究—野中兼山関係の一史料. *Tosa shidan* 土佐史談, no. 99 (October 1960): 1–12.

Yokoyama Toshio 横山俊夫. "'Han' kokka e no michi: Shokoku fūkyō fure to tabinin"「藩」国家への道—諸国風教触と旅人. In *Kasei bunka no kenkyū* 化政文化の研究, edited by Hayashiya Tatsusaburō 林屋辰三郎, pp. 81–130. Tokyo: Iwanami Shoten 岩波書店, 1976.

Yonemoto, Marcia. "Silence without Secrecy? What Is Left Unsaid in Early Modern Japanese Maps." *Early Modern Japan* 14 (2006): 27–39.

Yoshimura Yoshiho 吉村淑甫. *Tenpō Shichinen Fujinamigū otabisho ojinkō kiroku* 天保七年藤並宮御旅所御神幸記録. Kōchi: Kōchi Shimin Toshokan 高知市民図書館, 1988.

Yui Katsumasa 由比勝正. "Tosa-han ni okeru hanso shinkakuka no dōkō" 土佐藩における藩祖神格化の動向. *Kainan shigaku* 海南史学, no. 42 (August 2004): 44–68.

Index

Numbers in **boldface** type refer to tables and figures.

About the Author

Luke Roberts earned his PhD in East Asian Studies at Princeton University in 1991 and is currently a professor of early modern Japanese history at the University of California at Santa Barbara. He is the author of *Mercantilism in a Japanese Domain: The Merchant Origins of Economic Nationalism in Eighteenth-Century Tosa* (1998) and a coauthor with Sharon Takeda of *Japanese Fishermen's Coats from Awaji Island* (2001). His abiding interest as a historian is in the region of Tosa and the theme of nationalism.

Production Notes for…

Roberts/*Performing the Great Peace*
Jacket design by Julie Matsuo-Chun
Text design and composition by
Julie Matsuo-Chun with display type in
Calisto MT and text type in Arno Pro
Printing and binding by
Sheridan Books, Inc.